RIVERS OF CANADA

RIVERS OF CANADA

HUGH MACLENNAN

WITH THE CAMERA OF JOHN DE VISSER

MACMILLAN OF CANADA / TORONTO

ISBN 0-7705-1172-4

A BIBLIOGRAPHICAL NOTE

In my research for this book I consulted so many works on geology and geography, so many encyclopedias, maps, and magazine and newspaper articles, that I am quite unable to remember them all. But I do wish to acknowledge the invaluable help of some writers and scholars who were before me.

First, of course, must come the journals and diaries of the original explorers: La Vérendrye and his sons, Sir Alexander Mackenzie, David Thompson, and John Macdonnell. Next, Francis Parkman's *The Oregon Trail*. Then Marjorie Wilkins Campbell's *The North West Company* and *McGillivray, Lord of the Northwest*, followed by John Gray's life of Lord Selkirk.

Of those who have written specifically of Canadian rivers, I owe much to Grace Lee Nute's *The Voyageur*; to Esther Clark Wright's books on the St. John and the Miramichi; to Marius Barbeau, Morris Longstreth, and Père Victor Tremblay for their various studies of the Saguenay region; to Donald Braider's *The Niagara*; to Mabel Dunham's *Grand River*; to Marjorie Wilkins Campbell's *The Saskatchewan*; to Bruce Hutchison's *The Fraser*.

In the general field of Canadian history, I am much indebted to Bartlet Brebner, Donald Creighton, A.R.M. Lower, Harold Innis, and Arthur S. Morton.

PICTURE CREDITS

All contemporary photographs are by John de Visser with the exception of the following: page 90 (bottom) by Barbara K. Deans; pages 228, 229, and 232, courtesy of Churchill Falls (Labrador) Corporation Ltd.; page 236, by Ted Gorsline.

Historical illustrations

Order of appearance in the text of historical pictures
is listed here, left to right, top to bottom:

28 Public Archives of Canada
29 Provincial Museum and Archives of Alberta; Public Archives of Canada; Public Archives of Canada
35 Notman Photographic Archives
69 Notman Photographic Archives
70 Public Archives of Canada; James Collection of Early Canadiana
71 James Collection of Early Canadiana; Public Archives of Canada
72 Notman Photographic Archives; Public Archives of Canada
73 Notman Photographic Archives
74 Notman Photographic Archives; Glenbow-Alberta Foundation
75 Public Archives of Canada

76 Ralph Greenhill from Miller Services
98 Public Archives of Canada
106 Metropolitan Toronto Library Board
117 Metropolitan Toronto Library Board
118 Public Archives of Canada
119 Metropolitan Toronto Library Board
120 Metropolitan Toronto Library Board
121 Glenbow-Alberta Foundation
122 Glenbow-Alberta Foundation
123 Public Archives of Canada
124 British Columbia Archives
128 Metropolitan Toronto Library Board
143 Metropolitan Toronto Library Board
145 Metropolitan Toronto Library Board
149 Metropolitan Toronto Library Board
151 James Collection of Early Canadiana
174 Public Archives of Canada

178 Manitoba Provincial Archives
179 Public Archives of Canada
187 Public Archives of Canada
204 Public Archives of Canada
205 National Gallery of Canada
206 Metropolitan Toronto Library Board; Public Archives of Canada
207 Metropolitan Toronto Library Board; Public Archives of Canada
208-9 Metropolitan Toronto Library Board
210 Glenbow-Alberta Foundation; Manitoba Provincial Archives
211 Notman Photographic Archives; British Columbia Archives
212 McCord Museum
216-17 Notman Photographic Archives

Printed and bound in Italy for the *Macmillan Company of Canada Ltd.*, 70 Bond Street, Toronto, Ontario.

TABLE OF CONTENTS

Thinking like a river 7

ALBUM:
Images of Canada 13

How the rivers run 21
The nation-makers 24
INTERLUDE 36

ALBUM: St. Lawrence 37

The St. Lawrence
The imperial river 53

ALBUM: Fun on the river 69

The Ottawa
Way of the voyageurs 77

ALBUM: Workaday water 85

The St. John
A lovely, lovely river 93

The Miramichi
Salmon and scriptures 102

Streams of Nova Scotia
The brooks of boyhood 110

ALBUM: Where the cities grew 117

The Niagara
One of the world's wonders 125

Waters of Ontario
Austere Albany, gentle Grand 140

INTERLUDE 152

ALBUM: The seasons of the river 153

The Red
River of paradox 169

The Saskatchewan
Streams in solitude 180

The Mackenzie
Into a future kingdom 188

ALBUM: The water road 205

The Saguenay
A river of surprises 213

The Hamilton
Miracle in Labrador 223

ALBUM: Force 237

The wild waters of B.C.
Through the promised land 245

Epilogue
And on to the eternal sea 265

Index 268

Credits 272

A map depicting the rivers mentioned in the text appears on the back end-papers

To Tota, who travelled these rivers with me

and
to John Morgan Gray, my publisher and friend
of so many years.

Thinking like a river

I first began writing about rivers in 1958, and that is much longer ago than it seems if you merely count the years between then and now. That first little book had been an enjoyable holiday after the extreme tension of the longest novel I ever wrote. As Conrad used to say, it is no small endeavour to create a world of your own and that is what any sizeable novel is. It may not be great, it may not even be good, but a world it is indeed and you have made it and after it is finished it is yours no longer and you are more than tired. You are empty and yearn to be filled.

The rivers came to my rescue immediately after I had finished *The Watch That Ends the Night.* They took me out of the small subjective world of myself and my characters into an enormous landscape which I thought at the time was eternal. Now I know it is not eternal and if you read this book you will see what I mean, and I hope you will also see why this book meant far more to my soul and my sanity than its simpler and much shorter predecessor possibly could.

Back in 1958 I had no idea that the crack was going to come in the very next year. I mean the crack in the human psyche—universal, terrible, possibly wonderful, affecting everyone on our planet—which produced the watershed of the 1960s and caused the rivers of human thought, emotion, and morality to flow in new and strange directions. Not even that humble agent of the Divine Force, Pope John XXIII, could have known intellectually the meaning either of his work or of his own personality. Nobody now living will live long enough to understand precisely what caused this upheaval or what it portends or why it happened at all. But happen it surely did.

The world of today is so different from the one we knew before 1960 that we have all but forgotten what the old world was like. A Canadian of 1945 could barely recognize the Canada of now. In the intervening years we lost more than our old sense of the value of money—a very dangerous thing to lose for the reason that money, as Somerset Maugham so shrewdly noted, is a sixth sense which conditions the functions of the other five. The poor did not lose their sense of the value of money; they never do. But this time the rich did. And worst of all, the governments lost it.

Most of us lost more than this in those years. We lost the reality of our immediate human past; ironically, we lost it during the very years when biologists and anthropologists were recovering for us what our historical ancestors never knew, a sense of the interminably long *human* past within the process of evolution. For these reasons and many others, the 1960s may turn out to have been the most important decade in all recorded history. Nor did it seem astonishing that as the churches everywhere collapsed, the spirit of Jesus Christ in sundry places experienced a new resurrection.

He told the people of two thousand years ago that He did not come to bring peace but a sword. He told them also that He was the son of God, but also was the son of man, thereby saying that all of us are sons of God and therefore a part of what, to a traditional socialist or small-l liberal, can only be regarded as a terrible and appalling personality. He told them also that this Personality pitied them as a father pities his children. As well He might, considering the glory, the shame, the pain, and the joy which are implicit in all human consciousness.

This is what the young at last accepted in the 1960s and it was too much for some of them, who often went crazy in their rage and contempt for an older generation which had ruined the cities and produced a system that looked like a cross-hatch of the assembly line and the boxes within the boxes of the modern high-rise. In those years I literally swam in the broth of students in the most harassed university in the land and I could not have dodged their anger if I had tried. Which I didn't. I learned that they were rejecting, either with fury or with despair, nearly all the values and many of the methods which had produced the stupendous power of humanity in the mid-twentieth century.

Like the melt of the glaciers, the retreat of the icy rationalism by which man had endeavoured to live for two hundred years was an agonizing transition. For parents and grandparents the sixties were pretty exhausting. In Canada the bright promise of the Centennial Year and Expo 67 did not last as long as the Centennial Year itself. During the kidnapping crisis of 1970 we asked ourselves how it was possible for such things to occur in what we had been accustomed to believe was the most orderly country on earth.

To be a novelist in these years was to be in extra-sensory perception with apparent chaos. By the time the decade ended, I knew I must pause for a new perspective. If the Beatles were forgotten within five years of the pronouncement by one of them that they were more popular than Jesus Christ, how could a novelist find any pattern whatever within the kaleidoscope of the sixties? I found myself longing for something older and more permanent than human beings, something not air-conditioned, not plastic, not high-risen, not bulldozed, not sky-hooked, not greased over by the platitudes of television, not made preposterous by the claims of politicians, advertisers, and propagandists. I wanted to return to the rivers, and please don't laugh at this: I wanted to try to *think* like a river even though a river doesn't think. Because every river on this earth, some of them against incredible obstacles, ultimately finds its way through the labyrinth to the universal sea.

Rivers are living things. Each has its individual history in terms of the geology, geography, and climate, and the fish, birds, and animals (including man) which have been associated with it. In its large or small way, every river is a geological agent.

So, of course, is Man himself, especially in recent years. He has caused many a stream to dry up because of his reckless cutting of timber in the feed areas. He has turned many into junk heaps and open sewers. Others he has threatened by the gargantuan cities he has built beside them. Others he has changed by dams, including a few I had written about a dozen years earlier. Though I have never much liked puns, I can't resist mentioning that quite a few dammed rivers have literally become *damned* ones.

No sane man is opposed to a dam on principle, but all sane men must oppose the building of dams just because dam-building became so fashionable that politicians were afraid of being forgotten unless they got into the act. What was done to a section of the Peace River is enough to make you weep. What was done on the lovely St. John River made many thousand people weep all too literally. On the other hand, what was done on the Hwang-Ho in recent years was perhaps the best example of creative control imposed upon any river in the world.

For centuries the Chinese had called the Hwang-Ho the Dragon River because of what it continually did to them. Descending in its 3,000-mile journey from Tibet to the Yellow Sea, it shifted its course constantly and flooded the plains of Honan and Shantung with a lethal regularity. This meant more than hundreds of drowned villages and towns. It meant cyclic famines, for after the waters subsided, the sun baked the farmlands into hard, cracked clay-pans which took years to recover. Now the Dragon River has been disciplined by forty-six step dams spread out over a length of some 2,000 miles, with a major dam at San Men for hydro-electric power. Here the world's yellowest river has been transformed into a deep, tranquil lake as blue as the ocean under a cloudless sky.

No Canadian river has been reconstructed on a scale like this, but there is no guarantee that none will ever be. Ambitious engineers have been talking blithely about turning some of them around and making them flow down into the United States. Some of our own tech-nocrats would dearly love to get busy on the Fraser, and if they are allowed to make a dam in the vicinity of Quesnel, how long will it be before they will be using this as a precedent to build a really spectacular dam in the Black Canyon? In New Brunswick they have already turned the central St. John into a lake and permanently ruined the river for salmon. In some streams I wrote about earlier, immense changes have been made by technology and the most dramatic of them all was made in a river I had never seen then, the Hamilton of Labrador. In this book I intend to call it the Hamilton despite the fact that the Newfoundland government of Premier Smallwood a few years ago renamed it the Churchill after Sir Winston. After all, one of the largest and most important rivers of exploration in the Canadian West has been known for years as the Churchill and it derived its name from an earlier member of Sir Winston's family.

In geological history, rivers have undergone changes that can only be called fantastic, yet for all their vulnerability to human depredations, throughout human history they have been more lasting than civilizations and far more permanent than nations. In a culture which has been systematically destroying most of the traditions and loyalties that created it, I find certain facts about rivers comforting. Most rivers are at least sane. Even the Niagara begins and ends in a state of sanity. Even some very small rivers are in fact very ancient.

Scientists have proved, for example, that both crocodiles and polar bears have been intimately acquainted with the English Thames. Only a few years ago they learned that there was a time when the Thames flowed through the Dogger Bank, now submerged in the salt water of the North Sea and littered with the rusting hulks of warships sunk in the First World War. It is pleasant to know that some crude version of *homo sapiens* used to hunt in the forests of the Dogger when it was dry land. But pleasantest of all is to look at a river or a lake and to know that men like ourselves, long since disappeared, have looked at it too, have drunk its water, made love on its banks when they were young, and rested their eyes on its shifting colours when they were old.

This planet is far more than a stage for man and his civilizations; it has a value far beyond ourselves, and considering its ferocious history in terms of chemistry and geology, it has been one of the supreme success stories of the entire universe. It has been amazingly durable. The Seine, the Marne, and the Garonne, except in the vicinity of the famous cities which have grown up along their banks and the volumes of sewage discharged into them, are just as they were when Julius Caesar informed the Roman senate that they divided Gaul into three parts. In the summer of 1944 General George S. Patton wrote in a communiqué that he had surprised the retreating Germans by using the same ford in the Loire that had been used more than two millennia ago by Titus Labienus, Caesar's best corps commander, when he surprised the advancing Gauls. When I looked up the incident in the *Commentaries* I discovered that it was Caesar himself who had discovered and used this ford, but that makes no difference. It was the same old ford in the same old river that still keeps rolling along.

How old is a river? This is a question I never asked myself until recently, when so many of us were informed with remarkable precision just how young is the human species itself.

Geologists classify rivers as "young", "mature", and "old" and when they do so they have in mind the history of the earth.

A "young" river has a steep-flanked valley, steep and irregular gradients in the bed, and these are legacies of the Ice Age. Most of the best-loved salmon streams of eastern Canada are very young rivers. They vary between still pools where the fish lie and rest and stretches of shallow turbulence over gravel where they nuzzle their way across as fast as they can. The most dramatic example of a young river I know is the Niagara. The most deceptive example is the upper St. Lawrence.

A "mature" river flows through a valley with a wide floor and flaring sides and its bed is more smoothly graded, which means that its flow is steady and generally serene. It has reduced its gradient so that its velocity is just sufficient to carry off all the silt and debris it has accumulated from its tributaries and its own main course. So long as its load remains stable, no river can erode its channel any deeper. Mature rivers are "graded" and have attained equilibrium. A thoroughly mature river has no rapids or waterfalls, and because its valley floor has been widened by the lateral swinging of the stream it can threaten its plains with flooding in times of high water. Such a stream is the St. John below Grand Falls. Even after the Mactaquac Dam was built, the low-lying meadows of Maugerville were flooded as they had been nearly every spring in the past.

Canada has no "old" river (though the Red occasionally behaves like one) for the famous "old" rivers of the earth exist in latitudes which the glacier did not invade. These are the ones which have finally succeeded in grading their floors down to base level and they run through what the geologists call a "peneplain", which is a land surface worn so smooth, generally by erosion, that it is a level steppe. Not a prairie in the Canadian sense of the word, for our prairies are mainly the result of the glacier.

Such a river is the lower Mississippi: so also are the Nile, the Tigris, the Euphrates, and the lower courses of all the great rivers of India, China, and Southeast Asia. When the Ganges and the Indus flooded, when the Hwang-Ho, the Yangtse, and the Mississippi broke their bounds, the results were always the same. Vast areas of level ground were transformed into temporary lakes. Before the step dams were built, the Hwang-Ho carried such a load of silt down into Shantung that the river bed in many places was twenty to twenty-five feet higher than the plain through which it passed. The stream was contained within its channel by the endless labour of the world's most enduring people, and before the river was tamed, a man standing on the farmland could raise his eyes and see the sails of junks coasting along above his head. Old rivers move in exaggerated loops and bends called "meanders" after the little river in modern Turkey and ancient Caria described by Xenophon in his story of the March of the Ten Thousand Greeks. But nobody has ever described the behaviour of an old river with such vivid accuracy as Mark Twain in his *Life on the Mississippi*:

> The Mississippi does not alter its locality by cut-offs alone; it is always changing its habitat *bodily*—is always moving *sidewise*. At Hard Times, La., the river is two miles west of the region it used to occupy. As a result, the original *site* of the settlement is not now in Louisiana at all, but on the other side of the river, in the State of Mississippi. *Nearly the whole of that one thousand three hundred miles of old Mississippi River* [italics Twain's] *which LaSalle floated down in his canoe two hundred years ago, is good, solid dry land now. The river lies to the right of it, in places, and to the left of it in others.*

Though most rivers even in countries visited by the glacier flow as they did through all recorded human time, the thoughts and obsessions of men are forever variable and unstable; it is these which combine with animal instincts to create the chimaera we call history. And this brings me back to the dilemma I found myself in when I began writing this book.

To anyone who tries to comprehend the meaning of even a fraction of what has happened since the defeat of Hitler, the end of the Second World War must seem an aeon ago. The thirty-seven-year-old man who was finishing the novel *Two Solitudes* when Patton's communiqué appeared in the newspapers was both more and less than the sixty-five-year-old who was flown with his wife in a small helicopter down the empty canyon where the Grand Falls of Labrador had thundered only a year before.

On a May afternoon in that same year I sat down in my study in McGill and began to re-read my earlier book, *Seven Rivers of Canada*. In more ways than one the experience was disturbing. I had barely glanced at the book since its appearance in hard covers eleven years earlier and now it came over me with a shock just how long ago in evolutionary time even 1961 was. Could I be sure that these original essays, at least in some of their parts and certainly in some of their thoughts, were anything more than artifacts of a discarded frame of consciousness?

"This is a book about one man's experience with seven rivers of Canada," I had written. "It grew out of a suggestion made to me by Ralph Allen, who then was editor of *Maclean's*, that I contribute a series of river pieces to the magazine. Over a period of two and a half years I did so, and it was a fascinating adventure in time and space."

I had been happy when I wrote that not very distinguished paragraph because I had had such pleasure with those rivers, but now when I re-read it what I felt was sadness and loss. Only yesterday, it seemed, Ralph Allen had been sitting in my Montreal apartment urging me to undertake his project. I could still see his ruddy face and red hair before me. We had been almost exact contemporaries, had shared many of the same thoughts and hopes for humanity. Ralph had been a front-line correspondent in the war. He had written some novels and had been one of the best editors *Maclean's* ever had. He was gone now and it was hard to accept that such a concentration of energy, integrity, goodness, humour, and intelligence was no longer here. Why Ralph and not me?

Inevitably another recollection followed—of Blair Fraser who had succeeded Ralph as editor of *Maclean's*. He was such a precious person to everyone who knew him. In Blair all the best elements in my own generation had fused and all the bad ones had stayed away. I remembered the night when he and I were sitting in the North Hatley cottage he then shared with Frank Scott while Frank projected onto a screen a long sequence of coloured slides he had brought back from a cruise down the Mackenzie. In those photographs the Mackenzie emerged as something incredible, far more wild, remote, and majestic than the St. Lawrence had seemed to Frenchmen and Englishmen in the eighteenth century. Among the pictures a young man kept reappearing. He had a wiry body, a lean, strong face, and a Roman haircut. When he appeared stripped to the waist, seated on a stool in the stern of a tugboat with a pile of books on the deck beside him, I finally asked Frank who he was.

"I thought you knew him. That's Pierre Trudeau."

To me at the time Trudeau was only a name connected with *Cité Libre*, which Premier Duplessis and most of the conservative press considered dangerously radical. Blair had known him well; he had also known a great deal about Canadian rivers. He and a number of friends, including Dr. Omond Solandt and Eric Morse, had formed a kind of voyageurs club, the idea being to spend vacations together on canoe trips over various streams followed by the canoe brigades of the old fur trade. They voyaged on the Rainy River; they once set out from York Factory up the Nelson, then up the Churchill and over the Methy Portage. Finally they paddled down several hundred miles of Mackenzie water and even explored the frigid grandeurs of Great Bear Lake.

Canoeing in white water is always risky, as we are reminded by the casualty lists published in the press after many a summer weekend. In the end it was fatal for Blair Fraser. In the spring of 1968, when Pierre Trudeau was fighting his first federal election as Prime Minister, the friends went to the Petawawa to tone up their muscles for a longer journey later on. They found the river swollen and fierce, but they launched their canoes on it. In the rapids Blair lost control and his canoe carried him over a fall.

A few days later my wife and I were at his funeral in Ottawa and the small church was crowded. Only one pew was empty and it happened to be directly in front of ours. Just before the service began, a lithe man with a bronzed face and an expression of stern, intense grief darted into that empty pew. It was the Prime Minister. While he remained bowed in prayer, I reflected that he had interrupted a campaign schedule in Alberta in order to be there. And a few years later, when the integrity of our Arctic was threatened by the international oil companies, I heard him quote over television Blair's beautiful passage about the Canadian north:

> Yet we have in Canada an environment, a stimulus perhaps hackneyed but equally provocative too, a milieu in which not merely forty centuries (as in the case of the Egyptian pyramids) but three hundred centuries look down upon us with the same imperturbable indifference that greeted the first man over the land bridge from Asia, just after the latest retreat of the glaciers. We have accessible to us something that until the day before yesterday was accessible to man almost anywhere, but that now is increasingly rare—the cleansing experience of solitude. The temporary disappearance, or at any rate the illusion of disappearance, of those barriers that man has contrived to place between himself and Reality.[*]

I thrust my old book aside and went out for a drink of water. Glancing in the mirror in the room where the water was, I examined what I saw there. My face had more lines than had been there a dozen years ago and they were deeper; my forehead was an inch higher. But though my hair had been conducting an orderly retreat, there was now more of it on my head than there had ever

---

[*] John Fraser and Graham Fraser, eds., "Blair Fraser Reports", *The Macmillan Company of Canada Ltd.*, 1969, p. 302.

been. If I was not really with it, I was at least ready to concede that long hair on men was here to stay for quite a while. I noticed that my eyes had changed. Now they had the rueful expression I had seen in the eyes of so many of my contemporaries who had been forced to admit, without really being able to credit it, that what they had confidently assumed was the true current in the great river of evolution had in fact been nothing but the furious eddies and cross-flows that had swept its surface ever since we were born. Fathoms below these the main stream had been flowing, its course meandering as always, its velocity varying, but flowing inexorably on toward the unknown sea. That was why so many dreams of the idealists, and so many schemes of the scoundrels, and so many theories of the economists, and so many careers of politicians and intellectuals, had been caught in the eddies into which they had swum so confidently and there they had foundered, or had swirled indefinitely around and around like logs trapped in eddies of the Fraser. It was the fate of my generation to have been born in the death-throes of a civilization that had supported the West for nearly two thousand years. It was our tragedy that hardly any of us had understood what this had meant. Sometimes I wondered, especially when recalling our blithe dreams of a Welfare State, whether we had not been like the man who went over the falls backward while all the time his brave little yacht, its sails set to catch the wind, had been cutting a modest bow wave in the current.

I returned to the corridor and some students were there, including a pair with their backs to me walking along hand in hand. They were equally tall, the hair of each of them was tied in a pony-tail, they both were in jeans and sweaters, and verily I could not tell the boy from the girl. Not even a glance in the direction of where I assumed their shoes would be was of any help, for they were in bare feet. Then appeared an indubitable girl. She was wearing glasses and her expression was grave; she was also in hot pants and a thin, skin-tight jersey outlining a lovely young bust with the nipples at the salute. She was one of my own students, a shy girl, very intelligent, and a hard worker. While I tried to answer some question about her work, it occurred to me that if any girl dressed like this one had appeared on a Canadian street a dozen years ago she would have been arrested by the first cop she met.

When women's fashions change it means nothing much unless they decide to bury themselves in petticoats or walk around nearly naked. But when men's fashions change to the degree they did in the sixties, it always means revolution. But revolution toward what?

We all knew what it was against. As one student put it to me, it was against "the whole God-damn phony mess". By which he may have meant that in everything from the projected nuclear war which didn't happen to the saturating triumph of television which did, the sixties was the decade of the overkill. Even now it makes me dizzy to remember it.

In those ten years, so my scientific friends assure me, the volume of scientific knowledge doubled itself. Because we had all been trained to regard any increase in knowledge good in itself, it was hard to admit that this was appalling, since it meant that man's astonishing brain had so far outstripped his wisdom and instincts that he had virtually lost control over his own abilities. No wonder that marvellous art-form, the novel, dribbled off into pornography and incoherence during the sixties. Drugs, hard rock, acid rock, Vietnam, presidential murders, bombs, arson, kidnapping, and boys and girls lying in their thousands stoned on the grass in the rain. The end of an epoch, the dawn of something else and nobody knew what. But toward the end of the decade a wonderful thing happened, and I'm not referring to the moon landings. Man finally discovered his own origin; or rather, he was at last willing to admit it.

This may explain why, out of such a caricature of living history, there had emerged in the early seventies the weirdest-dressed young generation there ever was. Its worst members, and they were many, were so soft, spoiled, and self-degraded that when you saw them on city streets you could weep for them, for they were casualties of a culture essentially schizophrenic, being at once suicidally permissive and suicidally over-organized. Yet I knew from experience that the best of this young generation had a cleanliness of mind that comes from a kind of acceptance my own lot had seldom possessed.

They had not been educated to be ashamed of their own humanity. They did not believe that man is a fallen creature. What they did believe, or rather, what they knew, was something infinitely more revolutionary than the political dreams of a Jefferson or a Marx. It was a knowledge absolutely new which even had a place in it for Jesus, and it marked out this generation from all the ones which had preceded it. The Greeks and Romans believed they had degenerated from gods. The Church Fathers asserted that if man's life is hard, it is because of the original sin of his human parents which caused the Almighty to drive them with a curse from the Garden of Eden. But now, toward the end of the sixties, a simple truth of incalculable importance to human sanity had finally permeated the consciousness of the young and they were at home with it. Man is not a fallen innocent but a risen animal. In spite of all his follies and crimes, on the balance he has more reason for pride than for shame. So I could at least hope that these young, given time and luck, had a better chance than my own generation had ever had because it was natural to them to think of themselves as organic parts in the great chain of Being. Long after I am dead, I thought, this new knowledge could evolve into a new sense of relationship with the Mystery our ancestors called God, and man may return from his long exile.

During this whole decade, as during all the time when man was able to talk, the rivers had been flowing along, draining the land of its excess water, preserving and restoring it, liquid homes to the fish and the birds. Only a few miles from me flowed one of the greatest of them, though it was hidden from me by the glass and cement of the newly risen air-conditioned tombs. The St. Lawrence would still be there when the human race recovered from its present madness. The algae and sewage, seasoned with the occasional cement-wrapped corpse reposing on the river bed, would have disappeared. There would be no more land speculators and the people living in the river-city would enjoy it again.

Yes, it was indeed possible to regard the rivers of any land as precious in themselves, as more than raw material for human convenience. Yes, I was ready for another adventure in time and space.

Space—much of North American art used to be obsessed by it in the days when the only space that concerned people was global. How to use it in design, how to proportion human beings to it, how to reveal the effects of immense land horizons on the descendants of people whose poetry and traditions had stemmed from little towns in ancient Greece and Palestine, from German and Scandinavian farmland, from small cathedral cities in small countries like France, Italy, Belgium, Holland, and England. The artistic problems created by space in our continent have been much more difficult than Europeans have ever been able to recognize, though a Russian or a Chinese would understand them immediately.

For in Russia and China, as in the New World, the major rivers make all western European streams save the Rhine and Danube look inconsequential. Beautiful the Seine and the Arno certainly are, and their very smallness enables them to slip comfortably into the human comprehension. Famous some of them certainly are, and involved in more history than even the Mississippi. The Thames was, and still is, "a tranquil waterway leading to the uttermost ends of the earth", though the section of it described by Conrad in his marvellous overture to *Heart of Darkness* is not a river but the salt estuary below the Isle of Dogs.

Of our Canadian rivers, only the St. Lawrence is still a waterway leading to the ends of the earth, though in the days of the clipper ships this could have been said of a variety of very small streams in the Atlantic provinces. Our other major rivers thread half a continent. In a most intricate pattern of space they link the Atlantic to the Pacific and even to the Beaufort Sea. These long rivers of exploration and settlement wind through forests and plains, one of them charges for hundreds of miles down mountain gorges, some swell into tranquil lakes and then resume their steady descent to a distant ocean. The country through which some of the largest pass is still almost void of human habitation and on the prairies space seems boundless, literally without the suggestion of a frame, but space not dead because those living currents flow through them.

There is also time, mysterious companion of space, and anyone with the most elementary perceptions had to believe that in Canada more than in older lands we had utterly lost our old sense of time. It was first shaken by the railway age, but not destroyed by it. In the end it was the airplane that did that. In July 1972 nearly a million Canadians were flown by Air Canada alone. Air travel has actually narrowed our space because the machines flash over the seas and lands taking us from one collection of high-rises to another. This new way of life, this entirely new way of perceiving the earth itself, has not grown out of us. It has been imposed upon us by technology. Ours is not the only nation which has out-travelled its own soul and now is forced to search frantically for a new identity. No wonder, for so many, the past Canadian experience has become not so much a forgotten thing as an unknown thing.

A knowledge of our rivers will recover at least a little of this earlier sense of space and time in the land. It may even bring back a little of the old Canadian experience.

It was an experience literally dependent upon the rivers, for before the railways were built, they were the sole means of lengthy communication in the country. David Thompson describes rivers with the careful exactitude of a tourist guidebook describing the condition of roads.

The use of the rivers to overcome the problems of Canadian space produced a new kind of man, the voyageur, whose courage, endurance, and resourcefulness were such that no modern man could believe that such a way of life had ever existed were not the evidence so detailed that it actually did. The early Canadian experience can only be described as epic. In a sense, each voyageur was his own Odysseus, though none of them ever found Circe's isle or any kind of Lotus Land. The record is there to read in the journals of voyageurs, explorers, and travellers from Champlain and Hennepin until the middle of the nineteenth century, when the trails originally blazed by the canoe-men were followed by the builders of the Canadian Pacific Railway, and later by the airlines.

IMAGES OF CANADA

Reflections on the Gatineau suggest a world arising from the mists of its beginnings.

Cartier called it "the land God gave Cain". Voltaire wrote Canada off as "a few acres of snow". Britain almost swapped it for Guadeloupe. This is a testing land, no doubt, but—if the mirror doesn't lie—along the river ways it also has a surpassing beauty.

In the incomparable looking-glass of nature

The Appalachian interior of Newfoundland, where John de Visser found this living painting,
is almost as remote and unvisited today as when Yorkshire's Captain James Cook,
the renowned Pacific discoverer, traced its rivers and glacial lakes in the 18th century.

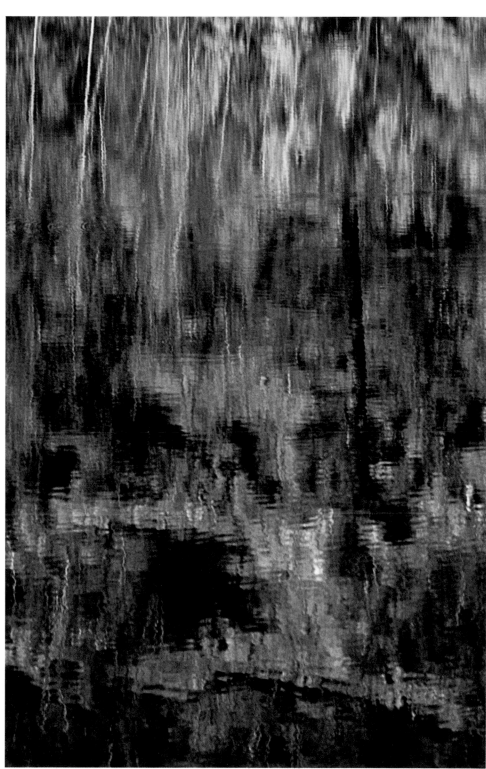

*Abstract art? This is an uncharacteristic rill of the
Fraser, that most violent of Canadian rivers, shortly after
it exits from the canyon between Lytton and Yale.*

Explorer country still awaits today's adventurer

Northern Ontario?
If it starts at North Bay
(just 223 miles above
Toronto)—as most Ontarioans
might guess—then it runs
another 700 miles to beyond
Fort Severn on Hudson Bay,
and all the way west to
Lake of the Woods, a scant
120 miles from Winnipeg.
It is a forgotten kingdom
of 360,000 sq. miles,
almost empty of people above
the fringe of settlement
around the Great Lakes.

Here is the great granitic
curve of the Precambrian
Shield, dappled with countless lakes, drained by
the Albany, Ekwan, Winisk,
Attawapiskat, Severn—some
of the world's loneliest
and longest rivers.

Prospectors hardened to
the attack of black-fly and
mosquito, a few Indian
bands, well-to-do hunters
and fishermen, these are
the only men who break the
mirror stillness of lake
and river. Geologists agree
that the mineral wealth
of the territory is still
barely scratched, awaiting
only world demand and
practical access to be
developed. With a drop of
2,183 feet from Alva to
Hudson Bay, huge resources
of hydro power await the
dam-builders of the future.

Portrait of the Thompson

Our greatest geographer, Welshman David Thompson, never saw the twin rivers named for him—although there's not much else in the British Columbian interior he did not know. The North and South branches join at Kamloops, heading for the Fraser.

This album offers an image of Canada as
a lonely, unpeopled land and, in a crowded world,
this is fundamentally true. There is one
square mile of territory for every six Canadians
(in England, 900 per sq. m.).
Few Canadians have seen the Yukon River (*above*)
flowing 2,000 miles to the ocean.

How the rivers run

An American reviewer once remarked that a novel of mine had a Russian atmosphere; he said the book was pervaded by what he called "a true northern melancholy". This he deduced not from the lives of the characters, but from the effects on them of living in a huge land far in the north.

At first his acceptance of the old stereotype annoyed me. Canada, at least the parts of it where most of us live, is not northern in terms of latitude. It is no land of midnight suns and midday dusks. My home town of Halifax lies approximately on the same meridian as Milan, and Windsor is almost as far south as Rome. Even Lake Athabaska lies well to the south of Leningrad, and Edinburgh is farther north than our most northerly large city.

But when I recall a summer I spent in Scandinavia and Russia, it occurs to me that this American reviewer was probably right. Nearly all the moods of Canada can be duplicated in Russia and in the Scandinavian regions. Most of New Brunswick is very like Karelia, in the Laurentian forests a Swede would feel completely at home, the British Columbia coastline has often been compared to the fjords of Norway. Russia itself, at least so far as the landscape goes, is more like central Canada than any other country. The civilized portions of Canada may not be northern in terms of latitude, but climatically they are, and also in appearance, because of three phenomenons of nature from which Europeans are exempt. One of these is the ice cap on Greenland, another is the ice cover on the Canadian polar sea, the third is that the results of the ice ages are visible in the western hemisphere much farther south than in the eastern.

The effect wrought on the Canadian climate by the huge refrigerators on Greenland and the polar sea is peculiar: they make eastern Canada much colder, in proportion to its proximity to the pole, than the far northwest. Northern Ungava, though it is no farther north than Great Slave Lake, is a true arctic country. But though the delta of the Mackenzie is more than a thousand miles to the northwest of Great Slave Lake, trees grow all the way down the river because Pacific airs reach the Mackenzie Valley and some Pacific water enters the Beaufort Sea through the Bering Strait. Arctic experts tell me that the Belcher Islands in Hudson Bay, though they are scarcely farther north than Edinburgh, are as truly "arctic looking" as Ellesmere. A Pole I met on the Slave assured me that the country in that region is pure Siberian. This he well knew, for he had escaped from a concentration camp on the Yenisei.

In no respect do Russia and Canada seem more akin than in the appearance of their great rivers. I have never been in Siberia, and I suppose I should thank God that I haven't, but judging from photographs and from the accounts of people who have been there, I think it safe to say that the great rivers of eastern Russia, despite their immense lengths, are remarkably similar to the Yukon, the Slave, the Mackenzie, the Peace, the western Churchill, and the Nelson. The Volga and the Don, flowing through the Russian wheat lands, have the movement and colour of the Saskatchewan, the Moskva wiggles through the Russian capital just as the Red wiggles through Winnipeg, and the Dnieper in places reminds one of parts of the St. Lawrence. However, there is no river in Russia, and to the best of my knowledge none in the world, which resembles the Fraser.

The chief point I am seeking to establish here is that the principal rivers of Canada are northern in nearly all of their general aspects. The glaciers have affected the terrains of nearly all of them, with the result that some of the largest flow through country almost devoid of habitation. The most common trees along their banks are spruce, pine, birch, and—in the west—cottonwood, and the viridian of evergreen forests, splashed here and there by the white trunks of northern birch, gives a sense of vastness, of solitude, of melancholy utterly unlike the lushness of the lower Mississippi or the wildflower and grassy loveliness of the English Thames. The only real lushness I ever found on a Canadian river is in the Thousand Islands section of the St. Lawrence, where the stream sucks through the maze of the archipelago and in summer the air is hot, humid, and after dark as influential on the young as flutes and fireflies under the moon. Even in the little province of Nova Scotia, too small to contain a river longer than fifty miles, the trout streams have the clean austerity of burns in the Scottish Highlands.

One of the first things I learned from a study of Canadian rivers is the pointlessness of the old quiz-show gambit, "What is the longest river in the world?" In my own quiz-show days we used to be asked this question once a year, and if I remember correctly, the answers varied. Sometimes it was right to say the Nile, sometimes the Yangtse, sometimes the Ob-Irtish and usually you could get by with the Mississippi-Missouri. The last of these answers gave the whole thing away. This practice of combining the Missouri with the Mississippi in order to give the United States the world's longest river in addition to the world's highest building merely sharpens the absurdity of the old school-book approach to fluvial geography.

Why, I wonder, did they stop with the Missouri? Why not the Mississippi-Missouri-Ohio-Arkansas-Yazoo-Red and several dozen more of the tributaries? No river like the Mississippi can be a simple thing, for it is a united system draining a third of a continent. A river's "greatness" cannot be measured by its length but by the area of its drainage basin, and above all by the accumulation of water which it carries off. In this latter sense every river in the world is minor compared to the two jungle systems, the Congo and the Amazon. Since the bore of the Amazon is visible hundreds of miles out in the sea, anyone particular about measuring this river's "length" should begin with a spring in the Peruvian Andes (if he can be sure of finding the right one) and end at a variable point in the Atlantic between South America and Africa. Any "great" river, to repeat, is a system of waters draining a basin.

If none of the Canadian systems is remarkable for the length of its main stem, this is because of a series of accidents of geography. The north-south continental divide lies in the United States just below the Canadian border. This means that all the important Canadian rivers except the Columbia and the Fraser trend toward the north. Even the St. John runs north for a while before it bends to the east and descends to the Bay of Fundy. Owing to the huge indentations in the northern and eastern coasts of Canada, most of the rivers find their terminus in some body of water not far distant, in global terms, from their sources. The vast, briny tongue of Hudson Bay, extending far south into the Canadian heartland and serving as a funnel to convey polar airs into southern latitudes, catches the Churchill (nearly all of which flows through a grim wilderness) after a run of a thousand miles. It also receives the Nelson, Hayes, Severn, Attawapiskat, Albany, Missinaibi, and Abitibi, and on all but the first two and the last of these there is no settlement marked on a small-scale map, though the ruins of famous York Factory lie four miles from the mouth of the Hayes. The Albany, flowing through the absolute wilderness of northwestern Ontario, is 610 miles long, which makes it all of 210 miles longer than the St. John and only 210 miles shorter than the Rhine. The St. Lawrence, pouring easterly out of Lake Ontario and then northeasterly through its trench on the edge of the Laurentian Shield, has not many hundreds of miles to go before it encounters the salt water thrusting into the estuary from the gulf. The Saskatchewan has enough water to flow on and

on like the Nile, but less than a thousand miles from its source it strikes Lake Winnipeg, through which some of its water issues finally into the Nelson.

Yet—and this has been and still is a matter of great consequence to the nation—Canada contains more inland fresh water than any other country in the world. It is estimated that eight trillion tons of water fall on Canada every year in the form of rain and snow. Apart from the four Great Lakes which she shares with the United States and the large shallow ones of Manitoba (Lake Winnipeg's area is greater than Lake Erie's) there are thousands—probably hundreds of thousands—of small lakes in the Shield and the Northwest Territories. These, of course, are glacial legacies. The river systems of Canada, properly speaking, only in rare instances can be said to include these lakes, but the voyageurs used the lakes as interconnecting links which enabled them to take their canoes from one river system to another across the country. Incredible though it sounds, the canoe parties which used to leave Montreal in the late eighteenth century were able to paddle nearly all the way to the Pacific coast. Their portages were many and exhausting, yet few of them were longer than three miles. So it came about, thanks to the maze of lakes in the Shield, that Canadian waters could be used as an east-west lateral avenue from the St. Lawrence to the Pacific *above* the American border. That is why it is accurate to say that without the rivers, the early nation could never have survived. The plains and British Columbia would have been fatally severed from the older communities of the Canadian east.

In the Maritime Provinces the only rivers which properly can be called systems are the St. John and the Miramichi, and as river systems go, these are very small ones. The great system of the Canadian east is, of course, the St. Lawrence. That of the central plains must be called the twin Saskatchewans together with the Nelson, for the Churchill flows too far north to matter much to settlement or to the development of the country. The second longest river rising in Canada is the Yukon, but most of it flows through Alaska before, after a weirdly erratic course, it reaches the Bering Sea. In the Rockies the two chief systems are the Fraser and the Columbia, and the far northwest is drained by the largest system of them all, the Mackenzie. In the prairies, however, and in the southwestern regions of the Laurentian Shield, there survive remnants of one of the vastest inland freshwater complexes in the history of the world, of which the old glacial Lake Agassiz was the heart. But more of this when we come to the Red River.

This brings me to a question which has fascinated me over the past few years, a question which I suppose is really metaphysical. What is a river, anyway? According to the Encyclopaedia Britannica, a river is any natural stream of fresh water, larger than a brook or a creek, which flows in a well-defined channel. As such, it is a basic geological agent. But though the river carves the channel, its water is always changing—the reason why Heraclitus used a river to illustrate his definition of reality, "Everything flows." Nobody, as he truly pointed out, can bathe in the same river twice.

This old idea recurred to me many times when I contemplated the Columbia Icefield. Out of this massive survival of the ice age flow two of the major streams of Canada: the North Saskatchewan and the Athabaska (which merges into the Mackenzie system). Because the icefield straddles the Great Divide, this makes it possible for the ice to feed rivers which flow, theoretically, into three different oceans. Thus we are told that rivulets leave their source in the icefield and carry the water to the Pacific, that the Athabaska water reaches the Arctic Ocean by way of the Mackenzie, and that the Saskatchewan (since Lake Winnipeg drains into Hudson Bay through the Nelson system) carries some of the icefield, converted into water, as far as the Atlantic.

But do all these things happen in just this way? Do these little trickles of melt one sees seeping out of the ice really travel all the way to those distant oceans, or are they absorbed into the atmosphere?

Incredibly, we must presume that some of the water from the icefield really does go all the way down to the various oceans. For consider the Nile which floods regularly, and carries its melted snows far north through the hottest and most arid desert in the world, yet still has an abundance of water to discharge into the Mediterranean. Yet it is certain that a vast weight of Nile water evaporates, and so must a great deal of the water in these northern streams. So once again, what is a river?

The water which evaporates, of course, turns into clouds, and the clouds into rain and snow which may fall as the winds carry them and rejoin the oceans and other streams quite different from their originals. When Shelley wrote *The Cloud* was he not in a sense also writing of rivers? Is it fanciful to imagine that all the rivers of the northern hemisphere, if not of the world, are in this sense interconnected?

Mother of mountain streams: Crowfoot glacier, Banff National Park.

The nation-makers

If any modern Canadian is curious to know how his country was valued two centuries ago, all he need do is recall some of the sentiments it inspired among famous men at that time. Voltaire's dismissal of the St. Lawrence Valley as "a few acres of snow" is almost too well known to repeat; it is less well known that Montcalm, who now is a Canadian hero, loathed the country he fought to defend. The British never valued Canada for herself. Just before the peace conference which ended the Seven Years War there was strong pressure in England in favour of trading Canada back to France in return for Guadeloupe. This little Carib isle grew sugar which makes rum, and because many people like rum, rum will always have an economic future.

But in early days few people liked the Land of Cain or the Land of Snows, nor did many believe that it could possibly have an economic future worth mentioning. Had it not been for the strategic necessity of securing the St. Lawrence as a high-road into the Ohio Territory, and also of protecting the northern flank of the rich Thirteen Colonies, Guadeloupe might easily have been England's choice.

Nor would the British of that time have been absurd if they had made such a choice. Canada may have had, as Dr. Johnson remarked of Lapland and the Scottish Highlands, "prodigious wild and noble prospects", but the Age of Reason saw nothing beautiful in wild and noble prospects, and certainly nothing useful. Least of all could the British recognize any economic future in a terrain shaggy with evergreens and horrid (to them the word meant "bristling") with the rocky outcroppings of the Precambrian Shield. In addition to all these disadvantages there was the Canadian climate, which was colder then than it is now. The journal of a British governor of New Brunswick, just before Confederation, records a temperature nearly 30° below zero in Fredericton in the first days of May.

Once more we cannot consider the British to have been stupid. The gold and practical metals of the Shield were still locked there, hidden, awaiting a twentieth-century technology to make them available to men. Two centuries ago nobody understood the value of petroleum, least of all did they know that a lake of it existed under the Alberta plain. From the servants of the Hudson's Bay Company the English might have picked up some vague information about prairie soils, but they would have presumed them unfavourable to any large creatures except the buffalo which browsed and multi-plied in the knee-high grass of a pasture a thousand miles wide. After fearful hardships the Selkirk settlers managed to keep themselves alive in Manitoba, but for decades they were the most isolated farmers in North America. Railways had to be built, farm implements mechanized, grain elevators invented before wheat-growing could become the huge industry it is today. As for the timber of the Canadian east, it never transcended a local use before Napoleon sealed off the Baltic ports from British shipping and made it profitable for Canadian business men to export timber for the masts and decks of the Royal Navy. Most of Canada, just like Siberia, had to wait for the age of technology before it could be developed.

Two centuries ago—and this the English understood when they toyed with the idea of exchanging Canada for Guadeloupe—the sole profitable Canadian enterprises were fur trading and the coastal fisheries. Of these, only the former was of real and continuing interest to the capitals of Europe.

Far different was the situation south of what is now the Canadian-American border. With climates ranging from temperate to sub-tropical, the American English soon developed an economy of considerable variety. Towns and cities flourished on the fertile lands between the sea and the Appalachians. The ports were all ice-free and in easy contact with Europe and the West Indies. By the middle of the eighteenth century a mature urban culture had grown in Boston, New York, Philadelphia, Baltimore, Charlottesville, Richmond, and Charleston, and its capacity to offer outlets to a variety of human resources and talents was soon proved by the kind of men it produced. The careers, interests, and abilities of men like Benjamin Franklin, Thomas Jefferson, John Adams, Alexander Hamilton, and John Jay were of a kind that could not have been developed in the Canada of that time, any more than the careers and abilities of men like Peter Pond and Alexander Mackenzie could have been developed within the Thirteen Colonies. Sophistication is the product of universities and the variety of urban life, epic adventures of a society much more primitive.

In the early days the Canadian experience *was* epic, and the price of such an experience is roughness and lack of education. As late as 1800, James McGill wrote to the Governor of Lower Canada that not one boy in five in the Montreal area could write his own name. Reading and writing was of no use to a canoe man (nearly all the *engagés* in the fur trade signed with an X) and for a hundred and fifty years young French Canadians had been growing up along the St. Lawrence expecting to earn their livings on the rivers leading into the west.

For this reason alone, urban growth in Canada was extremely slow, and the seniority of a few Canadian cities is no indication whatever of a cultural maturity. Though Quebec was founded some dozen years before the landing of the Pilgrims in Massachusetts, and in the mid-eighteenth century had an imposing presence on its rock above the river, it was really more fortress than city. Louisbourg in Cape Breton Island was rightly named the Gibraltar of America: nearly all of its citizens were soldiers. Halifax, founded in 1749, was originally intended as a naval and military base and only developed into a true city after the American Revolution. As for Montreal, up to the end of the Napoleonic Wars, when its population was verging on 20,000, it could almost be described as a supply depot and base camp for the fur trade carried on in the interior.

But early Canada possessed one asset the Americans lacked: the St. Lawrence River. Its rapids halted sailing ships just above Montreal, but the river struck directly through the gap between the Laurentian and Appalachian chains, and the French Canadians used it. While the Americans remained penned between the mountains and the sea, it was the high honour of the French Canadians that their boldest spirits sallied out from the St. Lawrence to explore and map nearly all of the continental interior which Americans and English-speaking Canadians now occupy. Many Americans today believe that their own West was unknown before the mountain men went up the Missouri, but French-Canadian voyageurs had been there long before the mountain men. When Francis Parkman went out on the Oregon Trail in 1846, the epic period of French-Scottish-Canadian exploration was over. But the reliable guides Parkman found in the Missouri country were all French Canadians. They were the last in a long chain of frontier adventurers whose abilities had been developed by the fur trade.

By its very nature this was a river trade. The rivers brought the traders and the Indians into contact with each other, and from the beginning the French had a wonderful naturalness in getting on with the Indians. The tributaries and backwaters of the great river systems were breeding grounds for the animals, and most of the valuable fur-bearing animals are amphibious. In early times the beaver was the animal whose fur was most highly valued in Europe, and for a curious reason: it served as raw material for the hat trade in a period when the wearing of costly hats was deemed essential to a man's status as a fine gentleman. By another of history's ironies—and Canadian history has been a huge congeries of ironies—this wild and dangerous trade owed its support to a temporary fashion in the capitals of Europe.

The dominance of the fur trade conspired with conditions of soil and climate to retard the development of a true Canadian culture. Not only was fur trading a nomadic occupation; it discouraged settlement everywhere because settlement drove off the animals. It could never afford to employ a large body of workers in the field, and the great majority of these were ignorant men who regarded themselves as a class apart, very much like mercenary soldiers in the old days. Though some of the leaders—Alexander Mackenzie, for instance, David Thompson, Alexander Henry, and William McGillivray— had intelligence and sensitivity, and hated the harshness and semi-savagery of life in the field, the goal that urged them onward never failed to give them a mental and moral dominance over the men they led.

Even the habits of the beaver tribe conspired to turn the early Canadians into rovers who departed further and further from civilization. The beaver is not a remarkably prolific animal: if let alone, the beaver population is said to increase only 20 percent annually, though the explorer David Thompson, who certainly knew the ways of the beaver a century and a half ago, asserted that each beaver pair produced from five to seven young every year. When the Europeans first arrived in America there were, according to later computations, about ten million beaver on the continent, their numbers varying between ten to fifty per square mile in the regions where they bred. This was not a large number considering the destructiveness of the trade. The beaver's habits made it impossible for him to escape his enemies because he was not a migrant. He lived in lodges. As Thompson noted, the beaver "could be attacked at any convenient time and in all seasons, and thus their numbers were reduced."

They were reduced so rapidly that in the Maritime Provinces the fur trade was virtually dead after a few years of European depredation. As early as 1635, only twenty-seven years after the founding of Quebec, beaver had almost vanished in the region about Trois Rivières, despite the fact that the St. Maurice is a great tributary which still, for most of its course, flows through uninhabited land. Champlain himself recognized that if he hoped to retain the interest of his home government in the colony of New France, the fur trade would have to be carried into the interior. *His* primary interest may have been to find the Northwest Passage to the Sea of Japan, but he was practical enough to see that if this venture was to be financed, it would have to be paid for in beaver.

It was Champlain who was the first European to recognize that if Canadians were to move in a forested country they would have to forget about horses and even about European methods of navigation. Cartier had been stopped at Lachine, and so was he:

> The water here is so swift that it could not be more so . . . so that it is impossible to imagine one's being able to go by boats through these falls. But anyone desiring to pass them, should provide himself with the canoe of the savages, which a man can easily carry.

So began, with Champlain's first tentative journey in a crazy birch-bark canoe above Montreal, the first chapter in the long saga of voyaging. The canoe, as has sometimes been suggested, would make as accurate a symbol on our coat of arms as the beaver, and the birch tree a truer emblem than the maple. Canada is one of the few countries which did not depend for its early development on the horse. In the Canadian bush a horse could neither eat nor move; if you merely tethered him there the mosquitoes and blackflies would kill him or drive him mad. But the birch-bark canoe could go wherever there was a foot of water to float it, and was so light that even the largest could be carried by a few men. The canoe made possible the careers of generation after generation of explorers who were to follow the rivers of America from Montreal to the Gulf of Mexico, to the Beaufort Sea, and finally to the Pacific Ocean.

It was Champlain, as Bartlet Brebner suggests, who invented the strange trade of voyageur, with its even stranger derivative, the coureur de bois. The difference between them was technically a legal one. The coureur de bois was an individualist who operated without a licence, and when he first appeared in the west, the servants of the Hudson's Bay Company called him a pedlar. But voyaging, as it was conceived by some of the greater spirits who engaged in it, was more than fur trading. Though men like Radisson, LaSalle, La Vérendrye, Samuel Hearne, Alexander Mackenzie, David Thompson, and Simon Fraser were certainly in the fur-trading business, essentially they were explorers.

Once Champlain had begun the fur trade along the interior waterways, the voyages multiplied with a rapidity which still astonishes the historian. So mobile was the canoe, so enticing the next bend around the river, so dominant the human instinct to know what lay around it,

that within the course of a very few years the voyageurs of French Canada were in the heartland of the continent. The names of some of them ring like bugle calls in the North American story— some of them the greatest in continental history before the age of Washington.

Etienne Brûlé, one of Champlain's "young men", almost certainly reached the Chaudière Falls on the Ottawa as early as 1610. Two years afterwards he became the first European to reach the Sweetwater Sea, as Lake Huron was then called.

Radisson, with his brother-in-law Groseilliers, was probably west of Lake Michigan by the mid-1650s. During this period (the dates are uncertain) the pair entered Lake Superior and discovered a portage over which other unknown voyageurs, probably Indians but possibly French, had passed before them! Soon after this they were in Minnesota at the top of the drainage basin of the greatest river on the continent. When the government of New France, which seldom had the quality of its greatest subjects, confiscated the furs of Radisson and Groseilliers on the excuse that they lacked a licence to trade, they went over to the English, and one result of that was the founding of the Hudson's Bay Company.

The two priests, Marquette and Jolliet, descended the Mississippi as far as the Arkansas in 1673, and thereby established beyond doubt the existence of a water avenue from the St. Lawrence to the Gulf of Mexico.

They were followed a decade later by Cavelier de La Salle. In 1680, La Salle was on the upper Mississippi with Père Hennepin, and in 1682 he reached the delta of the river and claimed the region later known as the Louisiana Territory for the French king.

About two decades later Sieur de Bienville, who may have been born in Montreal, became the first official governor of Louisiana. A road had been found and developed, though it was very thinly held, from Quebec City to the Gulf of Mexico. The French, using the rivers as only they knew how, had drawn a vast loop about the English colonists who still were confined to the Atlantic seaboard.

The last of the supremely great French discoverers, and surely one of the most interesting, was Pierre Gaultier de Varennes, Sieur de La Vérendrye. Born in Trois Rivières in 1685 (the same year, incidentally, in which Handel and Johann Sebastian Bach were born) La Vérendrye first served in colonial wars, then went to Europe to fight in the War of the Spanish Succession. After his final return to Canada, a man over forty, he took to the rivers. Armed with a monopoly for the far western fur trade, La Vérendrye was at Grand Portage in 1731 with a party of fifty including three of his sons. He worked out a successful route through the maze of small streams, lakes, and muskeg of the western Shield, and in

1734 the first white man's fort stood on the black earth of Manitoba. The vast central plain lay open to him. The Assiniboine and the South Saskatchewan wound across it and led men of the La Vérendrye party to a sight of mountains, possibly the Rockies, a little more than one hundred and thirty years after Brûlé reached the Chaudière Falls.

Nothing in later years was as epic as the sustained efforts of these early Frenchmen. It could not be. In later years the white men were better armed, and though the Indians in the Canadian west could be dangerous, they seldom if ever displayed the appalling cruelty and military vigour of the eastern savages who tortured Brébeuf to death. After the Hurons killed Etienne Brûlé, they ate him.

These facts are familiar: I repeat them only to underline the desperate nature of the early Canadian experience. There was no discharge from this war, at least not for the dedicated man. The isolation of the voyageurs, the knowledge that they were self-condemned to a life of hardship and danger before which, ultimately, their physical and moral powers were bound to fail—these thoughts haunted the bravest and boldest among them. They lacked the consolation of soldiers who risk their lives, for what they did was done without an audience, without the support of a disciplined regiment or army. They could not even communicate their experiences to civilized men, because civilized men lacked the knowledge and background to understand what they meant when they told them that the winter had descended before they could reach a base camp, or that such and such a number of portages had been made or rapids run in such and such a number of days.

Thoughts like these were in Radisson's mind when he wrote a passage with the force of poetry:

What fairer bastion than a good tongue, especially when one sees his owne chimney smoak, or when we can kisse our owne wife or kisse our neighbour's wife with ease and delight? It is a different thing when victuals are wanting, worke whole nights & dayes, lye down on the bare ground, & not always that hap, the breech in the water, the feare in the buttocks, to have the belly empty, the wearinesse in the bones, the drowsinesse in the body by the bad weather you are to suffer, having nothing to keep you from such calamity.

When New France fell and was ceded to England in 1763, the control of the Canadian fur trade passed from the French forever. English-speaking men, most of them Scottish Highlanders, now appear in the trade working with the experienced French-Canadian voyageurs who served under them in the North West Company as *engagés*. It was a partnership vital for the future of Canada, and the beginning of the Scottish influence in Canadian affairs.

For it was about this time that the Highland Scotch had finally reached the end of their long, brave, but self-damaging struggle for independence against the Anglo-Saxons of the south. The English had conquered them in 1745 and doomed the clansman's way of life. At the best of times it had been a poor life in a poor country: it has been remarked more than once that only the Highlanders and the French Canadians had the necessary background of poverty to qualify them for work on the Canadian rivers. Already the Hudson's Bay Company, scouring the British Isles for men hardy, desperate, and disciplined enough to entice into the trade, had been recruiting Orkneymen from the rocks of Ultima Thule, shipping them by the northern route into Hudson Bay and putting them to work there.

Simon McTavish, the master of the North West Company, lived in Montreal like a lord and had something of the temperament and style of a Highland chief of the better sort, though his Scottish ancestry was probably less exalted than he liked to pretend. All of these Highlanders—as distinct from the patient Orkneymen—had the intense personal pride of a race never noted for its emotional balance. This may have been one reason why they had so little sympathy for the slogans of the democratic revolution then brewing in the Thirteen Colonies. That revolution came out of the middle classes, and the Highlands had never had a middle class.

The fire, the imagination, and the boldness of these Highland leaders transformed the whole character of the fur trade and turned it into an enterprise in which business considerations, at least as seen by a cool-headed man, very often took a second place to dreams. When the American Revolution broke out, James McGill (a Glasgow man originally) instantly recognized that if the Americans won the war the southwest of the continent would soon be closed to the Canadian fur trade. When he realized that the Americans were on the point of victory, he sold his shares in the company. But Simon McTavish met the challenge by pushing it right over the edge of the map. He bet his fortune on the Athabaska region. The tenacity of McTavish and his colleagues in the face of appalling obstacles can almost be called sublime. Under the best of circumstances, fur trading was a gamble in which the margin of profit over cost was never very great. Though a few large fortunes were made in it, they were acquired by penny-pinching and a driving of the *engagés* to a degree which would horrify a modern labour union. But McTavish and his associates did not hesitate. Not even the complete success of the American

A swift century of river craft evolution

An Ojibway family in its birch-bark canoe (c. 1820).

Men doubled as mules to "track" barges upriver.

A supply scow shoots a chute on the Athabaska River.

The tough black hide of the shaggy moose sheathed this workboat on the Mackenzie River (c. 1927).

The birch-bark canoe was the brilliant invention of the first Canadians, gladly accepted by the European arrivals. To tote heavier supplies, first the "bateau" and then the York boat appeared. Until the 1920s, the stately paddlewheeler was queen of the far rivers.

Settlers on the way to Lloydminster, via the North Saskatchewan. These barges were broken up for timber on arrival.

Paddle steamers stacked with cordwood and ready to go at Fort McMurray.

Replica of *Don de Dieu* at Quebec, 1908.

Revolution lessened their compulsion to expand. Ironically, it was the blind obstinacy of these Highlanders which limited the plans of some of the shrewdest American statesmen who ever lived.

When Benjamin Franklin, John Adams, and John Jay met the English diplomats in Versailles in 1783 to draft the treaty which ended the Revolutionary War, one of their chief objects was to destroy permanently the British ability to threaten the new republic. The British were still entrenched in Nova Scotia and the St. Lawrence; the Americans had not yet moved out in any large degree beyond the Appalachians. The question of the boundary between the United States and what remained of British North America was therefore the most vital question at this conference.

The boundary to which the British finally agreed was a triumph for the United States and a permanent disaster for Canada. The British were so ignorant of North American geography they did not understand what they were giving away, and they had invited no Canadians to the conference who might have told them. Ever since 1783, the Canadian population has been penned between the Shield and the border in narrow strips. The St. Lawrence and the four northern Great Lakes were split down the middle between the two countries. Montreal was cut off totally from the Ohio Territory and the Mississippi Valley, and as a final touch, Grand Portage was slipped in just underneath the new border so that it reposed in the United States. However, the British did insist on gaining equal rights along the Pigeon and Rainy rivers, and this was to be of vital importance to Canada. It left open a canoe route to the prairies and the far west.

The Montreal fur-traders had few illusions about what this border would mean to them. In time, and the time would not be long, they would be forbidden to do any business at all in the wilderness south of the border which Canadians had explored and opened up to trade. Even Grand Portage would be closed to them. So the North West Company moved their inland base to a new site at Fort William. The cost of doing so came to £10,000 in an age when sixpence would buy you a good dinner in a London restaurant.

From this time until the North West Company was absorbed by the Hudson's Bay Company in 1821, the Montreal traders met one of the most remarkable challenges in the history of commerce. As they depended on the far northwest for their furs, they were now committed to an operation in which the supply lines were stretched to a limit which would make any normal, hardheaded man of commerce turn pale. The pelts had to be paid for in trade goods conveyed three-quarters of the way across the continent in birch-bark canoes. The pay loads had to be paddled and portaged back to Montreal over a distance of some three thousand miles. The market, nearly all of it in Europe, was still another three thousand miles to the east across the Atlantic Ocean.

Speed and efficiency of the highest kind, supported by an *esprit de corps* among the canoemen as intense as that of a championship hockey team, were the sole possible replies to a challenge so stern. The travel schedules set for the voyageurs seem incredible to the modern imagination.

Leaving Lachine in "brigades" of three to four canoes, with an experienced guide in the leading craft, the voyageurs from Montreal first set out for the Grand River, as the Ottawa was then called. At Ste. Anne de Bellevue they always stopped to pray in the chapel to the saint who protects travellers on water, and this rite gave rise to Thomas Moore's famous poem:

> *Faintly as tolls the evening chime*
> *Our voices keep tune and our oars keep time,*
> *Soon as the woods on the shore look dim*
> *We'll sing at St. Ann's our parting hymn,*
> *Row, brothers, row! The stream runs fast,*
> *The rapids are near and the daylight's past . . .*

This poem, written in soft music by a cultivated visitor to Canada, using the word "oars" instead of "paddles", depreciates its subject. The Homer of the *Iliad* might have risen to the experience of the voyageurs, but not the sweet poet of Ireland.

After paddling and portaging the Ottawa as far as Mattawa, the canoes turned south toward Lake Nipissing, crossed it, and descended the French River into Georgian Bay. Then they paddled west along the North Channel above Manitoulin Island, working in the dead or choppy waters of the lake and often losing several days if the winds were contrary. They called the wind *la vieille* (the old woman), and if she was behind them they could raise a sail. But if she was heavy against them—and the prevailing winds in the region are contrary to westbound canoes—they often had to put up on the shore because the high, steep waves of the inland lakes would break the backs of their canoes. When they went to Michilimackinac they were expected to reach their destination within a period of from thirty-five to forty days, and the same time was expected when they were bound for Grand Portage and Fort William. This voyage was accomplished with canoes fully loaded with trade goods, and there were thirty-six portages between Lachine and the Lakehead, some of them longer than a "league". In the voyageur's language, a "league" was roughly two miles. If express canoes without cargo were used, as they sometimes were on special occasions, the time was much faster. A letter survives dated in Montreal on May 6,

1817, which was received at Rainy Lake beyond Fort William on June 3.

What these voyages involved in hardship, labour, and moral stamina can no more be revealed by the historian's method of stating the facts than the truth of a battle can be conveyed by the communiqué issued by the high command after the fighting is over and the dead have been counted. From Julius Caesar to the P.R.s of the Pentagon, the truth of life and death has always been hidden behind facts and statistics. That is the trouble with history. It is probably an unavoidable trouble, but it certainly explains why so few people learn much from it.

"Our men moved their camp, marched twenty miles, and at night they placed their camp in a suitable place" — how many of us welcomed lines like these when we studied the *Gallic Wars* in school! They occurred so often we did not have to pause to work out the grammar. But they told us nothing of the realities.

On every step of that twenty-mile march, probably through hostile country, the legionaries had to carry their weapons and food, their armour and personal necessities, a total weight close to a hundred pounds per man. When the "suitable place" was reached, it was usually on a hill with a forest nearby. While one detachment marked out the lines of the camp, another dug a trench about it and still another went into the woods to cut trees. After the trunks had been trimmed, sawn up, and sharpened at one end, they were dragged to the suitable place and staked into the ground just behind the lip of the trench. Only after all this work was done could the soldier wrap himself in his cloak and fall asleep on the ground.

A similar recovery of reality is essential if any modern man is to understand the truth about life on the Canadian rivers in the voyaging days.

On May 25, 1793, a young Scot called John Macdonell set out from Lachine on his first voyage with a brigade of the North West Company. He has left a diary of that voyage written in the usual terse language of the communiqué, and he has also recorded, with the distances distinctly stated, the nature of each of the thirty-six portages between Montreal and Grand Portage—here the carrying place was nine miles long—as well as the character of the streams and lakes. With the help of the imagination, the record is a fascinating one, the more so because this was a routine voyage.

On this stage of the journey into the west, the larger canoes carried loads varying from three to four tons and were manned by crews of eight or ten men. The middle men, using short paddles, sat two abreast while the bowman and steersman were placed higher and were equipped with paddles much longer. The Montreal canoe was thirty-five to forty feet long made entirely of the bark of yellow birch placed over ribs of thin white cedar with thwarts numbering between four and nine and boards four inches wide secured just below the gunwales as seats for the paddlemen. The bark was secured by melted pine gum, and after a heavy rapid or a day's paddling the seams had to be regummed to prevent leaking. The canoe used by Alexander Mackenzie, and specially designed for his exploration of the Rockies, was so light that it could be carried by two men. But the weight of a large canoe out of Montreal was much greater than this, and required at least four men on the portage. The whole operation of portaging brings up an interesting calculation in the mathematics of labour, sweat, and tired muscles.

Superlatives have bothered me all through the writing of this book, but I cannot avoid them without diminishing what seems to me the truth. Every new thing I have learned about the Canadian voyageur seems to me more incredible than the last. His deeds originated the Paul Bunyan myths of the American northwest, and Paul Bunyan was an inheritor of Hercules and Mercury in folklore. But the true and proved facts concerning the life of the voyageur are such that I can only say that if I, physically, am a man, he, physically, was a superman.

On portages the load that had to be moved, divided up among the crew, usually totalled more than four hundred pounds per man not counting the canoe. Every man of the crew was expected to carry at least two "pieces" of goods, each weighing ninety pounds, but so great was the emulation among them that some individuals often carried three pieces or even four. They did not walk with these loads: *they carried them at a dog trot* bent half-double with the pieces on their backs and secured there by a leather band, called a tumpline, which was passed around their foreheads. More than one traveller conveyed by voyageurs in the canoes has testified that without any load at all he could barely move as fast as these men did with two hundred pounds on their backs. Finally, because they worked at the height of the insect season, the voyageurs were encased over the carrying places in humming, stinging envelopes of mosquitoes and blackflies.

In addition to the portaging there was the tracking of canoes against heavy currents and the running of rapids. The rapids were always risky, and crosses marked the graves of drowned voyageurs on the banks, clusters of them all the way from the Long Sault on the Ottawa to the mouth of the Winnipeg River. Tracking could be a nightmare. The men had to get out and haul by ropes attached to bow and stern (two ropes were essential to prevent the canoe from yawing in against the shore) and this meant slithering over wet rocks slimy with vegetable growth, stumbling over the usual litter of fallen trees, and sometimes wading breast high in the stream. As I know from personal experience, the silt along the banks of the Assiniboine, Saskatchewan, and Mackenzie is deep and soft, and after rain it has the consistency of porridge and sometimes the texture of axle grease. Along the Fraser when the men had to do a great deal of tracking under appalling difficulties, they wore out a pair of moccasins a day and had to make themselves new ones. While tracking canoes, the men were more plagued by insects even than when they portaged, because there were usually more of them along the water's edge. So paddling in a free river or in an open lake came as a marvellous release, and when the men swung into the stroke they broke into song. That was when time was made up. The mileage from Montreal to Georgian Bay was little more than the mileage from the mouth of French River through the Sault to the head of Lake Superior, and here the figures of John Macdonell tell their own story. It took his brigade thirty-one days to reach Lake Huron from Ste. Anne. But though they lost a day through a storm on the lake, they reached Grand Portage from French River in just under ten days! Look at the map, remember that most of the time they were travelling against the wind, and try to believe that this was merely a routine voyage!

At Grand Portage or Fort William the Montreal men ended their runs. The company's agent met the wintering partners from the northwest, and the trade goods were forwarded over the height of land by a special body of men to the company's fort on Rainy Lake, the eastern terminus of les vrais hommes du nord who had come down across the plains from the Athabaska country. At Grand Portage or Fort William the Montreal crews had a brief time for carousing and eating, then they reloaded their canoes with the furs and set out on the return trail to Montreal with the pay loads. If they did not get back before winter, they were frozen in and had to survive as best they could. A failure to return in time also meant a disastrous financial loss to the company.

At Rainy Lake the true Northmen took over, and these were the elite of the service. They paddled through Lake of the Woods and by a series of smaller lakes and interconnecting streams (the Winnipeg River was exhaustingly cursed by rapids) into Lake Winnipeg itself. In earlier times canoe parties used to paddle from there up the Red River into Minnesota toward the sources of the Mississippi, but after the American Revolution the goal was the northwestern edge of the North American map, Lake Athabaska and the Peace River country. The Saskatchewan and Athabaskan brigades paddled north up Lake Winnipeg to the mouth of the Saskatchewan River and then—after some very severe portages—they worked up against the current of the North Branch to Cumberland Lake and thence to Frog Portage, which

made a bridge to the Churchill River. This powerful stream, against which they also had to paddle, led them to the Methy Portage (or Portage LaLoche), a very tough one with a sharp height of land at the end of it. The Methy took them to the Clearwater, a tributary of the Athabaska, and then they coasted down that great river of the northwest into Lake Athabaska and reached their chief northwestern base at Fort Chipewyan. In the later years of the North West Company the brigades went even beyond this. They paddled up to Fort Vermilion on the Peace, and later still the fur-traders established themselves in forts on the Fraser and the Columbia.

This final leap across two-fifths of Ontario, across Manitoba, Saskatchewan, and some or all of Alberta, all of it trending north, was a race against time even more intense than the run from Montreal to the head of Lake Superior. So close was the margin between the meeting with the Montreal canoes and the coming of frost that a delay of a few days might ruin a whole voyage. According to Alexander Mackenzie, the Athabaskan brigades generally left Rainy Lake on the first of August, and had to reach Chipewyan inside two months.

What of the canoes and of the men themselves?

By the time the North West Company was established, the art of canoe-handling had so matured on the rivers that the French Canadians were much more mobile than the men of the Hudson's Bay Company. British as they were, the Bay men clung for a long time to wooden bateaux. The Nor'westers used two types of canoe which they called the canot du maître and the canot du nord, the former for the run out of Montreal, the latter, which was lighter and carried less than a ton and a half of cargo, for the run west of Fort William where the streams were shallower and tracking more frequent. The canot du nord often carried a crew of no more than five men.

But the canot du maître was a considerable craft. It had a wide beam, a remarkably high strake, and high, curved bows. It was gaily painted and travelled with a pennant blowing out from its stern and often with the picture of an Indian's head on its bows. A variety of pictures of these larger canoes survive and one of them has a feature which—at least to me—was more interesting than the canoe itself.

This was no less a personage than Sir George Simpson, the "Big Bourgeois" of the Hudson's Bay Company, the chief destroyer of the Nor'westers, and in his old age one of the richest men in Montreal. After the Bay absorbed the North West Company they not only employed the skilled Canadian voyageurs; even before that time they had adopted the classic Canadian canoes. In this picture Simpson sits in the middle wearing a top hat of massive proportions, as did many of the bourgeois (this was the old French name for the proprietor or company partner) while *en voyage*. The top hat was a mark of their quality and station. In Simpson's canoe the paddle-men are seated as usual two abreast and the bowman and steersman are in their usual places. But directly behind Simpson, who wears a grim expression on one of the most haughty faces in Canadian history, are a pair of undersized, wildlooking characters blowing bagpipes.

The presence of these pipers in Simpson's canoe gives the Big Bourgeois an extra dimension. People who worked for him knew that he was the toughest employer there ever was in a notoriously tough trade. He pinched pennies, he was ruthless, he squeezed out of his servants the last ounce of work, he paid them as little as he possibly could. One knows that Simpson understood the value of every square foot of every canoe or York boat in the service of his company. And yet, there sits that pair of private pipers! The Scotch are a peculiar people, and never more so than when they try to out-English the English in cold calculation after they have gone into business and made a success of it. But the old wildness never quite leaves the pure Scot. Behind the granite features of George Simpson, underneath his brutal surface callousness, the primitive heat burned, and hence that pair of pipers. Without them, the *canot du maître* could have carried at least two hundred more pounds of trade goods. Yet Simpson sacrificed money for the pipers, and I like to think of him sitting there in his stove-pipe hat, the mosquitoes buzzing in his hair, the canoe swaying down a rapid through the forest wilderness, and that pair of wee pipers behind him blowing his ears off.

But there were no pipers, no luxuries, for the average *engagé*—the paid voyageur of the fur-trading companies. Day after day from dawn to dusk, sometimes for eighteen hours daily, they drove those loaded canoes back and forth across the continent. As they paddled they sang the old French songs and some others of their own making. In favouring currents they could swing the stroke easily, but in adverse currents or dead water their paddles bit hard. The average rate of stroking was forty to the minute, but often they stroked at the rate of one per second, in perfect time and with only a few stops in the course of the day. The stops were called "a pipe", and their length depended on the state of the men. Travellers carried in canoes have testified that after twelve hours' paddling, with only three rests of ten to fifteen minutes each, those incredible French Canadians refused to stop because they were still "fresh". Their sense of competition with one another was Homeric. Duncan McGillivray once witnessed a race in Lake Winnipeg between Athabaska men and a rival brigade. The men paddled all out *for forty-eight consecutive hours without once leaving their canoes!* A steersman collapsed into sleep, fell overboard, and would have been drowned had not his own canoe

gone back to pick him up; he was sinking under the weight of his clothes and in a state of shock from the frigid water. In this race as the men stroked, the guides cut off hunks of pemmican and thrust them into the mouths of the paddlers.

What manner of men were these—giants? Actually, they were built more like gnomes. In 1826 an American, Thomas L. McKenney, visited the trading routes of Canada and described the voyageurs as follows:

> They are short, thick set, and active, and never tire. A Canadian, if born to be a labourer, deems himself to be very unfortunate if he should chance to grow over five feet five, or six inches—and if he shall reach five feet ten or eleven, it forever excludes him from the privilege of becoming voyageur. There is no room for the legs of such people in these canoes. But if he shall stop growing at about five feet four inches, and be gifted with a good voice, and lungs that never tire, he is considered as having been born under a most favourable star.

Freedom, T. E. Lawrence once wrote, is man's second need: here is the sole explanation of those men's willingness to engage in a trade like this, which in time was sure to break them. Though there were many instances of river men keeping on working into late middle-age, the voyageurs as a rule died young. They were lucky if they were not double-ruptured and suffering from spastic backs before they were forty. But at least they were free from the forelock-tugging kind of poverty their class had to endure in Europe. They had the pride of champions which is the surest of all proofs of an inner sense of personal value. Freedom has always been the most expensive possession in the world, and the price for it has been paid in different coin from age to age. In the early days of Canada, the coin was hardship and endurance.

There were rains and cold nights, and the only women of the interior were virtual savages. The food the men ate on the rivers makes the diet of a modern Canadian work camp seem like the fare of a Roman emperor of the decadence. On the eastern run to the Lakehead the voyageurs were called *mangeurs de lard*, or pork-eaters, and the French word gives us a good idea of the quality of the pork. In the west pemmican was the staple diet, and no more nourishing one was ever invented, but even with wild rice added, boiled pemmican at the end of sixteen hours of labour is not much to look forward to. If the schedule was not too exacting, the men fished and hunted and searched for birds' eggs, but if food ran out they would eat anything. Often they literally ate crow. The poor French voyageur, especially in the early days, usually had nothing better to eat than a kind of hominy made of split dried peas or corn impregnated with fat.

But of all the ordeals faced by the river men, that of the winterer was the worst. He was the one who had to stay out in the wilderness perhaps two thousand miles from his base. The Indians brought him furs, and though he often had an Indian wife, he sometimes was entirely alone. If game was abundant he ate well, and there was usually plenty of fish preserved from the fall through the winter. But if game failed or fish rotted, starvation or dysentery was his fate. If he fell sick there was no help for him, and his loneliness was total in a six months' winter when the prairie was nothing but a white death.

Narrow this life was, uncivilized and uneducated, but on the whole it was less brutalizing than the life in the lumber camps in the Victorian era. At the principal bases of the Hudson's Bay Company all the men were required to attend prayers regularly. There is a poignant memorandum dating from the early eighteenth-century records of the Bay which enjoins the company's servants "to live lovingly with one another not to swear or quarrel but to live peaceably without drunkenness or profaneness." The Nor'westers had a rougher tradition but more personal independence within the service; less consciousness, perhaps, that they were suffering a thankless exploitation by rich men who never troubled themselves to know at what price of human stamina and hardship the profits were earned. Nearly all the Montreal partners in the company had served at least some time on the rivers. The French-Canadian voyageur, though not fond of washing *en route*, was a considerable dandy whenever he neared a post. Even though the only women in the post were savages, he washed and put on his best clothes. He had a Gallic courtesy to counteract his almost incredible toughness, and Francis Parkman writes feelingly of the human quality of his *Canadien* guides along the Missouri. As for the Highlanders in the service of the fur trade, one of them wrote the "Lone Shieling" poem, possibly the most haunting verses ever composed in Canada.

The fur trade failed in the end; it was doomed the moment the settlers began moving into the west to farm. Long before that time there were men engaged in it who had seen the writing on the wall. Sometimes when I walk up the avenue of the McGill campus and reach the Founder's tomb, I think back on the life he led and the shrewd Lowland caution which prompted James McGill to take his money out of the fur trade in time. He had never been a true voyageur, merely a poor boy from Scotland who had entered the only Canadian trade which offered him a living. He had earned his place in the Beaver Club by a winter spent alone near the headwaters of the Mississippi, but he got off the rivers before the life on them broke him. McGill lacked the transcendent imagination of Simon McTavish and the last-ditch loyalty of William McGillivray, but he had much com-

mon sense. Unlike most of his old colleagues in the fur trade, he did not die broke. His life had taught him that civilization could never grow in Canada under the conditions he had known in his youth. Though he was well off by colonial standards, he would never have been accounted an especially rich man in England. He left just enough to make it possible to found a college. Until a few years ago, McGill University lay like a quiet pattern of order in the roaring tumult of modern Montreal; it is still the most important visible monument to the North West Company's great adventure.

For the economic contribution of the fur trade after the American Revolution has surely been exaggerated. It is a common argument that furs saved the country from being absorbed by the United States because they provided an east-west trade, all Canadian, in a continent where the normal lines of economic communication run north and south with the greater power and population of the United States sucking the wealth of Canada southward. I cannot believe this. The fur trade may have bridged an economic gap for a number of years, but the true reason why it saved Canada from absorption was not economic. It was political, and none of the explorers understood this as well as did David Thompson, who detested Lord Ashburton for surrendering to the United States land which he himself had won by the rights of prior exploration.

Not only did the voyageurs explore most of North America; after 1783 they staked out Canadian—or, at that time, British—claims to the whole northwestern hinterland from the head of the Lakes to the Pacific. When the tide of homesteaders fanned out from the railheads in the American mid-west in the nineteenth century, the Canadian west would surely have been occupied by them, and subsequently claimed as American territory by the American government, had not the ancient rights of prior exploration, which the Americans respected, bound the land to Canada. The lonely posts were on the plains, in the Fraser and Columbia valleys, on the Pacific coast, and the Union Jack flew over all of them. Yet only a handful of men achieved this result. At the height of its power the North West Company may have employed as many as five thousand men, but less than two thousand were in service in the field between Montreal and Chipewyan. It was not their numbers that counted, but what they did. And in the long run what was done by the dreamers mattered the most.

David Thompson was probably the greatest geographer ever developed in North America; without his work, backed by Simon Fraser's voyage down the river which bears his name, it is hard to believe that British Columbia would now be a Canadian province. And of course there was Alexander Mackenzie, the boldest of all the Canadian explorers after La Vérendrye, but David Thompson, the most accurate and thorough of all individual surveyors in continental history, was the key man.

A dozen years before Lewis and Clark, Mackenzie reached the Pacific through North America. He threaded to the end the Northwest Passage. Its reality bore no resemblance to the European dream of a great gorge which would float sailing ships from the Old World through the continental land mass of the New. It was simply the chain of rivers, lakes, and portages which enabled canoes from Montreal to move all the way from the St. Lawrence across Canada to the northern and western oceans.

"Alexander Mackenzie, from Canada, by land, the twenty-second of July, one thousand seven hundred and ninety-three"—this celebrated understatement, scrawled in a mixture of vermilion and grease on a rock in Dean Channel after Mackenzie's passage down the Bella Coola, wrote *finis* to a quest begun exactly three hundred and one years earlier when Christopher Columbus set out across the Atlantic from Palos. The reality found by Mackenzie served only to dissipate the dream. But it introduced a new reality, just as Columbus's lost quest drew an entire hemisphere into the story of civilization. How strange that a Canadian birch-bark canoe without a name, last in a long succession of canoes from Champlain's first one, should have earned a place in the company of ships like the *Santa Maria* and the *Golden Hind*!

A lost skill. William Notman (1826-91) recorded construction of a Montagnais canoe.

Interlude

Forsan et haec olim meminisse iuvabit—no, it does not always follow that in later years it is a pleasure to remember hardship, passion, and suffering. In the eighteenth century, when Englishmen for the first time in their history could afford to relax and begin to enjoy life, there was a general and polite forgetting of the heroic age of Elizabeth and the struggle for popular freedom against Charles I. When hardships are unavoidable they can sustain a man, but once they have passed, after he has had time to understand them with his mind, the pain rises and hurts.

Shakespeare's insight recognized this when he wrote the passage in which Othello, speaking of his first meetings with Desdemona, tells of the desperate strugglings and sufferings of his younger days:

> *'Twas pitiful, 'twas wondrous pitiful:*
> *She wisht she had not heard it: yet she wisht*
> *That heaven had made her such a man: she thanked me;*
> *And bade me, if I had a friend that loved her,*
> *I should but teach him how to tell my story,*
> *And that would woo her. Upon this hint I spake:*
> *She loved me for the dangers I had past,*
> *And I loved her that she did pity them.*

It was so difficult, it was so terribly difficult, to build a community, much less a nation, in Canada's harsh terrain. What wonder when the railroads were built, when the buffalo herds vanished and the Indians were retired to reservations, that a people rapidly becoming middle class should no longer wish to think much about the truth of the early days. Step by step in the nineteenth century, leap by leap in the twentieth, Canadian society has fled from its past.

I think of Sir John Macdonald, still Prime Minister but an old man, sitting on the cow-catcher of one of the first C.P.R. locomotives and travelling in exultation up the Kicking Horse, over the Great Divide into British Columbia. The barrier of those mountains had haunted his entire political life. On the conquest of them had depended his country's survival; Canadians alone had had to build that railway through their own Rockies. On the day when Sir John first rode through, he must have felt like a man who has always been poor, always stretched to the limit, always been required *to prove* that his country had a right to exist, and then suddenly, beyond expectation, knows that at last both he and the country have not quite failed. With the coming of the railways, most of the rivers ceased to be avenues of travel.

Yet even in the present century there have been men who used them as such, just as everyone did in the old days. Charles Camsell was one of these, and he died only in 1958. Born in Fort Liard in the Mackenzie country where his father was a factor in the Hudson's Bay Company, Camsell grew up beside that vast, lonely river of the Northwest Territories nearly two thousand miles away from any organized community. When he went to school he had to go all the way to Winnipeg, a distance of eighteen hundred miles, and he did so by canoe, York boat, Red River cart, and his own feet. When his education was over, he spent many years of lonely exploration in the Mackenzie and Yukon regions; he nearly lost his life to a polar bear, to hostile Eskimos, and even to hunger. Years later he became Deputy Minister of Mines and Resources, and in this capacity he once flew with Punch Dickins over some of the territory he had covered by canoe and dog team. It was like leaping from the primitive past into the technological future in the span of a few years of life. Camsell remarks, without further comment, that he and Dickins accomplished in two hours a journey which once had taken him half a year.

But the rivers of Canada are still there, and their appearance and character have changed little or not at all in the last century and a half. It is only our use of them that has altered. Now we fly over them, build dams on them, fish in them for sport, use them for municipal water supplies, and some of them we have poisoned with sewage and industrial effluents. We even give them a passing glance when we cross them on government-built bridges or drive beside them at seventy miles an hour.

But the rivers are as worth knowing as they ever were, though none of us will know them as the voyageurs did. The art of canoe-handling, in which Canadians once excelled the world, has so vanished in Canada that at some Olympic Games contests our few competitors have been overwhelmed by Russians from the Dnieper and by Germans and Austrians from the Rhine and the Danube. But the memory of the canoes is there, however buried, and in the past few years, many young Canadians are taking to them again. A small party of McGill students in the late sixties even went down the Fraser on an unsinkable (but not untippable) raft made of some combination of rubber and plastic.

A great river, after all, is more than a personality in its own right. It is a vital link with a people's past, and also it is a mystery. The eternal river is always a new river yet forever the same; just as men are new in each generation but forever the same, and always must relearn what the others learned before them. As I did myself, at least up to a point, when I found out that a personal discovery of the rivers of Canada was also a discovery of the country which had given me a home.

ST. LAWRENCE
THE RIVER OF KANATA

Across the outfall, where river becomes gulf, the noble St. Lawrence is a sea in all but name.

To the early seafarers, the great waterway beckoned as the entry to the Northwest Passage, leading to the riches of Cathay. As Cartier entered the portal, he gave the name of the martyr St. Lawrence to a sheltering harbour; the mighty *fleuve* was to him the river of Kanata, the Indian term bequeathed to the whole land. In this album, the camera of John de Visser retraces the upstream voyage of discovery.

Past the dark mouth of the Saguenay

In the hundred miles from Bic up to Murray Bay, the St. Lawrence shows the traveller the mountains of Notre Dame to the south, the Laurentian Highlands to the north, and, in the stream, the verdant relief of Ile Verte and Ile aux Lièvres—where Cartier's men chased hares for the pot. In the age of exploration, the white beluga whale was plentiful in these waters and "fish like horses which go on land at night". Translation: the walrus.

The harbour at Bic.

Where the Saguenay joins.

At St. Fabien.

Baie Ste. Catherine.

St. Siméon: rugged and remote.

Brave little towns
on brooding shores

*The lonely spire of St. Siméon guards
the mouth of the tributary Noire on the North
Shore. Here, the highway swings away
for Chicoutimi, 70 miles up the Saguenay, and
the Lake St. John country of Maria
Chapdelaine. In the navigation season, a car
ferry crosses the river from St. Siméon
to Rivière du Loup, via the Ile aux Lièvres.*

A blazing sun sets over Rivière du Loup, the former Fraserville, 120 miles below Quebec City. This lumbering centre on the lower South Shore is the jumping-off place for the rugged Temiscouata country and the Madawaska valley of New Brunswick.

Notre Dame du Portage is one of a string of popular summer resorts (Trois Pistoles is another) along the South Shore in Rivière du Loup County. The Du Loup and Trois Pistoles rivers drain this territory, adding their water to the giant flow of the St. Lawrence firth, estimated at 400,000 cubic feet per second at the mouth.

The camera swings again to the Côte Nord, to Port au Persil, close by Murray Bay, an area pioneered by Captain John Nairne in 1761 after the British victory at Quebec. Nairne lived on his seigniory for more than forty years. Champlain had labelled the harbour mal baie ("bad bay") but that's never deterred the tourists.

Baie St. Paul: where sea and river mingle

At the head of its deep inlet on the North Shore, Baie St. Paul marks the furthest reach of the fresh water that has poured through half a continent. Here, where the Du Gouffre ("Whirlpool") River tumbles into the mainstream, the St. Lawrence is brackish to the taste, but still salt enough to encourage the seaweeds that decorate the rocks of the Precambrian shore.

Hugging close to the northern coastline, the historic Ile aux Coudres splits the stream. Here, Jacques Cartier and others, diet-weary after the long Atlantic buffeting, stopped off to sample the wild hazel nuts. The six-mile-long island is the accepted locale for the first mass said in Canada; a stone cross marks the spot. The date: September 7, 1535.

From this point onwards, as the river begins to command the sea, ships from all the ports of the world seek the 35-ft. channel that lies open to them clear up to the humming docks of Montreal.

"The river is one of the noblest in the world"—the writer is gentle Frances Brooke in that first of all Canadian novels, The History of Emily Montague (1769). But the St. Lawrence is first of all a workaday river, as the scenes below describe.

Sentinel of stone: "Kebec . . . where the river narrows"

Every traveller who approaches Quebec by sea reaches for his own superlatives. A symphony of a city. The only walled city on the continent. At the core of the modern capital lie the stones of Champlain's fortress, founded a dozen years before the Pilgrim Fathers saw Plymouth Rock. At every vantage, the St. Lawrence River fills the eye, and the camera's lens. Across one thousand yards stands Lévis, southern bastion of what was once veritably the "gateway to the New World". But the sea is definitely here too, with tides rising eighteen feet at the docks.

Cape Diamond: a Gibraltar in the west.

The settled shores of a mature stream

Quebec City: bridges old and new.

Pulp for tomorrow's papers.

Close by Lotbinière.

From the bridge, Trois Rivières.

The spires and shrines of a devout people

At Cap Santé.

The shrine at Cap de la Madeleine.

A streamside sanctuary.

Quo vadis?

Up from Montreal: a river in harness

With Montreal and its mountain as backdrop, an ocean-going freighter skirts the sail roofs of Expo as it moves silently into the neck of the St. Lawrence Deep Waterway— the "Seaway" as everyone calls it. The foaming rapids that once blocked the way at Lachine are by-passed by canal and others drowned by dammed-up water. Proceeding by river, lake, and higher canal systems, the freighter is offered a 27-ft. channel clear to Thunder Bay, at the head of Lake Superior.

Below: a Russian liner visits Montreal.

Below: *At Prescott, where Ontario shares the river with New York State, one of three dams helps to create the artificial Lake St. Lawrence, smothering the Long Sault rapids and providing a head of water for hydro plants producing 2,200,000 h.p.*

The North American laker, 730 ft. long and 75 ft. wide (made to fit snugly into the locks), takes a million bushels of wheat past Morrisburg, Ontario, on its way to Montreal. On the way back, it will bring 25,000 tons of iron ore from Sept Iles.

Overleaf
The fifty-mile run of the St. Lawrence between Brockville and Kingston, as the river threads the Thousand Islands, is hurdled by the graceful Ivy Lea Bridge.

The watchdog at the gate

*The St. Lawrence begins here, and still guarding the door—as it once did
in earnest—stands the stone pile of Fort Henry (at the tip of the central point).
The city of Kingston lies beyond, treasuring memories of Frontenac, La Salle, and
Montcalm, equally proud of Bradstreet, Simcoe, and Macdonald. From these coves bigger
warships than Nelson's "Victory" sailed out to give battle on Lake Ontario.*

The St. Lawrence

THE IMPERIAL RIVER

To think about the St. Lawrence as a separate entity in a book of this nature is impossible; leaving out the Colorado and the Rio Grande, its story is connected with that of every other important stream in North America west of the Appalachians and even with the rivers of British Columbia, Idaho, Oregon, and Washington. It was the St. Lawrence which led the explorers to all of them. It was to the St. Lawrence that they returned with their furs and the news of their discoveries, it was into the St. Lawrence that the men and supplies were brought, and over various sections of it that the armies battled.

So much is known of the St. Lawrence that it is unnecessary to discuss it in detail. Yet this best-known river, like so many other fundamental influences in Canada, is remarkably taken for granted. As happens with all truly great river systems, the experts differ about its dimensions. But the old question, "How long is it?", while unimportant in itself, in the case of the St. Lawrence is worth asking, for it serves as a pointer to some of the unusual aspects of the system as a whole.

The St. Lawrence basin is the third largest in North America, its area generally computed at 365,000 square miles. But the system is underestimated by such a figure because it contains a feature unique among the rivers of the earth: the five Great Lakes which are a part of it. Their total area comes to 95,000 square miles, which is almost twice the area of England. If they were not reservoirs transferring their excess volume into one another and finally into the stream, if all the water in the system found its way to the sea through the St. Lawrence channel, this river would rival the Amazon. But, of course, such a thing could never happen because nearly all the water in the five Great Lakes is ponded.

There is certainly an immense amount of it. The maximum depth of Superior is 1,302 feet; of Huron 750; of Michigan 923; of Erie 210; of Ontario 774. The lakes are set in the land in a series of four tiers. Superior's height above sea level lies between 602 and 623 feet, which means that most of its bottom is well below the surface of the sea. The reason why the surface height varies is the pressure of the winds, which on occasion can force the water against one shore while the surface in another area is depressed; it is wind, not the attraction of the moon, which has led many people to believe that Lake Superior has a tide. Huron and Michigan share the second tier at a height of 580 feet. Erie, on the third tier, has a height of 572 feet. The height of Ontario at the point where it overflows into the channel of the St. Lawrence proper is 245 feet.

These drops from tier to tier are extremely gentle except in the region between Erie and Ontario; there the Niagara which links them rushes in a furious rapid to plunge over its falls. But along the forty-mile-long St. Mary between Superior and Huron the total drop is only thirty feet at the most, while Lake St. Clair and the St. Clair River drop only eight feet between Huron and Erie. As for the river proper, the drop from its egress at the eastern end of Lake Ontario until it merges with the sea is only 246 feet. The Great Lakes, the river's source, are also its main stabilizers.

These figures explain why the St. Lawrence system has become the greatest inland traffic avenue the world has ever known. Were it not for the rapids it would have been too good to be true, for nowhere else has nature made travel and transport easier for restless man. The lower St. Lawrence flows with just enough velocity not to be sluggish, and only in its rapids with too much velocity to be navigable. So wide is its channel, so even its flow, that in spring freshet it never floods higher than ten feet unless piles of ice act as dams to its current. For these reasons, no less than the fact that it leads directly through the gap between the Appalachian and Laurentian chains, it is no wonder that the St. Lawrence has become the life stream which sustains so much of North American industry and commerce, with the great cities of Chicago, Milwaukee, Cleveland, Detroit, Toronto, Montreal, and Quebec supported by it, with grain and ore floating through it in such quantity that even before the International Seaway was built, the traffic on the St. Lawrence system was more than double that of the Rhine and five times that of Suez.

But how much of the St. Lawrence system can truly be called a river?

When David Thompson first began his long work as astronomer and surveyor for the North West Company and established the true longitude and latitude of the source of the Mississippi (ignored by Lord Ashburton when he negotiated the Webster-Ashburton Treaty which cost Canada some extremely valuable real estate), he held that the head of the St. Lawrence was "at the falls of the St. Maries, the discharge of Lake Superior . . . which flows into Lake Huron".

Most modern atlases and encyclopedias give the ultimate source as the little river St. Louis which rises near the head of the Mississippi and drains easterly into Lake Superior. Calculating a line through the heart of the Great Lakes and the central channels of their connecting streams, then down the main channel to the Gulf to a point in the vicinity of Anticosti, they arrive at a figure of 1,900 miles.

It so happens that Thompson also explored and described the St. Louis River and one of his observations offers one of the many proofs of his marvellously precise mind. He noted a marshy area "somewhat like a height of land between the Mississippi and the River St. Louis, as from its west side it sends a brook into the former, and from its east side a brook into the latter." The St. Louis itself he describes as "a bold stream of about a hundred yards in width and eight feet in depth, and the current three miles an hour. . . ." After passing through a number of rapids and falls, the St. Louis does indeed discharge into Lake Superior.

The single fact, that the same tiny "height" of marshy land can feed both the St. Lawrence and the Mississippi systems, indicates as well as any example I have ever come upon how extremely delicate can be the geographical balances.

But to return to the St. Lawrence proper. There can be no doubt that all five Great Lakes, reservoirs though they may be, are an essential part of its life. Yet if we accept the definition which says that a river is "any natural stream of fresh water which flows in a well-defined channel", I do not see how anyone can deny that the St. Lawrence is the shortest stream of great importance in the whole of Canada. It can easily be proved that it is shorter than the St. John.

For consider its course. It becomes a true river only where the channel leaves Lake Ontario and enters the bay of the Thousand Islands. From this point to Quebec City the distance is slightly under 400 miles. Though the "river" certainly continues for many miles below Quebec, the moment the stream has embraced the Ile d'Orléans its waters cease to be entirely fresh. The pulse of the distant Atlantic thrusting into the Gulf through Cabot Strait is felt by the fresh water even as high upstream as Trois Rivières. At Ile d'Orléans, a full 650 miles away from Cabot Strait, tides have been recorded as high as nineteen feet. Ocean fish abound in the river between Murray Bay and Rivière du Loup, and though the water here is to some extent brackish, there is true seaweed along the shores. So this majestic reach of the lower river, steadily widening until at the estuary the width is ninety miles, is not a river at all but what the Scots would call a firth and the Norwegians a fjord.

But no matter what name we apply to it, how incomparable the St. Lawrence is! Sky-blue on fine days it comes out of Lake Ontario into the maze of the Thousand Islands on into its great driving curve with the weight of the lakes behind it. So impetuous was the rush of the upper stream that it had to be controlled by the Cornwall Power Dam and the Long Sault Spillway dam

on the American side; before the dams were built it virtually hurled itself through the Galops and the Long Sault into the tranquillity of Lake St. Francis, at the end of which it has been again controlled by the Beauharnois Canal and lower down by some other works. It passes on into the calm bight of Lake St. Louis southwest of the Island of Montreal, then through the famous rapids of Lachine into still another stabilizer, La Prairie Basin, which is flanked on one side by the Seaway and on the other by Montreal itself. After the city is passed there are some lovely islands, some fair old towns like Verchères on the right bank that almost compensate for the hideous, foul-smelling, polluting congeries of heavy industries and oil refineries at Pointe aux Trembles. Soon afterwards the river swells into the seven-mile-wide Lake St. Peter where hundreds of thousands of waterfowl bred for centuries and until very recent times people lived a semi-aquatic life in the little bayous. Deep purple-blue, it has the nobility of the Strait of Gibraltar as it moves past Point Platon. It is deep, strong, and in light breezes laced with the finest of white foam as it flows through the narrows under the rock of the old fortress city (the word *kebec* was Algonquin for "Narrows"). After it embraces the Ile d'Orléans it enters its firth which widens steadily with the flanking hills rising, finally, to the height and dignity of true mountains.

The physical impact of the lower St. Lawrence is always tremendous. Here nature has been the cruellest of spendthrifts. Though there are some rich bottoms along the stream, the fertile valley is astonishingly narrow. So much space, so much water, and so little of it useful to farmers. Trying to describe the St. Lawrence below Montreal in my novel *Two Solitudes* I wrote a bravura passage which in spite of some geological inaccuracy, still seems valid so far as it goes:

Nowhere has nature wasted herself as she has done here. There is enough water in the St. Lawrence to irrigate half of western Europe, but the river pours right out of the continent into the sea. No amount of water can irrigate stones and most of Quebec is solid rock. It is as though millions of years back in geologic time a sword had been plunged through the rock from the Atlantic to the Great Lakes and savagely wrenched out again, and the pure water of the continental reservoir, unmuddied and almost useless to farmers, drains untouchably away. In summer the clouds pass over it in soft, cumulus pacific towers, endlessly forming and dissolving to make a welter of movement about the sun. In winter when there is no storm the sky is generally empty, blue and glittering over the ice and snow, and the sun stares out of it like a cyclops' eye.

The Gaspé takes its name from the Indian
gespeg — the "end of the world".
Here, the St. Lawrence greets the sea.

An exaggeration, perhaps, but not a big one. I went on to speak of the old Quebec farms hugging the shores between the rocky uplands and the stream; of the roads on either side of it (this was long before the Trans-Canada Highway) like a pair of village main streets linking the settlements, one street nearly a thousand miles long if you follow it from the Quebec-Ontario border all the way down to the tip of the Gaspé Peninsula. I wrote of the manner in which the land was divided in early days between seigneurs and their sons, then between tenants and their sons, with the result that sections of the lower river's slim band of farmland remind you of the course of a gigantic steeplechase, the fences making long rectangles as they run inland, the farms established in these long narrow patterns because a river frontage was vital in the days when the river was the chief means of communication. Finally I wrote of Montreal where the original Canadian ethnic groups met without really mingling, the pulse of their encounter throbbing from east to west across the land.

Even the climate of the lower St. Lawrence is violently dramatic in its contrasts, because the river valley serves as a funnel between the airs of the high arctic and the sub-tropical climate of the lower Mississippi. In the late summer of 1937, most of which I spent in Russia, I came home up the river on the old *Empress of Britain*, which was bombed to death only three years later. At seven in the morning in the lower stream the temperature on deck was only 42 degrees and the surface of the river was covered with a swirling pattern of fog. But when we docked at Wolfe's Cove in mid-afternoon we could hardly breathe; the temperature verged on 100 degrees. Late that night we reached Montreal saturated with sweat to find that the heat in our apartment was 84 degrees at midnight. So it continued for twelve days—we lived in the west end of the city then—until on a Sunday afternoon at five o'clock, the thermometer at the window reading 94 degrees, finally the storm broke. We watched the lightning flashing out of huge thunderheads and then with a roar the wind came and the whole city was hidden by the rain. An hour later the storm ceased and looking at the thermometer again, I saw that the temperature had plunged to 38 degrees. Is there any other part of the world where you can get climactic shifts as sudden as these? I doubt it. And somehow they seem symbolic of Canada, subject to invasion by both north and south, but with the balance of power always in the north.

It is the lower St. Lawrence which has the tributaries, the gentle upper river being a kind of geological afterthought. The chief one is of course the Ottawa, but I find it hard to call this river a tributary because millions of years ago it was the master stream. Each of the tributaries has a legend and a history of its own. The Richelieu,

draining Lake Champlain and entering the St. Lawrence at Sorel, has the richest farming valley in the whole of land-poor Quebec. During what the Americans call the French and Indian Wars, it was the invasion route for a century and a half of warfare until at last Gentlemanly Johnny Burgoyne marched down from Montreal to suffer at Saratoga one of the most decisive military defeats in the history of the world. Since then the Richelieu has suffered the usual attentions at the hands of humanity. A little canal was built out of Chambly long ago to avoid its rapids; the canal is so narrow that only pleasure craft use it now. The river's flow has been somewhat dammed and of course it has been turned into an open sewer. A similar fate was suffered by the St. Francis and the twin Yamaskas, rivers of the Eastern Townships with their deep volcanic lakes and rolling hills like the Scottish Lowlands. There is the wild Maurice down which the logs come to the polluted air of Trois Rivières, followed by the lumbermen roaring into the towns when the season's work is done; the Montmorency with its falls like a stained white scarf hanging, apparently stationary, against a cliff 265 feet high; finally, the Saguenay.

But the Saguenay is not a true tributary of the St. Lawrence, though it is often described as such. It is a genuine system in itself. Yet, like the St. Lawrence, the Saguenay is certainly a part of that vast area the geologists call the Laurentian Upland, and the remembrance of those contorted hills twisting northwest from the north shore of the St. Lawrence fjord brings me inevitably to the awful forces which made them what they are and left to more than ninety percent of the Canadian land-mass a virtually soil-less cover.

In the huge region spreading westward from Labrador and southward into Mediterranean latitudes—geographically, Montreal is close to the latitude of Genoa—the glaciers were merciless. Formidable remnants of them still exist farther north.

Four distinct sheets of ice, possibly even five, have formed in different periods over the St. Lawrence, the Laurentian Upland, and indeed over virtually all of Canada. They advanced southward like some terrible curse of a cold and angry god to cover the territory of the Great Lakes and the upper Mississippi basin. The human imagination has little difficulty in understanding that the sun is a chain reaction of H-bomb explosions; nothing sentient has ever existed in the sun. But we do live on this earth and millions of us have identified ourselves with parts of it that we have loved. The poetic fallacy is a part of our human nature and the poet in all of us can feel for the earth as we might for a human being condemned to an aeon of Promethean torment.

All figures connected with the ice age are so vast we

cannot imagine them; we can accept them only as figures. During the last glacial period the ice sheet spreading from Labrador across and over Keewatin had an area estimated at 9,000,000 square kilometres, which almost equals that of the present Soviet Union. Its average thickness was 2,400 metres. Its volume has been estimated at 20,600,000 cubic kilometres. This whole mass lay with insensate indifference over the land where we now live. It lay for thousands of years in absolute silence because there were no living creatures to hear the winds or the crack and rumble of shifting ice. The cold silence of the Columbia Icefield can still give a suggestion of what it was like then.

Was it from nature, I wonder, that the dramatic poets learned that the primal forces in a drama are always fatally simple? That more often than not, tragedy is the product of a purposeless logic?

The cause of the ice age was awesomely elementary. For some unknown reason the sun gave off less heat than it had given off before or afterwards. The sun at present maintains a precarious balance between heat and cold on the earth, a favour it grants to no other planet in the solar system. But there is no reason why anyone should rely on it doing so forever. When a blizzard strikes the Montreal region in mid-May, when drift ice clogs the Gulf of St. Lawrence in the first week of June, anyone can imagine how it was when the ice age began. There arrived a time when more snow fell in the winter than melted in the summer. It was as simple as that. That first fatal summer lowered still further the temperature of the earth, just as, in 1972, the ice fields that formed in May in the Gulf of St. Lawrence lowered the mean temperature of the water in August by more than 8 degrees Fahrenheit from the temperature of the August previous. Another and another cold season into thousands of years. As the ice cap rose higher and higher to a final height of between 6,000 and 10,000 feet, the monstrous weight of it crushed down the land. All the rivers in what now are the temperate zones of the northern and southern hemispheres were frozen solid under the ice and discharged no more water into the seas. So the seas dropped far below their present levels.

Then, as the ice grew still heavier, it began to move, and it moved at first with unimaginable slowness—perhaps no faster than four feet a year. It moved also with a power and momentum equally impossible to imagine. It acted like a grading machine with the mixed attributes of a plough, a bulldozer, and a colossal hydraulic press. If most of Manitoba is billiard-table flat, it is because an icepack nearly 10,000 feet high squashed it flat. If its black earth is wonderfully fertile, it is because myriads of octillions of creatures died in the ice and later in the waters that formed into a huge lake when the ice cap was

receding. If the lower St. Lawrence is not a river but a fjord, it is because the ice carved out that fjord in its glacial progress.

There are few regions of the earth where the geological story is more wonderful and obvious than in the St. Lawrence System. Not even the Great Lakes were always there. In pre-glacial times their present beds were wide valley basins created by rivers which vanished long ago. Those streams flowed at a height of from 400 feet to 600 feet above the ocean level of that time, which we infer from the elementary fact that it is impossible for any river to flow below the level of the seas. Yet today, as we have seen, the bottoms of all the Great Lakes except Erie are from 300 to 400 feet *below* the present sea level. How did this change occur?

Once more we return to the mindless architect of the north, the glacier. Its godlike weight with a base shod with rock scarred and eroded the surface of the earth and at the same time crushed it down. When finally the glacier melted, the same depressions it had created were ready to receive and pond the water, and in the area of the Great Lakes the ponds became literally inland seas. While all this was happening, what is now the demure little Grand River of Michigan came into its own. It drained volumes of glacial melt across the southern peninsula of what now is the state of Michigan into the great lake forming there.

Even more fantastic, as every student of elementary geology knows, was the story of the main St. Lawrence Valley. Everywhere the melting ice was causing a rise in the oceans until finally they rose higher than the shores which had previously contained them. Saline water came flooding up the St. Lawrence and formed the inland body of brackish water the geologists called the Champlain Sea. This began to form as recently as 13,000 years ago and for close to 4,000 years the St. Lawrence Valley up to Lake Ontario, the Ottawa Valley, Lake Champlain, and most if not all of the Eastern Townships were flooded by it. During this time New England, New Brunswick, and Nova Scotia formed an island separated from the rest of the continent by a shallow sea which ran out in a strait to the Atlantic along the valley of the present Hudson. As I write these words in an eastern township I can look out my window at a deep lake which once was a part of the Champlain Sea. If I climb the nearest hill I can discern the line of the distant mountains of Vermont and New Hampshire which once formed the shoreline of the New England-Acadia island. Marine shells are still imbedded at the foot of some of those hills.

After the terrible load of ice had disappeared, the land rose in the north just as a sponge will rise after it has been crushed by a human hand. Slowly, but in geological time very quickly, the land rose to a final lift, in places, of

Man fights the gelid grip of winter

While the rest of the nation huddles to its central heating, the icebreakers of the lower St. Lawrence shatter the white silence as they force passage across the Gulf. John de Visser took these pictures in March as the "John A. Macdonald" kept ore cargoes moving.

59

2,400 feet. As the land rose, the force of gravity pulled the Champlain Sea out of the upper St. Lawrence and the Hudson-Champlain lowlands into the Atlantic whence it had risen. We can imagine the St. Lawrence rumbling and foaming in a vast spate to the sea through the main channel. If there were thousands of years of ice silence on the Laurentian Upland, how boisterous must have been the noise of the waters as they went home again to the sea, whence they would succumb once more to the power of the sun and rise into clouds which would drop rain and snow onto the recovering earth?

Then it was that the present St. Lawrence System came into being. It supplanted the Ottawa, which previously had carried off the inland waters. As all the Great Lakes diminished, the present drainage system of the three upper ones established itself through the St. Clair and the Niagara on through Lake Ontario into the upper St. Lawrence channel. So it came about that while the St. Lawrence below Montreal is a very old channel, the St. Lawrence above the city is a young one with the usual attributes of a young river—an uneven gradient alternating between calm stretches, lakes, and tumbling rapids.

As the St. Lawrence in geological time was usually more than a mere river, so also it has been more than a river in the few years during which *homo sapiens* has been trying to inherit and dominate the planet where he lives. The St. Lawrence has made nations. It has been the moulder of the lives of millions of people, perhaps by now of hundreds of millions, in a multitude of different ways. At some time in my middle years I realized that the river and its people have been the principal catalyst in my own microscopic existence.

A number of springs ago, on the fourth of my five voyages on the lower St. Lawrence, standing by the greasy taffrail of a Manchester freighter drawing out from Quebec for its journey down to the sea, the idea came to me that my life would have been totally different had it not been for my long association with this river. Though all my ancestors were in British North America long before Confederation, I am myself—if words mean anything—almost as much a New Canadian as any immigrant. A Nova Scotian from the Atlantic shore, I was all of twenty-eight years old before I came to live in the country my great-grandparents had called "Canada".

They used to speak in awed tones about the St. Lawrence. Though I suppose I was taught in school that the river forms the boundary between the United States all the way from Lake Ontario to Cornwall (the American

negotiators in 1783 made sure they would own at least half of it, which in the eyes of John Adams signified that soon they would own all of it), the river always seemed to me as Canadian as the Rhine is German though it rises in Switzerland and reaches the sea in Holland. Socially and politically this comparison is particularly apt, for the Rhine, from Julius Caesar to now, has profoundly affected the history and the collective character of the divers peoples who have lived beside it. Its very position in the European landscape destined it to become an imperial river, for it was at once an avenue for commerce and a frontier between rival cultures. It even created what in Quebec is called a "language problem". Ask any Alsatian what *that* has meant to him.

Like most Anglophone Canadians in the thirties, I had no understanding whatever of the weird social complexities of Laurentia before I went there to live. I arrived in Montreal in the fall of 1935 because a boys' school had offered me the only job I could find anywhere. It paid me twenty-five dollars a week, gave me the use of a tiny room with a truckle bed and a desk large enough barely to hold a typewriter. Though it also gave me three meals a day, the supper was usually such thin pickings that I often had to eke it out with a late snack at a Honey Dew restaurant a mile away. When I began the job there were only two Canadians on the staff—the French master and myself, and he was a French-Canadian Protestant. All the others were Englishmen and many of them "went home" the day after the summer term ended. Not bad for an introduction to Laurentia.

I wanted to become a writer but I did not know how to write and I had to eat, so for ten years every morning I rose at 6:45, taught school from 9:00 till 3:30 in the afternoon, then coached the boys in football in the autumn, (coming from Nova Scotia I did not know the Canadian game), in hockey in the winter, and in the summer term it was cricket which I could not play at all. Every afternoon I spent an hour marking papers and on my duty day I held the boys in detention and sat over them in prep after supper. The rest of the day was my own for writing.

Later on my wife and I lived downtown and this meant that eighty of my precious daily minutes were spent with the Montreal tramways being trundled back and forth between home and school. We had a four-room apartment in a mid-Victorian mansion belonging to the estate of a rich French-Canadian family whose heirs had moved to a better district. It had high ceilings, two fireplaces, a tiny dining-room, and a kitchen somewhat smaller than the galley in a railway dining-car. The house next door was large and commodious and when I asked the janitor why its shutters were always closed, he explained that it was one of the three highest-class (his words) bordellos in Montreal.

"Only the best people are allowed in there," he told me. "No sailors. No roughnecks or students. You gotta have connections to get into that one."

He claimed to know all about the place because one of his four brothers-in-law was its janitor.

"Men from the best clubs," he said. "The cream of Montreal. Some of the judges. You know, some big politicians. It's got the protection. Four years ago the Old Madame she die and there must have been fifty of them come down to the wake. Some of them even went to the funeral."

Here biculturalism and bilingualism flourished without the help of a royal commission.

"All the girls in there," said the janitor, "they speak French and English. They got to for their profession."

Half of my old block is gone now. The last time I saw it there was a huge parking-lot of black asphalt, inevitable precursor to the inevitable egg-crate high-rise.

In those early days I learned Laurentia as a child learns to speak a language—without even knowing I was learning it. Every evening in those years I wrote between 7:30 and 10:30 and every weekend also. But before going to sleep I usually relaxed by walking through the central city for half an hour, which you could do then without anxiety about the intentions of whoever was walking immediately behind you. You could get a good seat in the Forum for a dollar, and once a week we saw a hockey game and it was much more fun than it is now. There was a section called "the Millionaires' Section" where the admission was fifty cents and it was solidly populated by working-men, mostly French-speaking but well intermixed with "les Anglais", including, often, myself and my wife.

I had come to Montreal assuming I would be speaking French inside of a year, and almost immediately I discovered that unless you were a young boy living in a district with French boys, your chances of learning French from conversation would be just as good in Chicago. Every French Canadian I met, on streetcars or socially—and the English and French rarely met socially then—invariably spoke English to me and apparently desired me to speak English to them. It was a most amiable city, amiable even in its corruption.

"He's all right," one heard of various politicians. "Ten percent, that's all. You know where you stand with him."

To anyone who had learned in Nova Scotia and later in Greek and Roman Literature that citizenship is a prime virtue, the kind of citizenship I found in Laurentia was unique. In retrospect it was not half as bad a citizenship as it sounds when you write about it in cold print. Again, it was amiable. French and English shared a very real love for Montreal and Quebec and were proud of their *status quo*, which they considered to be a mature

sharing of powers based on an absolute recognition of each other's territory, in precisely the same way that civilized animals like wolves (who politically are extremely mature) respect each other's territory. Territorial respect was automatic then. Incidentally, not even the Silent and the Sexual Revolutions of the 1960s have entirely obliterated it. Many French Canadians were shocked when the Separatists marched on McGill in 1969. It was deliciously apposite that when Team Canada defeated Russia in 1972, "O Canada" was sung spontaneously in English in Place Ville Marie and in French in Place Victoria.

But never again will we see the almost glacial divisions between the so-called founding races that confronted me when I came to Montreal before the Hitler War. A diluted version of the British Empire began at Guy Street and ran westerly into well-farmed fields which now, alas, are covered with nondescript housing developments. *Le Fait français* began at Rue Bleury and ran easterly and northerly embracing the substantial Jewish community (even at that time breeding poets and millionaires) which Mordecai Richler, then a child, was later to describe as a ghetto.

In between the two main populations lay the shopping district where the national department stores, and one local one, received customers from all over. They were all owned by Anglophones. Most of the banks were also controlled by Anglophones. In Old Montreal near the harbour, French was spoken in the Bonsecours Market and English in St. James Street, whose power men assumed that they controlled most of the nation's life. Above Ste. Catherine Street, stretching beyond Sherbrooke to the ridge of Mount Royal, reposed the massive Victorian mansions of the bankers, railway presidents, and vice-presidents, salted with a number of merchants, brewers, and corporation lawyers, most of them Anglophones. So many of these had high-coloured Scottish faces that an Edinburgh man confided to me that he felt more at home in Montreal than he ever felt in Glasgow, which he described as uncivilized. We *accepted* religious difference here, he said; in Glasgow they didn't. And he told me a story to illustrate the point.

In Glasgow a stranger stopped a native in Sauchiehall Street and asked him a question.

"Please tell me the quickest way to get to the Alexander Hospital?"

The native replied, "Gang awa doun yon side street, holler at the top of your voice 'To hell wi' the Pope' and ye'll be there in five minutes."

In Montreal in those days no Anglophone would dream of shouting "To hell with the Pope" in public, and whatever a French Canadian might have said about King George in private, he would not think of saying it aloud in the presence of his *concitoyens anglais*.

Men of the Seaway: a special breed

For three hundred years, while the St. Lawrence has borne the commerce of a growing Canada, hard-bitten men have worked the shores. Sons have followed fathers to the docks for generations. Since 1959, the deepened Seaway has brought the whole world to their river.

63

The district where the Big Money lived was then known as the Square Mile, and after the war much of the Square Mile has followed the dreary sequence of metamorphoses into lodging-houses, into boutiques, into parking-lots, into high-rises. Years ago the son of one of its denizens explained to me why the best society of English-speaking Montreal constituted a genuine nobility.

"Forsytes we may be," he said, "but in England the Forsytes had a titled gentry above them. In Canada *nobody* is above us."

"Toronto?"

A smile.

"Yes," said the sixteen-year-old daughter of a Square Mile family *after* the Hitler War, "it was fun spending a week in Toronto, but it does feel pleasant to be back in Canada again."

As for Westmount, now erroneously regarded as a symbol of the last bastion of Anglo-Saxon social and commercial domination, it was then, and still is, a pleasantly opulent suburb with gardens and fine elms. There is some big money there now, of course, but no such concentration of it as used to exist in the old Square Mile.

"I never believed it possible that a daughter of mine would ever have to live in Westmount," I heard a formidable old dowager declare as recently as 1948.

Complex Montreal certainly was in those years, the more so because the historic and probably insoluble problems which surfaced in the sixties were hardly ever mentioned. Politicians of City Hall, of Quebec, and of the Church were happy if the two solitudes kept as far as possible apart from each other. Anglophone Big Business was equally happy with the situation, because it had never encountered any difficulty in making what it called "the necessary arrangements" with the politicians and the Church. What did they care if Maurice Duplessis threatened at election time to nationalize Big Business so long as select Big Business men dined with him every Sunday in the Ritz? As one of them said to me, "You see, we have to protect the French against themselves."

It could not last. No way at all could it last after French Canada, between 1940 and 1960, finally and against every possible obstacle, created a large, affluent, and exceeding articulate middle class. I am no Marxist, but I believe that nobody ever uttered a truer statement than Marx did when he pronounced that in all history it has been the middle class which has made revolutions.

No need any more to describe the nature of the revolutions made by middle-class *Québécois* in recent years. They left the Church in droves. They plunged into art, literature, drama, film-making, industry, business, and every known variety of politics. They talked, and many of them still do, of separating Quebec from the rest of Canada. They flirted with General deGaulle, who got the shock of his life when he learned that the flirtation did not mean going the whole way. Some of their children experimented with bombings and kidnappings. The sexual *mores* of the *Québécois* turned upside down in the sixties. As late as 1959 the movie censors cut out the word "divorce" from the sound-tracks and ruled that no married woman could be kissed on the screen. Ten years later there were twenty-two skin flicks showing in Montreal theatres, many of them made in Quebec. When the war began, Quebec's birth-rate was the highest in North America. By 1968 the birth-rate of French-Canadian Quebeckers had become the lowest in Canada.

Yet during all this triple revolution Laurentia's eternal balancing act continued. After eight years of clamorous attacks against federalism, in 1968 French-Canadian voters rallied solidly behind the most adamant federalist in the entire country. Yes, Laurentia remains complex, and in a sense so profound it can almost be called instinctual. No matter how much he may long to be whole-heartedly one thing or the other, no true Laurentian can believe he can afford to do it. Given the choice between the cash and the credit, the Laurentian Anglophone has always settled for the cash. To be absolutely loyal to the Catholic Church, yet at the same time absolutely anti-clerical—this balancing act was automatic among most educated French Canadians for close to a century until finally the Church lost its power.

Lately, of course, the balances have become more precarious, and the cause of this has been the enormous inflow—as relentless as the inflow of the ancient Champlain Sea—of business and industrial power from the United States. Now it seems probable that this threat to Laurentia's duality may force the duality to accept itself finally. The English of Quebec know in their hearts that they would be nothing without the French. The French of Quebec know in their hearts that without the presence of the English, without the target the English so readily afford, they would inevitably so quarrel among themselves that they would soon be at the mercy of the multinational corporations, who would find it as easy to divide and rule them as they have found it in Latin America. The key problems of the modern world are ethnic and territorial and for this reason alone, Laurentia must be the most important region in all of Canada. Provincial it may be, but naive it can never be. Better than any other people in North America, the Laurentians understand the truth of the old Jewish definition of an idealist—a man who believes that because a rose smells sweeter than a cabbage, it will make better soup. The true Laurentian is the Hamlet of North America, and perhaps the same can be said, if to a lesser extent, of your true Canadian.

Douglas Le Pan once described the voyageur as "Hamlet with the countenance of Horatio," and Robertson Davies remarked that nobody had ever compressed into a single phrase more insight into the Canadian character. The phrase applies perfectly to the greatest statesman ever produced in the Laurentian region, which of course includes the upper St. Lawrence. One could almost say that Sir John A. Macdonald's entire career was the result of Laurentian tensions and needs. His whole life was one of Hamletian doubt and imagination, of Horatian self-control and endurance. Circumstances always compelled him to achieve his results without dramatizing them. I think of Macdonald at the Washington Conference of 1871, where neither the English nor the American delegates took him seriously because he was a colonial. All his life he had been forced to deal in a calculus of politics, and he did so then. He cared, but he did not let them know how much he cared, when his pride was insulted and his country scorned. He probably knew it would be like this when he went to Washington determined that Canada remain in the British Empire whether the British wanted her or not, determined also that the British garrisons should leave the forts along the St. Lawrence if their departure would result in a demilitarization of the frontier. To meld with the interests *both* of Britain and of the United States was the only way in which Canada could hope to become independent. If the others did not understand this, Sir John had always understood it, and he came home with the minimum of what he knew he required—the famous undefended frontier for which other statesmen were later to claim the credit.

As a Nova Scotian I find it impossible to believe that Macdonald could have succeeded had he been as dramatic as our own Joseph Howe. In Nova Scotia we had never felt any special need to bank down our native fires. The Royal Navy with a base in Halifax had sheltered us for years and our pride when I was young was a British pride. But in Laurentia this could never be so because it was a pocket in the continent's heart. The United States literally touched it. The orphans of three European defeats inhabited it.

"If we could only get ourselves included in a genuine western alliance, or even a genuine state, then, in the multiplicity of nations involved, we might be able to hold our own against our friends (*i.e.,* the Americans) a little better. As it is, locked up in the same house with them, we are necessarily their prisoners."

These words reached me in 1960 in a casual letter from a distinguished Canadian historian. Clearly, it is truer now than it was then. As late as 1963 a man who later became a federal cabinet minister, and who had many connections in Europe, told me there was real hope

that Canada might once again restore the old North Atlantic Triangle (Great Britain, the United States, and Canada at the slim apex) by becoming connected with the European Common Market. That hope surely disappeared with the later British decision to enter the Common Market.

"Locked up in the same house with our friends"—Laurentians have always had to accept that this was the best situation they could ever hope for. The river, which made their history, has compelled them to realize, and before most peoples, that in an overcrowded world, this has become the inevitable fate of all mankind.

The freighter felt the tug of the current flowing through the gorge between Quebec and Lévis, and looking around I felt the excitement this famous scene always gives me. The sky over the purple-grey city was turbulent, and the distant mountains were streaked with patches of brightness as the sun struck through clouds. Here, as everywhere in the central and lower St. Lawrence, was visible the perpetual Canadian frontier, the rocky hills of the Shield.

Travelling along the St. Lawrence aboard a working freighter is still the best way to know this river. On the upper reaches where the Seaway now runs it can be very intimate, the ocean-going ships sailing through farms and villages. Once years ago, before the Seaway was built, stealing past the little Ontario town of Cardinal, I seemed to be looking into everyone's home. We slipped noiselessly along in the dark virtually between the United States and Canada, and I will never forget the startling beauty of a lighted window behind which a young girl, smiling secretly to herself, was brushing her hair. Nor again another night in 1940, the month that France fell, the feeling of hope and security when I looked across that river-frontier to the lights shining in the most powerful country in the world. Standing now on the freighter below the pile of Quebec City, I wondered how anyone could believe that a nation containing a city like this is really young at heart.

Quebec, to me at least, has the air of a city that never was young. No community in America, few in Europe, give out such a feeling of intense, rain-washed antiquity as does Quebec's Lower Town. A little like Calais, perhaps, but far nobler with its rock and wilderness behind it and the great river at its foot. Those stern grey walls with their Norman and Mediterranean roofs two centuries ago sheltered an embattled, isolated people who lived as long and as hard in a decade as most communities live in a century. Even their religion contributed to their tensions, for the Quebec of Bishop Laval was a product of the fierce intolerance of the Counter Reformation, in turn a riposte to the equally fierce intolerance of Protestantism.

I looked up at the palisade of the Citadel polished smoothly grey by wind, rain, snow, and ice with the river sheer below it, and remembered an evening not long before when I had stood on the grass of the King's Bastion beside a famous English statesman with whom we had been playing croquet. A corporal's guard had marched round the corner of the blockhouse to the flagstaff. Wind tossed the clouds and across the river rain was falling on Lévis. The soldiers were guardsmen in red coats and bearskins, and as the flag came down one of them sounded the British Last Post over the river whence, two centuries ago, British shells had whirred into Lower Town, smashing it to a shambles. I saw tears in the eyes of the English statesman and heard him murmur:

"If Winston could see this, he'd talk of it for hours."

Our host, who happened to be the Governor General, said with a quiet smile: "If he knew those guardsmen spoke French, I fancy he might talk about it half the night."

But Quebec, as everyone knows who has ever lived in it as long as a week, is no monument. The noble convent of the Ursulines looked as it always did; the belfry bells seemed to ring incessantly; the black soutanes of the priests flapped in the wind round the corners. But the Plouffe Family lived here along with their furiously energetic creator. Maurice Duplessis had ruled here for years with a personal authority which almost, but never quite, verged on a dictatorship. Here also the statesmen, generals, admirals, and airmen of the Western Alliance had met to set their seals to the master plan which won the Second World War. And here, in this so-called monument of the past, Albert Guay had conceived and executed the most thoroughly modern murder of the twentieth century, the first destruction of a commercial aircraft by a deliberately planted time-bomb. Here also, when the Queen came in 1964, the streets had been double-lined by troops and police to protect her from the possible act of a political fanatic.

The ship turned into the channel leading round the southern tip of the Ile d'Orléans, the sun broke through the clouds and slowly set, and again I found myself recalling Conrad's chapter at the opening of *Heart of Darkness*. Conrad's scene was a river even more famous, the Thames, but the thoughts it evoked in the novelist seemed to fit the St. Lawrence better than any of my own:

The old river rested in its broad reach unruffled at the decline of day, after ages of good service to the race that people its banks, spread out in tranquil dignity to a waterway leading to the uttermost parts of the earth.

Ages of good service! At least three centuries of varied service the St. Lawrence had given, and not the least of its gifts had been the knowledge the problems it created have taught the people who have been involved in its story. The chief lesson of all is that history is invariably ironical, that the greatest men of action seldom understand the true meaning of what they do, that the results that flow from their lives are seldom as they planned them. Irony has been connected with the St. Lawrence from the very beginning.

Jacques Cartier seems to have been as practical a mariner as ever sailed from a Brittany port, but when he entered that enormous estuary in 1535, when he sailed on and on up the fjord, what else could he have assumed than that the St. Lawrence was the Northwest Passage? What importance he attached to the wild grapes he found in abundance on the Ile d'Orléans! Was he disappointed, or was he stricken with awe when he stood on Mount Royal after his ship had been halted by the rapids and stared into the unpeopled land into which the great river disappeared? And why did his own government, when he returned with the news of his discovery, do nothing about it for nearly a full century? Had France moved promptly then, the whole of North America would have been hers.

Irony has haunted most of the great lives connected with the St. Lawrence. LaSalle, seeing the rapids boiling past his seigneury on the southern shore of Montreal Island, may not have been as naïve as the jokers who called the rapids "Lachine" in mockery of his dream, but China seems to have been his dream-goal when he paddled and portaged all the way to the delta of the Mississippi. The meaning of the river's future was clearly closed to Jean Talon, or at least to the French government who employed him, when he established along its banks a replica of a European feudal system. Was it not in the New World that the first decisive blow against the old privileged classes was struck? Laurentian facts quite baffled Laval's dream of a Catholic-American empire with a cross on every hill from the Gaspé to the Gulf of Mexico. The same river which led the French canoes into the interior also invited the Royal Navy in behind them, and at Quebec the French were trapped.

Irony also haunted the Europeans who thought about the St. Lawrence. The cleverest man in the eighteenth century is remembered in Canada chiefly for one epigram which is repeated only to make a fool of him, namely that along the St. Lawrence two empires were fighting for a few acres of snow.

But what of the English conquerors of Quebec—what did their victory on the St. Lawrence achieve for *them?* The English experience with the river was the most exquisitely ironical of all.

In the middle eighteenth century when Lord Chatham studied his maps in London, it seemed very clear to him that if Britain could become master of the St. Lawrence, the whole of North America would be hers permanently. The river was the sole avenue into the Ohio Territory from which the English of the Thirteen Colonies were barred by the Appalachians. Imperial France was in a bad condition internally with a corrupt government, a weak navy, and a worthless king. So Pitt made his decision and mounted the greatest overseas armada in the history of Europe up to that time. Louisbourg fell and the American auxiliary troops razed it. The St. Lawrence was open, no longer did a French fortress lie across the British lines of communication, and the French at Quebec were cut off from a discouraged and (for the moment) decadent motherland. Whether or not Wolfe would have preferred to be the author of a minor poem than to have taken Quebec is a matter in some dispute. He certainly took Quebec, and four years later the government of France ceded Canada to England.

This must be the most fatal victory any country ever won. For now that the Laurentian threat was removed, the American revolutionary movement grew rapidly. When the Quebec Act, the most liberal document ever granted to a conquered people up to that time, came into effect in 1775, it fired the mine in the southern colonies. The French Canadians had been the enemies of the British Americans for a century and a half. The French Canadians were as militantly Catholic as the Americans were militantly dissenting Protestants. The Revolutionary War broke out and the Americans, as has occasionally been mentioned, won it.

So came about the greatest irony of all: at the end of the war the chief North American region flying the British flag was Laurentia, the home of Britain's ancient enemy. And as a component part of *that* irony, the Protestant United Empire Loyalists, ousted from their American homes, now had to trek north to build new homes in the wilderness along the upper river, and from then on were doomed to share the river with a people they had always accounted their enemies. Their foolish attempts to dominate the French in the next century and a half served only to make their own lot more difficult. For the French waited. The endless patience enforced upon them enabled them to wait and wait until now, in the mid-twentieth century, Quebec is theirs. It was said in ancient times: "Greece, captive, led captive her captors." The French Canadians were too shrewd to say as much in public, but they said it in private many times. By waiting, by enduring, by yielding again and again on small issues but never on a vital one, they saw their concept of a dual culture accepted by the English-speaking compatriots whose ancestors considered them a conquered people.

An imperial river—the St. Lawrence has always been that. After the first commercial empire of the St. Lawrence withered, the empire of timber took its place. Then came the railway empire, and soon the prairies discovered by the voyageurs became virtual provinces of the Laurentian cities, their tribute manifest in the Victorian castles built on the southern slopes of Mount Royal. With the coming of hydro-electricity, empire moved from the railway barons and the forest industries to the manufacturers. Now the power bred out of the St. Lawrence System began to change in a few decades the whole nature of traditional French-Canadian life, turning an erstwhile race of simple folk into one of the most highly organized industrial communities on the continent, with results to their character at first exciting, then painful, and still unpredictable.

Finally, with the opening of the International Seaway, the rapids were conquered and ocean-going ships of more than 20,000 tons began moving into the continent's heart. The power project connected with the Seaway was sure to create still another Laurentian empire along the former agricultural reaches of the upper river. What course this one will take I still would not presume to guess; there have been enough bad guesses connected with the St. Lawrence as it is. But in 1960 it seemed certain to me that the St. Lawrence, breeder of nations though she had been, could never tolerate a narrow nationalism in North America. Just as the French and the English would have to sink their differences in order to share the river, so now, more closely than ever, Canada and the United States seemed permanently tied together by the river which theoretically divides them. But in the 1970s, is even this assumption still a safe one?

Strangely the St. Lawrence has changed its appearance very little over the years. The lower Thames is overwhelmed by London, the lower Hudson is utterly dominated by the towers of Manhattan, the Elbe disappears into Hamburg. When you fly out of Dorval on the London or Halifax plane, the river below you is so enormous that even the Seaway looks no more than a trivial scar along the south bend of La Prairie Basin. At night Montreal is a scintillating wash of coloured lights pouring in a sluice of brightness down the long slope of the mountain to the stream, but in daylight the new high-rises, even La Place Ville Marie, remind you of a nursery town built out of a tinker-toy set.

In a matter of minutes you leave Montreal behind. The river is still too big to be dominated in its landscape by anything human connected with it. Below Quebec there are long reaches which look exactly as they did to Cartier. Even along the upper river, even in the section of the old International Rapids where the engineering work connected with the Seaway and the power project has been most spectacular, the changes wrought in the landscape are still relatively small compared to the landscape's vastness.

My freighter turned into the channel round the Ile d'Orléans and an incoming ship broke out her lights. We passed her and went on into the gathering darkness of the stream. After dinner I came out on deck and began counting the ships we passed, but as I could see nothing but their lights I could only guess at their nationalities. For hours I walked around the decks looking at the lights of the old parishes slipping by, and leaning over the side I could hear the hiss of brine along the plates of the ship. The water was almost entirely salt now, but we were still many miles inland from Father Point. I went to bed and slept eight hours, and in the morning we were still in what the maps call the river. A school of white porpoises flashed about us very close and a deckhand told me they were unique to this region. A steward contradicted him and said they can also be found in the estuary of the River Plate and probably he was right, for he was torpedoed there in the war. We passed Anticosti and entered the Gulf, but we were still, at least in the geological and transportation sense, within the St. Lawrence System as

we passed slowly north along the flank of Labrador where yet another empire connected with the St. Lawrence was a-building. Newfoundland appeared on the starboard bow as I was going to bed. The next morning broke cold and foggy, I dressed and saw the icebergs in the Strait of Belle Isle. Some time in the forenoon we rounded Cape Bauld and were out of the St. Lawrence transportation system at last.

Ten days later, after coming down from Manchester in an English June, I found myself in London again after many years. Alone and caught by a bus strike, I spent hours of every day walking the famous old streets. As a young man in Nova Scotia I had not looked west but east, and London had been the first great city I had seen. Now I found myself looking at London with fresh eyes, and because I have moved about a good deal in my life, I began asking myself if there was any city I knew remotely like it. There is only one London, of course, and it still is the greatest city on earth; in time it will probably become as eternal as Rome. But I noticed one thing about myself in connection with London I had never felt before. I felt at home. I was prepared now for its scope and attitude. One evening walking down the Haymarket toward Trafalgar Square I remembered an essay about London by V. S. Pritchett, the one in which he said that the word evoked in his mind by the image of Rome was "murder", the word by the image of Paris "feminine", but the word brought forth to fit London was "experience".

I had it then. "Experience", above all other words in the language, is the one which seems to me to fit the city of Montreal where I live now. It still is, and always will be, the commercial capital of the St. Lawrence. Its character has been formed by the river which made its existence possible and its importance inevitable, and in 1967, our Centennial Year, Expo 67 came close to making it the most interesting city in the entire world.

An end and a beginning: the hallowed ground of the Plains of Abraham.

FUN ON THE RIVER

A member of a Montreal snowshoe club gets "bounced" in this William Notman photograph, taken Jan. 30, 1902.

At the turn of the century, the world seemed new and full of marvels. The Canadian was still an outdoorsman, only a holler from pioneer days, and filled with innocent, uncomplicated fun. The rivers and lakes offered everything he could ask—swimming and fishing, canoeing and sailing. Picnics by the shore. Horse-racing on the ice of winter. Respectable ladies, hatted and gaitered, skated demurely in pairs, but when they donned a neck-to-knee bathing costume, they were rushed by pop-eyed beaux.

At a club picnic beside an Ontario lake, it was striped blazers, pipe-clay pants, and that "in" item of the times, the mandolin. The strummer at left is H. M. Mowat, later M.P.

A regatta down by the old mill stream. Gents in their boaters crowd the stand on the Humber River, near the Toronto landmark, the Old Mill. The year? About 1909.

The siren of Sunnyside Beach. One sizzling summer's day in 1910 this unknown girl tugged down her daring costume and laughed at the photographer behind his bulky tripod.

The Great War was over, but there was still a martial spirit about—among the teenagers, at any rate. The village cadet corps sets out for a community picnic.

Ah, yesterday! Look at those fish the young lady has on the gunwale! Look at the bamboo chair she reclines in as the boatman paddles about the Thousand Islands!

Not everybody's idea of fun, but shooting the rapids at Lachine was the biggest thrill Canada could offer. Champlain did it, and so did the rich Victorian tourist.

Gentlemen rowed in the 19th century for the sheer pleasure of it. These stalwarts belonged to the Lachine Boating Club.

It is March 1902. The horses blow plumes of steam in the frosty air around the track on the Ottawa River.

What a thrill to zip across the breadth of Lake St. Louis! These craft, seldom seen today, hit 60 m.p.h.

Left
If this skating party seems a little stiff—it should. It's one of the famous composites posed in the Montreal studios of the Scottish-born William Notman, in 1873. Each person was photographed separately, or in small groups, then the prints were assembled on a painted background and rephotographed.

Right
When this race was staged on the Fraser, British Columbia had not yet joined Canada.

Below
Carried west over the new C.P.R. tracks as far as Fort Qu'Appelle, these militiamen marched on to suppress the Riel Rebellion, 1885. They made good use of the "fishing lakes"

The Frenchman Blondin (Jean-François Gravelet) had made the whole
world tingle when he crossed the Niagara gorge on a tightrope. In
1859-60, he went over blindfold, carrying a man on his back, pushing
a wheelbarrow, and on stilts. The feat still drew a mighty crowd
in 1873 when Maria Spelterini tripped across in baskets. Since then,
several people have dared the Falls in barrels. Some even made it.

The Ottawa

WAY OF THE VOYAGEURS

On an autumn day I was strolling on the embankment above the Ottawa River just below the point where the stream enters the Lake of Two Mountains. A cold wind was mournful in the pine grove, and I remembered how different everything had been the first time I had seen this grove. I was in the company of the same old gentleman I was with now, but it had been twenty years earlier, and summer. Everything had been delicious: a lace of foam was visible where a light breeze blew against the current, a lace of shadows lay on the pine needle floor of the grove. But our hearts were cold that day because France had just fallen. Everything in that summer of 1940 was so lovely except the one thing we thought about.

Now on this autumn afternoon of cold winds and grey skies the region had the grim look of early November in Canada without sun. But our hearts were light then. The old gentleman, no older in spirit than he had been twenty years before, but with twenty more years of distinguished service behind him—two ambassadorships and one high-commissionership—had just learned from Oxford that his translation of Dante's *Inferno* had been accepted with enthusiasm. He had always written poetry as a hobby. Now in his retirement he had completed the finest translation of the *Inferno* I had ever read.

He chuckled. "The publishers insist that I do the *Purgatorio* for them. In fairness I had to warn them that there is every likelihood that I will arrive there in person before I finish it."

He asked me what I was writing now, and I told him I had been spending the last two years trying to turn myself into a river. Trying to *feel* like a river, even; now I was trying to feel like the Ottawa.

He had lived in this place near the Trappist monastery at Oka every summer of his life for nearly forty years. As he was studious in all things, I assumed that he knew much more about the Ottawa than I would ever learn. In front of his property, he told me, he had water rights extending far into the lake, and with a charming smile he said it was very pleasant to own a part of a river like this.

"But of course," he added, "this is the unknown river of Canada."

"That much I've already discovered."

Though I had lived in Montreal for a full generation, had crossed bridges over the Ottawa so often I could not count the times, and had even worked one summer in the capital, I had taken the river for granted as everyone else seems to do. The old question about its length was revealing only in so far as it underlined everyone's ignorance about the river itself. I had been asking people how long they thought the Ottawa was, and one man gave a length of a hundred miles, another of two hundred, and a third went so far as to say it would not surprise him if it was as long as two hundred and fifty. I remarked that the Ottawa's chief tributary, the Gatineau, was nearly that long, and he looked at me in mild surprise. "Is it?" he said.

My friend smiled: "That's so typical. Somehow or other the Ottawa got lost when the St. Lawrence took its place. But it's a river full of character. It's most unusual, you know. And it's much senior to the St. Lawrence. But then, I suppose you've found that out for yourself."

It so happened that I had found it out, but only a few days previously. A geographer I know had told me that the St. Lawrence was a geographical afterthought. Once upon a time it was the Ottawa, not the St. Lawrence, which had drained the Great Lakes. Its channel had been the old voyageurs' route through French River, Lake Nipissing, and the Mattawa, and it discharged an immense volume of water into the channel now claimed by the St. Lawrence below Montreal. But changes had occurred in the contours of the land, there had been an upthrust of the earth, and the lake water had found itself the new channel which now is the upper St. Lawrence. It is significant that there are no northern tributaries of the St. Lawrence above the point where the Ottawa now enters it. The little Rideau River, together with its lakes, is really a kind of water bridge between the Ottawa and the St. Lawrence, for though it tumbles over its cliff into the Ottawa, its flow is very gentle and at the southern end there is a still stretch on the Rideau which receives water from the bay just below the point where the St. Lawrence channel drains out of Lake Ontario.

Today, of course, the Ottawa is regarded as the chief tributary of the St. Lawrence system. Yet *la grande rivière*, which once was itself the master stream of a great system, has retained a genuine air of independence. It also possesses, as my friend had said, some features very unusual, and its own northern tributaries come through wild country.

Years ago my brother-in-law paddled down one of these, the Lièvre, which is the Ottawa's second-longest tributary now. Locally the Lièvre is pronounced in French as "Lever" because, after its original discovery and naming by French explorers, nothing was done with it until some Scotch people came to it after the Conquest. The Scotch mispronounced the French name, and when French Canadians moved in later, they accepted the mispronunciation. The Ottawa story is charged with anomalies like this and with forgotten episodes. However, this canoe trip down the Lièvre was one of the most vivid recollections of my brother-in-law's life. In places the Lièvre is very dangerous with fierce rapids, and for long stretches it runs through a forest as lonely as it was in the days when the hunter Algonquins roamed it. My brother-in-law had studied the contours of the Ottawa system, and he gave me what I believe is the only sensible answer I have received concerning its length.

"I don't think anyone knows how long the Ottawa is," he said.

If I talk about the Ottawa's length now it is only as a means of describing the character of a stream more unusually constituted than any I have studied. Usually the river's source is given as the head of Lake Temiskaming, and the distance from there to the Ste. Anne de Bellevue Passage is roughly 696 miles. But what lies behind Lake Temiskaming? At least one official Quebec map shows the thread of the *Rivière Outaouais* winding far back into Quebec toward the northeast, deep into the Laurentian forest through a chain of weirdly shaped lakes all the way to Lac au Bouleau in the La Vérendrye National Park.

As no single lake can be described as the original source of a river which flows through a long series of lakes, and is fed by most of them, it is therefore quite impossible to determine how long the Ottawa is. But these lakes give the Ottawa its uniquely repetitive character. The river usually enters each lake with a mild current, and with the pressure of the lake behind it, discharges into the ensuing channel in a short, heavy rush. That is why there were eighteen portages on the Ottawa between Lake of Two Mountains and the mouth of the Mattawa, and why the journey up the Grand River was such a hard one for the canoe parties.

The voyageurs estimated the Long Sault at three leagues—in other words, at about six miles—and they made it in three portages. Though some of the bolder men tried to shoot the rapids coming down stream, this was very dangerous. John Macdonell, on his voyage up the Ottawa in the spring of 1793, noted a cross on one of these portages marking the grave of a young Christian Indian who had been drowned while trying to save time by shooting the rapids in his canoe. He also reports that several canoes of his own brigade of expert commercial voyageurs were damaged on the river and that the work of portaging was very hard. The carrying place about the Chaudière Falls was a troublesome one. The longest on the river was called LaMontagne; a mile long, it was also very steep. Macdonell says it took his party twenty-four hours to clear it. But the rushes of swift water out of the lakes are generally quite short. The one at the Allumettes, for instance, was measured at fifteen to twenty paces only, and in the slack waters of the lakes paddling

was easy and rapid, especially if a wind was behind the canoes. But though the voyageurs wore the carrying places smooth between Ste. Anne de Bellevue and the Mattawa, the Ottawa above this point was virtually left alone in the fur-trading days. It is little visited now except by people in the lumber business.

Still less familiar are some of the eleven tributaries. Everyone living in Ottawa City knows the lower Gatineau, and everyone knows the Rideau. But one of the most interesting of the tributaries, it seems to me, is the Coulonge. It is 135 miles long and flows south for all of its course. But if you trace it to its origin, what do you find? You find the Coulonge issuing from a section of La Vérendrye National Park where the water pattern is so intricate that you can almost persuade yourself that the Coulonge draws some of its source waters from the same swampy Lac au Bouleau which is often considered the prime source of the Ottawa itself. It would be pleasant to imagine that it does, for then one could argue that for most of its course the Ottawa flows in a circle, and that the final stretch from the mouth of the Coulonge in Campbell's Bay is merely the tail of a vast, fluvial Q. But enough of these paradoxes. Think of the Ottawa as a chain of elongated lakes with a current connecting them and flowing through them and you have the general character of the river as a geological agent.

In a wider sense I think of the Ottawa as a complex of contrasts, all of them inherent in the pattern of the Canadian nation and the Canadian land.

Most of the lakes on the central and lower Ottawa are gentle with reeds through which the water sighs and among which hundreds of thousands of wild duck breed. Were it not for the rapids the lakes would make navigation from Montreal as easy as it is on the St. Lawrence, and plans have been considered for the construction of an Ottawa Seaway. One of these days they will probably be realized. But now we have the tranquil lakes succeeded by the quick gush of rapids at the end of them, and this is the first of the contrasts.

The next one, it seems to me, is the difference between the north and the south bank. The Ottawa forms the boundary between Ontario and Quebec all the way from Lake Temiskaming to the confluence with the St. Lawrence, and for much of the distance the contrast between the two terrains is absolute and visible. Southward in Ontario are rich farms and rolling hills, with a wealth of hardwood trees. But the moment you cross the river and enter Quebec, you are in the rocky Laurentian highlands among the conifers, and the land is so useless to farms it has remained just about as wild as it always was.

"Do you mean there are *wolves* here?" I asked a man on Allumette Island a few springs ago.

He had been asked the question before, and in the same tone of voice.

"Over there"—and he pointed to the high bush country, "there are so many wolves that I don't like going far into those woods without a rifle. Let me tell you a story about our wolves."

I was sceptical, having heard the remark attributed to an editor at Sault Ste. Marie that he had yet to meet a man who had been eaten by a wolf, but this man looked solid and responsible. He was an American, a professional hunter and guide, and he had come here years ago from Pennsylvania because he had always liked wild country.

"Only last year," he said, "in August, I drove a tractor up there to take out a fishing party. In there among the hills a few miles, some Americans were fishing a lake. The fish were biting and on toward twilight the party didn't want to leave. I told them they'd better get moving on account of the wolves and they laughed at me. 'Wolves up here?' one of them said. 'Wolves in August? Wolves within a hundred and twenty-five miles of Ottawa City?'

"Well, I did a very foolish thing. I knew the deer had been taking a bad beating from the wolves lately because a few nights before some wolves had crossed the river and killed cattle on farms on the south side. That meant they were getting pretty hungry, for a wolf has to be desperate to enter a lighted country after dark. But anyhow, I went over to a birch tree and cut off a strip of bark and made myself a moose call. 'Listen and see what happens,' I said, and I began calling. Almost right away I heard a wolf howl. The howl was answered and I felt like the whole mountain was coming alive. 'Let's get out of here,' I said. 'Let's get out of here fast. I've only got three cartridges to my rifle.'

"So we got aboard the tractor—I had a trailer attached with some hay in it—and went down that trail as fast as she would move, which was only about thirty miles an hour. The tractor had no light and the trail was rough. There are hundreds of trails like that on the other side of the river leading to abandoned lumber camps. Pretty soon the wolves came out of the trees and began following. Then some more came in from the sides. It was like being hunted in a war, the way they came they seemed so organized. I don't mind saying I took them more seriously than my party did. How many there were I don't know, but there were enough to have torn us to pieces. They were closing in. They were getting confident when we came round a bend in the trail and there was a light in an Indian's cabin. I figure that light saved us, for they faded out."

I murmured something about not knowing the country was so wild.

The man smiled: "Across there it's just about as wild as it can get in Canada. The lumbermen haven't been working there for years, and their old bunkhouses make pretty good lairs. Once I found some wolf cubs in the ruins of an old bunkhouse and began playing with them and the next thing I saw was a pair of lobos staring at me."

I had heard the word "lobo" before, but not in Canada. In the States, lobo used to be the name for a solitary wolf, a smart wolf that preyed on cattle. The name is still used in states which have wolves.

"If I hadn't had my rifle," the man said, "I wouldn't be talking to you now."

This story I relate just as it was told to me, and to the best of my knowledge it is true. But a hundred miles lower down on the Ottawa, nobody thinks about wolves.

The contrast between the settled and the wild—so typical of many parts of Canada—yields to a pattern of contrasts even more complex in the capital itself. There almost every influence in the country is visible and many of them are at odds with one another. The nation's capital is at last developing into the beautiful, ordered thing the National Capital Planning Commission intends, but for years its mixture of rawness and dignity reminded one of pictures of Washington at the time of the Civil War, except that the contrasts were all Canadian.

Parliament Hill stands nobly on its bluff with the foam-flecked river swirling below out of the Chaudière toward the mouth of the Gatineau and the Rideau Falls. Here, miraculously captured by the architects, are visibly united the three separate heritages which originally formed the nation. Nobody can look at Parliament Hill, especially in the evening from the little park behind the Château Laurier, without being reminded of ancient France, of Westminster, and of Edinburgh Castle. For years, that splendid composition stood isolated in the commonplace red brick of old Bytown, and faced across the river not only to the Laurentian wilds, but also to one of the biggest lumber stacks in the country. I remember when there shone at night, on top of that hideous industrial congeries in Hull, in brilliant Neon, a huge advertisement for toilet paper.

The Ottawa is not easy to picture, is almost impossible to define, and nowhere is its pattern more complex than at its end. Just before the confluence with the St. Lawrence, the river swells into the last and most beautiful of its many lakes. But out of Lake of Two Mountains, Ottawa water gushes into the St. Lawrence not by one channel but by four. On the south it flows around Ile Perrot through gaps at Dorion and Ste. Anne de Bellevue, and this was the route of the old voyageurs. But the bulk of its water goes north-about and enters the St. Lawrence below Montreal. This archipelago is not a true delta,

Pomp and pulp.
The Ottawa River,
by John de Visser.

though sediment brought down by the river has certainly made its contribution to the rich topsoil of some of these islands.

At this point the map is further confused because the Ottawa (like the Rhine and the Yangtse) emerges under an entirely new set of names. The channel separating the mainland from the northern flank of Ile Jésus (the second largest island in the Montreal archipelago) is called Rivière des Mille Iles; as the name implies, it is a rusty-brown stream sucking along through a welter of tiny islets. The other channel dividing Ile Jésus from Montreal Island is marked on the maps as Rivière des Prairies, but English-speaking Montrealers have further confused things by calling it "the Back River". Re-uniting, these two channels again become "the Ottawa", and after embracing the little Bout de l'Ile, the river finally merges with the St. Lawrence. But it does not lose itself. The Ottawa's amber hue—product not of mud but of root stain and iron stain—colours the main stream all the way down to Quebec and beyond, until finally the waters of the entire Laurentian system blend with the tides in the great firth below the Ile d'Orléans.

Before Queen Victoria selected Bytown as the capital of the Dominion of Canada, the Ottawa River served this continent, and also the French and British Empires, in several distinctly different ways. Its role as an avenue of exploration and trade has already been discussed. But even before the fur trade died out, the river became the centre of one of the world's largest lumbering industries. The south side of the valley, with its rolling land and good soil, offered a homeland to large contingents of settlers, most of them United Empire Loyalists and retired officers on half-pay, and over the years their quiet labour has helped to make Ontario our richest province.

The constructive influence of Americans on Canada has been profound from the day of Peter Pond to the age of Clarence Decatur Howe. So it was along the Ottawa. The creator of a farming and industrial society along *la grande rivière* of the voyageurs was neither a French Canadian nor a Scot of the North West Company; he was the Massachusetts Yankee, Philemon Wright.

Wright first visited the Ottawa in the last year of the eighteenth century, liked what he saw, and returned with a small colony to break land. But this man was destined for a career larger than farming. Wright possessed the Yankee talent for complex organization which sees one activity dovetailing into a dozen others. He was a surveyor, a farmer, a woodsman, a lumber man, and in the end he was a shipping and financial tycoon deeply involved in international affairs. Nor was anyone in Canadian history luckier in the coincidence of his private dream with a pressing public need.

When Wright surveyed the Ottawa forests he found an abundance of white pine standing two hundred feet tall—useless if nobody wanted them, a fortune if anyone did. Here also were oaks, hickories, maples, butternuts, and cedars, and a strong, broad river flowed through them. Wright dreamed of "a fleet of a thousand ships carrying Ottawa timber to the sea", and with this end in mind, he conducted the first systematic survey of the river. The voyageurs had never done this because they had not found it necessary, and their maps were less adequate than most Montrealers believed. In Montreal, Wright was told that he could never succeed in driving logs economically. Heavy ships could not pass the Long Sault, and log rafts could not be conveyed through the Ste. Anne de Bellevue Passage or controlled in rapids as violent as the Lachine. But Wright searched elsewhere, and found what he wanted in the north-about route past Bout de l'Ile which the voyageurs had neglected.

At this very time, and for the first time in history, the demand for Canadian lumber became exorbitant. Napoleon had countered the British naval blockade by imposing the Berlin Decrees which forbade the use of all continental ports to British ships. The Royal Navy, controlling the high seas, was able to convoy to England all necessary supplies but timber. For this they had depended for years on the Baltic ports of the Scandinavian countries. The very existence of the fleets—both naval and mercantile marine—depended on timber and the Admiralty became alarmed. In 1801 Nelson fought the Battle of Copenhagen to prevent the French from seizing the Danish fleet. In 1807, the British seized the remnants of the Danish fleet and held them as hostages. But still their shipyards were denied the use of Scandinavian timber.

Philemon Wright knew this well, and it was in that very year that his first shipment of Ottawa timber reached Quebec and was transferred to ocean-going vessels which carried it to England.

This was the beginning of a huge lumber industry which transformed the Ottawa Valley and made Quebec City the chief lumber port of the world. There was an old sea shanty sung in British, American and Canadian ships through much of the last century:

> *Have you ever been in Quebec*
> *Piling timber on the deck?*

Great fortunes were made in Ottawa timber over a period of a century and a half, and in modern times the industry has expanded to include pulp and paper, so that you cannot travel far along the Ottawa without smelling sulphur or seeing the tell-tale plume of yellow smoke that marks a pulp and paper factory.

But lumbering, though not so nomadic as fur-trading, by its very nature is bound to keep a human community frozen almost indefinitely in a state of cultural infancy. The lumbermen of the Ottawa cut over a territory and moved on, leaving the cut-over land until a new generation of trees grew up in sufficient quantity to make it profitable once more to destroy them. This meant that the lumbermen built nothing for permanence. Their communities were not towns but work camps, their buildings were not houses, but structures almost as temporary as the shacks they nailed down on the huge rafts they kept sending down the rivers. Nor were the men engaged in lumbering in the early days the kind who would ever build a cultivated society. They spent their lives in forest slums, and most of them were illiterate.

In the heyday of the lumbering business in the last century, the Ottawa was one of the toughest regions of North America; at times, one might think, almost as bad as in the days when the Iroquois war parties hunted the Algonquins and Dollard des Ormeaux conducted his famous defence at the Long Sault, for there was a feeling of basic hopelessness among most proletariats in the last century. Until very recently the poor and uneducated—the people described in the Statue of Liberty's inscription as "the wretched refuse of your teeming shores"—performed most of the work now done by machinery, and were treated as such. Considered as economic units, machines were all they were. The work gangs along the Ottawa were almost the size of regiments, and matters were made worse by the practice of recruiting them racially, whether because the men preferred to work with their own kind, or because their employers instinctively followed the old principle of divide and rule. The hardness of their lives, the quality of their food, their isolation from normal society, the absence of family life, the feeling that they were spending their strength for an old age of poverty and loneliness—all these things combined to make them permanently quarrelsome. The Irish fought with the French, and feuds between shanties and shantymen endured for years while the character of the lumbermen remained the same. Generation after generation along the river, they cut the trees, drove the logs, cleared them from jams, took them over waterfalls, and subsisted on a diet that exposed them to scurvy and boils: pea soup, pork and beans, scouse if they were lucky, and gallons of tea the strength of lye.

It was directly out of this background that the present capital of Canada developed, and whenever I see the civil servants walking down Wellington Street with their brief cases, I marvel at the human capacity for rapid change.

For old Bytown, even old Ottawa, was a barbarous place. In 1832, when Colonel By and his Royal Engineers had completed their six-year job of digging (with the help of Irish labourers) the Rideau Canal with its forty-seven locks, the town named after him was a huge work camp containing more than two thousand human souls. Hideous and semi-savage, it rapidly grew into the largest lumbering centre on the river. Its streets were muddy tracks leading from sawmills to taverns, and drunken brawling made them dangerous after dark. Bytown endured everything. Its filth was such that even typhus developed, and in 1847 an epidemic nearly decimated the population. Cholera was common and typhoid even more so. Then, only a few years after the name of the place had been changed to "Ottawa", its fortune brightened. In 1857 Queen Victoria nominated Ottawa as the capital of United Canada.

The decision was not as absurd as it looked. If at last the two old rivals, Upper and Lower Canada, were to have a common government, a seat for it must be found in which neither province was favoured at the expense of the other. Quebec and Montreal were ruled out because the former was almost totally French and the latter was largely so; Toronto because it was English. Kingston might have served had it not been so close to the American border. At that time the fear of invasion from the United States hung constantly over Canadian heads; it was this that had caused the government to build the Rideau Canal, the purpose of which was purely military. In the event of American invaders seizing the upper St. Lawrence, the British planned to move troops up the Ottawa, then down the canal to consolidate a defence about Fort Henry at the place where the St. Lawrence channel issues from Lake Ontario. So Kingston would not do. Nor would any place else, for the simple reason that Ottawa was then the only neutral community on the one river which was shared through most of its navigable length by both the provinces.

But it was a mortifying choice, just the same. American journalists, hostile to all things British and supremely contemptuous of the Canadians for clinging to poverty under the British Crown, gave hoots of merriment when they heard the news that this new united Canada, this second nation produced by the American Revolution, had decided to place its capital in one of the most notorious work camps on the continent. The English wit Goldwin Smith described Ottawa as "a sub-arctic lumber village converted by royal mandate into a political cockpit".

In the Ottawa of that time everything seemed ugly, undignified, and ridiculous, even the way things were done. Splendid new Houses of Parliament were planned, but the only suitable place for them was occupied by the abandoned wooden barracks of Colonel By. Instead of tearing the barracks down and carting off the lumber, the work gangs simply dumped them wholesale over the cliff into the river. But the work continued, the Houses of Parliament were built pretty well on schedule, and in

1860 the capital of Canada received the first of what was to become a long series of royal visits. The Queen's son, Edward, Prince of Wales, arrived to lay the cornerstone of the main building.

A primitive but extremely vivid photograph recalls not only the occasion, but the nature of Ottawa in those days. The Prince stands there, trowel in hand and with no expression on his Hanoverian countenance. About him is a semicircle of politicians in top hats and frock coats. But the scene, so far as this photograph is concerned, is stolen by the citizenry. There they are, hundreds of workmen in shirts and checked trousers, ankle deep in mud, all set to give three cheers the moment the old Bytown Brass Band has finished playing "God Save The Prince of Wales".

Now most of the human aspects of the Ottawa Valley have changed out of recognition. The lovely seigneury of the old rebel Papineau has become a famous luxury hotel. The lumbermen in the forests eat as well as eighteenth-century gentry, and Ottawa has become the most sedate city in the land. All has changed, apparently, except the old habit of taking the Ottawa River for granted, and this brings me to a story which illustrates better than anything else what the results of that habit can be.

In 1960 the Supreme Court of Canada had to consider one of the most complex and romantic cases ever to come before a Canadian bench, and the Ottawa River was the cause of it.

A few years earlier the Hydro Electric Commission of Ontario decided to build a dam to enlarge the lake in the Joachims sector, the site of portages numbers 14 and 15 in the days of the voyageurs. Despite the protests of some lumbering interests, agreement was reached between the Ontario and Quebec governments and the dam was completed. The Ottawa got a new lake, most of it artificial, some ninety miles long. As the river's current is now dead in the lake, lumbermen must tow their logs in barrel booms instead of driving them, and this greatly increases their costs. Naturally they took legal action for compensation, but at the beginning of the case neither plaintiff nor defendant seems to have been aware of the entanglements into which the ancient history of the Ottawa River would leave them before the case was settled.

For the Ottawa in this section not only belongs equally to Quebec and Ontario; many of the rights along the river depend on leases older than Confederation. Here, as is inevitable, English Common Law as practised in Ontario clashed with the old Civil Code in force in Quebec.

Nor was this all, for the practice of driving logs down rivers is much older than the discovery of Canada. Log-driving, which most Canadians assume is native, goes all the way back to Biblical times: "And Hiram sent unto Solomon, saying . . . I will do all thy desire concerning timber of cedar and concerning timber of fir. My servants shall bring them from Lebanon unto the sea: and I will convey them by floats unto the place that thou shalt appoint me."

Log-driving was never practised in England and was unknown in the continent of Europe until 1549, when it was introduced into France. A century later the Intendant Jean Talon introduced the practice into North America when he had logs driven down the St. Maurice and the St. Lawrence to Quebec. Although the Ottawa River received little settlement in the French regime, it seems certain that the French drove logs on this river in the 1740s, so that Philemon Wright was not the first man to introduce lumbering there. He certainly adopted the practice of log-driving from the French; for that matter so did all the English; it was, in modern times, a French invention.

Hence it came about that this case between the Ontario Hydro Electric Commission and the Upper Ottawa Improvement Company was heavily involved with a cluster of French legal practices antedating not only Confederation, but even the Conquest. The Supreme Court was handed a case where some of the legal concepts lay completely outside the scope of English Common Law; where some of them, in fact, went all the way back to legal precedents which first were developed in the time of Henri IV. How valid these were I did not know. But it fascinated me to think that the history and locality of the Ottawa River compelled their Lordships to consider them. Inevitably the lumbermen lost their case. The law so often surrenders to a *fait accompli*, especially when the *fait accompli* involves millions of dollars and thousands of jobs.

Of all the streams I have studied in Canada west of the Maritimes, the Ottawa on its lower reaches is the gentlest. Except in the rapids it flows calmly; birds haunt its many marshes; the water sighs through billions of reeds and past pleasant green islets. In summer along the river near Papineauville the whole scene appears, sometimes, to be resting in a trance. Here it is a mature river indeed.

But from the air you see a different prospect, and on the whole a truer one. You see the Ottawa as a strong avenue equal almost to the master stream of the present system. In broad curves it sweeps into the northwest, and from the air you see it as a boundary clear and absolute between the settled country of gentle Ontario and the Laurentian wilderness which, in all likelihood, will always remain as uncultivated as it was in the time the Algonquins hunted in it.

WORKADAY WATER

We hold 3,845,144 sq. miles. But this mass has an equally enormous blessing in rivers and lakes. These have coursed a lifeblood into the nation's endeavour. To some, the stream in its verdant valley calls for poetry but as these photographs confirm, the rivers are still mostly workaday water.

Since the square-timber days of the 19th century, the rivers have been vital to Canada's forest industries.

As the river runs, the pulse of the country quickens

Livestock thrives on the fertile meadows near where the St. Lawrence accepts the waters of the Richelieu. In more commercial mood, this confluence also supports shipbuilding, steel-rolling mills, and a smelter for titanium ores shipped from Labrador.

Below: The rushing millstream (this one's at Kincaid, Ontario) supplied the only power the first settlers knew. Grist mills ground wheat into flour and sawmills provided timber for housing. Before steam arrived, Upper Canada had 1,400 water-powered mills.

Ile d'Orleans (once Bacchus Island) rides in the St. Lawrence just below Quebec City tethered by a handsome bridge to the Beauport shore. François Xavier de Laval, first Bishop of Quebec, once extolled its fine soil and mild climate to immigrant farmers.

Below: The Rockies create an unforgettable frieze for this Albertan farm, in a fold of the upper valley of the Bow River. In semi-arid southern and eastern areas, a million acres are under irrigation, bringing prosperity to beet growers and truck farmers.

From the silt of the St. John, food for a hungry world

Along the swinging reaches of the St. John, New Brunswickers take a heavy harvest of potatoes, mixed crops, and fruits from the intervales. Ten million bushels of potatoes are sold from this rich dirt every year, mostly from Carleton and York counties (founded 1786). The province is 85 percent forest (a percentage that is increasing) and vast quantities of pulpwood float down the mainstreams, most of it conifer. Half of all New Brunswick industry is based on lumber, and without rivers like the St. John, Miramichi, St. Croix, the Petitcodiac, Nepisiguit, and the Restigouche, the raw material could not be moved economically to market. At the mouth of the St. John, where the river drops over the famous Reversing Falls, stands salty Saint John (note the spelling!), the first city in Canada to be incorporated—1785.

Water work . . . and play

Our history is essentially the story of our rivers. To stay-at-homes, it comes as a surprise to see their fellows at work or play on river, canal, or bay, responding (even unconsciously) to the central theme of the national saga. The pleasures of the canal network are still little known. Apart from the shipping links through the Great Lakes, there are five other systems which give small boats a marvellous cruising range.

Capilano, Lynn, Seymour, and a dozen other streams pour into Burrard Inlet, scene of Vancouver's hustling maritime trade.

Factory smoke joins scudding cloud over Saint John, New Brunswick. River joins sea in this ice-free port, discovered by Champlain and De Monts on June 24, 1604, settled by American Loyalists in 1783. The famous tides of the Bay of Fundy surge into the harbour, rising as much as 70 feet.

Lock-keeper at work
on the Trent Canal.

Panning for gold in
the Yukon's Bonanza.

Low tide, Grondines,
lower St. Lawrence.

The rivers provide winter sport, both on the ice—and through it. Skating,
ice-boating, curling, and snowmobile racing have their devotees, and fishing
from portable huts is popular everywhere. This photograph was taken at
Ste. Anne de la Pérade, where winter cod attracts fishermen from far and near.

Like England's Thames, the Seine of France, Germany's Rhine,
the Canadian river has always played its full part
in the working life of the nation. Fish for table and commerce
is supplied by these Newfoundland waters (*above*) while
the appetite of B.C. industry is met by river and sea-going craft.

The St. John

A LOVELY, LOVELY RIVER

For myself, a return to the St. John River is like a homecoming. Deep and splendid though the river is, it is not like any of the others of the country which we Maritimers, in my grandfather's day, referred to as "Canada". The old Maritime provinces have changed less than any part of North America. What they have lost in prosperity, they have gained in coherence, and on the whole the life there is the quietest and happiest in the country. Everything here is on a small scale easily comprehended, close to the English or Scottish past of the people, and the whole region still abounds in the eccentric characters which only small old places, sure of themselves emotionally, seem able to afford.

Years ago I heard one of those Maritime province stories which nobody verifies for fear it will turn out to be false. On a tributary of the St. John River, around the turn of the century, quite a few lumbermen were owners of dress suits with all the fixings: boiled shirts, starched wing collars, white ties and gloves, black silk socks, and patent leather pumps. They had acquired this apparel from a man they respected as the best fly-fisherman, the best bird-shot, and the best still-hunter they knew in a district where standards in these activities were high. He was an Englishman and a remittance man, and each year his family had his former tailor and haberdasher send him the kind of garments they presumed he required in the St. John River country. The remittance man, who lived in a shack and wore nothing but work clothes, passed on the parcels to his friends. He spoke little about himself, but whenever anyone asked him why he had chosen to live there, his answer was always the same.

"One lives like a gentleman here. One has all the fishing and shooting one wants at one's door. This is a happy land."

I hope the story is even half-true, for happiness is the word which always comes to my mind when I think of the River St. John. It is the shortest of our principal streams, being only about 420 miles long, and its system is a small one. Yet it offers so much variety of scenery that a stranger travelling along it encounters a surprise every twenty miles or so. The St. John is intimate and very beautiful. On fine summer days the colours in its lower reaches shift from ocean blue to delphinium blue to a deep quivering violet according to the intensity of the light given out by the sky. A sudden rain in the Aroostook country can make the upper St. John look as brown as the Red while the lower stream is still clear, and indeed the depth lower down is so great, the current so gentle, that the silt from the upper river tends to sink to the bottom, with the result that the water of the lower St. John is beautifully clear most of the time. Sunsets in the Long Reach are as majestic as sunsets in a deep fjord of Norway. At dawn and in the evening some of the settled sections have pastel hues soft as in southern England. "Tenderly, day that I have loved, I close your eyes"—I thought of this line of Rupert Brooke the last time I heard the bells of Fredericton chime across the stream after sunset.

The happiness associated with the St. John, especially in the older communities lower down the river, is of a kind the world is losing everywhere. It proceeds from a life closely entwined with the river and with woods which are still wild and abundant with game: with family farms, small towns, neighbourly villages, and plain people living with nature at their doors and not much troubled by ambition. Most of the intensely ambitious Maritimers emigrate; most of those who remain regard the living of a good life as more important than the using of a life for the sake of achievement. The St. John River country is old-fashioned; it makes you think of the serene, green growing years of eastern America.

There are several reasons for this. Not only is New Brunswick a geographical offshoot of New England; the people inhabiting the St. John Valley from Woodstock to the Reversing Falls are nearly all descended from the original Anglo-Saxon stock which pioneered the United States. After the first tentative French occupation petered out, the Loyalists came to the valley at the end of the eighteenth century and settled it. With them they brought, along with a reinforced loyalty to the Crown, most of the habits, virtues, and limitations acquired by their ancestors in the first century and a half of the English-American experience. But because they were a twice-transplanted people, the lower St. John is much younger in terms of settlement than Massachusetts or New York, and from the visual standpoint this has been a calamity. The old New England towns were built in the most exquisite period of domestic architecture ever known, but most of the St. John River towns suffer from the bad taste of the nineteenth century with its ugly angles and harsh red brick. But their way of life is not reflected in their buildings. It still belongs to an earlier period than survives in any place I know in the northern states of the American east.

"I come to Canada regularly," a retired American general said to me, "because it reminds me so much of home when I was a boy. I can close my eyes and hear the old folks talk."

The St. John River people along the lower reaches are such staunch retainers of the past that "conservative" is too weak a word to apply to them. There is something endearing in their stubborn dislike of change. There can be something paradoxical about it, too.

Few Canadians have contributed more to the speed of modern living than Rupert Turnbull, who invented the variable-pitch propeller, built the first wind tunnel in Canada, and was the first man to close the wing in aircraft. Although for a time he did research under Edison in Menlo Park, for most of his career Turnbull worked in his private laboratory at Rothesay where the Kennebecasis comes in to share Grand Bay with the St. John. In his personal life this singular inventor was so averse to change that he lived like a country squire of the last century. He sailed, he fished, he shot ducks into his early eighties. He disliked speed, and when he reluctantly bought an automobile, he never drove it faster than twenty-five miles an hour. When New Brunswick in the early 1920s grudgingly changed the rule of the road from left to right (in other words, from English to American) he so disapproved of the alteration that he tried to ignore it. Finding progress difficult with the traffic coming from the opposite direction, he at last accepted a compromise. Instead of driving on the left hand side of the road, he drove in the middle, and in a region full of individualists, he was not only condoned, he was applauded.

For years this conservatism of the St. John River country, until recently the heart of New Brunswick province, was responsible for the fact that New Brunswick had one of the lowest average income figures per capita in the whole country. Power plants came late to the St. John. Though the river has a great weight of water and the most spectacular cataract east of Montmorency, it was 1925 before a power plant was opened at Grand Falls. This plant, together with the development of the pulp and paper industry higher up at Edmundston, changed the economy of the upper stream, and also made its appearance much less attractive. To this day there are people living lower down the river who regret that a pleasant village like the old Grand Falls should have been converted into a factory town with wide streets and a movie house. It was not until 1950 that engineers undertook an exhaustive survey of the St. John River basin in search of power sources for a province finally forced to admit that it was suffering the fate of all raw producers in the technological age, and it was only in 1958 that the dam at Beechwood came into operation. The engineers installed fish ladders for the salmon swimming up to the spawning beds on the Tobique, but salmon cannot so easily be guided back the same way, and a great number of fingerlings are sure to perish in the turbines. Knowing the region pretty well, and knowing the Maritime province mentality since childhood, I was not surprised to encounter a good many negative opinions about the Beechwood dam just after it came into operation.

"What's the use of installing new manufactures here?" said one man. "I'd like to ask you what good *that* is going to do New Brunswick. The rest of the country has fixed the freight rates against the Maritimes, so even if the dam does anything—and it probably won't—what difference? We'll still be outsold one way or the other."

And another said: "This was the most beautiful salmon river on the whole Atlantic seaboard of America. Then some engineers come along and ruin it."

And another: "Do you really want to know why they built that dam? For precisely the same reason the Egyptians and the Burmese and Ghanaians want to build dams where dams never were. It's become a status-symbol for this crazy modern world that knows how to do anything else except be sensible and happy. That dam isn't worth an hour's fishing."

These conversations occurred in 1959. They form a gentle praeludium to the close-lipped fury of many New Brunswickers when they talk about the much newer dam built at Mactaquac. As dams go, this has been quite efficient in producing hydro-electricity, but I have yet to meet a St. John River man outside of the government with a good word to say for it. Maritimers are not accustomed to the bureaucratic ruthlessness of modern governments in the so-called Welfare State, and they found it hard to believe that the personal rights of so many people could be totally disregarded for the sake of an engineering project.

Fourteen miles above Fredericton, the little Mactaquac River flows into the St. John on its left bank and here the dam was built. When completed, the result was a head pond extending sixty miles up the St. John River to within three miles of Hartland. This was one of the loveliest sections on the entire river. The islands and intervals were famous, they were beautiful and they were fruitful. They were all drowned out. Communities, settlements, historic landmarks, cemeteries, houses lived in by the same families for over a century were obliterated. Some people moved away, others built new homes farther back on what was left of their properties. Some people died. Altogether, upwards of three thousand men, women, and children were displaced.

As power dams have no effect on flood control, the Mactaquac was useless to prevent the flood in the spring of 1973, the worst in fifty years of the river's history, when the stream swelled over its high banks in Fredericton and even flooded the ground floor of the Lord Beaverbrook Hotel. The flood of course subsided, but the life of the river has been changed forever.

There was something grisly in the government's behaviour to the salmon that swam up from the sea to congregate in bewilderment at the foot of the Mactaquac Dam. There many of them were netted, hoisted ashore, and dumped into tanks filled with water. The tanks were then carried miles upstream by trucks and were emptied into tributaries so that the salmon would provide sport for wealthy anglers. A number of fish swam up the Nashwaak to spawn. Some born in the St. John were reported in Nova Scotian streams like the Stewiacke and even the Annapolis. But the St. John's days as the greatest of all eastern Canadian salmon streams are now ended.

Thank God the dam did not spoil the river's beauty. Many new sand bars have appeared lower down, but the river is still lovely to behold, though the hearts of some of its greatest lovers will be sore for the rest of their lives. Naturally, the log-driving on the upper river has ended.

The St. John River people can at times be vague about their first New Brunswick ancestors—not *very* vague, but vague because their ancestors, when they think of them at all, seem so much like themselves today that there is no point in talking about them. The ancestors of nearly all of them were United Empire Loyalists, many of them soldiers in King George's American regiments during the Revolutionary War. Their present descendants have inherited their conservatism. They do not dislike Americans—how can they, being in some senses more authentically American than most American citizens of the present? They admit the United States has been as successful as Mr. Jefferson hoped she would be, but at the same time they feel that the price of success has been too high. With the pride of the unappreciated they accept it as a compliment when bustling moderns of a city like Toronto accuse them of lack of enterprise. They are proud of the simple dignity of their own past, and of the dignity of this river they have so carefully preserved. The American general knew what he was talking about when he said that the country-dwelling Loyalist is a survival of the old American society.

Sometimes I amuse myself by imagining the feelings of famous Americans of past eras if these same Americans were reincarnated into the present. What would Longfellow say of the motels, beach cabins, billboards, and roadside eating stands of Maine's U.S. 1? Emerson in modern Boston, Whittier in Peyton Place—the thought of these grave old Americans in the society which developed after them fills the one-eighth of me which is Loyalist with a quiet amusement. Pre-industrial New England smelled of harbours with rope walks and caulking irons, of kitchens warm with fresh bread, of root cellars and

October leaves and crab-apple jelly and scrubbed churches where incense never burned. Many places in the St. John River country still do. At Market Slip in Saint John City, Longfellow could still discover the beauty and mystery of ships as they were before ships turned into a combination of huge machines and floating Grand Hotels. Fredericton today is not unlike Emerson's Concord, though the equivalents of State Street and Washington Street are here called Queen Street and Regent Street. In Maugerville (pronounced "Majorville") there must still be a few of Whittier's barefoot boys. All along the lower St. John from Woodstock to the mouth are people bearing names well known in colonial America. Nearly all the Winslows who were descended from the only Pilgrim Father to have his picture painted have disappeared in the United States after a long record of service in which one of them was admiral of the United States Pacific fleet. But along the St. John River today there are quite a few Winslows living there simply.

This is a wonderful country for growing boys, as was the old New England of chores and fishing and rural schools. Here a growing boy can live close to nature and at the same time see an integrated society reduced to a boy's scale. Until recently it was like this all along the St. John, and in some places it still is. No wonder so many Maritime province boys, grown into successful men in the large cities, sigh for home as the grown Adam sighed for the Garden. They had good childhoods there. Their selective memories have censored out the bad spots and the dull spots and have created the kind of poetry which Stephen Leacock, raised in a rawer community composed of the same stock, wove into his *Sunshine Sketches of a Little Town.*

The lure of this land to the expatriate is as strong as the invisible thread of Chesterton's Father Brown which could draw a man home from the remotest corner of the world. It is like the mysterious pull of the spawning beds to the Atlantic salmon, which do not die after spawning as the Pacific salmon do. Lord Beaverbrook, to judge from anecdotes and his own stories, never found in London the inner satisfaction he knew in his New Brunswick boyhood. To a Maritimer there was something charming in the provincial arrogance which caused this tough and difficult man, during a war-time conference with Roosevelt, Churchill, and Stalin, to force the great men to learn the old New Brunswick lumbering song about the Jones boys' sawmill. There was something touching in the salmon-like returns of this formidable old egotist to his native land, in his desire to make Englishmen admit that it is a wonderful place. But if I know the St. John River mentality, I suspect that they have always assumed, without having to mention it except to strangers, that Lord Beaverbrook was not quite one of them, having been raised on the Miramichi in a different part of the province. It would not surprise me if Lord Beaverbrook encountered with familiar exasperation that same built-in conservatism which originally drove him out. Fredericton built a statue to him, and the family has given much to Fredericton, but no part of New Brunswick would ever have given a man like Max Aitken a chance to succeed on his own terms. London's *Daily Express* could not compete in Fredericton with *The Gleaner*, and the average St. John River man, exposed to the *Express*, would wonder why anyone would want to read it at all. The *Express* is tailored deliberately to an incoherent metropolitan society, and its readers know nothing of a life where everyone is everyone else's real neighbour, where banker, barber, professor, cathedral dean, and odd-job man, each knowing his exact place, nevertheless feels himself bound to the others within a common coherence.

In a charming essay called *Paddlewheels on the Saint John* (the last river steamer carrying passengers was scrapped in 1946) Fred W. Phillips of Fredericton describes the life of the river in his boyhood:

> A family excursion to the great exhibitions at Fredericton or Saint John was then an ample reward for a summer's work on the farm. There would be the rising in the half-light of dawn, an excited breakfast and then the seemingly endless wait at the wharf. Finally there would come a long-drawn whistle from "beyond the point", and in a moment more a gleaming white hull would appear. And those hulls themselves—they breathed the very air of the communities they served. From below decks in those crisp autumn days of the fair excursions came the earthy smells of barrels of new potatoes and fresh apples, of sides of beef and carcases of pork; and permeating all else, the pungent odour of crackling pitch pine and hot machine oil.

Nobody should ever have called this river the Rhine of America. The Rhine is longer, larger, more dramatic, its banks are crowded with monuments and factory cities, its surface with coal barges and excursion steamers, and its ferocious history has a ghastly tendency to repeat itself from one generation to the next. Those romantic castles which glower at you from Rhenish islands were never beautiful. They housed tyrants, robbers, and torturers, and you can almost feel their wickedness as you pass them by.

But the St. John River knew little wickedness, and apart from small-scale Indian frays in the days when Malicete war parties roamed the river in canoes, the fighting along the St. John has never amounted to more than the ridiculous affair between La Tour and d'Aulnay Charnisay and the so-called Aroostook War of 1839,

when neighbouring Maine and New Brunswick lumbermen created an international crisis over cutting rights. Almost the only structures on the St. John islands are hay-barns, and on many of the islands the Malicetes still gather the fiddlehead greens. Only in the Long Reach where the river slants off at right angles northeast from Grand Bay does the St. John resemble any part of the Rhine, nor does it really resemble it here except in width, depth, and the form of the hills rising above the water. But the hills of the Long Reach are virgin forests glorious with colours in the fall, while on the Rhine they are terraced vineyards.

The St. John rises in the woods of northern Maine, it curves under the hump of the Laurentian-Atlantic watershed, and it reaches New Brunswick at the lower tip of the Madawaska County panhandle. Then it winds through forest country, mostly evergreen, northeasterly to Edmundston, then curves southeasterly down through St. Leonard and Grand Falls and so to Woodstock. From a point in Madawaska County just above the hamlet of Connor, to a point just above Grand Falls, the river forms the boundary with the United States.

These upper reaches of the St. John differ from the lower ones more than Quebec differs from Ontario. More recently settled—the original English population thinned out as it moved upstream from the mouth—the upper St. John is almost entirely French-speaking, Edmundston is as *Canadien* as Trois Rivières, but much rawer and with poorer dwellings, so that the huge church with the aluminum-covered roof dominates it like a castle. French Canadians, no less than the native New Brunswick Acadians, have been steadily moving down the St. John River for a generation and a half.

The river in its upper reaches is slim and graceful, a delicate band through the forests, and it looks quiet until you come to Grand Falls. There, abruptly, you see the power of it. The flume of the falls, utterly savage, hurls itself, twisted by the contour of the rock, into a huge slide of water before it plunges roaring into a gorge with walls more than a hundred and fifty feet high. No salmon could ever surmount the Grand Falls of the St. John, but logs can go down it without serious trouble. Only once in a century of lumbering have the falls been jammed, and then it was done on a bet.

From Woodstock down to Fredericton the river was not much wider than the Thames at Reading, before Mactaquac Dam was built. After passing the head of tide at Crock's Point and receiving the Nashwaak, it widens at Fredericton to nearly half a mile, passes under three bridges, and proceeds deep and generally still toward the splendid stretches lower down. The Long Reach is one of the fairest sections of river I have ever seen in Canada, and a little below it the stream swells into Grand Bay behind the city of Saint John. Here the Kennebecasis comes in from the east, not as a tributary but as a separate river which ages ago in geologic time flowed in the opposite direction. Below Grand Bay the St. John ends with the biggest surprise on any navigable river in America: it comes to the Reversing Falls between the city and the raw new suburb of Lancaster. When the tide is low, the river descends a gorge with a drop of fifteen feet into the Fundy. But when the huge Fundy tide lifts, salt water surges up the gorge and floods deeply into the river itself. So high is the Fundy tide that ocean-going oil tankers can sail inland when the fall is reversed.

A variable river this, but never a crowded one except when logs came down in the spring drive. Most of the logs recently were cut in the Maine forest near the headwaters and they had an adventurous journey of three hundred miles or more before they reached the plants at the river's mouth. They tumbled over Grand Falls, they were shepherded past the Beechwood dam, and finally they came to a stop in a jam three miles long against the great boom stretched between Oromocto Island and the eastern shore by Maugerville. Tugs towed mats of them downstream in barrel booms, and behind the drive came the Wangan boats, which are house-carrying scows powered by outboard motors and crewed by about twenty men. Within three weeks the Wangan boat men cleared the river of stray logs all the way from Beechwood to Maugerville, a distance of some two hundred miles. Thereafter the St. John was clear for pleasure craft.

To the selfish, one of the beauties of this river is that so far few American small-boat owners have discovered it; if they did, the stream would be crowded with craft from half the eastern states, for there is no river on the continent more suited to pleasure boats. Above Head of Tide it is too shallow for cabin cruisers, but from Fredericton down to the mouth it is deep enough to carry a ship and quiet enough for a child to be safe on it. A large proportion of people along the St. John own boats, but as the population is small and there is a great length of water, they have most of it to themselves.

The shores float by, the tall grasses are fragrant in the water meadows, ferns and wildflowers blow on the islands, shadows move along the hills. As a picnic party comes round the bend a flock of startled ducks takes to the air, and like sea planes alighting they splash back again after the boat has passed. "Look!" cries a small boy, and there at the water's edge, up-wind, is a deer with big eyes. As the sun sinks, the great hills above the Long Reach cast their shadows over a river violet-dark, and

later in Grand Bay, the water shrimp-pink and pastel-grey from reflected cumulus clouds, the yachts becalmed on the flood, the boat party sees the lights of the city which marks the journey's end.

Or perhaps the family turns off into one of the tributaries and camps under trees beside the Oromocto. Or perhaps it goes up the little Jemseg into the lonely expanse of Grand Lake. Or perhaps still another party in canoes is paddling the Nashwaak into the woods where the moose are, or still another is moving up the Tobique where the Atlantic salmon spawn. No matter where you go on the river today you can easily be alone. And if you own a cabin cruiser you can use the St. John as a sally port to any place to which a cabin cruiser can sail. Friends of mine have sailed from Fredericton to Port Arthur in the same boat. They went down the St. John and over the Reversing Falls into the Fundy, then they followed the coastline of New Brunswick, Maine, New Hampshire, and Massachusetts to Cape Cod, passed through the canal and so down the American coast to New York. Sailing past the towers of Manhattan they went up the Hudson and then, using a variety of American inland waterways, they reached the St. Lawrence system and sailed through the Great Lakes to the end of them.

Like any North American river the St. John abounds in geese and duck, and wild animals still drink on its shores. Not long ago a moose swam the St. John at Fredericton and spent some time wandering through the city's streets. Deer come out of the woods and eat garden greens as they do everywhere in the Maritimes in closed seasons. But it was in its salmon runs — before the Beechwood and Mactaquac dams ruined them — that the St. John was supreme among the fishing rivers of the eastern seaboard.

The salmon in Gaspé, Anticosti, Labrador, and Newfoundland, even on the Restigouche and Miramichi, may come upstream in larger runs than they did on the St. John, but there are not so many runs in the course of a season. Cedric Cooper of Fredericton, who had rights on the largest pool in the river, told me that in the St. John there used to be nine salmon runs in the course of a year. The first entered in early May a few weeks after the ice breaks, when the river is so widely flooded that the Maugerville farmers sometimes have to put their cattle in the lofts of the barns. These fish were bound for the Serpentine Branch of the Tobique, where they spawned. The last run entered in November just before the river began to freeze. So the salmon here were so plentiful that they were exported. If they sell you fresh salmon in the Montreal markets today, they always call it "Gaspé salmon". But not often did the "Gaspé salmon" eaten in Montreal come from any other place but New Brunswick.

"The Saint John is a fine river equal in magnitude to the Connecticut or Hudson" with a harbour at the mouth "accessible at all seasons of the year, never frozen or obstructed by ice."

Such was the first report of the agents of the Loyalists who had come to Annapolis Royal in Nova Scotia in the fall of 1782, had crossed the Fundy and proceeded up the St. John as far as the Oromocto in search of farm land for a desperate people. The Revolutionary War was over in the United States, and the victors were earning the distinction later conferred upon them by the historian Arnold Toynbee, who notes that the Americans were the first people in modern times to expel thousands of men and women of their own race, sharing their own religion and experience, because of their political activities. The president of the Board of Agents for the Loyalists bore one of the most famous names in the State of New York: he was the Reverend Dr. Samuel Seabury.

Americans had of course heard of the St. John long before the Revolution. The river had been established on the map as early as 1604, when Champlain entered it while still a member of De Monts' expedition. La Tour had built a fort at its mouth in 1635, d'Aulnay Charnisay had taken it from him ten years later, and nine years after that, Charnisay had been displaced by an English expedition operating in the name and authority of Oliver Cromwell. After the fall of Louisbourg a force of two thousand men under Colonel Robert Monckton had arrived at Partridge Island, rebuilt the old French fort, and renamed it Fort Frederic. Four years after this a Newburyport merchant had built a post at the river's mouth for burning limestone and for fishing, and through his efforts a small trade was begun in fish, lime, lumber, and fur. But no real development of the St. John was attempted before the British forces were defeated in America. When the agents of the Loyalists arrived, the population of the post at the river's mouth was only one hundred and forty-five. A year later the city of Saint John had come into being.

The Loyalists who settled the St. John Valley were proud, indignant men with a bitter sense of wrong, nor had many of them been rich or privileged in the south. A census of the first settlement shows that every trade was represented from lawyer to carpenter and odd-job man. But they belonged to the defeated party. Some had been "inflicted with the Punishment of Tar and Feathers". Some had "sheltered themselves in the Mountains". One had been "Fined, whip'd and Tried for his Life". One had been "Robbed and maimed by the Rebels". Many could prove that "A valuable Dwelling House had been burnt up by a malicious Set of Men." Edward Winslow wrote to his son on June 20, 1783: "The violence and malice of the Rebel Government makes it impossible even to think of joining them again."

It was ever thus after brother has been divided against brother in a civil war, and in the long run the victors probably did the kind thing when they decided to drive the Loyalists out. They felt toward them exactly as the victorious Soviets felt toward the White Russians in the 1920s.

Sir Guy Carleton, still in control of the port of New York, requisitioned transports for an exodus in those days unparalleled. By late November 1783, more than 35,000 people had been convoyed to Nova Scotia, and the total number reaching Saint John (New Brunswick was then a part of Nova Scotia) was 14,162. Along with the civilians there arrived at Saint John some 3,396 officers, N.C.O.s, and privates of the British North American regiments, and the settlers had need of their discipline and team spirit.

"It is, I think, the roughest land I ever saw," wrote one of them. "We are all ordered to land tomorrow, and not a shelter to go under."

But by the year's end the location had been divided into lots, trees had been cut, trimmed, and planed, stumps had been burned out, fireplaces built, and frames raised. The skeleton of the city of Saint John existed, and with the river and pine forests behind it, the community rapidly grew.

Less than a century after its founding, Saint John was the fourth ship-owning city in the world, and her clippers were famous on all the oceans. One of the most famous lines that ever floated, the White Star, had its birth in Saint John. Had it not been for a disaster, Saint John might well have become the chief city of the Maritime provinces. But in 1877 the worst fire in Canadian history gutted the city's heart, and in a sense Saint John never fully recovered from it. From the visual standpoint this was a tragedy. Old Saint John must have been beautiful, for all of its principal buildings and dwelling houses were in the splendid style of the first Loyalists. Rebuilt in one of the ugliest periods of architecture known to man, and rebuilt in a hurry, Saint John today is angular red brick and salt-stained clapboard.

But Fredericton, smaller and more secluded, preserves intact the image of Loyalist New Brunswick. Situated on St. Ann's Point about ninety miles upstream from the Bay of Fundy, the provincial capital is a mirror of the Loyalist mind. Here, in a Canadian terrain different from any in England, different again from the warm fields of Westchester County, eastern Pennsylvania, and New Jersey whence they had set out in Carleton's transports, His Majesty's loyal Americans erected a living monument to their determination to keep alive on this continent the British Fact.

Fredericton's little Anglican cathedral is an exact replica of St. Mary's Church in Snettisham in Norfolk; it is also claimed to be the first cathedral foundation established on British soil since the Norman Conquest. Fredericton's Legislative Building contains portraits by Sir Joshua Reynolds of King George III and Queen Charlotte, the Legislative Library has a copy of the Doomsday Book. And the bells of Fredericton still chime across this Canadian river with a sweet English sound.

They kept it alive here, the British Fact in America; they kept it alive from the end of the eighteenth century until today. But they are threatened now and they know it.

Just below Fredericton is the new Gagetown camp, the largest military camp in the Commonwealth, with a permanent troop concentration seldom under ten thousand, with battle ranges embracing every known kind of terrain but mountains, with soldiers from all over the nation. "Canada" is moving into the lower St. John, just as French Canadians have been moving steadily downward from the upper reaches of the river, and the power techniques of modern America are producing electrical energy from a stream sufficient to supply power for dozens of factories.

"I guess," said an old Frederictonian to me the last time I talked with him, "I guess I've seen about the last of it. Fredericton may be the capital of New Brunswick, but so far as I can see it's soon going to be a suburb of Gagetown. They tell me there are now eight of these hydro-electric stations in the province. And do you know what they've got in Gagetown now? They've got *a shopping centre!*" (A few years later, Fredericton had one, too.)

He shook his head, and I thought again of the legendary English remittance man who stayed here because this was a gentleman's country, his notions of a gentleman being a man who did not work in a factory or shop, but had all the fishing and shooting he wanted at his door, and no boss to tell him he could not afford to enjoy it except on Saturday afternoons. I thought again of those old days—I myself am old enough to remember the last of them—when the farm people went up and down the river with the paddlewheels of the steamboats chunking, and everyone knew everyone else, and there was no confusing knowledge of psychiatry, and sin was sin, and churches were not semi-theatres.

It had to go, of course; the old order had to change or rot. But along the St. John a growing boy can still experience the simple things, and learn without thinking the fabric of a coherent society. The great salmon, firm from the cold Atlantic, brace themselves against the currents at the pools, the geese and duck come and go with the seasons, the moose and deer haunt the forests which Charles G. D. Roberts described so well.

"A lovely river," the old man said. "A lovely, lovely river!"

Along the St. John. Here, on a summer forenoon, the peace of time past.

The Miramichi

SALMON AND SCRIPTURES

"Are not Abana and Pharpar, rivers of Damascus, better than all the waters of Israel? May I not wash in them, and be clean?"

The famous retort of Naaman the Syrian to the prophet Elisha reached me in a letter some years ago from, of all people, Lord Beaverbrook, and what he had in mind was the Miramichi. Why had I not written about it? Even though its three main branches, all of them shallow above tidewater, have a total length of under 200 miles, the Miramichi was Lord Beaverbrook's own personal river. He was the most famous of all the men who had grown up beside it and if he had moved in the company of the great of the world, why should not his river belong in the company of giants like the Mackenzie and the St. Lawrence?

It was also in character that Lord Beaverbrook should have begun his letter with a quotation from Scripture. His father had been the Presbyterian minister in Newcastle-on-Miramichi, and though it has sometimes been noted that his son in later life disregarded the teachings of the manse, the evidence is overwhelming that he never forgot them. Indeed, he so thoroughly incorporated them into his own immense and complicated ego that he felt himself qualified to write a biography of Jesus Christ, which he published under the title of *The Divine Propagandist* — a title that is singularly appropriate in Beaverbrook's case because he himself had served as Minister of Propaganda in the British War cabinet in 1918. He wrote another biography called *Courage*, now out of print and a collector's item, which is a good deal more revelatory of himself and the Miramichi region. Its subject was his lifelong friend Sir James Dunn, another famous son of the New Brunswick North Shore, and in this long and curious account of Dunn's many financial triumphs, quotations from the Scriptures and John Calvin also abound.

Territory, or the desire for it, has always been a potent element in the power-instinct, so Beaverbrook's choice of that biblical text was remarkably apt. Though Naaman "went off in a rage" after Elisha told him to wash in Jordan, a more mature consideration of his problem convinced him that Elisha was probably right, so to Jordan he went after all, he bathed in it and behold, his skin became as pure as the skin of a new-born babe! Though the Miramichi was certainly the river of the young Max Aitken, the river beside which he ultimately established his career turned out to be the Thames. And here is a perfect allegory of the tragi-comedy that besets able men who grow up in a colonial society.

That the colonial attitudes of Loyalist Canada tended to produce a long series of tragi-comedies, I learned long ago; I became acutely conscious of it through conversations with Peter Aitken, Lord Beaverbrook's younger son. In 1933 I played a lot of tennis with Peter when he was sent out to Nova Scotia by his father to work for 28 cents an hour in a pulp and paper mill. "The idea is to toughen me up," Peter explained. He told me that his father used to wax scriptural once every month and in these moods he never failed to remind Peter, whom he had sent to Eton and Cambridge, that no such advantages had attended *him* in his youth along the banks of the Miramichi, that life in northern New Brunswick was real, it was earnest, and so on and so on. Peter had the idea that the Miramichi was his father's touchstone of pristine virtue, as Pugwash seems to have been for Mr. Cyrus Eaton. Men of wealth and power who were born in the Maritimes are the greatest lovers *in absentia* that those austere provinces have ever had.

If I appear to be ironical it is because irony is the essence of the situation in the Maritimes. No matter where men like Lord Beaverbrook or Sir James Dunn might have been born, nothing but an early death could have prevented them from acquiring power and wealth, but the Maritime atmosphere of the late nineteenth century gave them a schizophrenic attitude even toward themselves. In his biography of James Dunn, Beaverbrook writes: "In the days of his wealth and power he rejected the meagre standards of New Brunswick — except for one thing. Like almost every boy in the province, he had been bred on the Shorter Catechism."

This statement ignores the large number of Acadian Catholics who never heard of this atrocious work of John Calvin; it even ignores a substantial number of New Brunswick Anglicans who were spared from it. But no matter. The Acadians of the Maritime provinces have so far produced no tycoons, nor, to the best of my knowledge, have the Maritime Anglicans. But let Lord Beaverbrook continue in his own words: "In the questions and answers to the Eighth Commandment [Thou shalt not steal] the Shorter Catechism says that this commandment 'requires the lawful procuring and furthering of the wealth and outward estate of ourselves and others.' This is a positive injunction. Negatively, the catechism forbids 'Whatever doth or may unjustly hinder our own or our neighbours' wealth or outward estate.' "

Beaverbrook concludes by saying that his old friend James Dunn of the north New Brunswick shore learned these words at the same time as he learned the multiplication tables and that "the man who denied his rights was hindering his wealth and was therefore a sinner." He ends this chapter with the grimly cryptic sentence, "We do not escape easily from the pit whence we were digged."

All this poses a very interesting question, since Beaverbrook was undoubtedly one of the best-known native Canadians of the entire twentieth century. Would his career, as well as those of a few other famous New Brunswickers, have taken the same directions they took had they been born in Ottawa, Montreal, or Winnipeg? Being a Maritimer myself, I am inclined to think that they wouldn't have.

English-speaking New Brunswick has been the most colonial-minded society in the whole of Canada. It has been so ever since the first Loyalists appeared after the American Revolution. The town of Chatham on the Miramichi estuary was founded by the New England Loyalist Francis Peabody who arrived there in 1800 in a schooner from Halifax with a cargo of "wet and dry goods". He found a handful of settlers and promptly named the tiny community after the ruling prime minister of Great Britain, who incidentally was one of the greatest war leaders Britain ever had.

The tradition of automatic, uncritical loyalty to Britain remained, and often it took curiously predictable courses, especially among some able New Brunswickers born in the last decades of the nineteenth century. Most of them admired their province for its loyalty, but at the same time despised it for its lack of opportunity for wealth and what Lord Beaverbrook called "gracious living". So emigration to England seemed the perfect solution to the problems of some and emigration to the United States the solution to the problems of others.

Of Lord Beaverbrook's famous New Brunswick contemporaries, Bonar Law went to England and became the only man born in a dominion who reached the British prime-ministership. Beaverbrook's own career everyone knows. James Dunn went to England early in the century, made a fortune in London, won a baronetcy, and returned to Canada and the Algoma Steel Company only a few years before the Second World War. R. B. Bennett emigrated first to Calgary (Beaverbrook and Dunn once had the same idea, but Dunn decided there was more money to be made in the East), then became prime minister of Canada; but after his defeat by Mackenzie King in 1935, Bennett shook the Canadian dust from his feet, sailed to England, and there was inducted into the House of Lords. New Brunswick's last man of wealth and power, K. C. Irving, would seem to be an exception to

the general New Brunswick rule, for he made his great fortune in the province. Yet in the end he was not so much of an exception after all, for he left New Brunswick to become a citizen of Nassau, objecting to the new provincial inheritance tax. As Lord Beaverbrook said of Sir James Dunn, "the man who denied his rights was hindering his wealth and was therefore a sinner."

New Brunswick is a strangely divided province: the rich and gracious farming valleys of the Petitcodiac and the central and lower St. John are utterly unlike the Dunn and Beaverbrook country of the north shore. The glacier scarred the Miramichi country almost as savagely as it scarred Labrador. There is scant good farmland there, and though Newcastle and Chatham are old towns for Canada, they have the tired air of disappointed men who have grown old without ever having grown up, men who know it was not their own fault, but simply fate and circumstances. It was always difficult to get any enterprise started in this region. Its best days were in the mid-nineteenth century when the people were able to build sailing ships using the timber of their own forests, and for a time there was real prosperity for a few. The old dwelling-houses of Chatham are roomy, solid colonial-Victorian, and one can imagine the rich Turkish rugs and the heavy mahogany furniture on the inside.

Victorian is therefore the word which inevitably fits the Miramichi's most famous son. He was the logical product of his time and place, consistently viewing the present through the mirror of the past, which meant that the larger meanings of the twentieth century constantly eluded him, leaving him with nothing but his indomitable will and energy.

The last authentic tycoon of British citizenship, Lord Beaverbrook was sure he had hitched his wagon to the morning star of the future, when in fact he had double-bolted it to the evening star of a dying empire and era. If New Brunswick seemed meagre to his friend James Dunn, Canada at no time seemed ample enough to serve as a stage for Beaverbrook. Nor did the British Establishment ever really accept him. Though many of them were happy to take his wages, they smiled behind his back at the constant assertions of his rugged colonial self-respect. How significant it was that his closest English friend was Winston Churchill, who was so Victorian that he even wrote in the style of Macaulay! And how characteristic it was of Lord Beaverbrook, when he was at one of those ghastly war-time summit meetings where the leaders of the Grand Alliance played poker with the lives of millions, that he made Stalin join him in singing a Miramichi folk song called "The Jones boys", all about brothers called Jones who had a sawmill on the river! But though the newspapers he founded are still read by millions of Britons, the gospels he used to make them preach have faded into ghosts; in Canada they have become memories as quaint as the small-town wooden bandstands where bandsmen in high tight collars and bristling moustaches used to play "Colonel Bogey" on Saturday nights. The Newcastle of Lord Beaverbrook's boyhood still has its King Street, Queen Street, and Duke Street; nearby Chatham, to which he used to drive his buggy for a change of scenery, still has its King Street, Duke Street, and Wellington Street. But even there, Lord Beaverbrook's brand of boisterous free enterprise has merged into the faceless, computerized multi-national corporation, while the England of his youthful dreams of glory merges into the European Common Market. Did he ever learn, I wonder, that a mother-civilization in decay or mutation can never be regenerated by a colonial reared in the full faith of that civilization when it was still vital, or that not all the will-power in the world can graft a monkey gland into its changed organism?

Ironically, New Brunswick is perhaps the only place where Lord Beaverbrook's name is still held in honour and affection. He gave much to the province, including an art museum and ample bequests to the University of New Brunswick, nor can anyone look at his statue in Fredericton without knowing that this was no small man. He never exploited any part of the province he loved, which is more than can be said of a number of others who made their wealth there. Esther Clark Wright, historian both of the St. John and the Miramichi, has written that "the Miramichi has suffered always from being regarded as a field for exploitation; it has been mined by successive individuals and firms who have left it for more profitable sources from which to drain wealth when the mine ceased to pay." The word "mine" is of course figurative, for there are no mines of any sort on any of the Miramichi's branches.

When you visit the Miramichi today, you will notice the flag of the now-reigning empire is flown only by the motels seeking tourists from south of the border. It is assumed that you will know that most of the river's fishing rights have long been owned by Americans. The air of Newcastle and Chatham now reeks with the effluvia belched out of the giant chimneys of a variety of multinational branch plants. When you stand on the riverbank you can see the prevailing winds carrying long pennons of smoke downstream, and when the wind blows strong from the west, the two old river towns crouch under a veritable chinook arch of sulphur. The last night I spent in Newcastle, a young filling-station attendant said, after I had mentioned it, "They don't even

have to care. Everyone knows it's a choice between them and unemployment." After supper that day it was so bad that my wife and I couldn't stand it, so we drove out of town past the belching mills into a glorious sunset. At the confluence of the Northwest and the Little Northwest branches all was peaceful and pure. The last bird songs floated in the fragrance of a New Brunswick evening beside what used to be one of the finest salmon rivers on the continent.

The Miramichi is an intact system, a very small one, archetypal of most of the rivers in the Atlantic provinces, the St. John alone excepted. All of them are both young and small and nearly all of them have deep tidal estuaries carved out by the receding glacier. The Miramichi alternates between quiet pools of a depth of over twelve feet in July and turbulent rapids, and washes over gravel or among large rocks where canoes have to be poled or pushed, and most of the fishing in the Boiestown and Doaktown regions is done by men in waders as in the burns of Scotland.

There are three main branches to this river which drains central New Brunswick east of the height of land which divides it from the St. John Valley.

The Northwest Branch has five small tributaries and three very small tributary brooks. The Little Southwest has five tributary brooks and unites with the Main Southwest just above Newcastle. The Main Southwest is at once the longest of the three and the best salmon stream, and not far from Boiestown there is a little airstrip where fishermen from the big cities arrive in small planes after flying by jet to the large Chatham airport. The Main Southwest rises near Plaster Rock, flows south, then southeast, then fairly consistently northeast by east, and its three main tributaries are also good salmon streams. These are the Bartholomew, the Dungarvon, and the Renous. When all three branches are finally united, they discharge into the estuary just above Beaubear's Island (a corruption of Boishébert?) and the estuary in turn widens out into the broad Miramichi Bay. At Chatham it is deep enough to enable ocean-going ships to dock beside the bank.

So many regions of the Atlantic provinces have grown old without ever having had the chance really to fulfil themselves. Nearly three centuries ago, in 1688, Richard Denys, Sieur de Fronsac, wrote that "Miramichy is the principal place of my residence." He was the first to settle in the region and 1688 happens to be the year of "the Glorious Revolution" against James II.

The story of the Denys family is not untypical of the

expansive but unrealistic colonial policy of France under the monarchy. Richard's father Nicholas Denys (a small stream in Cape Breton still bears his name) was granted the entire coast from the Strait of Canso to the Gaspé Peninsula by the Company of New France in 1653. It must have been the most extensive seigneury of them all, and the only defect in the arrangement was that there was hardly any settlers to develop it. The company granted "to him and to his assigns" the countries, land, woods, coasts, ports, and islands with the right of the fur trade with the Indians, as well as the fishing rights for salmon, mackerel, herring, sardines, sea cows (walrus), seals and other fishes "found throughout the extent of the said country, the coast of Acadia as far as the Virginias, and the adjacent islands."

Wow! On paper that beats twenty times over William Penn's grant of Pennsylvania in lieu of bad debt of £16,000 owed by Charles II.

Life was lonely and isolated for Richard Denys. He owned a small wooden fort with eight four-pounder cannon and lived off the country. At the time there was a great deal to live off there. Abundant game in the forests, flights of passenger pigeons in their many thousands at a time alighting in meadows and on the sandbars in the river. Let modern salmon fishermen, dreaming in their nightmares of Danish trawlers on the high seas, make what they will of this passage written by Richard Denys:

"If the pigeons plagued us by their abundance, the salmon gave us even more trouble. So large a quantity of them enters this river that at night one is unable to sleep, so great is the noise they make in falling upon the water after having thrown or darted themselves into the air. This comes about because of the trouble they have had in passing over the flats, on account of the paucity of water thereon; afterwards they enjoy themselves at their ease when they meet with places of greater depth."

With the death of Richard Denys, European settlement on the Miramichi disappeared for quite a while and the Indians roamed the forests and streams as they had done for thousands of years.

The first permanent settlement of the region began in the mid-eighteenth century and it was tragic, cruel, and harsh. After the Acadians were expelled from Nova Scotia in 1755, the Marquis de Vaudreuil in Quebec ordered the Sieur de Boishébert, his lieutenant in the territory now known as New Brunswick, to encourage deported Acadians to settle in the Miramichi. About 3,500 of them did so, starving and in miserable condition, but even here the war pursued them. At the mouth of the Miramichi they would be able to furnish a base for any French warships that entered the Gulf of St. Lawrence, and the British feared that this would pose a threat to the convoys they were planning to send against Quebec.

In the summer of 1758 the fortress of Louisbourg fell and the Gulf was open to the British. Colonel James Murray was then ordered to destroy all the French settlements on the northern shore of the Gulf and he set out to do so with vigour. In mid-September of that year he reported to General Wolfe:

"In Obedience to your Instructions embarked the Troops, having two days hunted all around Us for the Indians and Acadians to no purpose, we however destroyed their Provisions, Wigwams and Houses, the Church was a very handsome one built with stone, did not escape. We took Numbers of Cattle, Hogs and Sheep, and Three Hogshead of Beaver Skins, and I am persuaded there is not now a French Man in the River Miramichi, and it will be our fault if they are ever allowed to settle there again, as it will always be in the Power of two or three Armed Vessels capable of going over the Barr, to render them miserable should they attempt it."

In its small way this reads like a communiqué from Vietnam. Then, as now, military communiqués seldom correspond to much reality. The Acadians and Indians had taken to the woods when they saw the British coming; they returned to the ruins after the British had departed. However, after Quebec fell in the next year, the Acadians who settled on the Miramichi were to have little control over the affairs of the region until nearly two centuries later. For the American Revolution came hard after the fall of New France, and expelled and embittered Loyalists soon found their way to the Miramichi.

It continued to develop very slowly. Fishing and shipbuilding were the chief industries along the estuary; lumber in the interior; and the Forks was the dividing line between two very different ways of life. During the Napoleonic Wars the Royal Navy came to the Miramichi for timber, principally for masts, and well before the middle of the nineteenth century the shipyards of the estuary turned out a large number of barques, brigs, and schooners. The business here was much as it was in Nova Scotia. A Miramichi ship would carry local products, mostly timber and salt fish, to the eastern United States and the West Indies and returned with cargoes of goods not available in the Miramichi. In one season in the mid-1860s a single shipyard employed as many as two hundred workmen. This was Muirhead's, and in 1864 the *Chatham Gleaner* reported that "on the morning of Tuesday last, William Muirhead, Esq. launched from his Shipyard another fine vessel. She was named the *Tirzah*. She is the largest hacmatac [i.e. tamarack] vessel ever built on the river, her register tonnage being 1,564 tons." This would have been a full-fledged clipper capable of sailing around the Horn.

An 18th-century engraving, after a sketch by Captain Hervey Smyth, depicts shallops of armed redcoats "showing the flag" along the forested Miramichi.

The shipbuilding trade, with its attendant lumbering, soon bred a small number of tycoons who tried to live in the style of English noblemen. The most famous of these was Joseph Cunard, brother of the famous Samuel Cunard of Halifax who founded the greatest shipping line there ever was—and, like Lord Beaverbrook and Sir James Dunn, left the Atlantic provinces to live in England. Joseph Cunard built himself an enormous house with a large garden, ornamental trees, and peacocks strutting on his lawns. When he and his wife drove to church at Chatham Head they went in a coach with liveried coachmen and footmen. Whenever he returned from one of his frequent business trips to England, he was saluted like a returning emperor with cannon fire, bonfires, bell ringings, and cheering crowds. Again it was the fatal colonial pattern, all the way down to the logical colonial end.

Joseph Cunard was in England with his brother Samuel in 1839 when the Cunard Steamship Line obtained from the British government a contract for carrying the mails. When he returned home to the Miramichi, he sent a courier ahead of him to Chatham to prepare the populace for the wonderful news that was in store for them. He was greeted on his arrival by the entire town, a fusillade of cannon salutes, and a chosen deputation of citizens who presented him with an address praising him for his enterprise, for the great things he had done for the Miramichi and the wonderful results that were to follow "the general use of steam power".

Wonderful results did indeed follow the general use of steam power, but it doomed the only lengthy prosperity the Miramichi had ever known. Joseph Cunard himself went broke soon afterwards, though it was his own mismanagement that was responsible. The wooden ships and iron men of Nova Scotia continued the tradition of sail until the end of the century, but by 1870 shipbuilding along the Miramichi was virtually done.

What most people think of now when the name "Miramichi" is mentioned is not the potent mills of the branch plants on the estuary. It is the beautiful, unspoiled salmon water flowing through the forest trees. The Northwest Branch is navigable in small craft from twelve to fifteen miles, the Southwest from fifteen to twenty, depending on the height of the water, and the tidal pulse is felt as far up on the Southwest as the confluence with the Renous. Every season the canoes and guides carry their wealthy passengers to the salmon pools, and it would be a fine journey for anyone even if he failed to catch a single fish.

For some time now it has been a very real fear that the day is at hand when nobody will catch an Atlantic salmon anywhere from Norway to the Restigouche and the Moisie. The moment the meeting-place of the salmon in the ocean was discovered, the trawlers and factory ships moved in and literally sucked them up by vacuum machines. It is horrifying to think of them at work, literally scouring the sea bottom, picking up all manner and sizes of fish, crustaceans, and everything their technology can acquire. Every species of Atlantic fish, with the possible exception of the ocean perch and flounders that cling close to shore, is in danger of extinction unless some kind of international controls are imposed and accepted. In the summer of 1972 it was almost impossible to buy a single pound of fresh haddock in Nova Scotia. Halibut was so rare that if you asked for any fresh halibut you were greeted with a look in which indignation was mixed with contempt. Even cod was growing scarce, and I saw salt cod selling in Montreal at $1.10 a pound, which was the price of fresh salmon in Nova Scotia only a dozen years ago.

In that same year the Canadian government made a belated and perhaps despairing attempt to save what was left of the Atlantic salmon. They forbade netting at the mouths of the rivers and also forbade (at least according to what I read in the papers) the commercial selling of salmon for a number of years. Did that explain why it was easier to buy salmon from the merchants than to buy any other species of fish except cod and flounder?

Or did the species make one of those inexplicable efforts at survival that species sometimes do? At any rate, it was a fact that in 1972 more salmon and grilse returned to the rivers of the Atlantic provinces than had been seen for years. "I saw more fish in one week this year than I did all last summer," said a veteran fisherman of the Little Southwest Miramichi. And the New Brunswick newspapers rejoiced that the salmon were back again.

Apart from those caught by New Brunswickers who happen to live beside the Miramichi, nearly all of these returning salmon will be taken by visitors, some of whose rights have been willed from father to son for several generations. I cannot believe that these fishing rights can be valuable much longer. The lovely Miramichi will continue to flow as it has done since the recession of the glacier, the dawns will lift the heart and the evenings will soothe the soul, but so long as *homo sapiens* continues to over-populate his planet, pollute his rivers and oceans, and in general behave like *homo insanus*, there will never be a situation on this or any river on earth such as there was when Richard Denys complained of the salmon because their splashings kept him awake at night.

The wooden ships from the Fundy slips
once won premiums across the Seven Seas.
Today, a mere handful of craftsmen remains.

Streams of Nova Scotia

THE BROOKS OF BOYHOOD

I was born beside one of them, a very little one in Cape Breton Island, during a tremendous blizzard in a cold March. My mother subsequently told me that she had a hard labour while the wind shook the house and snow lashed the panes and a mile away a wild ocean thundered against the cliffs.

The doctor in attendance was an able and formidable Victorian clad in the medical uniform of the day, which consisted of a black frock coat, a starched white collar, a black necktie, dark grey trousers, and a black vest enlivened by the twin loops of a heavy watch chain. This is accurate; after I grew up I was shown a picture of him.

In mid-afternoon there was a break in the sky, a green blink followed by a flash of gold, and the doctor turned to the woman on the bed. "Madam," he remarked factually, "I think we are going to have a little sun."

My mother had an acute sense of humour—born twenty years before the death of Queen Victoria she needed it—and nothing ever seemed to her so funny as a solemn male making a pun without knowing he was doing so. She exploded with laughter and out I came, howling, into the twentieth century. In the way that mothers have, she later said that I came into the world on a laugh and a beam of sunshine, which was charming of her. Anyway, this may explain why, to date, I have not gone insane, for I was born in time for nearly all of the twentieth century up till now: from Edward VII's empire on which the sun never set to Elizabeth II's tight little Welfare State on which it sets within less than a single time-zone; from the Dowager Empress through Chiang Kai-shek to Mao; from Sir Wilfrid Laurier through Mackenzie King and Diefenbaker to Pierre Trudeau; from the Kaiser through Hitler to Brandt; from samurai swordsmen to Toyota salesmen; from Pius X who condemned modernism to John XXIII who embraced it; from Nicholas II through Lenin and Stalin to the hockey team that nearly gave us a collective heart attack in 1972; from William Howard Taft to Nixon Agonistes.

Against such a background of events and personalities, I suppose I should find it astonishing (though actually I don't) that most of the people I have encountered over those years have been people I liked.

Vaguely out of my infant recollections there lingers the music of that little stream that flowed through a small, wooded intervale just between our house and an embankment where small locomotives hauled coal cars to and from the Caledonia mine. It was little more than a brook, but it once had trout in it and I remember there was a drake with ducks and ducklings. It had only a mile more to go before it reached the sea, but in my semi-infancy it seemed to me a great river. In the evening it was a cradle song, in the morning a madrigal, and the Century of Progress destroyed it. Fifteen years ago I made a special pilgrimage to see it once more, but all I found was a slimy wash tinctured with an iodine-coloured pollution (probably from rusted cans) and littered with broken bottles, sodden cartons, and empty tins bearing the inspiring names of Seven-Up and Schooner beer. But small though it was, that little brook of ours was typical of most of the streams of Nova Scotia. It had a very short course amid trees, it was intimate and musical, and it would still be alive if a sizable industrial town had not grown up beside it.

All but a very few streams in Nova Scotia are glacial legacies, but I never knew this when I was young. It did not even occur to me that Nova Scotia had been as unmercifully mauled by the ice sheet as any part of Canada south of the tundra. I once thought that glaciers were only for the arctic, as jungles are only for the tropics. The Nova Scotian climate is on the whole a mild one. Though the Labrador Current is uncomfortably close, the Gulf Stream is never far away. I slept in a tent in the family backyard in Halifax from the age of eleven to twenty-one, and I loved it. In January and February I usually woke to find the topmost of my four blankets white with a fine dust of snow formed by my breathing, but I can't remember any night colder than 18 degrees below zero. Glaciers here?

The remnants of the Ice Age are as omnipresent in Nova Scotia as in the Saguenay or Labrador. Look at those long, rugged headlands jutting seaward to give that little province more natural harbours than exist between Yarmouth Light and the mouth of the Amazon. Granite whalebacks along the Atlantic coast, near Halifax a rocking stone so accurately balanced that though a boy's hand can move it, a gang of a hundred strong men could not push it off its base. Halifax Harbour, with its tidal head in Bedford Basin, is a perfect glacial scoop-out, and into the basin flows another typical Nova Scotian stream, the little Sackville River, near the mouth of which, just before the Hitler War, I have seen as many as seven silver salmon leaping into the air within the same minute. (They were frustrated; some kind of construction, probably from the railway, made it impossible for them to ascend the Sackville to spawn.) The Citadel Hill in Halifax is a drumlin; so are McNab's Island and George's

Island in the harbour itself, and they act as natural break-waters against the terrible seas piled up by easterly gales in fall and winter. So deep is the trough of this harbour, so fjord-like sheer do its sides drop down from the shore into the sea, that when the *Olympic* used to dock at Pier II throughout the course of the Kaiser's War, her great bow seemed almost to jut into the city. The ironstone bedrock of Halifax, typical of all the Atlantic coast of Nova Scotia, has so little topsoil that it takes a maple fifty years to grow as high as a maple grows in ten years in the Eastern Townships of Quebec, where I spend my summers now.

Yes, the glacier was here all right. The Wisconsin, grinding its way off the continent into the sea, carved, gouged, twisted, and scooped out so many bays and inlets that though the over-all length of the province, Cape Breton Island included, is less than 500 miles, the total length of the shoreline is close to 5,000. The ice carried nearly all the topsoil overboard onto the continental shelf, thereby bequeathing to all the Atlantic provinces save little Prince Edward Island the mixed blessing of a meagre and scattered agriculture and a small population. If the happiness of a people can be measured by its sense of community and the frequency of its children's laughter, the populations of the Atlantic provinces should be grateful to the glacier after all. It permitted very few men to become rich enough to be unhappy, or any province of the four to grow a megalopolis.

The glacier may even have been the cause, at least to some extent, of the curious shapes of these provinces which in turn determine the courses and characters of the rivers. New Brunswick has the form of a massive beef chop in which the butcher left two small bones protruding on the western and eastern ends, and it is the only one of the four provinces with sufficient land to enable at least one great river to form. Newfoundland on the map looks like a pork chop gnawed by rats. Nova Scotia is a lobster and Prince Edward Island comes close to having the shape of a tropical fish whose name I cannot remember. Paradoxically, Canada's smallest province has the heaviest population in proportion to its area of any province in Canada, and this is because its soil is wonderful. Presumably it lay under the waters long enough to be fertilized and to acquire a fine topsoil from thousands of dead generations of marine life.

The longest main pipe of any Atlantic province river outside of New Brunswick is Newfoundland's Exploits, which travels for 153 miles in a general northeasterly direc-

tion from its source in King George IV Lake to reach the salt water of the Atlantic in Exploits Bay. The central Newfoundland plateau is a lower version of Labrador's and the Exploits has a total drop of 1,000 feet from source to sea including the steep plunges at Grand Falls and Bishop's Falls, Grand Falls inevitably being the site of a large pulp and paper development, an industry which in northern climes is another glacial offshoot.

Newfoundland's most famous salmon stream is the Humber, which also happens to flow through a fine valley containing the only good agricultural soil in the whole island. But the Humber runs for barely twenty miles before reaching salt water and at its mouth stands Cornerbrook, brightest of all the jewels in the crown of the Bowater empire of pulp, paper, and sulphur fumes.

There was a Danish writer called Henrik Pontopiddan who won the Nobel Prize for Literature in 1917. He once wrote a book on Iceland in which each chapter was titled so as to form an inventory of every aspect of that country's flora, fauna, geography, achievements, and attributes. The book is memorable for one reason only: it contains the shortest chapter in all known literature. Under the title of OWLS, Pontopiddan inscribed a single sentence containing six pregnant words, all but the last a monosyllable: "There are no owls in Iceland."

With almost equal truth it must be said that there are no rivers in Prince Edward Island, and this grieves me because the island is so lovely. A few brooks and rills; quite a number of leaks. But the watershed of the island, which is very gentle, runs lengthwise and the width of the island is simply too small to permit moving water to grow into a river.

So, having dealt elsewhere in this book at length with the St. John and the Miramichi, the two main rivers of New Brunswick, and with the Hamilton, which at least belongs to Newfoundland and must therefore be considered its greatest river, I come to rest in my native Nova Scotia. But I do so with the admission that none of its streams would be called a true river by anyone whose idea of a river is something that can be navigated even by a canoe. Only in the scattered small pools where the fish lie can a canoe float in a Nova Scotian stream without striking bottom. All you need to fish these waters is a pair of waders.

Though Nova Scotia when seen on a map resembles a lobster, its geological form is actually a whaleback. This means that the general watersheds are east into the Atlantic and west into the Fundy and the St. Lawrence Gulf. As the provincial mainland is seldom wider than sixty miles, with the watershed running like a spine through the centre, it follows that any Nova Scotian stream is doing pretty well for itself if it has a fresh-water course longer than fifteen miles.

All the streams of Nova Scotia that flow into the Atlantic and the Gulf of St. Lawrence are what in Scotland are called "burns". They tend to be noisy and tumultuous in freshet, gently musical in summer, and some of them go almost dry in September. Where their waters are drinkable, only two or three of them are more impressive than sizable brooks, and whenever they look like a true river—the Lahave below Bridgewater, for example—they are invariably narrow inlets of the sea. Only two Nova Scotian streams have any kind of delta. These are the Baddeck and the Middle River of Cape Breton which rise in the semi-mountainous interior of the island and cascade down into beautiful valleys which have accumulated enough topsoil to enable the streams to collect a little silt. If they discharged into the ocean, the tides and storms would have carried the silt off, just as on an infinitely vaster scale the Gulf Stream keeps reducing the otherwise enormous delta of the Mississippi. But these two streams discharge into the salt water of the tideless upper Bras d'Or Lake. So it happens that the delta of the little Baddeck River is a tiny miniature of the delta of the Mackenzie, while the more regular delta of the Middle is like the delta of the Nile divided by a million.

The longest of all the Nova Scotian streams must be the Annapolis, a fact which surprised me when I took the trouble to look it up, for this river is so unobtrusive that you often do not notice its presence when you travel through the valley. It is so modest a stream that in slack water a good pole vaulter could probably clear it without wetting his feet, and it is utterly different in character from any of the streams that flow into the Atlantic or the gulf of St. Lawrence. It is a brown river flowing gently through the most fertile land in the whole province. The low ridges called the North and South Mountains, which enclose the Annapolis Valley, permit the stream to swing slowly down to salt water at the head of the Annapolis Basin. It drains what certainly is one of the loveliest valleys in all Canada.

This is one of the very few regions in the Atlantic provinces where nature is gentle. For many years the valley was the finest apple-growing region in North America and until 1939 it supplied England with most of the apples the English ate. The subsequent loss of the British market changed the balance of agriculture in the valley so that today there is mixed farming, though in May the blossoms extend for miles in the sun. When Chamber-

lain and Levine flew over it in 1927, a few weeks after Lindbergh, they described it as "a dream of beauty". After you have crossed the harsh whaleback of the province from the Atlantic shore, you find it hard to believe you are still in the same province. Near Wolfville they are now growing grapes for wine.

Here, of course, is some of the most historic country in Canada. De Monts' expedition established Port Royal on the Annapolis Basin in 1605, and though De Monts, Poutrincourt (and, at that time, Champlain) were all Huguenots, the Acadian settlement which spread out of Port Royal up along the course of what now is called the Annapolis River was entirely Catholic. They built the first dykes about the rich meadows where Grand Pré looks out to Cape Blomidon, and when Longfellow wrote in *Evangeline*, "Neither bolts had they to their doors, nor bars to their windows," he was telling the literal truth about one of the gentlest nests of simple God-fearing people who ever lived together in the western hemisphere. Unlike the French Canadians of Quebec, so many of whom came from Normandy, the Acadians all came from Brittany or the Biscay coast of France.

What was done to them during the Seven Years War was one of the most disgraceful episodes in all North American history. When I was young, most schoolboys on the continent knew the story, for in those days *Evangeline* was required reading in almost every grade school of Canada and the United States: how the helpless people were rounded up by British troops, largely owing to pressure from New England which wanted the valley for settlement for the overflow of population in Massachusetts; how they were herded into transports and taken south to the swamps of Louisiana; how after desperate hardships some found their way home to Acadie, only to discover that their lands had already been pre-empted by English colonists, so that those Acadians who remained scattered to the rocky shores of Yarmouth County, to the milder shores of western Cape Breton, or to the north shore of New Brunswick. The crime rate among them is almost non-existent to this day. In the Pubnico region of Yarmouth County, where so many descendants of the original Acadians live today, there is not even a jail.

The Massachusetts people who took over the valley after the expulsion built their houses in the colonial style of New England, and unlike the Scotch in northern Nova Scotia and the Germans of the South Shore, they painted them white. As early as 1713, when Nova Scotia was ceded by France to England, the valley's name was changed to "Annapolis" and the fort built to defend it on the Annapolis Basin was called after Queen Anne. The New Englanders who settled here, later called by the novelist Thomas Raddall, "His Majesty's Yankees", made no attempt to rebel in 1776. Why should they have?

Not only did they have better land than any that can be found in Massachusetts; they were also protected (or were prevented) by the Royal Navy.

Quite a few Loyalists joined them later and it was they who brought to Nova Scotia, and also to New Brunswick, the first colleges—King's at Windsor and the University of New Brunswick in Fredericton. One of the descendants of these was Joseph Howe. Another was Howe's friend, Thomas Chandler Haliburton, the first internationally known writer who lived in what now is Canada. Lately his *The Clockmaker* is having a considerable revival among college students, which is hardly surprising these days when Sam Slick the salesman, the amiable, shrewd, and kindly old con man, has multiplied several million-fold.

The other rivers which flow into the Fundy are the Shubenacadie with its tributary Stewiacke, the Cornwallis, and the Avon. All flow through rich, fruitful country with a clay soil, and the Cornwallis Valley under a harvest moon is so lovely it would make a pool-room owner frightened. In their upper reaches these streams are mere fresh-water brooks, but through their lower courses they widen out and are open to the tremendous tides of Minas Basin. When the tide is rising or ebbing, the lower courses of these rivers are deeper and browner than the Missouri, the white foam on the surface like lace, the whole river a seething of liquid salty mud. When the tide is out, only a few runnels of muddy water remain between the high, slimy, brown banks, and at Windsor, on the estuary of the Avon, ocean-going ships lie high and dry in wooden cradles which are a part of the wharfs. I know of no other rivers in the world quite like these, though there may be a few in countries I have never seen.

For the rest of the Nova Scotian streams, the tell-tale model must be the Musquodoboit (pronounced "Muskadábit") which reaches the Atlantic in Musquodoboit Harbour some twenty-five miles east of Halifax. Its name defines the nature of nearly every Nova Scotian stream that empties into the Atlantic, for in Micmac *musquodoboit* means, "after a narrow entrance, suddenly widening out at the mouth". In other words, a brook-sized river enters a glacial scoop-out of the coast. Cape Breton even has a small fjord: the mouth and lower course of the North River which enters St. Ann's Bay and once was famous for its trout fishing.

Whaleback in many versions is almost the basic form of nature in Nova Scotia. Near Peggy's Cove at the mouth of St. Margaret's Bay (the vista as you look inland uncannily similar to the great scene that confronts you when you stand beside the temple of Poseidon on Cape Sunion and look westward toward Athens) you will find some granite whalebacks forming the coastline itself.

And just inland from the cove are some the tide never reaches and these are fascinating. Sea winds and sea spray, together with the rains and snows of thousands of years, have cleansed these rocks to the ever-so-slightly pebbled surface of true granite beside a northern ocean. They have a fine, pungent fragrance caused by a mixture of salt and growing things. They are a beautiful colour of pale grey spotted with greenish-grey patches of lichen. They also have superficial cracks in their surfaces to the depth of several inches and these have collected the only dust in the region, a dust formed out of the powder of dead alder leaves and ground cover. On a rainy afternoon I studied one of the largest of these whalebacks and discovered in its cracks a few tufts of coarse grass, an alder six inches high, and a pair of wild irises. This was better than Blake's

> To see the world in a grain of sand,
> And heaven in a wild flower;
> Hold infinity in the palm of your hand,
> And eternity in an hour.

For here, caught in a rock formation literally the shape and size of a right whale, was visible much of the process of creation, including the origin and forms of rivers. The rains had descended and the fogs had congealed, they had moistened the dust caught in the cracks of the granite, seeds had blown into them and germinated, and now as the rain gently fell, I watched in the smallest of miniatures a Nova Scotian stream working its way in a silver thread along the irregular course of the largest crack, picking up a few tributaries as it went along, and finally disappearing into a delta three inches wide in some thin sand at the base of the rock.

Most Nova Scotians have their own favourite streams and generally they flow near where they live. As an exile from the province since the age of twenty-one, yet a man who tries to return for at least a few weeks every year, I think I can claim to have seen all but a very few reachable areas in the whole province. Have I any favourites?

First, the Baddeck (pronounced Baddéck). Its main stream rises in the remote Baddeck Lakes in the high plateau of the central island, whence it flows down a narrow but beautiful valley for about twenty miles until it enters its little delta in the St. Patrick Channel of the Bras d'Or Lakes. The North Baddeck is formed by three brooks, one of them only about a mile distant from the Baddeck Lakes, and just before it joins the main stream it offers one of the loveliest sights east of the Jalbert Valley.

The boisterous "burns" of Nova Scotia
freshen the few fertile valleys that
flourish with fruits, cereals, and—along
the Annapolis—grapes for the winepress.

You walk up a narrow mountain forest trail with the little stream purling near you, climb over fallen trees, brush blackflies out of your ears, and see the occasional track of a moose or a deer in the soft earth. You smell the moss and find yourself in a kind of tunnel among the spruce and birch, the light filtering through as it does in the paintings of Emily Carr. Then you find yourself at the foot of a mountain and hear the noise of a cataract. On hands and knees, literally, you scramble upward over the rocks and fallen trees, work your way around a corner, and there, very close, very white, the spray-moistened air fragrant, is a narrow waterfall a good deal higher than Niagara. This is the Uisge Ban Falls, which in Gaelic means "white water".

After the forks have been passed, the main stream of the Baddeck flows through a small, fruitful, and intimate valley in the lee of mountains about a thousand feet high, which seem much higher than they actually are because they rise virtually from sea level. It is lovely to fish there in the evenings hearing the bells ringing hollowly when the cows come home, seeing the black pools and the white shallows filling with the rings of feeding trout and fry, smelling the alder, and finally, when the fishing is done (it's no longer a river prolific with fish) the moon blooms white in a twilit sky. In all these Cape Breton rivers there are two kinds of trout: those that winter in the Bras d'Or Lake and have meat when cooked of the soft, greyish-pink colour of a Madame Butterfly rose; the other, the sea trout, often called "salters", which are small and bright as shining silver coins. They cook to a salmon pink and are as fast and game as any fish you are likely to find.

The people of this region, as along every Cape Breton stream except the Cheticamp, are almost entirely Highland Scotch and in this particular region the most common names are MacLeod, Mackenzie, and MacDonald. When I was young most of them spoke Gaelic and they still have Gaelic accents when they speak English. So, for that matter, do I myself, though I have spent nearly all my life but its earliest years outside of Cape Breton.

Nova Scotians and Newfoundlanders are the greatest story-tellers and yarn-spinners in the whole of Canada, if not in the whole of North America. Indeed, the Cape Breton Highlanders see life in such a perpetual frame of anecdote that many exasperated Anglo-Saxons have come to the conclusion that they are incapable of telling the truth because they literally cannot distinguish between fact and fiction. The following story I cannot entirely vouch for because I was ten minutes too late to be present at the incident which occasioned it.

In the summer of 1971, Prime Minister Trudeau and his bride visited Nova Scotia and Cape Breton. He was then at the height of the popularity from which he was to begin to fall only a few weeks later. Was there any connection, I have often wondered, between the announcement of the new Nixon economic policy that August and the whispering campaign against Trudeau that swept Canada immediately afterwards? To use the favourite phrase of Ontario farmers and small-towners, "It's hard to say."

Anyway, Pierre Trudeau got a great reception in Cape Breton. The Scotch and the French have always got along together and Pierre is at least one-quarter Scotch himself. At Cheticamp, my favourite village in all Nova Scotia, the Acadian fisher-folk and their Scotch neighbours really turned out for the man and, it being midsummer, there were also many American tourists in the crowd.

When I entered George's store in the Baddeck main street the day after, I heard a Gaelic voice holding forth: "This American lady was in here and my ghlory, did you ever hear anything like that? She was in hysterics almost. 'I touched him!' she said. 'I touched him!' 'Who was it you touched?' I asked her. 'Him!' she said. 'Your Prime Minister. I touched him.' 'Whell, what was he trying to do to you?' Nothing!' she said. 'But do you know it? I live in Washington, and nobody can get inside of a mile to President Nixon.' "

In the region of the Baddeck River, as indeed in most of Cape Breton, nicknames were not only at a premium because you might find a whole village filled with the representatives of no more than five clans; they were also inherited. They were handed down from father to son. And here is another Cape Breton story I acquired from the most prolific anecdote-and-story-teller I ever knew, my mother.

She had engaged a fine old gentleman named MacLeod, a carpenter by trade, to dig a cess pit for her place in Baddeck. He was a man whose humour was as quiet as his gravity and when he worked he always wore a dark waistcoat with watch and chain appended. He had three other men with him, two of them MacLeods, the fourth a MacDonald. The MacDonald bore the nickname of Johnny Hot, either from the colour of his hair or the temperament of his family. One of the MacLeods had the prosaic name of Black Angus (in Gaelic it would have been Angus Dhu), but the nickname of the other was unique even for Cape Breton. It was Neilly Tits.

Mother got into a long argument with Mr. MacLeod over the bill, she insisting that she pay more, he that she pay less, and he finally won the argument by stating, "If you was like herself down the road, we wouldn't be working for you at all." Being alone with him, Mother finally got around to asking how Neilly Tits had acquired his name.

"Do you remember them old Nova Scotia spelling

books, Mrs. MacLennan? Do you remember them spellers?'

She remembered them.

"Whell, it wasn't Neilly himself, it was his father."

She waited.

"He was a good man but he was pretty slow and the teacher was a good-sized woman. So they came to this word in the speller—I remember it myself—it was 'quadruped'—and when she asked Neilly what it meant he could not say. So then she tried to draw him out so he would find out by himself, so she asked him, What is it a cow has four of that I only have two of.' So Neilly came up with an answer and that is why that family got the name of Neilly Tits."

The road along the Cabot Trail from Baddeck turns inland from the Bras d'Or Lake just after crossing the bridge over the Baddeck River and leads you over Hunter's Mountain into the valley of the Middle River, broad well-farmed meadows with many wine-glass elms, and it was here that my forebears on my father's side settled after their escape or deportation (it was never discussed what it was) from Kintail. They were closely allied and entwined with the MacRaes (a more numerous clan) both in Scotland and in the Middle River Valley, and at the centre of the community stand side by side two small white churches, one belonging to the United Church of Canada, the other to the Presbyterian Church in Canada. Here, as in other parts of Nova Scotia and Ontario, the old Church Union controversy of the 1920s for a time came close to splitting communities in two.

"And they did it," said an aunt of mine, "without there being a Methodist within a hundred miles. They did it, and what did that do but make the church of our fathers a branch of the T. Eaton Company of Toronto?"

You pass out of the Middle River Valley, you skirt Lake O'Law which used to be framed by white birches before they cut them down to widen the road, you cross the height of land—and it is a considerable height of land—and come out into one of the loveliest and peaceful scenes in all eastern Canada, the valley of the Margaree.

This is the noblest stream in all of Nova Scotia and its name is pronounced Már-garée. It has three branches. The Southwest Branch rises at Lake Ainslie and flows almost directly northeast for a distance of about thirteen miles. The Northern Branch rises in the interior mountains and flows almost directly southwest for about 18 miles; the little Northeast Margaree is barely five miles long, but its valley is beautiful. The two main branches unite with the Northeast at Margaree Forks and the united stream runs for about nine miles until it enters the Gulf of St. Lawrence at Margaree Harbour.

Once upon a time this was one of the great salmon streams of the Atlantic provinces, but netting at its mouth, combined with the depredations of Danish trawlers in the high seas, has reduced the salmon terribly.

One more Nova Scotian stream I must at least mention—the St. Mary's River of Guysborough County which drains the chain of the Lochaber Lakes, the highest of which is in the county of Antigonish. This may well be the best salmon stream in Nova Scotia now. It has a flow of water at least equal to the Margaree's and reaches salt water at the small but old village of Sherbrooke, named after the same cantankerous British army officer who is remembered also in the names of the principal street of Montreal and the third-largest city of the Province of Quebec.

So now I must end or I will be producing a catalogue of rivers. I love these Nova Scotian streams because they are so intimate. The air about nearly all of them is delicious with the fragrance of alders and wild flowers, especially clover, in some times and places so strong it is overpowering. In my boyhood, when most of my serious reading was in Latin and Greek, I discovered quite unselfconsciously that the classical lyric poets had described the streams of Nova Scotia just as vividly as Homer had described the Nova Scotian coast. "Cephisus, the fair-flowing river" is not unlike the Margaree; it passes through the Plain of Chaeronea where Philip of Macedon dealt the death-blow to Athenian democracy and the Roman Sulla, a few centuries later, destroyed the army of Mithradates. The Inachus, "river of Argos", whose sounds mingle with the pipes of Pan as it descends from the mountains of Arcadia (they really do; I heard them myself one evening when I thought I was lost there), has a sister stream in the little northwest Baddeck. As for Horace's *O fons Bandusiae splendidior vitro* ("O fountain of Bandusia more shining than crystal"), I know of several such in Nova Scotia that are marked on no map. Only a person who believes that high-rises are more important than thatched cottages would insist that a river must be as large as the Mississippi to have value. The truth is that with the exception of the Nile and the giant rivers of India and China, the rivers most intimately and nobly connected with civilization are generally modest: the Thames, the rivers which divided ancient Gaul into three parts, the Po, the Arno, and the Tiber, to name only a few. For that matter, is there a river in all our Western world more justly famous than Jordan? Yet it is barely two hundred miles long and only seventy feet wide at its mouth.

When the pioneers came to roadless Canada, the cities sprouted where the rivers branched. Fredericton was chosen as capital of New Brunswick partly because it was far enough (90 m.) up the St. John River to escape raids. The idyllic scene at left is dated 1838; it seemed even more serene when John de Visser made the camera study below, 134 years later.

WHERE THE CITIES GREW

La vieille Québec

On its lofty rock, almost girdled by two rivers, Quebec was a magnet to artists from the golden days of the Sun King. The coffers of the Bourbons and of the rich Jesuits provided gold to erect the spacious public buildings and the spired churches, then so notable against the evergreen wilderness beyond. Time soon healed the scars of war — for this has been a fighting fortress — and the two foundation cultures now share proudly in the city's renown. Thankfully, modern builders have preserved many of the old storied stones within a vibrant new city.

A THE FORTRESS	G HOTEL DIEU
B FRANCISCAN MONASTERY	H BISHOP'S PALACE
C HARBOUR BATTERY	I A REDOUBT
D JESUIT CHURCH	K THE HOSPITAL
E THE CATHEDRAL	L ARRIVAL OF TROOPSHIPS
F THE SEMINARY	

The bold capital of New France: early 18th century.

Trois Rivières: a street as old as Canada.

Quebec City today: a gift from time and tradition.

118

A thousand miles from the open sea, at the head of natural navigation of the St. Lawrence, Montreal was destined to be one of the world's greatest ports—even allowing for the closure of the river in winter. Here, in 1809, brewer John Molson built the first Canadian steamship and ran to Quebec City (fare: down $8, up $9). In the 1820s, service began to Britain. At the end of the Victorian era, Montreal had a population of 328,000. Today, the docks stretch for a dozen miles and population is at 2,500,000—and growing.

Montreal at water's edge: a Victorian view.

The Habitat housing hive in modern Montreal.

Celebrating Confederation in July 1867, Ottawans enjoy a regatta.

Ottawa: a queen's choice

We may owe the selection of Ottawa as the national capital to Queen Victoria (she preferred it to Toronto, Kingston, Montreal, or Quebec City), but the city wouldn't be there at all if the Duke of Wellington hadn't decided to have a canal dug to connect the Ottawa River with Lake Ontario. The Duke— he was then British Minister of Defence—feared the Americans would close the upper St. Lawrence if the War of 1812 was resumed. By 1832, Colonel John By's Royal Engineers had dug enough rock between the streams and the lakes of the Rideau Highlands to allow the steamboat *Pumper* to make the first through trip to Kingston. By had set up his camp where the Rideau River fell into the Ottawa and his name was fixed on the roistering lumber town that sprang up there. When it was dubbed a city in 1855, it took the name of the great river that gave it life. The Gothic-style Parliament Buildings, dramatically perched on a high bluff over the river, are comparatively modern, being extensively rebuilt after fires in 1916 and 1952.

From the Peace Tower, De Visser sets the Library spire against the river.

Winnipeg: western crossroads

The Red and Assiniboine rivers meet on the Manitoba plain close enough to the very centre of Canada. The first Scots in the settlement that is now Winnipeg fought their way upstream from Hudson Bay. The adjoining St. Boniface had Swiss-German beginnings, then became a French-Canadian city. Today, Greater Winnipeg is an exciting 256-square-mile melting pot of races.

Winnipeg: the year the C.P.R. reached the Red.

A regional and a provincial capital, Winnipeg dominates Canada's Mid-west.

Where Elbow meets Bow: Calgary in its birth year and (below) the oil capital today.

Riverside towers of Alberta

By the reckoning of history, sober-sided Edmonton (*this page*) and rambunctious Calgary (*opposite*) seem to have leaped almost overnight from the palisades of the frontier forts. Where the rivers of the plains take their oxbow swings, the Hudson's Bay Company and the North West Mounted Police sited posts easy to defend by land, easy to reach by water. Both of these have known Indian attack and pioneer hardship—and some of those who look up today with disbelief at the soaring concrete towers along the river banks were already grown men when the cities were incorporated.

Those western symbols, York boat and Red River cart, wait before Fort Edmonton, 1871.

The deep gorge of the North Saskatchewan throws a moat around the heart of Edmonton.

Shantytown to shining city

Sea and river, mountain and ever-changing sky combine to pour blessings on Vancouver, Canada's gateway to the Orient. The frame shacks of Gastown (*above*) were burnt to ash in 1886 and the new city, named for discoverer George Vancouver, was sited at the orders of William Van Horne, the American whip-cracker who punched the Canadian Pacific Railway through to the Pacific.

The Niagara

ONE OF THE WORLD'S WONDERS

So many stories are told about Niagara and its Falls that I suppose there is no harm in telling another. It concerns an Englishman named Pilkington, who during the Second World War had been navigator of a Lancaster bomber piloted by a Canadian from St. Catharines. After the war the two men corresponded with each other occasionally and a few years ago Pilkington wrote to say that at last he intended to visit America. His work had taken him all over Europe, even to the Near East and Africa, but he had yet to cross the Atlantic.

The Canadian, now a high official in Air Canada, cabled to say that he would meet Pilkington in Toronto and arranged with the airline's London office to send a complimentary ticket. The flight would arrive in Toronto just after dark.

When the visitor cleared Immigration and Customs, the two old war comrades drove south in the Air Canada man's car and came to rest at a motel on a side road near Stoney Creek. After a drink and some more conversation they went to bed.

The next morning at breakfast the Air Canada man seemed irritated. He had just received a summons to return to Toronto immediately. 'I'm damned sorry about this snafu, Nigel. The controllers may really go on strike this time and I'll have to meet them. With any luck I'll be back here in time for dinner. Meanwhile I've asked the Tilden people to bring you a car. Why don't you just drive around and see some of the country?"

"Where should I head for?"

"From here? I'd suggest Chippawa."

The Air Canada man drove back to Toronto, the Tilden car arrived, and Pilkington set off. He soon got lost and opened the glove box to look for a map. There was no map, so he continued to roam and gradually the idea came into his mind that he was dreaming all this. In fact, he doubted if he was in Canada at all.

So might anyone, even from the Canadian west or the Atlantic provinces, if he did not know it *was* the Niagara Peninsula and if nobody had told him what the peninsula is like. Pilkington's notion of Canada may have been a stereotype, but on the whole it was not inaccurate: huge forests, wide open prairies, Rocky Mountains, and the British Columbia coast where one of his uncles lived in retirement. The land through which he now was driving corresponded to nothing he had ever heard of in connection with Canada. The elms and oaks were as stately as any he had seen in England, and the land had the cultivated air of his native Cambridgeshire.

After a while he saw the upperworks of an enormous ship moving across the fields. A canal certainly. But what canal except Suez and Panama could carry a monster like that? He came on a bridge, crossed it, and wondered if this might be the St. Lawrence Seaway. A little later he realized he was driving through vineyards and rubbed his eyes. He knew that wine— not very good, he'd been told— was grown in the States and he had heard that it is as easy to cross into the States from Canada as from Scotland into England. Then he struck a superhighway roaring with trucks, trailers, and cars and was almost sure he was in the States. He *must* get a map.

In hope of finding a filling station (he had read that American thruways have none) he took the first exit which led (according to the signboard) to a place he had never heard of. Still roaming, he found himself in what appeared to be an immense park. It was the first week in June and lilacs and tulips were in full bloom. The lawns were so ample and well kept he assumed they belonged to one of those great estates that only American multimillionaires can afford to keep up. This park seemed to extend for miles, but now there were swarms of people and hundreds of parked cars, most of them with American plates. Soon there were thousands of people and Pilkington abandoned his idea that this was a millionaire's estate. He parked his own car, got out, and moved among the people. He passed a party of Japanese, each of them with a camera; East Indians with their women in saris, each of the men with a camera; a short, thick, and very black man with an air of authority speaking an African language and surrounded by what looked like an entourage, they also with cameras. Then he heard it and wondered what it was. Then he saw it and knew what it was.

If only any of us could discover Niagara Falls as this Englishman did! For the first sight of them, like the first sight of a great painting, can be almost everything. A linked rank of liquid wheels more than a half-mile across turning on an unseen axle of unheard-of dimensions, turning over and down with the overwhelming indifference of nature herself, wheels of chartreuse green bound together by narrow hoops of the most delicate liquid snow, unchanging, never brusque, never plunging, just rolling and rolling and rolling and rolling forever down into the white roar of its cloud.

Well, I've done my best. To try anything more along

this line would be as futile as to use words to describe a great music or a perfect love-making. So many have tried to describe the Falls and all have failed, for the reason the poet Thomas Moore recognized after he had been to Niagara for perhaps a half-hour. "The former exquisite sensation was gone. I now saw all. The string that had been touched by the first impulse, and which *fancy* would have kept forever in vibration, now rested in *reality*." You can only experience the Falls of Niagara. They annihilate thought, which may explain why so many honeymooners keep coming to them.

The Niagara is the best-known river on earth and the second most-famous. People hardly think of it as a river at all, but as one of the world's wonders along with the Pyramids, which stand beside what without question is the world's most famous river. The Falls have captured the imagination of civilized man from the moment when Père Hennepin's description of them was circulated throughout Europe by the publication in 1683 of the memoirs of his explorations with LaSalle. They have held men's imagination ever since, in spite of all the corniness and commercial publicity built up around them. You see those Falls and all the vulgarities vanish from your mind.

The river has also fascinated scientists. Geologists have found here one of the most important of keys for unlocking the mystery of what happened to the land after the glacier retreated. To historians on both sides of the international border which runs down the centre of the river, the Niagara is an indispensable area of research. If Wolfe guaranteed the existence of the United States by beating the *ancien régime* at Quebec, just as certainly Brock made possible the existence of Canada by beating the Americans at Queenston Heights.

In its perennial attraction for tourists, Niagara has come close to rivalling Paris for the past hundred years. In the nineteenth century many Europeans made the costly and often hazardous Atlantic crossing solely to see the Falls, somewhat in the spirit of devout Muslims journeying to Mecca. The Falls fitted perfectly into Rousseau's veneration for nature, and Rousseau's vision was very powerful in nineteenth-century Europe. Today it is estimated that at least nine million people a year come to Niagara and that the Falls have been more photographed than any other single place on earth.

The moment the Industrial Revolution incorporated electricity, the mouths of technologists watered at the very thought of those tremendous Falls. In 1877 Karl Wilhelm Siemans, a famous pioneer in hydro-electric power, calculated the total weight of liquid that "ran to waste" over the Falls at a million tons an hour; he also estimated that this weight of water, combined with the further energy created by its drop, was so stupendous that it would require 266,000,000 tons of coal to produce an equal amount of energy by the use of steam. If people smile because a simple priest like Hennepin overestimated the height of Niagara Falls by some 350 per cent, why is it, I wonder, that nobody smiles at a famous technologist's overestimation of the power potential by nearly 500 per cent? But power is there, and in abundance. When Nicola Tesla discovered the principle of the alternating current, Niagara was selected as the natural place to put it to the test, and Buffalo became the first of the world's cities to be illuminated by the power of moving water.

The least remarkable thing about Niagara Falls is their height. The Angel Fall in Venezuela is more than twenty times higher than Niagara. The Takakkaw in Yoho National Park is more than seven times higher. Even the delicate Uisge Ban Fall on the north-west branch of the little Baddeck River in Cape Breton Island is at least as high as Niagara. Indeed, one of my encyclopedias lists the Niagara as only forty-ninth in height among the notable waterfalls of the world.

But it is not the height that has made Niagara famous; it is its volume and the beauty of its symmetry, the power of a major river going overboard in all of its totality. The most awe-inspiring of all waterfalls is of course the Victoria on the mighty Zambezi. The mind boggles at the very thought of them: three hundred and fifty feet high, more than a mile wide, and behind them the weight of a river that has originated hundreds of miles back in the African rain forest. But those prodigious Falls discovered by David Livingstone lie between Rhodesia and Zambia, and relatively few people have yet been lucky enough to see them. Hemingway nearly lost his life trying to view them from the air. But it was the luck of Niagara to be located on a continental cross-road. All the explorers after LaSalle and Hennepin saw them; possibly Etienne Brûlé saw them even earlier. And since the invention of the automobile, the tourist migrations regularly take in Niagara from south-west to east and from east to south-west.

There is an even simpler reason why Niagara is the best-known river. It *can* be known. Who but a river pilot could really "know" a stream the length of the Mississippi or the Mackenzie? After travelling a few hundred miles along any really great river, your powers of perceiving it become numbed. Its rhythmic bends—nature's braking system—become hypnotic; your memory of its details blurs. But the Niagara is only thirty-four miles long—thirty-five if you accept the other measurement frequently given—and here are assembled more facilities for seeing and studying a river than can be found anywhere.

You can see the Niagara by crossing its bridges, by

walking on paths in its gorge so close that the Whirlpool seems like a tidal wave about to snatch you up, by standing so close to either of the Falls that you can almost touch them. You can drive the length of the river on either side by landscaped roads, you can watch it from park benches, you can watch it go over its brinks while eating a *filet mignon* in a revolving restaurant 755 feet high, you can see it illuminated in the night. You can glide over the Whirlpool in an aerocar. You can don the famous black waterproofs, rubber boots, and sou'westers and throb up to the very verge of the Horseshoe's cauldron in the *Maid of the Mist*, and who but an oaf would permit his fastidiousness to refuse the *Maid* because at least fifty million people, many of whose acquaintance he might not enjoy, have done it before on a long succession of *Maids of the Mist*? For it is only down there that the Horseshoe does itself full justice. Literally, it seems to come rolling down out of the clouds of heaven, and on an overcast day, literally its own cloud of spume rises up to merge with the real clouds above. As for the American Fall, which has often been scorned because its volume is so much less, now that the engineers have repaired its brink and removed the debris caused by the last heavy rockfall, it has become so beautiful you can hardly believe it. The place to see this one is full face. Male and female a poet might call these twins, and it may not be entirely ironical that the Canadian is the male and the more disorderly.

The Falls do queer things to people, some of whom have had, and obeyed, the impulse to jump in.

"I felt as if I could have *gone over* with the waters," wrote the author of *Uncle Tom's Cabin*. "It would have been so beautiful a death; there would have been no fear in it. I felt the rock tremble under me with a sort of joy. I was so maddened that I could have gone too, if it had gone."

Mrs. Stowe has never been my favourite author, despite the fact that the man I consider the greatest novelist who ever lived (Tolstoy) believed that *Uncle Tom's Cabin* was the greatest novel ever written. But to repeat, the Falls can do queer things to more people than Harriet Beecher Stowe.

In that dank tunnel under the Horseshoe I was stopped by a stranger who asked me if I felt all right. I said yes. He said he didn't feel all right. He came from California and he wanted to know if this was earthquake country. The noise in his ears reminded him of the noise at the beginning of an earthquake and this might be the start of one. But the tunnel's rumble, for no reason I could discover that made any sense whatever, made *me* think of something on the whole more sinister than an earthquake—of the engine room of H.M.S. *Hood* into which I was conducted when she visited Halifax in the 1920s.

She was then the largest warship ever built and was believed to be the mightiest. The *Hood* was not a happy memory underneath Niagara Falls. On May 24, 1941, she was vaporized when a fifteen-inch shell fired by the *Bismarck* exploded in her magazine. She had aboard at the time a crew of more than 1,200 men.

With the Falls rumbling over my head and the opaque grey water streaming down a few yards from my eyes, I next remembered the 185,000 tons of rock (four times more massive than the *Hood*) which broke off the American Falls in 1954 and crashed down into the gorge; remembered also that the escarpment of the Horseshoe, in which I was then encased, recedes at the rate of four feet a year. Onward to other grisly thoughts. How many human beings actually did go over them? How many animals?

"The Niagara River is very deep in places," wrote Père Hennepin, "and so rapid above the great fall that it hurries down all the animals that try to cross it, without a single one being able to withstand its current." That seventeenth-century visualness—"it hurries down all the animals". So naturally a sequence of pictures of desperate moose and deer, their antlers twisting in the rapids; of little dogs, squirrels, and raccoons, of frantic bears, wildcats, and panthers, even of rabbits. In 1827, long before the parks were made, hotelkeepers on either side of the then-defended border, prophets of the commercial brotherliness that was to flower so fully later on, together conspired to create a spectacle of callous vulgarity not even a twentieth-century showman could hope to rival, if for no better reason than that the laws of no civilized nation would now permit it. Far and wide they advertised it. An old ship would be filled with "ferocious animals" and for a price the public would be able to see these ferocious animals. Then the ship would be loosed onto the upper rapids and the current would take it over the Falls. The only creatures the hotelkeepers managed to obtain were a bison, two bears, a pair of raccoons, a dog, and a goose. All but the bears were put in cages. An enormous crowd, estimated at its maximum at thirty thousand souls, assembled to see this entertainment. Some of them travelled for hundreds of miles to see it. The two bears jumped overboard in time and managed to swim ashore, but the other beasts went down with the ship. And that scow that broke loose from its tow in the upper river in 1918, was caught by the current, and went whirling down until the crew managed to open her seacocks just in time so that she grounded in white water almost on the brink of the Horseshoe—when I first saw the scow, I took it for one of the eroded rocks in the river, so many of which are shaped like scows and coffins. It was only when genuine towing bits emerged in my binoculars that I whispered to myself "My God!" Was it true

Niagara has always dazzled the beholder. No two artists ever agreed in their portrayals of the world's most famous cataract.

[*Compare this engraving by Carl Bodmer in 1834 with the De Visser camera study on page 135.*]

Looking across to Buffalo from his native shore, a Canadian nationalist might wince at the sight of an extremely prominent sign on the American bank—the Curtis Screw Co. Most unlovely, insalubrious, and odoriferous is the effluvium of Buffalo, polluted also is Lake Erie's water which once was pure and delicious, the chief culprits being the cities of Buffalo, Erie, Sandusky, Cleveland, and Toledo, and, behind Lake Erie, Detroit, Windsor, and Sarnia, assisted to the best of their abilities by a number of lesser towns. But from the banks you do not actually see this pollution. The upper Niagara looks calm and gentle. A little stream joins it at the place where William Lyon Mackenzie left Canada to seek refuge in the United States, intending to raise a force of guerrillas to make a comeback later in Upper Canada, a mad scheme which ended in débâcle on Grand Island.

The river swells into a sizeable bay, it divides calmly to embrace the egg-shaped six-mile-wide Grand Island with two separate streams, the right branch taking in as a tributary the small river called Tonawanda Creek. When the rivers rejoin at Navy Island the channel is now a mile and a half wide, quite shallow but swift. On the Canadian side it takes in the little stream called Chippawa Creek and then . . .

Suddenly the Niagara turns into an allegory of a peaceful creature visited by a demon which drives him insane with pain and fear. Like Hercules in his poisoned cloak it writhes and roars, the surface of the Upper Rapids like a sea in a hurricane, but flatter; it leaps suicidally over its cliffs on either side of Goat Island only to discover that the leap has not killed it; it thunders down its gorge tearing at the stone as it goes—in 1956 a collapse caused by erosion in the rock a half-mile below the Falls sent two-thirds of a power station crashing down into the stream. In the Whirlpool, which is probably caused by a deep hole hammered out by the Falls when they were located at this point, the river becomes its own torture chamber. Driving at velocities up to thirty-three miles an hour, it contorts backward and around, so loosened by the air sucked into it by its speed and turbulence that it even loses its natural buoyancy. That is why Captain Matthew Webb, the first man to swim the English Channel, was drowned when he tried to swim the Niagara Whirlpool. He sank like a stone and disappeared like so many of the fish and animals that came over the Falls, were buried in the river, and were later spewed out on the shores mangled and torn. Then the river is torn out of itself by the same invisible and relentless force of gravity until, as suddenly as its torment and madness began, they cease. Calm and navigable it flows the short remainder of its course from Queenston down to Niagara-on-the-Lake. It slips into Lake Ontario as innocently as a quiet Victorian lady coming home from a tea party.

In geological language, the Niagara has finally succeeded in uniting the drainage basin of the upper St. Lawrence System to the lower.

Donald Braider's recent book on the Niagara is one of the best-written and most exciting in the long *Rivers of America* series, and to a Canadian he writes with a refreshing candor and objectivity about the river's long and complex history. Speaking as an American, Mr. Braider holds that the Niagara "shares with the Rio Grande the distinction of being one of our two most political rivers"; that 'The Niagara story embodies, too, many of the great and little lies that have so long comprised the myth we have chosen and have, until all too recently, accepted as 'American history'. For possession and management of the Niagara have contributed some important chapters to the generally appalling narrative of the European white man's rape of the western hemisphere."

In a short narrative like mine it is impossible to offer more than the briefest of summaries of the long and involved history of the Niagara, and perhaps the best way to begin is to state categorically that its political and military history has been over for a long time. The Niagara is still a political frontier, but if a time should ever come when a serious political or military crisis should develop between the two nations now sharing it, it would have no strategic significance whatever. Concrete highways and invisible airways are now the invasion routes for what Gibbon called "the civilized and polished nations". Radar and sensors are their telescopes and signallers, computers their tactical high command, rocket launchers their longbows and muskets, high-flying and far-ranging aircraft their cannon.

All these developments are of course very recent. The excellent condition of Fort Henry at Kingston, the livableness of houses built in the vicinity of Fort George and Fort Niagara when these were serious military installations, indicate just how recent technological warfare is.

It is now believed that the Niagara was a trading-centre for the Indian tribes as long as six centuries before the first European arrived in the New World. It was fated to become a crossroads, because the old portage route on the right bank near modern Lewiston, which was nine miles long, became inevitably a meeting-place for trading Indians from the north-east, the south-east, and the west.

The Five Nations (Cayugas, Mohawks, Oneidas, Onondagas, and Senecas) were able by reason of their federation to dominate all the tribes adjacent to the Niagara district and there they built longhouses—some say as early as fourteen hundred years ago. The nature of the river and the general levelness of the plain surrounding it furnished them with their own interpretation of the Eternal Mystery. They worshipped two gods: one they called "the Holder of the Sky", the other "the Great Voice". They were there when Hennepin found them (and the Falls) on LaSalle's journey of exploration in 1669.

From that point in time, the fate of the Niagara Indians can now be seen to have been predictable. The failure and ultimate betrayal of Pontiac's Rebellion in 1763-4 extinguished their last hope of any real independence or control of the Niagara River. The English settlers, who sixteen years later would be calling themselves Americans, forced the Indians to cede to them two strips of land four miles wide on both of the river's banks.

The Indians still lived mainly by hunting, while the eighteenth-century Europeans depended on agriculture. The white settlers of the United States hungered and thirsted after land with the same passion of their descendants who hunger and thirst after exploitable minerals, oil, and natural gas. As a way of life, hunting has always had to yield to agriculture because the two activities cannot co-exist in the same place. So the Indians went through the same turnstile that Esau did in his famous bargain with his brother Jacob, who is generally conceded to have been the smartest Jew who ever lived. The Indian sold his land for a similar mess of pottage to traders who were literal readers of the Old Testament and consciously took Jacob as a model.

When I was a boy in Halifax, my family attended St. Matthew's Presbyterian Church in Barrington Street close to the harbour, next door to Government House and across the street from the old British colonial cemetery for garrison soldiers. St. Matthew's claims to be the second-oldest non-Catholic church in Canada. On either side of its pulpit are two large, framed slabs of white marble on which are engraved, with the dates of their incumbency, the names of all the clergymen who were the church's ministers since 1750. The first name on the list is that of the Reverend Aaron Cleveland, who arrived in Halifax the year after it was founded, in the exact middle of the eighteenth century. Nor was the congregation to which he preached at that time Presbyterian. They were dissenters, and for a short time the church was known as the 'Protestant Dissenters' Meeting House" and a little later as "Mather's Church" after the Rev. Cotton Mather, celebrated as one of the chief Salem witch-hunters, son of the equally famous Rev. Increase Mather whose philosophical study of the prevalence of witches was so influential in New England. Aaron Cleveland remained in Halifax for only a few years. He later went to England, was ordained by the Bishop of London into the Church of England, obtained a good parish in Delaware, and died shortly afterwards in Philadelphia in

the house of his friend, Benjamin Franklin. His great-grandson, Grover Cleveland, became President of the United States a little more than a century later.

More pertinent to our story is the fact that Aaron Cleveland had a brother called Moses, who spelled the family name "Cleaveland". This Moses Cleaveland, as every native of Ohio knows, became the founder of what for many years has been a very large, rich, and smoky city. Moses Cleaveland was a prime pioneer in a long succession of energetic Anglo-Saxons who saw a future in Manifest Destiny long before it occurred to a later generation to adopt the phrase as a slogan to justify their seizure of much of Mexico and their threatened seizure of British Columbia. The operations of Moses Cleaveland began as unobtrusively as the buy-up of shore properties in Nova Scotia and Prince Edward Island in 1969. They were to lead to developments which soon brought on the War of 1812, in which the Niagara was the chief battleground.

In 1790, only seven years after the end of the War of Independence, there were virtually no white Americans in the Niagara district. In the years immediately after the peace treaty that divided the Niagara River between the new Republic and the British Crown, few white Americans dared settle in the district because the Indians distrusted them, fearing that the citizens of the Republic which had been conceived in liberty and dedicated to the proposition that all men were created equal would soon come to the conclusion that some men are more equal than others. The Indians strongly suspected that the United States would repudiate the treaties drawn between themselves and the British king. National boundaries as such meant little to them, but the fact that they trusted Governor Simcoe was to mean a great deal to Upper Canada in the war that was bound to come. At this time Simcoe governed Upper Canada from Niagara-on-the-Lake, which he renamed Newark. Moses Cleaveland's activities must certainly have contributed to Simcoe's decision, a few years later, to transfer his capital to the safer locality of York.

At any rate, Cleaveland arrived in 1790 in the Niagara district with a party of forty-seven men and two women to see what he could do for himself on the western frontier. Passing through Niagara to the south shore of Lake Erie, which of course was within American jurisdiction, he contrived to purchase from the local Indians some sixty-five square miles of land bordering on the lake. To a people who used virtually no money and had not the least understanding of its value, Cleaveland paid out $500 and a hundred gallons of rot-gut booze. Since then he and his seed have prospered so well that it is difficult to confute their conviction that Moses did that which was righteous in the sight of the Lord.

Inevitably, Cleaveland's settlement opened the gates to many more, and as the white tide moved in, the Indians were cleared out along with the forests which were cut down to make room for the plough. Many of them crossed the Niagara into Canada filled with hatred for those who had dispossessed them. As more settlers arrived from the American East, the feeling grew among them that they might as well take over the land on the British side of the river while they were about it. Powerful politicians abetted them and in June 1812 President Madison and the Congress declared war on Britain.

At the moment, the price seemed about as right as any price could be. Napoleon, apparently at the height of his powers, was attacking Russia with the largest single army ever seen in Europe's history. Wellington was heavily engaged in the Spanish Peninsula. There were only 5,000 British regular troops in all Canada; no more could be spared. The Royal Navy was stretched to its limit in ships and manpower, and a few of its captains had been obliging enough to enrage American opinion by searching American merchant ships for deserters and even impressing a few American citizens. It was taken for granted that the Canadians would not defend themselves; indeed that they would be eager to become Americans. To President Madison the entire situation looked like a kind of historical godfather making him an offer he could not refuse. The risks seemed negligible. The ultimate prize was no less than possession of the entire continent west of the Appalachians.

The politics that led to the War of 1812 are responsible for the term "War Hawks", which was to be resurrected again in the Vietnam War. The principal "Hawks" of 1812 were John C. Calhoun and Henry Clay, the former of whom was subsequently held responsible, more than any other individual, for the American Civil War. Clay's name was long associated with a popular cigar, and in our own time his memory has been erased by the pugilist Mohammed Ali, who believes himself a direct descendant of Clay. (As a member of the great Adams family of Boston once remarked of Thomas Jefferson, "He dreamed of freedom in the arms of a black slave.")

Though Calhoun and Clay were the most famous instigators of the War of 1812, I am indebted to Donald Braider for a less-known "Hawk" who in his own way is more interesting to the student of practical politics. This was Congressman Peter O. Porter, a businessman of Fort Schlosser whose ambition it was to gain a total monopoly over the portage trade of the Niagara River. This he could not do because the best facilities were on the Canadian side. A timely war would make them his. So Porter wangled himself a seat on the House Foreign Relations Committee along with Clay and Calhoun. Most of what followed is history too familiar to repeat. The majority of

John de Visser's study of Niagara; the Canadian (Horseshoe) Falls on the right.

the American people had no enthusiasm for the war; they felt they had been conned into it. The generals in command of the invading forces were the most incompetent in all American history, and their aggression immediately ran into three difficulties their politicians had never anticipated: the release of energy given to the Canadians by the territorial imperative, the tremendous support and awesome fighting qualities of the Indian allies led by Tecumseh, and the accidental presence of a genuine alpha fish who focussed all these energies into decisive action. Isaac Brock, a native of the Channel Island of Guernsey, outmanoeuvred the Americans repeatedly, led the charge at Queenston Heights, saved the Niagara and thereby saved Canada.

Brock came close to accomplishing even more than this. As nothing is so execrated as an unpopular war which fails, the New England states were almost up in arms against the War Hawks. After Napoleon's surrender in 1814, which released the full strength of the Royal Navy, New England saw its trade threatened with ruin. Admiral Cockburn captured Washington and burned it in reprisal for the American burning of York. Had not peace been made early in 1815, it is not impossible that all New England would have seceded from the Union.

Of the many stories surrounding Brock, none is more moving than an incident which occurred at his funeral immediately after the battle of Queenston Heights. Suddenly guns were heard booming from Fort Niagara across the river and the first thought on the Canadian side was that a new attack was impending. It turned out to be something very different. American gunners were firing a salute to their dead enemy. And indeed it is true that before the war there had been warm friendship between the officers of the two garrisons at Fort George and Fort Niagara. Territory alone would guarantee it, for these isolated, lonely men shared the same region.

After the War of 1812, the Niagara entered into an era of rapid development, much of it caused by the barrier to travel created by the Falls and the rapids of the river itself. If the West was to be opened up on either side of the border, canals were necessary to transport the people and stores inland, for the waterways were still the main avenues of travel.

The first and most ambitious scheme was made in the United States with the projection of the Erie Canal. As early as 1818 the first Canal Commission was formed and after the war was over, work on the canal proceeded so fast that the first voyage was made in 1825, on the completion of which Erie water was ceremoniously poured into the Atlantic in New York harbour. The total length of the Erie Canal was 352 miles from Albany on the Hudson to Buffalo Creek. Its prodigious success did more than turn Buffalo into a boom town with the usual trimmings of all boom towns, where most of the men are bachelors or without their families and most of the women are professionals who are there for that very reason. The canal enabled New York City very quickly to supplant Boston as the commercial capital of the United States and it also played an immense role in the rapid settlement of the American Middle West. By the mid-century it ran into the cut-throat competition provided by Commodore Vanderbilt's Erie Railroad, and as more and more railroads were built, its utility faded out.

Very different was the fate of the Welland Canal in Canada, not because Canadian tycoons were that much purer than their brothers across the border, but because of the nature of the St. Lawrence System, of which the Great Lakes are a part, with the Niagara River a vital link. The Erie Canal was shallow and narrow compared to what the Welland later became.

The Welland leaves Lake Erie at Port Colborne and enters Lake Ontario at Port Weller, just outside St. Catharines. It is only twenty-seven and a half miles long. The first Welland Canal was built between 1824 and 1833; the second between 1872 and 1887; the present one, at a cost of $122 million, between 1914 and 1933. It is three hundred feet wide; it has eight separate locks with a total lift and descent of 325 feet over its entire length; each lock measures 800 feet by 80 feet, so that the canal can accommodate very large grain and ore ships in addition to those which have crossed the Atlantic and entered Lake Ontario through the Seaway. There was another intruder which the builders of the canal never foresaw—the lamprey eel. It has finally come close to exterminating the wonderful lake trout and whitefish in which all the Great Lakes used to abound.

Shortly after the Niagara had survived the frontier wars, it suffered an invasion more insidious, and a good deal of that invasion lingers still. The fame of the Falls attracted more people than those who came with reverence to witness a natural wonder. It attracted many more whose instinct for a fast buck was as sure as a vulture's for a wounded animal. Phineas Barnum saw the Century of the Common Man, at least in embryo, more than a hundred years before that unhappy slogan passed the lips of Franklin Roosevelt's Vice-President, Henry Wallace. To Barnum's original, 'There's one sucker born every minute," he was later to add, "And most of them live."

By the mid-nineteenth century the whole Niagara region had been turned into an earlier version of Coney

Island with con and carney men encamped everywhere. Well into our own century, fools were going over the Falls and down the Whirlpool in barrels and were encouraged by the local hucksters to do so. One exception, I suppose, was the amazing Blondin (né Jean-François Gravelet) who earned a small fortune by crossing and recrossing the Whirlpool Gorge on a tightrope, sometimes with another human being on his back, sometimes on stilts. If stunts like these have vanished from the Falls it is not entirely cynical to deny that this is evidence that humanity's fascination with the macabre has diminished. Anyone who wants to see somebody killed before his eyes need only buy a season ticket at an auto-racing track. For that matter, television can bring a *bona fide* war into everyone's living room.

The cities and towns which grew up along the Niagara River were of various kinds. Youngstown, Lewiston, and Queenston probably owe their origins to the portage route and the river. As we have already seen, Buffalo was the creation of the Erie Canal. Both of the cities called Niagara Falls grew out of the collection of hotels built to accommodate tourists, and after the power came in, both became industrial. Last, though first in time, were the little military communities on either side of the river: on the American side Fort Niagara and Fort Schlosser, on the Canadian, Fort Erie, Fort Chippawa, and Fort George, with the adjacent town of Niagara-on-the-Lake.

Man's obsession with literality has caused many modern Canadians to describe Niagara-on-the-Lake as "the birthplace of Upper Canada" because it was the province's first capital. But it was never that. Upper Canada as a political necessity was born south of the present border in the minds of His Majesty's Yankees, who were so stubbornly conservative that they were unable to believe that it is in any way self-evident that all men are created equal and endowed by their Creator with certain inalienable rights, among which are life, liberty, and the pursuit of happiness. They held that though life may indeed be a gift, it certainly is not a "right". Had the electric hare been then invented, they might even have compared self-conscious pursuers of happiness to the greyhounds who chase the rabbit they never can catch. Upper Canada was conceived in the Loyalists' profound suspicion of intellectualism, which their descendants have never lost, as they once again proved when they repudiated Pierre Trudeau in the election of 1972. Finally, Upper Canada was born out of the settlers themselves who had been driven from their homes by the victors. Many of *their* immediate offspring never lost the half-guilty feeling that the victors may have been right. But no

original Loyalist would have found fault with a remark made to me recently by a dear friend, the direct descendant of the second and sixth American presidents, that the American War of Independence was never a revolution, but a commercial and constitutional quarrel between Englishmen.

For all of that, Niagara-on-the-Lake is surely one of the most lovely and interesting towns in all Canada. Its old buildings combine grace with robustness, as do so many British colonial homes of that period. As for Fort George, it was reconstructed between 1937 and 1940 by the Niagara Parks Commission and in 1969 it was declared a national historic park.

As I happen to have grown up in a city where several British colonial forts were in actual use during my lifetime, I am a mild connoisseur of them. The Citadel Hill in the centre of old Halifax, now a museum, would have been a formidable obstacle to any invading force before the invention of high explosive. It is quite similar to Fort Henry at Kingston. Even as late as the Second World War, Fort Ogilvie in Point Pleasant Park, Sandwich Battery on the heights just eastward of old York Redoubt, and Fort Chebucto at the harbour mouth some ten miles out from Halifax were all armed with 6-inch and 9.2-inch guns; these latter are still the chief ordnance at Gibraltar. All these forts were built of thick stone and masonry buried deep into the ground. Like the Citadel at Quebec, they were on guard against an attack from warships. Then, as now, naval guns were the heaviest there were.

Fort George is much more primitive than any of these. Its barracks and blockhouses were extremely vulnerable to fire for they were all built of timber. It is surrounded by a stockade and a modest dry moat, with ports for its cannon, and it could defend itself reasonably well against the small and largely amateurish militias that could be brought against it by the Americans of the interior. It never could have survived a bombardment by a ship of the line or even a frigate.

Fort George is memorable most of all because it was for a time the headquarters of General Brock, and in its annals it is recorded that Brock, a merciful man, was disturbed by the severity of the commandant to his troops. Beside the guardhouse there stands an artifact to remind us of the true nature of British discipline in the eighteenth and early nineteenth century. It is a post about nine feet high with two iron rings attached to it near the top. Such a post was standard equipment in every British garrison of the time. Flogging imposed by British officers in Canada was notoriously cruel, as sadistic as anything that could be found in Prussian and Czarist armies of the same period. Queen Victoria's Germanic father, a pop-eyed man not so much cruel as totally unimaginative— European aristocrats assumed that the lower classes were partial animals and Wellington's opinion of the character of his troops is too well known to repeat—once condemned his best sergeant to suffer 999 lashes in the Quebec barracks square, a torture which Sergeant Rose miraculously survived. His crime? He had left the barracks without leave, possibly to see a girl, and had been picked up at Pointe-aux-Trembles. While the same Duke of Kent was military governor in Halifax, the citizens used to be wakened regularly in the mornings by the screams of soldiers being flogged on Citadel Hill.

The cruelty on the upper St. Lawrence may well have been even worse. For one thing, desertion across the river was a constant temptation. For another, the boredom of garrison life on the western frontier was all but unbearable. There were virtually no women and drunkenness was probably as common among the officers as among the men. The flogging ritual at Fort George was particularly odious. The soldier was stripped to the waist and tied up to the whipping post. Behind him stood a powerful N.C.O. with the lash; behind him stood the Regimental Sergeant-Major with orders to hit the N.C.O. if he failed to lay on hard enough. Behind the R.S.M. stood an officer whose duty it was to hit the R.S.M. with the flat of his sword if the R.S.M. failed to hit the N.C.O. who in his turn was failing to hit the soldier hard enough with a knotted cat-o'nine tails so heavy that two dozen lashes were usually enough to strip a man's back muscles down to the naked spine. I am not implying that things were so much better in the Great Democratic Republic. The whipping post was standard equipment in most New England towns, along with the pillory, and in the American War of Independence Washington "found it necessary" on occasion to sentence a soldier to 500 lashes.

While searching the files in the McGill Library of the very large number of books and treatises on the Niagara, I came upon a title which arrested me for a reason purely personal: *Journal of a Tour to Niagara Falls in the year 1805, by Timothy Bigelow, With An Introduction by his Grandson.* Though written in 1805, the book did not appear in print in Boston until 1876. It was the name Bigelow which so caught my attention that I read the book—all of it.

When I was a very little boy in Nova Scotia I stood in awe of my great-grandmother, a Victorian lady of formidable morality only a few years younger than Queen Victoria herself. She stood five foot one, wore black widow's weeds and a tiny white tippet, and when she sat at table her frail little back was ramrod-straight. She read the Scriptures constantly and had such an obsession with sectarianism, inherited from her forebears, that she had been successively an Anglican, a Baptist, a member of the Salvation Army, and in her old age a Jehovah's Witness. In 1916, when my father was overseas, she once led me to an old-fashioned globe of the world my grandfather kept in the house. She took my index finger in her own aged hand and placed it firmly on a small red blotch in the waters off the European coast.

"Great Britain!" she said. "Great, great, GREAT Britain!"

She then turned the globe around until the huge area marked UNITED STATES came full face and this she contemplated in grim silence.

"They will regret it!" she said in her quavering voice. "They will *regret* it!"

Genetically, so I understand, I am three-quarters Highland Scotch and one-eighth Welsh, a combination which is not believed to make for stability of character. But thanks to my great-grandmother, I am also one-eighth old Massachussetts. Her maiden name had been Abigail Bigelow and the first Loyalist Bigelow to arrive in Nova Scotia had been a Massachussetts shipbuilder whose parents had christened him Amasa. He came north penniless and without good prospects and settled in Pugwash, hoping to start another shipyard there. Rightly or wrongly I picked up the idea that his other Bigelow relations had joined the American Revolutionary side because they wanted to get their hands on Amasa's shipyard. So this Mr. Timothy Bigelow presumably shared a few genes with me.

I regret to say that Mr. Timothy Bigelow failed to show the least signs of regret because his father had opted for the revolution, nor could I detect the smallest indication in him of a democratic attitude as it is now understood among his latter-day countrymen. Setting out from Boston by stage-coach on July 8, 1805, "in company with four other Boston gentlemen", he kept a meticulous record of his entire tour.

"Our first stage was to Wheeler's tavern in Framingham, twenty-three miles from Boston, to dine. This is a very good house; both Wheeler and his wife are industrious and obliging. We proceeded next to Jennison's in Worcester, to sleep, nineteen miles. Jennison himself is coarse, clownish and stupid; but his wife is active and obliging, and it is entirely owing to her that this is a pretty good house." Six days later they reached Schenectady "to breakfast fifteen miles, Beal's tavern; a good house. . . . It is not disagreeable to us to be informed that this road, and indeed all the other turnpikes we met with which required uncommon ingenuity or labor, were constructed by Yankees. Schenectady seems not a word fitted to common organs of speech. We heard it pronounced Snacketady, Snackedy, Kanackidy, Knsactady, Snackendy and Snackady, which is most common. To Ballston, Bromeling's, sixteen miles: a most excellent house."

On July 23 they reached "Ransom's in Erie, to breakfast. Making proper allowances, we fared very well at this house." On July 25 they set out from Buffalo Creek to the Falls of Niagara, proceeding down the river. It had taken the stage-coaches sixteen days to transport them from Boston to the Niagara River.

The Bigelows of Boston were all, apparently, possessed of a precision of mind that this mini-descendant of the original Massachussetts Bigelow lacks, and a passing glance at any American encyclopedia is ample proof that they took to heart the old copybook adage:

> Count that day lost
> Whose low descending sun
> Views from thy hand
> No worthy action done.

Timothy Bigelow's description of the Falls, the rapids, and the Whirlpool is as relentless in its accuracy, detail, and factuality as an engineer's survey report and is set down without the slightest emotion of any kind. One is left, however, with the impression that he regarded the Falls as worthy of himself and his family and well worth the time and expense he had expended to reach them. But his *Journal* does not cease with Niagara. He and the other gentlemen intended to return to Boston by way of Montreal.

On July 28 aboard a brig in Lake Ontario, "we could discern the mountains of Toronto behind York on the northern shore." Kingston impressed him favourably because of the number and quality of its houses but there "we saw considerable numbers of Messessaga [sic] Indians. They are filthy, indolent and miserable wretches, free as Paine himself would wish, and a fine specimen of the infinite perfectibility of man." They had been given to understand that the journey from Kingston to Montreal could be accomplished in only two days, "but we soon found this was a vain expectation." Finally they hired a *bateau* with a French-Canadian crew "who make it an invariable practice to blackguard and insult other crews they pass with the most sarcastic and abusive language they can invent." They ran the rapids of the Long Sault, "a frightful place", but when finally they reached the island of Montreal, they did not attempt to run the rapids at Lachine. They disembarked and drove into the city by coach.

In Montreal, Timothy Bigelow was entertained by "some considerable gentlemen of the place" to whom he had been furnished with introductions, one of them being William McGillivray, who also showed him through the warehouses of the North West Company. Another was a Mr. Sewall. "His mother, who was at table, a pleasant and facetious old lady, was a daughter of Edmund Quincy, Esq., and the wife of Jonathan Sewall, Esq., late King's attorney-general in the Province of Massachussetts Bay. She yet smarts from the confiscation of her husband's estate during the revolution." At this point I was certain that Timothy Bigelow did not smart from the confiscation of Amasa Bigelow's shipyard, if indeed he or his had anything to do with it.

On August 6, "We employed the morning by perambulating the town. . . . Considering that Canada has been a province of the British Empire for half a century, it is surprising that the English language should not have made a greater progress among its inhabitants. Not one in five of the people in Montreal can speak it. It is said that the French inhabitants refuse to be taught to speak English, even when instruction is offered to them *gratis*, and that they still cherish the prejudices against the English for which their ancestors were distinguished, insomuch that the government is of the opinion that, if the French should attempt an invasion of Canada, they would be gladly received and assisted by the great body of its French inhabitants."

Bigelow was also surprised, and not displeased, to learn that all Americans were called "Bostonians" by the French people of Quebec. For that matter, even today the translation of "New Englanders" into the French of the Quebec press is *les Bostonais*, a small point which might suggest a certain element of Canadian unity despite the language difficulty, for when I was young there were still some Nova Scotians who called the U.S.A. "the Boston States".

After several days in Montreal, Bigelow left for home. He took a stage-coach to Saint-Jean on the Richelieu, noting with satisfaction as he travelled that the "husbandry in the valley was most inferior to the husbandry in New England." He even said that the *habitants* did not understand the principle of crop rotation. The moment he reached Vermont, "we were satisfied to observe on all sides a diligence and prosperity sorely lacking in the British territory to the north." They arrived in Boston six weeks after their departure, having "terminated an excursion which had afforded us much diversified entertainment, and had also been attended by some inconveniences. For the encouragement of future travellers, however, we may with propriety affirm that the tour was interesting throughout, that it produced more pleasure than pain in the performance, and that it still yields considerable amusement in retrospect." In a footnote he adds that their direct distances totaled 1,190 miles and their deviations 165, making a grand total of 1,355 miles in six weeks.

So, with Timothy Bigelow, we follow the Niagara all the way down to the opening of the ancient channel of the St. Lawrence below the city which is still the question mark of Canada's future.

Waters of Ontario

AUSTERE ALBANY, GENTLE GRAND

Rivers define the character of every land through which they flow and in Ontario they are witnesses to the schizophrenic geography of our richest, most populous, and second-largest province. The gentle streams of the settled south remind you of English shires and the broad valleys of central Germany. But to find anything resembling the rivers of the Ontarian north you would have to go to Lapland or Siberia.

The vast wilderness extending from the foot of James Bay to high up on the western shore of Hudson Bay is void of anything that could be called human settlement. The rock and bush are seeded with thousands of lakes ponding glacial melt. Much of what passes for soil is muskeg. In summer, mosquitoes and blackflies; in winter, temperatures sometimes below the North Pole's. Along the indeterminate border between the wilderness and the outskirts of civilization there is a saying that you must never offer a Swede or a Finn a length of strong rope in the month of April.

In this largely forgotten region are found the only sizeable rivers in the whole province except for the Ottawa, which Ontario shares with Quebec, and the upper St. Lawrence, which she shares with the State of New York. These northern rivers are surely the loneliest in the world. The Lapps have fished and travelled on their streams for centuries, and in recent years Stalin saw to it that millions of his countrymen received extensive lessons in the geography of northern Siberia. But hardly anyone except a few trappers, prospectors, Indians, surveyors, and airborne fishermen and hunters ever visit the north-west of Ontario.

The longest of these wilderness streams is the Albany, only 115 miles shorter than the Rhine. Emerging out of a labyrinth of inter-connected lakes, it flows easterly for 610 miles through an absolute wilderness to enter James Bay. In all those miles of its course there is only one place-name on the map—Ogoki. Does it mark the habitation of even seventy human beings? Yet this river has ancient and famous associations. Discovered three centuries ago by Hudson's Bay Company explorers, it was named after the brother of their patron Charles II, the Duke of York and Albany who later became James II, and in 1683 the company built Fort Albany at the river's mouth. Albany, of course, is the ancient poetic name for Scotland; according to legend, one Albanuktos was given the kingship of Scotland by his brother Brut, king of Britannia, who in turn was supposed to be the descendant of Trojan Aeneas, legendary founder of Rome. Though Brut was king of England only in the

imagination of Geoffrey of Monmouth, I find eerie even this nominal association between one of the world's most solitary rivers and the cradle of western civilization.

Eerie also was the early story of the rivers of the Ontarian north, each of them with a trading fort at its mouth. Three centuries ago all white men anywhere in North America knew they were existing on the edge of the unknown, but on the shores of Hudson Bay they were in literal limbo between eternity and the ice. Yet even here, obedient to their European masters, they went through the old routine of killing each other and destroying each other's posts.

During the second-last of Louis XIV's wars, Fort Albany was captured by De Troyes and was later reoccupied by the English. Then appeared in Hudson Bay a man who came close to changing the history of the North American continent.

Pierre LeMoyne d'Iberville, perhaps the greatest French Canadian who ever lived, was born in the seigneury of Longueuil in 1661. During the course of five expeditions into Hudson Bay, D'Iberville captured all the English posts from Fort Albany to Fort Nelson. In a sea fight he sank one English warship and captured two more. It chills the soul to think of the only Europeans within two thousand miles of any other Europeans fighting each other in the frigid water of Hudson Bay. Two years later, with the capture of St. John's in Newfoundland, D'Iberville made France for a short time master of all the northern approaches to North America, and he was maturing his plans for the capture of Boston and New York when Louis XIV ended the war in 1698. In the nine years of its duration, James II lost the throne of Great Britain and William III occupied it. And as every Irishman knows, William's first act was to rout James' attempt at a comeback in the Battle of the Boyne, thereby bequeathing to Ontario a social and political legacy of which it did not rid itself until 1950—the Loyal Orange Organization, which has done more to promote Canadian disunity than any other political body which has so far afflicted us.

Peace brought no rest to D'Iberville. Before the year was out, his ships were in the Gulf of Mexico. He sailed into the Mississippi and was the first white man to explore its delta. He established a French settlement at Old Biloxi, moved it three years later to Mobile, and placed it in the charge of a man almost as able as himself, his younger brother Jean-Baptiste de Bienville.

But peace never lasted long while Louis XIV was alive. The Sun King, whose self-regard was so singular that he required the presence of his courtiers to witness him moving his bowels, in 1701 launched Europe into a war even more disastrous to France than the former one. When it was over, Marlborough had crushed four French armies, Rooke had captured Gilbraltar, France had lost control of Bavaria, and Nova Scotia (which then included New Brunswick and some of Maine) had become British territory. But while Louis's armies were losing in Europe, D'Iberville captured St. Kitts and Nevis and might well have attacked and captured New York and Boston had he not been stung by an *aëdes aegypti* mosquito and died of yellow fever. After his death, his brother Bienville founded New Orleans and colonized Louisiana.

From D'Iberville's time until a few years ago the Albany River was virtually forgotten, along with the other large rivers of northern Ontario, the chief of which are the Attawapiskat, the Winisk, and the Severn. Their thin lines waver across provincial maps with hardly a place name within hundreds of miles of them. The Winisk empties into the bay through an area called Polar Bear Provincial Park, which is almost as large as the southern Ontario peninsula. Wasted rivers, it has been said of them. Useless rivers. But for all this they have served the province and the continent. They are homes to millions of fish and birds; they are essential agents in the precarious climatic and ecological balance of North America. Now the chances are that they may become geographic agents of an entirely different kind.

Technocrats and merchants of technology have recently been looking at the rivers of Ontario's north with thirsty eyes. Since it is technologically possible to reverse their courses, is it not technology's manifest destiny to do so? Why not make these useless rivers flow south instead of north, down into Lake Superior, where the ultimate destination of their waters will be the power-hungry, over-powered cities of the United States?

For some time now the usual propaganda has been blaring. The rivers contribute nothing at present to the production, distribution, and consumption of material wealth. The engineering work will provide thousands of jobs. The sale of the water will help the Canadian government with its balance of payments, and above all it will be great for technology and science. This could be the most formidable of all the arguments, now that Science-Technology has become the universal religion of the vast majority of human kind. If this religion had a formal creed, it would have to run like this:

I believe in Science, explorer and examiner of heaven and earth; and in Technology his oldest begotten son who was conceived by the Virgin Mathematics; he descended into the hell of the Industrial Revolution; thanks to humane legislation He rose again from the dead; He ascended into the Welfare State where He sitteth on the right hand of Science His Father Who is on earth whence He will come to solve the problems of all mankind: I believe in the communion of technocrats, in the repeated resurrection of the Gross National Product, and the life everlasting of the Dow Industrial Average. Amen.

But some powerful voices have been talking back for some time. In 1967 the late General Francis McNaughton, who was also an eminent scientist, had this to say about the kind of technology which would handle our water resources solely within the context of civil engineering:

Even the slightest changes may have far-reaching effects; the danger lies in the fact that if water flows were altered, the related climatic changes could affect vegetation and biological life. With decreases in local stream-flow, the climate of a region could assume a more continental aspect—hotter during summer months and colder during the winter and fall. Because of temperature changes, plants might not be able to survive the heat of summer and the cold of winter. Conceivably, such changes in climate might also alter the water supply, because of a change in the régime of precipitation.

Then there is the question of permafrost, which occurs in Canada in large lenticular masses embedded in the soil at considerable depths. If these are subject to inflow of heat by flooding of the surface, the permafrost will melt and constitute a dangerous foundation upon which to impound the vast masses of storage water which have been indicated [by the technologists].

No technologists are likely to waste much time over the gentle little streams of southern Ontario because there is not enough power in them. Niagara alone excepted (its ferocious power is not caused by the general character of the land but by a geological accident), these rivers have little to recommend them except their beauty and tranquillity. They flow through a country of hardwood trees and marvellously rich topsoil. It is no wonder that one of them is called after England's Trent, one after the Humber, one after the Thames, one after the Avon, and still another after the Severn, which latter gives to Ontario two rivers, totally different in character, named after the beautiful stream which flows through western shires of England into the Bristol Channel. Inevitably, there is a city called Stratford on Ontario's Avon and a city called London on Ontario's Thames which rises just to the east of Woodstock, a town which in turn derives its name from the English Woodstock on the little Glyme, only eight miles from Oxford.

The Ontarian Thames winds its tranquil way down to Lake St. Clair for a distance of 163 miles, and only one violent event is connected with it—the Battle of the Thames in 1813 in which a future president of the United States, William Henry Harrison ("Tippecanoe") defeated a smaller force of British regulars and Indians and thereby saved his country from total defeat in the War of 1812. For in this battle Tecumseh was killed, and with his death the pro-British Indian Confederacy fell apart.

For years I used to wonder vaguely why so many parts of southern Ontario gave me feelings of nostalgia. Finally, I understood why.

Like many eastern Canadian boys born in the first decade of the twentieth century, I grew up on books written in England for English boys. Chief among them was the *Boy's Own Annual,* which arrived every Christmas and was often read by my father before it was given to me. The *Boy's Own* was not averse to the occasional story about the Mounties or the Klondyke; it was very partial to tales about Victorian and Edwardian Englishmen adventuring with lions, tigers, leopards, snakes, and natives in Africa and the Far East. But most of the *Boy's Own,* including the illustrations, exuded such a love of England that anyone who read it could only believe that England was a paradise. It never mentioned the slums of London, the pottery towns of the Midlands, or the mines of Lancashire. The England of my childhood reading was a land of exquisite towns and villages reposing by still little streams in whose pools were reflected the churches and colleges on its banks—*Under the crag where the ouzel sings / And the ivied wall where the church bell rings!*

Nor was this picture of England unreal; up to the Second World War it was at least half the truth of that country. England was so different from my native Nova Scotia that until I was nineteen I did not understand that there was any beauty worth talking about in the austere land where I grew up. Few lowing herds wound slowly over any of the leas I knew in my boyhood. No doves moaned for me in immemorial elms, nor did any Wordsworthian lambs bound for me as to the tabor's sound, though I do remember the time in Cape Breton when my mother phoned the butcher to ask if the lamb she had ordered that day would be ready by dinner time and he answered, "I don't know, but they're out chasing him."

Outside of a few counties, the soil of Nova Scotia is not soil at all; it is gravel, granite, and ironstone.

So in my ignorance I grew up feeling culturally poor, not knowing that the poets of ancient Greece had described Nova Scotia's beauty while describing their own rugged land. Truly I believe that much of the Canadian cultural inferiority complex springs from the simple fact that the poets we loved in our schooldays wrote of a land totally different from the kind of country most of us inhabit. It is a strange fact that it is the artists and writers who make people recognize the reality of their surroundings and thereby give them value in the imagination. I suppose that is what Rupert Brooke had in mind when he said that in the Rockies he missed the voices of the dead.

When I first went to Oxford all the things I saw, from the little Cherwell to the Cumnor Hills, seemed precious because poets and painters had depicted them. Constable and the artists of the hunting prints had caught rural England just as it was. Keats, Wordsworth, Tennyson, Arnold, and Housman—even Hazlitt with that wonderful description of the whole countryside pouring in over the hedges to see the great prize-fight between Bill Neate and Tom Hickman the Gasman. In my first Oxford term, willing to try anything once, I paid two shillings for an afternoon with the New College, Magdalen, and Balliol Beagles. As I panted mile after mile in their baying wake, I marvelled at the richness of the soil. The furrows shone as though exuding the oils of their own fatness. After about two hours the hounds cornered a hare beside a small stream, and when I recovered enough wind to speak, I asked an English student where we were. When he told me I felt great. For had not Matthew Arnold's Scholar Gypsy crossed "the stripling Thames at Bablock Hythe" many centuries ago?

Of course, this was pure adolescent romanticism and I got over it long ago. It is more fun to have your own chance to describe the Camsell Bend of the Mackenzie or the Black Canyon of the Fraser without having to compete with the mighty dead. I wonder if this explains why most of the Ontario writers after Lampman have shied away from descriptions of nature? If they grew up outside Toronto they lived in a country whose features had already been caught in perfect phrases long ago. If southern Ontario had been settled a century earlier, even its architecture would have resembled the architecture of rural England, but unhappily, the Industrial Revolution was already under way before even the first settlements in the province began.

There is, of course, much more to any land than mere description; there is the land as the background and scene of human evolution. It took a Polish exile with a British citizenship to cast the English Thames into a context which links it perfectly to those gentle rivers of

The streams of a new England

The names came easily to men dreaming of home:
Thames (at Chatham, *above*), Trent,
Humber (*below*), Avon — Ontario has them all.

southern Ontario: "And this also was one of the dark places of the earth . . ." Remember how Marlow in Conrad's *Heart of Darkness* described the Thames as it had been only two thousand years earlier, in a time when people living around the Mediterranean were reading Plato, Aristotle, Sophocles, and the poets of the Anthology, some of them even knowing that the basis of matter is the invisible atom? Roman camps in forests filled with savages; loneliness, fear, and terrible boredom; fog, rain, and sudden death. "They must have been dying like flies here." As for the aboriginal denizens of the Thames Valley, this is how Julius Caesar described them:

> All of them dye their bodies with the juice of a plant which stains them blue and makes them look very terrible in battle. They wear their hair long. . . . Those who are ill of any serious disease and those who engage in war and other dangerous occupations either offer up human beings as sacrifices, or make vows to offer up themselves. They think their gods cannot be appeased except by offering up life for life. They have public sacrifices of this sort. Some of them have huge wickerwork images which they stuff full of men and women and then set fire to the whole and burn them to death.

Born at the time when he was, Conrad could not have escaped reading Caesar's *Commentaries* in school, so it was natural for him to remember this passage when he was introducing his readers to that haunting story of the Congo and the life of equatorial Africa, which his narrator Marlow begins while sitting with a few friends on the deck of a cruising yawl becalmed in the Thames estuary. Undoubtedly he was also familiar with Stanley's account of his African explorations and Stanley's quotation from the psalms: "Verily, the dark places of the earth are the habitations of cruelty."

What have all these English and literary memories to do with those little rivers of southern Ontario? Much.

This region, reminiscent in so many places of England and central Germany, has no counterpart anywhere else in Canada except in the little Pereau Valley of Nova Scotia. If you drive through rural Ontario you understand why this has become our most prosperous and stable province, the most conservative, and (if you forget its intellectuals) the most self-confident. Yet this mild country, these slow-moving, English-scale rivers, these well-cropped hills with their stately hardwoods—this region also was one of the dark places of the earth. And not so long ago.

It was in this country, only two years before the founding of Harvard College, that Etienne Brûlé was killed and eaten by the Hurons, whose territories extended eastward as far as the upper Humber Valley. It

was here that Brébeuf and Lalemant were tortured to death. It was here that the Five Nations exterminated or scattered the Huron tribes and then turned south to exterminate the Neutral Indians in the region of the Grand River.

These were among the first significant events known in the history of southern Ontario. By history's irony, one of the chief reasons why this same region soon afterwards became civilized was the settlement along the Grand River of those same Iroquois who had come there to murder, torture, and burn only a few generations earlier. But by this time they had been converted to Christianity. The human brain is a mini-computer and so much depends upon how it is programmed. But the human mind, wrote Dr. Wilder Penfield, is a mystery which no knowledge of the brain has so far been able to comprehend by the technical methods known to science.

And so to the Grand River.

It never should have been called the Grand. This river is so unobtrusive that the majority of Canadians have never heard its name. If you ask the man at the desk of a Toronto hotel how long it will take you to reach Kitchener or Brantford he will be able to tell you. But if you ask him how long it will take you to reach the Grand River he will probably look blank.

If the Grand became one of the important rivers of Canada it is for the same reason that the Somme became important to France; it is one of the few streams of any size in an extremely important area. From the first records until close to the end of the nineteenth century, the Grand River has been vital in the history of Ontario. In the middle decades of the seventeenth century it linked Lake Erie to the old Champlain Road which led from Ville Marie up the Ottawa to Lake Nipissing and thence down the French River to Georgian Bay. Probably, though not certainly, it was used by Etienne Brûlé on his way to the exploration of the Susquehanna. The Indians called it Tinaaouta, and it was in the Indian village of that name that Jolliet encountered LaSalle in the company of the Sulpician missionaries Galinée and De Casson. Jolliet continued with LaSalle in his search for the Mississippi, but the two Sulpicians remained in Ontario. The month was October and they found the water in the Grand so low that they had to spend eight days paddling and poling. Galinée named it *La Rapide*, possibly for the same reason that modern Newfoundlanders called the slowest train in North America 'The Bullet'.

But Galinée loved the country of the Grand River. Moving westward through what now is Haldimand

In a province of 412,582 square miles, encompassing the
latitudes of Stockholm and Madrid, the rivers of Ontario
reflect the variety of climate and terrain. The Grand
(at Galt, *above*) rolls peacefully by steeple and meadow; the
French (*below*) was part of the voyageurs' route to the West.

County, he wrote that "the streams are full of fish and beaver. The grapes are as large and sweet as any in France [I wonder if they really were?] and game is abundant." Just what kind of game he does not specify, but there were certainly no deer living there then. It was only after farmlands developed that the white-tailed deer emigrated north out of Virginia. When the early explorers talked about roebucks in this region what they meant were the woodland caribou, now extinct.

Galinée and De Casson circumnavigated the southern Ontario peninsula—they were the first white men to do it—and after that, many years passed before Europeans took any interest at all in the Grand River Valley.

Draining some 26,000 miles of the southern Ontario peninsula, and today thoroughly polluted, the Grand rises in a large morass called the Luther Swamp, which embraces the two little townships of Luther and Melancthon. These two Protestant reformers are still venerated in several Grand River cities, notably in Kitchener and Waterloo, but that is not why one of the largest swamps in Ontario is called after them. The surveyor who named the swamp was a Roman Catholic, who added that it was the worst swamp he ever saw in his life.

Technically, I suppose, the Grand belongs to the St. Lawrence System because it discharges into Lake Erie, but in all other respects it is a little system in its own right, with five small tributaries. The Nith enters it at the little town of Paris; the Speed, after passing through Guelph, enters at Preston; the Conestoga and Canagigue come in through the farmlands above Waterloo; the little Irvine reaches it at Elora just south-west of the larger town of Fergus. The total length of the Grand is estimated at 180 miles, which makes it a few miles longer than the third-longest stream in England.

When I first set out to acquaint myself with the Grand I drove to Dunnville and thence down to the estuary at Port Maitland, where a tired signboard informed me that the village had been founded in 1820 with a population of seventy souls and that by 1967 the population had risen to a hundred and twenty. According to another item of local lore, a small party of seventeenth-century Jesuit missionaries once sheltered here after a storm on Lake Erie had nearly drowned them.

Those place names of Old Ontario are as eloquent of the nature of our two solitudes as the saint names of Old Quebec. Is there a single town in Old Ontario without its King Street, Queen Street, York Street, and Wellington Street? Is there any name even slightly famous in the story of the British Empire from the American Revolution to 1840 that is not remembered in Ontario? Little Port Maitland was reverently named after General Sir

Peregrine Maitland ("Now, Maitland, now's your time!") whom Wellington called on to turn back the last charge of Napoleon's Old Guard. Only a few miles away is Port Colborne, named after another hero of Waterloo. Anyway, it is at Port Maitland that the Grand River slips into Lake Erie through a man-made mouth, the water being channelled by concrete moles. It enters the lake without a bubble.

But in the lowlands behind Port Maitland the river looks quite impressive. There it has built up a ragged delta about seven miles long and five miles wide, with so many willows and rushes it must be a fine place for duck hunters in the fall. For a fair distance above Dunnville it is a good wide stream running remarkably straight. The Grand is lovely along this lower stretch with rich farmland, dignified houses nearby, and many willows along the banks. But once you are past Cayuga going north it narrows rapidly. At Brantford it is about the width of the Isis at Oxford and except in the spring there is less water in it. Four miles above Brantford is the little town of Paris; it should be noted that it was not named romantically after the City of Light but because a smart Yankee from Vermont found gypsum deposits near by and built a factory at the confluence of the Nith and the Grand to manufacture plaster of paris. Here again I had the illusion that I was in a small town of Europe. Ontario's Paris rises steeply from the river and its old stone houses seem to hug each other. It is just like a little town I knew near Grenoble in Dauphiné on a small tributary of the Isère.

Moving slowly north I kept marvelling at the Grand. How does it generate enough force to move at all? In Galt it could pass for a large drainage canal, and in Galt I was again back in an older country: those solid buildings made to last out of hewn grey stone; the Scotch names; the famous Galt Collegiate Institute; an old Calvinist hand like myself could almost smell the years of frugal living and high Presbyterian endeavour, earnest reading and worried small boys trying to memorize sections of the Shorter Catechism before they were allowed to go out to play. Then I saw a high-rise the colour of vanilla ice cream and reflected without enthusiasm that even Galt was getting with it in the first post-Christian era.

On through Preston into the twin cities of Kitchener and Waterloo and in the calm stretch of the river between Galt and Kitchener I saw with quite a lot of enthusiasm a flotilla of canoes manned by small boys. Passing through Kitchener and Waterloo the Grand almost but not quite gets lost. Out again into the farmland and it is still there, moving along imperceptibly until at Fergus you see a calm stream descending through a narrow channel. Here you can also see that some rivers, like human beings, acquire a few of their basic traits in the cradle.

Streams with low banks running through rich tillage can be very deceptive. They remind me of quiet, apparently docile women who periodically lose their tempers and are all the more terrifying because you don't expect it. The Grand River has a long history of losing its temper in the month of April. Descending from its swamp above Grand Valley, it has enough drop to gather more power than its banks can contain when the spring run-off is heavy. In 1929 there was a disastrous flood in at least three towns, and in the spring of 1972 it made the national television news. Millions of people saw it roaring and tumbling through Paris followed by the usual scenes of citizens paddling about the lower streets of the town in canoes and flat-bottomed boats.

Several small dams have been constructed along the Grand for flood control and the largest is at Belwood, just above Fergus. Built in 1942, it rises seventy-five feet above the river bed with a spillway one hundred and fifty feet across. It backs up some forty-six thousand acre-feet of water into a lake seven miles long and a mile and a half wide, and people can sail small boats on it. Here it is that the character of the country changes. The farmland so reminiscent of England begins to yield to pasture, the hardwoods to spruce, pine, tamarisk, and aspen. When at last you reach Grand Valley, you know you are close to the northern frontier.

Mabel Dunham, historian of the Grand River, begins her account of it in the Finger Lakes district of western New York in the time when this was the home territory of the most famous Indian confederacy on the continent, the Five Nations, whom the French had dreaded ever since that fatal discharge of Champlain's arquebus. Some of their descendants still exist proudly in reservations along the Grand River and in Caughnawaga, just outside Montreal, where the St. Lawrence Seaway made still another incursion into their territory. The Mohawks are still warriors, enlisting for Canadian wars in Europe, even for Korea and the American war in Vietnam, and their soldiers have some of the attitude and *esprit de corps* of the French Foreign Legion. Though they are also renowned for their apparent nervelessness on the high steel, they will quickly enough tell you that anyone who pretends to be without fear is a liar. The thing is to act in the presence of danger as though fear does not exist.

One bitter winter afternoon, with a wind blowing at thirty knots and gusting beyond forty, I had some business on the second-highest floor of the Sun Life Building in Montreal. Across the street the Royal Bank Building in the Place Ville Marie complex was under construction. I chanced to glance sideways and it took me at least twenty seconds to absorb what I was looking at. A workman was balanced on a girder on one leg, his other leg was bent, and he was scratching matches on the sole of that foot in order to light his pipe. He was a Mohawk.

The other tribes in the Confederacy, of course, were the Onondagas, Cayugas, Senecas, and Oneidas. When the Tuscaroras moved north from South Carolina and joined them early in the eighteenth century, the Confederacy became the Six Nations. With the possible exception of the Aztecs, they were the most savagely cruel warriors in the entire New World.

In 1708, in the middle of the War of the Spanish Succession (in English-speaking America it was called Queen Anne's War), a ploy on the chessboard of international power politics changed the ferocious character of the Iroquois forever. Though the armies of Louis XIV were faring badly in Europe, in America under the leadership of Frontenac and D'Iberville they were doing alarmingly well. The Dutch mayor of Albany, Colonel Peter Schuyler, came to the conclusion that if the Five Nations were to ally themselves with the French and attack the English colonies in the rear while the French were attacking New England and New York, the whole of North America above the Spanish possessions might fall into French hands. At the time he had good reason to fear that such an alliance might come about, for the famous Jonquaire brothers were then living as fullfledged braves with the Iroquois and their influence had almost erased the hostility created a century earlier by Champlain. Schuyler wrote to London suggesting that the Crown itself should invite some Iroquois sachems to London on a state visit.

As modern Canadians have learned more than once, the English have a unique instinct for the right moment to use the Royal Family to promote the political interests of Great Britain. Five Iroquois sachems were invited to England, and though one of them died on the voyage, the other four for a short time were the sensation of London. In their Indian dress with their enormous head-feathers they were followed by crowds wherever they went. They were guests of honour in the Haymarket Theatre at a performance of *Macbeth*, a play they would have found little difficulty in understanding. When the final curtain fell, the actor who had played Macbeth made a speech in their honour urging them to ally themselves with the English and to drive the French and the Catholic priests out of their lands. Finally, the Queen received them in person at court and by her orders their portraits were painted by court painters.

It worked perfectly, for never afterwards did the Iroquois desert the British Crown. Before leaving London, the sachems petitioned the Queen to send them a Protestant missionary, and the Queen turned the matter over to the Archbishop of Canterbury. Two years later there stood in the Iroquois territory the famous Mohawk Chapel, a tiny building with two windows on either side of the door, two windows on each flank, and a bell on the roof. Inside, flanking a reed organ, were two tablets inscribed respectively with the Lord's Prayer and the Ten Commandments in the Mohawk tongue. A large, leather-bound Bible was on the pulpit and twelve smaller Bibles were in the pews. There was even a double set of communion plate with the royal arms and the inscription *The Gift of Her Majesty Queen Ann, by the grace of God of Great Britain, France (sic) and Ireland and of her plantations in North America, Queen of the Indian Chapel of the Mohawks.*

One other thing the Mohawks gained which must have seemed most important of all, though history was to mock their descendants with it toward the century's end. The Crown signed a treaty confirming the Five Nations in permanent possession of their territory.

There was another strange result of this visit to England. While in London, the sachems were taken to Blackheath Common to see an encampment of Protestant refugees from the Palatinate. They had been driven out of their homeland by the war and were living in poverty and hoplessness in the open air near London. The sachems took pity on them, as it was hoped that they would, and promised them empty land between the Mohawk and St. Lawrence rivers. So began the great eighteenth-century immigration of German Protestants to the New World. And all this happened only sixty years after the Iroquois had exterminated the Hurons and the Neutrals just for the fun of it.

Some fifty years later came the first groundswells in the tide which led to the American Revolution. Inevitably the Iroquois Confederacy, now the Six Nations, was involved from the beginning. And of course, tragically.

In 1754 Benjamin Franklin observed their constitution and wrote down a thought very interesting in the light of his own activities twenty years later: "It would be a strange thing if Six Nations of ignorant savages should be capable of forming a scheme for union, and in such manner that it has subsisted ages and seems indissoluble; and yet that a like union should be impractical for ten or twelve English colonies."

But for all Franklin's admiration for the politics of the Six Nations, his attitude toward them as human beings was always one of cold calculation. Had he been active at the time the five sachems were invited to England to meet the Queen, he would certainly have approved of the motives behind the invitation. If the price of the alliance was a solemn treaty confirming the integrity of their territory, he would have accepted that, too. But while still a loyal subject of the Crown, he was never-

theless pondering ways and means of easing the Indians out, and he came to the conclusion that the best way of doing so was to feed them cheap rum. He had nothing against them personally. He merely wished the land to be farmed as skilfully as possible. With him, efficiency was at least nine points of the law, and a clever lawyer could take care of the last point.

It has often been remarked that Benjamin Franklin was the very prototype of the American WASP: intellectually honest, mechanically ingenious, politically shrewd, practical in all things, and judging men and events mainly by results. Nothing was more in his character than the observation that a prudent man in search of a mistress would do well to avoid beautiful young girls and take a plain and older woman who knew her business, a point of view which Lewis Mumford later described as no less disgusting because it was technically accurate. With men like Benjamin Franklin in the ascendant in what soon was to become the United States of America, the ultimate prospects of the Indians were bleak. But right up to the outbreak of the Revolution, the Iroquois were barely conscious of him. The white man they knew best was the Crown superintendent of the Indian Confederacy, a red-headed man whose temperament was diametrically the opposite of Franklin's.

Sir William Johnson, as he became in the mid-1750s, was one of the most unusual of the many unusual Irishmen of the eighteenth century. Born poor in County Meath, he emigrated to New York as a very young man and from there went up-river to Albany, where he was advised to establish a trading post in the Indian territory. He was soon on his way to one of the greatest success stories in colonial America. In his second year as a trader, Johnson met a German girl of the neighbourhood, a daughter of one of those Palatine families invited to America by the sachems. He hired her to keep the store while he was absent on trading journeys and soon she was pregnant with the first of the three children she bore him. She, too, enjoyed a success story of a kind, for though Johnson never married her, she was recognized in England as Lady Johnson when George II made her mate a baronet in 1755.

By this time Johnson had become a statesman, a soldier, and an administrator with uncanny influence over the Indians. In all possible ways he enjoyed being with them. He loved to dress up in animal skins and wardance with the braves. He is said to have sired no fewer than seven hundred half-breed children, which must have made him the champion father of his entire century unless some jungle king in the heart of Africa went him a few children better. After the death of his common-law wife, followed soon afterwards by the death of the only woman he married legally, the story goes that at a

To link the lakes, man makes himself a river

To bypass the Niagara cataract, allowing ships to traverse the 27½ miles
between Lakes Ontario and Erie, three canals have been dug over the past century and
a half. St. Catharines (*above*) is threaded by the waterways, old and new.

Mohawk picnic he saw a young Indian girl leap high off the ground with her hair flying and land secure behind the rider of a galloping horse. This was the celebrated Molly Brant, and when Sir William took her to live with him she became known as "the brown Lady Johnson". In eleven years she bore her indefatigable mate eight or nine children, one of them being Joseph Brant, who grew up to become as famous as his father and always retained his mother's name.

By this time Sir William was living in raffish splendour in a wilderness manor house he called Johnson Hall and it was here that he died. The year was 1774, one year before the passage of the Quebec Act lit the final match to the American Revolution. Historians have since wondered whether the Revolution could have succeeded had Johnson lived another five years in full command of his faculties, for his loyalty to the Crown was as remarkable as his political skill. His son Joseph Brant was with him when he died, and his last words are said to have been, "Control your people, Joseph. Control your people. I am going away."

After Sir William Johnson's death, Joseph Brant's control of his people was to lead them through seven years of guerrilla warfare and finally to their settlement along the banks of the Grand River.

Brant's life was a genuine epic. As a boy he had studied for two years in an Indian school kept by one Eleazar Wheelock in New Lebanon, Connecticut, but there is no doubt that his most important lessons were learned from his father. When he was only thirteen years old he accompanied Johnson on the Ticonderoga campaign and later fought with him on the Niagara and in Pontiac's Rebellion of 1763. When his father died he was in his prime at thirty-two years of age. After a mob of rebels broke into Johnson Hall, Brant and his white half-brother Guy Johnson travelled to England to beg help from the King himself, and George II promised that if the rebels did any damage to the Indian property, the British government would make reparations to them. At that time the British politicians took the same attitude to the American rebels as Napoleon forty years later took to Wellington on the morning of Waterloo. The war would be a picnic and would soon be over. It was on this visit to London that Romney painted the famous portrait of Joseph Brant. On his return to America he fought like an Indian Montrose, moving his guerrillas with lightning speed through the wilds to strike at the American where he was least expected. Personally, he was never defeated. The British defeats occurred elsewhere, and after peace was signed in 1783 the inevitable happened. Brant's petition to Congress to honour the old royal treaty with the Indians was rejected; after all, possession of the Indian reserves had been one of the many less idealistic motives

behind the entire War of Independence. Brant and his people were now in the same wretched plight as the white Loyalists.

But though the British government recklessly ceded to the new Republic all the continent between the present Canadian-American border and the Spanish possessions; though they gave away, partly in ignorance, far more than they need have given or ought to have given because most of the hinterland of today's United States between the Appalachians and the Rockies had been explored by French Canadians, they were at least in a better position to save face with their loyal friends in the New World, because north of the new border were vast empty lands which could receive the Loyalists.

The British government still retained title to the empty territories of Upper Canada. In no case, after their military defeat, could they have saved the Indian territories in western New York, so now they gave to Joseph Brant every assistance in settling his people north of the new border. In fact, they gave him the pick of Upper Canada, and the land he chose was in the Grand River Valley. Two strips of land six miles wide on either side of the river from its mouth to its source were guaranteed to Brant and his Mohawks by royal treaty. The Mohawks moved in and made the centre of the new settlement at Brant's Ford and there was built a new and larger Mohawk Chapel. It is there today. Before Joseph Brant died, he had translated into Mohawk St. Mark's Gospel and the English Book of Common Prayer.

But this remarkable man had also been extremely reckless in his guardianship of his people's new heritage in Canada. He could not understand the law; after all, he was an Indian chief rather than a politician like his father. By nature generous—it flattered his ego to be able to give splendid gifts—he was a soft touch for anyone who wanted some of his people's lands. The plain truth is not merely that he was most cynically conned; he laid himself open to being conned, and the Canadian land speculators had little to learn from anyone, not even from Moses Cleaveland. Toward the end of his life, Joseph Brant must have realized that he had failed in his last years; failed so badly that in the eyes of some American historians he was virtually a traitor. On his deathbed in 1808, he is recorded as saying, "Have pity on the poor Indian. [Did he—probably he did—think of himself as a white man?] If you can get any influence with the great, endeavour to do them all the good you can. O my father, the chariot of Israel and the horsemen thereof!"

So died on the banks of the Grand River a man who was as surely a father of the great province of Ontario as Simcoe or any other you can name. Frankly, it makes me want to vomit to hear educated men, skilful in the law and in business, condemn a man like Joseph Brant merely because he was naive and perhaps vain. Indeed, he had a great deal to be vain about. In his own way Joseph Brant was a minor miracle, his genes a mixture of Indian, Celt, and Anglo-Saxon. Born in a weird kind of manor house in a savage country to a wild Irish father of genius and a pure-bred Indian mother, he became a devout Christian and probably understood the religion of Jesus as simply and naturally as did the German and Balkan tribesmen of the late Roman Empire. It is at any rate something that the Mohawks still retain some of the old reserved land along the banks of the Grand River and that their reservation is the richest in North America. Though that is not saying much.

White settlement in the Grand River Valley began in 1798 with the sale by Joseph Brant to white speculators of six blocks of Indian land totalling 94,102 acres. The chief man in this posse of operators was the Methodist Loyalist, Colonel Beasley, and after some shady business on his part, the tract came into the possession of the most diligent settlers any young country could desire, German Mennonites from Pennsylvania.

Whole families came up in Conestoga wagons hauled by slow oxen, and in 1824 a substantial immigration began from Germany itself. Out of their labours, over the years grew the large and extremely prosperous twin cities of Waterloo and Berlin. Owing to the hysterical hostility of propaganda-maddened English-speaking Canadians in the 1914 war, the name of Berlin was changed to Kitchener, but in view of what we now know of Horatio Lord Kitchener, only a jingo could believe that the change of name was an improvement. Anyway—a matter much more important—the first lager beer to be brewed in Canada was brewed in Berlin in 1840, and out of a Waterloo grist mill there developed what now is the world's largest distilling company, known as the House of Seagram. Another native of Ontario's Berlin was a man who held power longer than any archon, consul, prime minister, or president in the history of democracy, William Lyon Mackenzie King.

As a result of the generally haphazard individual immigration that characterized the slow growth of Canada in the nineteenth century, the Grand River Valley acquired the pattern of the true Canadian mosaic. In 1816, Galt was founded by William Dickson. Eleven years later, Guelph was founded on the Speed River by John Galt. These two towns, together with Caledonia and Fergus, were predominantly Scotch.

So today, as you travel through this pleasant country, you see ruddy Scotch faces, paler English ones, robust German physiques, and the darker, more mysterious eyes of the first settlers, most of whom have become almost indistinguishable from their white neighbours.

The year, 1908; the place, Port Credit, Ontario.
Here, fifteen miles west of Toronto, the Credit River empties into Lake Ontario.
Today, there is a sleek yacht basin and marina here.

Interlude

Once upon a time there was a great city which tried to bury a small river. Its concrete and asphalt spread for several hundred square miles over lush farmland; its concrete, steel, and glass rose in narrow oblongs hundreds of feet into the sky.

The city's growth was the delight of investors, land speculators, producers of consumable articles, and the far-sighted men who had got into the construction business at just the right time. The sulphur dioxide of the city's high prosperity made the air its citizens breathed almost as tan as the skins of its richer ones when they disembarked at the airport after the Florida and Nassau vacations.

The city's suburbs grew out beside and over the little river, and the highways, thruways, crossroads, side roads, up-and-down roads, subway tunnels, and express routes twined in and around like the lianas of a tropical rain forest as it steadily became a graver problem to convey the hundreds of thousands of office workers from the high towers to the outlying dormitories. The river was almost invisible at the point where it entered the lake after its brief journey through the rich tillage out of lovely farmland doomed soon to be covered with more concrete growth.

The river was guided out of its beautiful little delta through a tunnel constructed underneath two mighty rivers of concrete over which thundered traffic so dense and constant that often it became two moving walls between the city and its lake.

Then came an autumn day when a hurricane which had originated two thousand miles to the south-west and had spent days churning the Atlantic into gigantic waves, suddenly turned toward the north-west and roared with full force over the continent to explode over the mighty city of concrete. The wind roared and the sky fell. Subsequently one of the city's many scientists computed that on a single day no less than 322 million tons of water fell into the city. On the chance that a visual comparison may assist a statistic-bludgeoned human imagination, it can be said that this was a weight approximately 280 times greater than the combined weight of all the ships in the largest navy the world has ever known—the Royal Navy of Great Britain at the end of the First World War.

Now where else could the water go except into the channel of that little river the mighty city had thought was tucked safely out of sight forever? The little river became more than a Niagara; inside of a few hours it turned into a flood. Houses collapsed into it, vehicles of all kinds disappeared in it, some not to be discovered until years later. More than forty of the bridges built over it to carry the roads and highways tributary to the city's concrete Amazons and Congos were swept away in the river. Chairs, tables, beds, mattresses, window frames, sides of wooden houses, and newspapers gushed through the river's little mouth into the lake and there they floated, with the occasional wild goose and wild seagull perching on them. Eighty-two of the city's citizens were drowned.

When it was all over, the city's computers translated what had happened into the appropriate statistics. The physical damage cost $17,699,280; fighting the flood and clearing away the debris cost $607,800; emergency relief including continuing provision for widows and orphans cost $836,500; emergency precautions against recurrence cost $5,500,000. Thus, when the bills were all in and tabulated, the total cost was $24,643,580.

The little river was the Humber and the mighty city was Toronto.

THE SEASONS

OF THE RIVER

The
land
stirs
to the
first
touch
of
spring

*St. John River,
New Brunswick.*

Renewal is promised in the shout of running water

Rideau River, Ontario.   *Credit River, Ontario.*

Summer brings fun to the river

Yukon River, Yukon Territory.   *Columbia River, British Columbia.*   Below: *Miramichi River, New Brunswick.*

Midsummer madness transforms an austere northern land

Columbia River, British Columbia.

Trout River, Newfoundland.

St. Lawrence River, Ontario.

Saskatchewan River, Saskatchewan

The cool of autumn: colour, thanksgiving, and preparing

Previous page:
Bow River, Alberta,

Musquodoboit River, Nova Scotia.

Next page:
Mackenzie River, Northwest Territories.

To
every
thing is
a season,
and a time to
every purpose
under the
heaven

ECCLESIASTES III.

Graveyard of the paddlewheelers, Yukon River, Whitehorse, Yukon Territory.

168

The Red

RIVER OF PARADOX

It is a tragedy of English letters that Rudyard Kipling's values were such that most of us feel we should apologize if we quote him. Actually, he had some remarkable insights. Such a phrase as "What do they know of England, who only England know?" may have been used originally as a mingled boast and sneer, but the idea behind it is universal. It can be applied to any country, province, or city on earth; it can even be applied to individuals. What do we know of ourselves, if we know no other people but our own families?

Kipling's well-worn sentence has constantly come to my mind in connection with the prairies. If a person has lived solely on the prairie, I don't think he can really know it—not in the context of the general human experience—unless he has lived elsewhere for a while. That is why nearly all novels of prairie life have been written by prairie people who moved to cities in the east.

But the reverse also holds true, at least in my own case. Having grown up in a little province by the sea, its experience to some extent recorded by the literatures of maritime peoples from the Greeks to the English, I was appalled when I first found myself on the prairie. It was as alien to me as the moon's surface. I wondered how anyone could endure life in a land which seemed to me so stark. Later on I realized that what I really feared here was the idea of my own littleness. Later still I learned that the prairie's monotony contains inner beauties and harmonies as subtle as those of a Bach fugue. But it is a challenge to the soul, just the same. It is also a challenge to the eye.

For the prairie can be wonderfully beautiful, once we have learned how to look at it. That is why Frederick Philip Grove's *Over Prairie Trails* is such a haunting book, a book so much more impressive than his novels. The beauty of the prairie sky is in it, and the mystery of the prairie winter. But I myself had to be on the prairie for a while before I could see it as Grove did. My whole attitude toward alien regions altered when I heard the prairie sing. And so to the Red River.

Before I became acquainted with the Red, I shared the general belief that it is the dullest river in Canada. It is not, of course. It is the most surprising river we have in the whole land. It is unlike any other I know.

To look casually at the Red in Winnipeg nobody would ever think this. Brown and lazy, it twines through the flat city with the motion of a convolvulus and then it wanders out again into the apparent sameness of the Manitoba plain. Not even after it has received the Assiniboine does its appearance alter much, for though the Assiniboine virtually doubles its volume, the difference in the river's size passes almost unnoticed in the huge land through which it flows. In Winnipeg the Assiniboine looks like the Red's identical twin, and before the two streams join in the city's heart, strangers frequently mistake one for the other. But from the air you can see quite a difference in their characters. Seen from above, the Red looks like a brown worm wriggling directly north through the grass. The Assiniboine, seen from above, has something of a sweep to its course: it swings out of sight across the western horizon with an air of adventure.

The Red River is not really a system, though it does have its tributaries. Nor, as North American rivers go, is it long. From its southern source in Minnesota to its discharge into Lake Winnipeg its total length is only 555 miles, some fifty miles less than the length of its chief so-called tributary, the Assiniboine. The parent stream issues from Traverse Lake in Minnesota under the name of Bois de Sioux, and when this little stream unites with the Otter Tail in the small town of Breckenridge, the Red River proper begins. In the United States they call it the Red River of the North to distinguish it from the larger Red River which joins the Mississippi in Louisiana.

Once the Red finds its true course, it proceeds directly north according to the map, but does so with a steady wriggling motion worthy of the ancient Meander. Sleek and muddy, its current is so sluggish that a strong contrary wind can bring it to a halt. Its banks are ominously low, and for nearly all of its course the Red seems utterly undramatic in normal seasons. It forms some of the boundary between Minnesota and South Dakota, and all of the boundary between Minnesota and North Dakota. It wriggles through Fargo, through Grand Forks, through a number of tank towns hard to tell apart into which farmers of Yankee, Scandinavian, Teutonic, and east-European origin drive from the prairie to attend church or the little movie house, to buy necessities and discuss prices of wheat, to grumble about the weather and listen to juke-boxes in restaurants operated by Greeks, Chinese, or anyone else who does not want to be a farmer. These main-street towns below the border have changed hardly at all since Sinclair Lewis wrote about Gopher Prairie. But they do have the Red River, which Gopher Prairie did not. The Red wriggles on, picking up a number of small prairie streams, most of them dried out in summer, all of them in rainy springs cataracting into the main channel in sluices of liquid mud. Just below the little town of Pembina, which claims to be "historical" and actually is (though the passing traveller would never guess so from its appearance), the Red crawls across the international border into Canada. Barely a quarter of its length is in Manitoba, but these final miles are by far the most interesting along the river's course.

I find myself able to describe the Red in general terms only in a series of paradoxes.

The first is the contrast between its colour and that of the prairie through which it flows: the prairie here is not red at all, but charcoal black. The reason for the Red's colour is the depth of its trench. It is a shallow trench compared to the Saskatchewan's—a most important point in the river's history—but deep enough to lie well below the black topsoil in which the Manitoba wheat grows. It is carved right into a subsoil clay which bakes hard in drought and in rain turns into a thick gumbo soup slippery enough to ski on.

The second paradox is more difficult to make clear, for to me it was the most surprising of all: the Red River, more than any other stream I have seen outside of England, reminds me of the Thames. As this statement would have sounded incredible if anyone had made it to me a few years ago, I should explain what I mean.

Manitoba is as unlike southern England as any country you could find outside high mountain ranges. Southern England is Constable country, and who could imagine Constable painting a Manitoba sectional farm? The southern English landscape is the subtlest, probably, in the world, and its valleys have enchanted the poets for centuries. But the Red River Valley is not a valley at all as people usually understand the meaning of that word. It is a colossal plain, table-flat. Ocean-like in size, but flatter than any ocean because it has no waves, it is black in spring, golden in August, white in winter. Its sole companion is a vast sky constantly changing above it, constantly moving above it.

Yet in this apparently stark setting the Red River again and again creates little aquatic scenes of pure loveliness. Splendid trees follow its banks sloping down with some undergrowth from the prairie table to the water's edge. As you drive along the plain and see these trees, if you did not know what caused them you would never guess a river was there. You come to the river suddenly; you walk or drive along the flatness, and abruptly you are at its trench. And more than once, standing on the prairie table to look down at a reach of the Red, I thought of the great reach the Thames makes at Goring. Once when an apron of soft green grass stretched out into the water, I even remembered Runnymede.

Then there is the delta. It contains more than a hundred square miles of brown marsh grass and water, with a few willows interspersed. Its expanse is as flat as the rest of Manitoba and it is virtually unsettled. As you near the forks where the three main channels of the river wind through the sedge into Lake Winnipeg, this empty region alive with swirling birds can seem as awe-inspiring as the lonely delta of the Slave. It can be incredibly beautiful, too. In late autumn and early winter the northern lights have a habit of rising above it, and their weird light, filtering through the man-high marsh grass, translates this whole region out of the world, translates it into patterns of unearthly lumination shifting through a landscape out of which all life has vanished save for the muskrats, otters, beavers, and fish. For when the brightest auroras shine, the birds of the delta have flown south.

Yet in this same delta, miles from any settlement, on a fine spring afternoon I found myself in a channel so small, still, intimate, and fragrant that I thought of the most civilized stream I know, the tiny Cherwell curving through may blossoms and bird songs under the wall of Magdalen, under Magdalen Bridge, and then through Christ Church meadows to the Thames. I could almost dream I was back there. Then there was a sharp slap on the water and the lad who was steering my boat rose and pointed. We had come to a beaver dam and the beaver had gone under water to hide.

The Red has other contrasts of a general nature, and not all of them are charming. This same river I have called both gentle and awe-inspiring can also, in its higher reaches, look as squalid as a dried-out irrigation ditch in certain seasons and vicissitudes of climate. During the great drought of 1934 there was a period of six months when the Red above Winnipeg virtually disappeared. In all that time not even a bucketful of water went through Fargo, though Fargo is about 150 miles from its source. When winds blew they set clouds of dust smoking along the river's trench, which seemed the most blighted part of the whole parched land.

Sixteen years later the Red ceased to be a river once more, but this time it turned itself into a lake.

Now, to combine all these contrasts into the single one which is the principal cause of the others — the Red behaves in this contradictory way because, geologically speaking, it is not a river at all. It is a surviving remnant of what once was the largest fresh-water lake in existence, at least in recent geological history.

Lake Agassiz—so the geologists call it after the Swiss scientist who studied the movements of ice caps—was the product of the last of the glaciers which shaped the present form of the central Canadian plain, together with much of Minnesota, all of North Dakota, and most of South Dakota. It is with the origins of Lake Agassiz that everyone must begin who wishes to understand the nature of the central prairie, of the prairie lakes, and of the Red River itself. The time to begin is a hundred thousand years ago (give or take twenty thousand) because it was then that the first ice age began. Since that time there have been four major advances and retreats of the polar ice cap in America, and the effects of them all are plainly visible in Manitoba today.

The prairie was not always as it is now. Once it was a normal, rolling land very like the terrain between Ottawa and Lake Ontario, with hills and depressions and little streams. But as quadrillions of tons of ice formed on it, the weight of the ice slowly crushed the land, and when the ice moved, it shaved off every hill and depression until the prairie as we know it was formed. In its progress south, the ice finally pressed against the height of land which extends just south of Traverse Lake in Minnesota. This small unremarkable elevation, today crossed almost unnoticed by thousands of tourists in their cars, is one of the most important land-heights in North America, for it is the north-south continental divide. It is the reason why the Missouri curves to the southeast to join the Mississippi, and why the Red and all the Canadian rivers flow toward the north.

But—and this is another curious contradiction in the Red's history—there was a time when the Red *did* flow south. While the glacier still existed in the north, south was the only way some of the water of Lake Agassiz could go, so there was a dribble over the continental shelf which eventually found its way into the Mississippi.

Now picture the scene in central Canada as it was during the many thousand years when the climate was growing warmer and the ice was melting. As the glacier withdrew and the southern ice turned into water, this water was captured in a basin bounded in the south by the height of land which now is the north-south divide, and in the north by the still existing wall of glacial ice. This huge catch-pit was Lake Agassiz, and for several aeons the Red—as has been explained—drained some of it off in a southerly direction.

In the period of its greatest extent, Lake Agassiz was more than seven hundred miles long and two hundred and fifty miles wide. Its total area exceeded that of the combined five Great Lakes today. It covered Northern Minnesota, the northeastern sections of South Dakota, and pretty well all of Manitoba. Until the ice retreated far enough into the north to enable the water to be carried off by Hudson Bay—the proximity of the bay explains why the glacier finally went off so quickly—Lake Agassiz drained into Lake Superior and for a time was a part of the St. Lawrence system, some of its waters reaching the Atlantic past Quebec.

As the glacier continued to retreat, mastodons and primitive men lived along the shores of Lake Agassiz, and the remains of millions of dead organisms sank to the bottom to enrich what later became the dry land the settlers put to the plough. Not until ten to fifteen thousand years ago—only yesterday in the time-span of a geologist—did the main body of Lake Agassiz finally disappear. Behind it remains sizable bodies of water called Lakes Winnipeg, Winnipegosis, Manitoba, the Upper and Lower Red Lakes, Lake of the Woods, Rainy Lake, and that maze of mosquito-breeding ponds, sloughs, and midget-sized lakes in the western Shield. Also there remained two important rivers, the Nelson and the Red. Today the Red, joined by lazy tributaries, worms through the central bed of old Lake Agassiz.

That is why, when certain weather conditions conspire, the Red River reverts atavistically to the behaviour of the lake which fathered it. In simpler language, when the Red flooded there was hardly anything the people could do to stop it under natural conditions. You can fight an ordinary river by means of dykes and levees, but nobody can stem the overflow of a river which turns itself into a lake on a continental plain where the highest elevation seldom exceeds twelve feet.

In the early spring of 1852, David Anderson, Bishop of Rupert's Land, was able to reflect with some reason that religion, civilization, and tradition were taking root in the enormous frontier diocese under his care. In his school near old Fort Garry one pupil had just completed the reading of Aristotle's *Ethics* in the original Greek. Several others had worked their way through Herodotus into Thucydides, four lads were studying the Gospels in Italian, most of the school knew them in French, and the whole school had recited a psalm in Hebrew and the Lord's Prayer in eight different languages "including the two leading dialects of our country." For a thousand miles around this little human island the wilderness and the empty plain extended, but within the colony itself the farms were prosperous, families were at least earning a livelihood, and the desperate hardships of the early days along the Red River were becoming memories.

But into this scene of peace, like a tocsin, came tidings the settlers dreaded, for they knew from experience what was coming to them. At Pembina, a hundred-odd miles to the south, the Red River was beginning to flood. Communications were slow and inadequate, and at first nobody knew for certain how serious the situation was. But they did know the habits of the river. The Red moves slowly, heavily, but with a fatal sureness. By May 2 the situation at Fort Garry was alarming and people began leaving their homes. The first bridges went as the river swelled, and a controlled anguish of panic was framed, as it were, in a scene of perfect peace. On May 8, Bishop Anderson noted that "the aurora borealis was brilliant at night, like a semi-circular arch of tailed comets." The next day he "awoke to the sweet singing of birds, and soon heard the news that the waters were stationary at Pembina." But they were not stationary, as the Bishop soon discovered.

"There has been today a peculiar noise, like the sound of many waters, such as one may imagine the distant sound of Niagara: it was the pouring of water over the plains." So sudden, so immense, was this flood that some of the settlers could not believe that a stream as innocent-looking as the Red could contain all that water. "They thought the Missouri was coming down on them," the Bishop noted in his diary.

But May 10 was another beautiful morning of singing birds, though the water was now flooding into the granaries and stores, and the people were working frantically to save the food on which they depended for their lives that summer. The Red River colony, even as late as 1852, was the most isolated civilized settlement in America; if catastrophe came to it, there was nobody but themselves to whom the people could look for help. The day passed into a bright Manitoba evening, but now the churchyard, "the seedplot of God", was entirely covered, and everywhere houses were awash or floating away. Three days later the Bishop noted that a tempest arose in the night, and that the resurrected Lake Agassiz roared like the sea. On Sunday a few days after the storm, Bishop Anderson's congregation rowed or paddled to a spot of dry land on the edge of the waters and there he preached a sermon on the destruction of Sodom and Gomorrah. At evensong on that same day he preached on Noah's dove, and the choir, standing in the open, "sang most beautifully Spofforth's *Te Deum.*"

But the waters, oblivious of the prayers of the people and the sermons of the Bishop, deepened, gained, and spread. On May 17 a boat was rowed through the churchyard gate and across the plain until it blundered into the main channel of the river, now foaming with a velocity of ten knots, and the boat was nearly lost in it. Wreckage floating everywhere reminded the Bishop to quote from the storm scene in the first book of Vergil's *Aeneid: Arma virumque tabulaeque et Troia gaza per undas*—"the arms of men, pictures and Trojan treasures in the waves". Now men, women, and children were drowning, cattle were floating feet up, stoves and ploughs lashed to rafts had been carried away and lost forever, some of them swept by the current down through the delta into Lake Winnipeg itself. But when dry land was reached, "violets and buttercups, raspberry and strawberry blossoms were grateful to the eye," and beyond the water's brink Bishop Anderson saw the men who had saved both ploughs and oxen working to the point of exhaustion to turn the sod before it would be too late to plant a crop. Mosquitoes, thriving in the dampness, formed clouds as thick as midges.

Four days later the flood reached its height and became stationary, and the Bishop, hoisting a sail in his "birch-rind canoe", went for a long voyage across the prairie in beautiful weather. The farmland was now transformed into a lake several hundred miles long and about twelve miles wide, with maples in full leaf protruding from it and birds singing in the branches, the gables of houses projecting from the water and families floating about in boats and on rafts. At 3:00 a.m. the next day "the sunrise was like a sunrise at sea," with the addition of the bird songs and the fresh green of the trees. Another Sabbath came. The day before it the Bishop had seen a flag hoisted to signify that the flood was abating, so his text was from Isaiah: "When the enemy shall come in like a flood, the spirit of the Lord shall lift up a standard against him." A few days after this, as the Bishop noted in still another Latin quotation, land began to appear above the waters. Quickly the waters drained off leaving a sea of slime which the sun soon baked to a scum, and into this miserable land the tired people returned.

Three weeks after the height of the flood, the first boats of the Long Portage brigade passed Fort Garry on their way west via the Saskatchewan to meet the brigades descending from the Mackenzie fifteen hundred miles away. With them they brought American newspapers from the south which told of a recent flood in Yorkshire in which nearly a hundred lives were lost. The Bishop reflected thankfully that the Lord had dealt with them graciously here, that "now the melody of former times may be renewed," and that in the future, when he took his seat in the hall where the daily worship was held, there would be "behind me the same engraving as before, that from the original of Andrea Sacchi, of Noah rearing his altar of thanksgiving, when saved from the waters of the flood."

This mid-nineteenth century description of a Red River flood can serve well for a record of nearly all of them. The flood described by Bishop Anderson was worse than the one in 1950 (the last severe flood the river will ever suffer). But the behaviour of the Red River in all of its floods has been pretty much the same. From 1776, the Red flooded seriously a dozen times, made a nuisance of itself often, and not once was it successfully combated. On each separate occasion the causes of the flood have been the same.

The first is the sluggish pace of the current: the drop in the Red from Fargo to Lake Winnipeg is so slight that the river's trench cannot carry off more than a normal quantity of water in a given time. The second cause is a series of heavy autumn rains followed by a quick frost which freezes the moisture into the prairie, preserving it for future action in the spring. Quick frosts of this sort are very frequent here; sometimes they occur in the first week of October and remain. The next cause is heavy winter snow. If these two latter acts of God are followed by a late spring, a sudden prolonged thaw, and heavy spring rains, the Red turns itself into a miniature Lake Agassiz.

In the flood of 1950, some 100,000 Canadians and 20,000 Americans were driven from their homes, fifteen thousand farm buildings and business blocks were inundated, and the loss of life might have been serious had not the Canadian Army taken over. On that occasion, as Winnipeg people vividly recall, the army was prepared to declare martial law and remove 320,000 civilians according to the plan worked out for southern England in 1940 if the Germans had crossed the Channel.

The stream looks so innocent; yet—because it is a survival of a lake—it can become deadly. As early as 1880, when Sir Sandford Fleming was in charge of the survey for the Canadian Pacific Railway, he recommended that the railway crossing of the Red should be located twenty miles below Winnipeg where the banks are higher and the flooding less serious. Winnipeg at that time was a small community and might easily have been moved, but people learn little from past experience and the citizens decided to remain where they were.

When I was in Winnipeg in the spring of 1960, it so happened that a convention of engineers was held in the hotel at the same time to make general recommendations for the construction of a floodway system to protect Winnipeg from further floods. After the catastrophe of 1950, the federal government had established the Red River Basin Investigation at the request of the province of Manitoba. Searching the records, the commission discovered that there had been several worse floods than the most recent one. In 1861, the Red had gone two feet higher than in 1950; in 1852 (the one described by Bishop Anderson) it had gone four feet higher; in 1826 it had gone six feet higher; and in 1776—a period in which no accurate measurements could be made—there had been a flood so enormous that it became a legend among the plains Indians. The evidence was clear that the Red can be expected to flood, on the average, every thirty-six years.

One of my uncles, an engineer who had done a good deal of work connected with the Saskatchewan, showed me the results of the conference, including the plans for a floodway which would divert the overflow of the river around Greater Winnipeg. The projected cost seemed so prodigious that I came away believing that the floodway would never be built, but in this I was wrong.

Two years later, in October 1962, under the premiership of the Hon. Dufferin Roblin, the work was begun and it was completed in 1968. During the construction period, mercifully, no flood occurred and when the next one comes, the floodway will take care of it.

The principle behind its construction is elementary, based on the nature of the terrain and the habits of the river. Under normal conditions, the Red will continue to wiggle through Winnipeg as it has always done, but if the water rises to a flow of 30,000 cubic feet per second, it will commence to divide naturally between the Floodway and the river itself. The Floodway is assisted by dykes built at strategic points. It is 29 miles long, its width varies from 380 feet to 540 feet, its depth from 30 to 65 feet, the channel being so designed that the maximum velocity of flow will be about five feet per second.

Recollecting that any river in its natural state is a geological agent, we can obtain from this man-made channel some idea of just what potent geological agents great streams like the Fraser, the Columbia, and the Mackenzie are. In order to make this Floodway Channel around Winnipeg, in flat, soft soil, the bulldozers had to remove 100 million cubic yards of earth, 30 percent more than was required for the excavation of the Canadian section of the St. Lawrence Seaway between Montreal and Ontario and 40 percent as much as for the Panama Canal. It took ten million man-hours of work, with most of the real work performed by the giant earth-moving machines.

People in the East think of the three prairie provinces as similar and lump them together under the general term "the West". Yet their histories are quite different. The Red River Valley, in antiquity of settlement, is much older than Saskatchewan and Alberta. Though all three provinces have a common background of fur trading, though the Vérendrye family explored them all (the elder La Vérendrye established Fort Rouge at the forks of the Red and Assiniboine in 1738), it is a fact of some significance that the homesteaders of the two westernmost provinces had the railways behind them at least most of the way, and that the nineteenth century was two-thirds over before serious farming began in Saskatchewan. But the Red River Valley settlement not only dates back to an earlier period in the story of western America; it emerged from an earlier stage in the social and moral evolution of the Europe from which the settlers came.

This is not the place to tell the story of the Selkirk Settlement, the full implications of which were greater than have been expressed in any local history of the settlement I have so far read. The story of the settlement began across the ocean. Originally, the conditions which made the settlement seem reasonable to Lord Selkirk arose out of conditions shameful to the ruling classes of the British Isles, whether English, Scottish, or Irish.

Departure of colonists from York Fort to Rockfort, Sept. 6, 1821.

Summer view in the environs of Fort Douglas on the Red River, 1822.

Winter fishing on the ice of the Assiniboine and Red rivers.

in 1812 came the first handful of pioneers

Among the Red River settlers enlisted by Scottish Lord Selkirk was the Swiss family Rindisbacher — father, mother, and six children. The second son, Peter, left us some of the earliest known pictures of the West (see opposite page). The Red was their only lifeline, leading up to Hudson Bay and thence to Europe.

Twenty miles north of Winnipeg, the Red skirts Lower Fort Garry.

Well before the end of the eighteenth century, the Highland Scotch were virtually finished as a force within their own land. Isolated for centuries in mountains which could never support a large population, living in warring clans ruled by patriarchal chiefs intensely jealous and for the most part devoid of intelligence, the Highlanders had believed they were braver than anyone else, and in the physical sense they possibly were braver than most. But it was not their valour which had kept their antiquated system intact for so long; it was the poverty of their country. Had it been worth enough, English and Lowland cannon would have taken it from them. A people whose concept of valour was the same as that of Achilles could never have held out against the military tactics even of a seventeenth-century English army. Montrose, after all, was not a Highlander. Though it is true that only Highland or Montenegrin troops could have endured as his did, their endurance would have availed nothing if Montrose's leadership had been of the usual Highland kind. Nothing was more typical of the old Highland mentality than the behaviour of their most powerful clan at the battle of Culloden in 1745. The Macdonalds, placed by blunder or jealousy on the left wing, refused to fight because the post of honour on the right had been given to another clan. Homer would have understood such people; indeed, he described them better than any Scottish writer has ever done, for he was not a sentimentalist.

No sane Scotsman could blame the English for treating the Highlanders as they did after the 1745 rebellion. Their blind loyalty to their chiefs, who in turn were blindly loyal to a worthless Pretender, had given the English no choice save to uproot and destroy the ancient clan system.

But these Highlanders were magnificent human material, and what was done to them when they were helpless was as disgraceful as what was done to the poor Irish by rack-renting landlords and stupid aristocratic brutes like Lord Lucan. They were enclosed so that landlords might turn the glens into sheep runs, and many of the landlords who committed this crime were not English, but Scotch. If the crimes committed against them were not denounced as were the crimes committed against the Irish, it was because the Highlanders took so long to be weaned from the family concept of society in which they were reared. Most of them covered up the selfish callousness of the chiefs who were supposed to be their fathers. They were too ashamed of them to complain in public after they were deported overseas to Canada or Australia, or left to starve. Seldom did a Highlander place the blame where it belonged, as did the unknown Canadian voyageur who wrote, somewhere on the western rivers, that he and his kind were exiles from their native land "that a degenerate lord might boast his

sheep." Yet even this poet, in the one verse of his song which everyone knows, uttered the permanent Highland home-sickness which stopped their lips from the final denunciation:

> From the lone shieling of the misty island
> Mountains divide us, and the waste of seas—
> But still the blood is strong, the heart is Highland,
> And we in dreams behold the Hebrides.

There was something Judaic in the Scotch of the north, just as there was something Judaic in their fate, and in their ultimate triumph when finally they learned to master the techniques and the culture of their conquerors. What Scotland lost, Canada was to gain: and Australia, New Zealand, and the United States also, but in proportion more was gained by Canada.

For these reasons it is difficult for anyone of Scotch descent to sneer at Lord Selkirk, despite what his recklessness, and at times his arrogance, did to many people. Lord Selkirk was one of the very few chiefs of his time who felt a genuine compassion for his people, and made it his life's work to help them. While everyone recognized that the old clan way of life had become economically impossible, and that ultimately most of the Highlanders would have to leave the glens, Selkirk at least tried to find a home for them. We can imagine him looking at the maps which were coming from the New World, perhaps even talking with Highlanders who had been west with the canoes, or with Orkneymen of the Hudson's Bay Company. We can imagine the great idea forming in his mind: across the sea, on the empty Canadian plain, was all the land his land-hungry people could desire, so why not send them there? But like many honest idealists, Selkirk was not informed of the realities his people would encounter on that empty plain.

More than once the Napoleonic Wars exercised an influence on Canadian history, but never more ironically than they did now. The Emperor's Berlin Decrees had all but ruined the fur market. When it was impossible to ship furs into the continent, the stock of the Hudson's Bay Company dropped from £250 a share to £60. Lord Selkirk saw his opportunity. Though he had no interest in the fur trade, he had a most lively interest in the country the Gentlemen Adventurers claimed to own. Taking advantage of the low price of shares, he bought control of the Hudson's Bay Company. Then he chartered a few small ships, filled them with homeless Celts, placed the party under the leadership of a stubborn man called Miles Macdonnell, and sent them with his blessing across the western ocean bound through Hudson Strait to York Factory at the foot of Hudson Bay.

In 1811 the first band of settlers reached York Factory, and there they wintered. The next summer they paddled seven hundred and fifty miles south up the Nelson River, then up Lake Winnipeg and the Red to its confluence with the Assiniboine. Though they did not know it, during those same weeks Napoleon was leading his *grande armée* across a land equally flat, and potentially almost as cold, from Smolensk to Moscow. Although the settlers were very few, and Napoleon's army more than half a million men, their experiences the following winter were not dissimilar.

No body of settlers in Canada ever endured more prolonged or terrifying suffering than did the Selkirk people. Idealists are seldom good planners, and Lord Selkirk was no exception to this general rule. His people arrived without ploughs, and pathetically they tried to scratch the surface of that gigantic plain with hoes and spades. Their sole line of communication ran back seven hundred and fifty miles to a tiny fort visited once a year by ships making a dangerous passage from home. Soon they were starving. Almost as bad as that, soon they were engaged in a civil war with the men of the North West Company, who themselves were engaged in a desperate struggle for survival against the Bay.

Settlement, as the Nor'westers always knew, is fatal to the fur trade, and here was a settlement encamped across their lines of communication. The Nor'westers attacked the homes of the settlers and burned some of them to the ground. The Indians, perhaps urged on by the fur-traders, attacked and killed some of them. In the Red River delta I have been shown hollows in the ground where some of the Selkirk people concealed their children, placing sods or marsh grass over them, when the Indians attacked. But somehow the core of the settlement survived.

For nine awful years, while Lord Selkirk, driven almost mad by a mixture of compassion, anger, and guilt, fought with the leaders of the North West Company, the wretched farmers on the Red River struggled to keep alive. They roamed up and down the river in search of buffalo. A decade after their arrival, small numbers of French Canadians appeared, made their little settlement at St. Boniface opposite Fort Garry, and shared the existence of their Scottish brothers. In 1826 the Red River itself rose against them, and in the worst flood recorded in its history, it washed away nearly all the meagre homes they had. For shelter, the survivors could only dig cellars in the plain, roof them with sods, and live through the winters under ground.

They persevered because this was all they could do. To return home was impossible. Summer was "a time of peace with hunger", winter a six months' white hell. In 1837 a plague of grasshoppers ate their crop and left them without seed for the next year. The winter following, two heroes walked a thousand miles to a point on the Mississippi where they believed that seed could be bought. They returned with two hundred bushels of wheat seed, a hundred of oats, and thirty of peas, and for the whole lot Lord Selkirk paid out of his own purse $600. Years later one of their descendants wrote: "Almost one might say that the Lord blessed that seed, for it saved the settlement."

The settlement which then grew and burgeoned was unique in America. Though the wilderness extended for a thousand miles in every direction around it, the moment the people "could eat their bread without weight and their potatoes without measure," schools and churches rose among them, books were imported from England, and some of their teachers were men trained in Edinburgh, Oxford, and Cambridge. In 1855, only three years after the flood described by Bishop David Anderson, an American journalist visited the Red River and on his return he wrote the following:

> There is a spot on this continent which travellers do not visit. Deserts, almost trackless, divide it from the habitations of men. To reach it, or once there to escape it, is an exploit of which one may almost boast. It is not even marked on the maps nor mentioned in the gazetteers.

Yet at the forks of the Red and the Assiniboine, this American visitor wrote that he had found dancing and good dining, several excellent wine cellars, one library, copies of *The Illustrated London News*, the latest novels of Dickens and Thackeray. "Intellectual conversation," he wrote, "might be had there as well as in Washington."

All these books, wines, and cultural influences had come to the Red River *from the north!*

The settlement remained isolated until several years after Confederation, its lines of communication now running south toward the head of steel in St. Paul. But one April day in 1871, there came floating down to Fort Garry a wooden scow loaded with eight men. They were "Canadians from Ontario"; they had bought the scow in the United States and come down the Red River aboard it intending to homestead on the plains. Though neither they nor the original settlers knew this at the time, those eight men were the advance guard of the homesteading avalanche which was to doom the fur trade, cause the two Riel Rebellions, accelerate the building of the Canadian Pacific Railway, and, by the century's end, turn the bed of Lake Agassiz into one of the richest wheat-producing regions on earth.

Today the Red River Valley is no longer "the West"; it is the geographical heart of Canada. It may also be the ethnic and social heart as well.

Here, facing one another across the river, are the two communities of Winnipeg and St. Boniface, one palpably Scotch-English-Canadian, the other palpably French-Canadian. But around these two original cores, indeed threaded through them, are the lines of a mosaic of peoples whose origins stem from all the nations of the Old World. In the little town of Selkirk just below the lower and larger Fort Garry, you can see this mosaic plain. The most prominent building is an onion-domed Ukrainian church. But within a stone's throw of it is a street called Britannia Avenue, the Anglican house of worship is called Christ Church, and there is even a street called after Toronto. In lower Fort Garry itself the style of stone cutting is pure Old Country, and the fort is as authentically British colonial as York Redoubt at the mouth of Halifax Harbour.

This continuance of tradition in the Red River Valley, it seems to me, has been and still is of priceless value. It has been one of the factors which saved Canada from becoming an amorphous melting pot with all sense lost of our ancestors' cultures in the Old World. Winnipeg has never seemed really provincial to me. For years, when John Dafoe was its editor, the Winnipeg *Free Press* was one of the most admired newspapers in the Commonwealth, and it spoke with an authority heard even in London. It seems to me a fact that the French-speaking people of Manitoba are less provincial in their attitude than are those of the parent province of Quebec. Did not

St. Boniface give to French Canada its finest prose writer in the person of Gabrielle Roy, who discovered Balzac as a little girl and became the first writer not a citizen of France to receive the *prix femina?*

Yet the Red River, though its settlements are now fairly old by western standards and just over three hours by air from Montreal, can still appear in one region so pristine that when you are there you can feel yourself the only man alive in the world.

On a spring morning I drove in a rented car to the delta, turned off at Petersfield into a little track leading inward, and came to its end in the Netley Marshes. It was the beginning of one of the finest days of my life, for there, at the end of the road, I found a camp with motor boats owned by a Canadian of Polish ancestry called Ed Chesley. When I told him I wanted to see the delta, there appeared in his face that look of friendship one sometimes sees in a man when a stranger reveals interest in the thing he loves. Quietly he asked his son Larry to prepare a boat, and while the fuel was being poured into the tank, we talked.

"There is so much to know here," Mr. Chesley said. "We spend our winters in Florida now, and I think I know every branch of the Everglades. But it is wilder

Early life at the Red River Settlement was a mixture of perils — from flood, famine, and savages. In these scenes, the young Rindisbacher catalogued the colonial types (Scotch, English, German, French, and Swiss) and depicted the murder of David Tulley and his family.

here, and there is more here. There is much, much more."

He told me of the Brokenhead Indian reservation just to the east of the delta, and a little about the flocks of birds. It was also he who showed me the depressions in the ground where the Selkirk settlers had hidden their children. Then his son called out that the boat was ready, I joined him, and Larry led me into the best duck-breeding area in North America.

The Red River delta, flat as the plain to the south of it, flat as the lake to the north of it, is an astonishingly large delta for a river relatively small. But the Red, one must remember, carries an abnormally large weight of silt in its waters. In that labyrinth of channels twisting through reeds and swamps a greenhorn would lose himself in fifteen minutes. But young Larry Chesley knew the delta as a man knows his own property. He took me into channel after channel while ducks of every species skittered away over the surface, or broke cover and took to the air. Marsh hawks, brilliant of colour and the size of eagles, beat slowly back and forth over that sea of reeds in which mice, rats, muskrats, otters, beavers, and fish lurk. Herons stood on one leg in shallow places; bush after bush was spangled with scarlet from the wings of roosting red-winged blackbirds; huge white pelicans, some of them weighing up to fifty pounds, floated on the water or rose with slow, heavy flappings of wings. We found the course of the Red River, sailed down it for a time, then turned off into one of its many little side channels—the one which reminded me of the Cherwell—went through the beaver dam I mentioned before and came out to another expanse where a game-warden's wooden tower stood in the marsh and in the flatness seemed as high as a skyscraper. We climbed it. Then in this new solitude the whole air was full of bird-songs for miles about, it vibrated with them, and as we returned to the boat a flight of mallard broke cover and flew away.

"In the fall," Larry said, "duck hunters come here from every place, and we take them out into the marshes. They jump-shoot from boats, or they shoot from blinds, or they use decoys." A little later he added: "Father and I go south after the birds leave here. Or did he tell you that? Last year in Mexico when I went shooting, some of the ducks I bagged may have been ducks I'd missed here a month earlier."

We reached the final forks of the Red where it divides into three channels, passed down the eastern branch, and entered Lake Winnipeg. We coasted along toward the mouth of the central channel which is almost invisible when you are out in the lake. The flat lake spread north over the horizon, the delta south into the prairie. The afternoon enclosed us along with hundreds of thousands of large fowl and the myriads of blackbirds and larks calling and shrilling in the higher light. Larry Chesley stopped the motor, and with the sinking sun streaming over the delta into our eyes, we floated absolutely alone on that sea-like remnant of old Lake Agassiz.

The Saskatchewan

STREAMS IN SOLITUDE

Of all the major rivers of this continent, the Saskatchewan seems to me the loneliest looking.
By this I mean the concept of it, the image of it
considered as a whole, for like any body of moving water
the river in section after section can be sprightly and full
of grace. In many places where I have sat beside it, the
Saskatchewan made me think of a smooth body pulsing
with life, a depth in it, a quiet tirelessness, and Marjorie
Wilkins Campbell has written well of the beauty of the
foam which washes down along its surface like white
lace.

Yet surely the Saskatchewan, when we think of it as a
whole, has within its image the great solitude of the
prairie it crosses. Endlessly winding, seldom dramatic
between the Rockies and the final spasm at Grand Rapids, the twin branches flow through the central plain in a
huge, wavering Y.

Often the Saskatchewan passes through bush and
parkland, and these were the regions most prized by the
fur-traders. But more often it winds through naked
plains, and the feeling of loneliness is in proportion to
the bareness of the land. The river is always below the
surface of the prairie and it seldom floods, for its trenches
are extremely deep. For hundreds of miles the trenches
of the two branches channel the waters easterly: hundreds of miles of tan, monotonous water with weeds and
wildflowers rife along the escarpments when sand-bars
protrude from the channels in late summer; hundreds of
miles of greenish-white ice against the flat white of the
plain in the six-month winter which seems so inter-
minable that the people in the river towns hold sweep-
stakes on the hour and minute of the spring break-up.
When finally the break-up comes it is the most awaited
moment in the seasonal life of the Saskatchewan. The ice
cracks, the floes pile up a dozen feet high, and occasionally bizarre.things can happen. Not long ago in Saskatoon a bewildered deer was carried through the heart of
the town on an ice pan while thousands of people
watched. Then, after a pause, comes the time of high
water when the twin branches race with foam as they
carry eastward the run-off from billions of tons of Rocky
Mountain snow.

The lonely feeling given by the Saskatchewan is different from what is felt on the Mackenzie because here
there are so many people. It is the nature of the prairie
landscape that a human being, a house, a grain elevator, a
moving train, even a village etched against the sky serves
only to enhance the sense of space. Standing on the
banks of the Saskatchewan, seeing it come out of one
horizon on its way into another, many a newcomer must
have felt he could go no farther into this enormousness
without losing all sense of who he was. The western Missouri used to give a similar sensation to many an American homesteader. But though the Missouri is a greater
river than the Saskatchewan, it lies farther south; it does
not have that final northern quality of making you feel
you are on the edge of nothing human. Stepping off a
train onto the wooden platform of one of those stark little
Saskatchewan river towns, many a settler must have
walked down to the river and watched the water coming
out of the prairie into the town—so tiny and alone in that
vast space—and then watched it going out again into the
prairie, and wondered if he would ever be equal to his
life in such a land. Some prairie people are indignant
when easteners use the word "stark" to describe their
towns. They shouldn't be. The very fact that towns like
Prince Albert exist and thrive in a place where recently
there was nothing but grass is a triumph. Can towns
become cities in two lifetimes?

For along most of the Saskatchewan, whether on the
North Branch or the South, the world has been reduced
to what W. O. Mitchell called the least common denom-
inator of nature, land and sky. There is also the effect of
the weather. It shifts constantly and with it the moods of
sky and land, and the river reflects all these moods with
total fidelity. Few sights in Canada are more peaceful
than the mirroring of the pastel sky-hues on the Saskatchewan on a fine summer day; none more chilling
than an eddy of snow in January when the thermometer
stands at forty or fifty below and the ice is too hard for a
curling stone. The winds here are visible: in summer you
see them as a throbbing radiance along a sea of grass, in
winter as a drifting lace of ice crystals along a sea of
snow.

My doctor father used to say that nature is usually
just, that what she takes with one hand she gives with the
other. The Saskatchewan country can be so bleakly stern
it shrivels the soul; it can also intoxicate with a deluge of
prolific loveliness that makes an English June seem
insipid by comparison. In the spring the voice of the
turtle is not heard much in this land, but the voices and
movements of a myriad of other birds, many of them
waterfowl, make hundreds of miles of clear atmosphere
quiver with sound and flash with colour and the very sky
thrill with the larks. The sloughs teem, the land deprived
by the long winter goes mad with the lust of recreating

the life the frost has killed. Moses would have understood this land. Had civilized men lived along the Saskatchewan three millenniums ago, the prairie country would have burgeoned with psalmists and prophets.

The Saskatchewan is not a simple stream but a system of waters having a combined length greater than that of the St. Lawrence or the Danube and draining a basin of 150,000 square miles, which includes much of the Alberta and Saskatchewan farmlands, a small corner of Montana, and (including the Nelson) much of northern Manitoba. The North Saskatchewan has a total drop from its glacial source of more than 7,000 feet, the South Branch a total drop of just over a mile. The river is seldom more than twelve feet deep, with many shoals and rapids, and after Prince Albert its average flow amounts to 56 million tons a day. To compare this with a man-made object, we can say that the daily tonnage of water carried by the lower Saskatchewan is sixty-four times greater than the tonnage of the S.S. *Queen Elizabeth I*, the largest liner ever built.

After the twin branches leave the Rockies, the most dramatic moment in their course occurs at Grand Rapids, just before the stream discharges into Lake Winnipeg. Here the river, five hundred feet wide between twenty-five-foot walls, flowing at a velocity of ten miles an hour, drops seventy-five feet over a distance of three miles.

In 1964 a dam was completed on the Grand Rapids section which produced the ninth largest man-made body of water in the world. In June of that year, to celebrate the completion of the dam, the engineers made an experimental shut-off which stopped the rapids entirely. The pools at the river mouth were filled with pickerel, northern pike, bass, goldeyes, and sturgeons and on that single day one commercial fisherman made a haul worth $1,400. The next day the gates were opened and the Saskatchewan flowed, under control, into Lake Winnipeg again.

Its strategic course as the principal prairie water route has made the Saskatchewan the second most indispensable of all the rivers which have played a part in Canadian history. The voyageurs followed one branch northwest across the plains toward Portage LaTraite and the Methy, while the other branch carried them southwest and into the Rockies by way of Bow Pass.

Though most of the Saskatchewan flows through the plains, its waters rise in one of the most spectacular regions of North America. The North Branch, fathered by the Columbia Icefield, comes out of the glacier on Mount Saskatchewan, and when you stand on the little bridge over the North Fork and look at the lithe, frigid stream, not glacial-green but milky from limestone, so narrow in August that a broad-jumper could clear it, you can have a strange sensation when you think how far this water has to go.

The analogy between rivers and lives has been over-worked, but only because it is unavoidable. The beginnings of both move us more than we care to admit because they show that all things are subject to accident. A chance in the human genes, a drunken driver, a virus so small it is invisible through a microscope, and a human life is stunted or killed. A tilt in the landscape, the proximity of a larger stream, and what might have been a famous river is only a tributary brook.

But this milky, cold brook we see bubbling down from Mount Saskatchewan survives to claim mastery over hundreds of brooks and even a few sizeable rivers. In the mountains it does not have the firm confidence of the young Athabaska, which finds the broad Jasper Valley soon in its career. In the mountains the North Branch is a nervous river. Its grey-green waters flicker down between Mounts Amery and Coleman, its wide gravel washes are littered with the bleaching bones of dead trees carried off in spring floods, and it finds or carves a narrow course through the ranges. It flows down to Rocky Mountain House where it takes in the Brazeau and Clearwater, then it swells in to the plain and flows on toward Edmonton, having gathered in several other mountain streams as it goes.

When the North Saskatchewan twists under the escarpments of Alberta's largest city, it is a master stream flecked with foam and haunted with wildfowl; it is about a hundred and forty feet wide under the bridges and the trench in places is deeper than a hundred feet. Its surface looks like tan silk, its current is visible with the life of the mountains still within it, its sound is a lisping whisper. But that this is already a river of the plains is proved by the amount of silt it carries. Floundering through rag-weed and mud the colour and texture of axle-grease, I made the primitive test of holding a silver quarter under the river's surface. As it disappeared at a depth of three inches, I presumed that even here the river carries more sediment than the Red. And yet it does not look so sleek and muddy, and its flow, of course, is more powerful.

From Edmonton the North Branch winds out into the plain through horizon after horizon with here and there a tiny village stark on its banks, and here and there a clump of cottonwood or birch. After crossing the provincial border above Lloydminster—when the first homesteaders arrived in the North Bend they found the prairie grass so rich and tangled they could scarcely walk in it—the river journeys some ten horizons farther into North Battleford. Here it takes in the Battle, bends south and then north to Prince Albert, above it the limitless sky, about and beyond it the empty land.

A little past Prince Albert, at The Forks, the North Branch finally meets its great partner from the south. Then the united Saskatchewan flows through the wilderness into Manitoba, past The Pas into Cedar Lake. Here through the ages it has deposited so much silt that Alexander Mackenzie, when he saw the region two centuries ago, predicted that in time all this watery expanse would turn into forest.

After Cedar Lake the Saskatchewan's journey is nearly done. With a swift rush of rapids, the waters swirl into the northwestern bulge of Lake Winnipeg at a point some three hundred and forty miles east of The Forks. Eventually some Saskatchewan water leaks out into the Nelson and reaches the brine of Hudson Bay, but it is wrong to claim, as some do, that the Nelson is a continuation of this river. Though in a sense it may be argued that it is now a part of the Saskatchewan's system, the Nelson, as was mentioned before, is one of the survivors of Lake Agassiz.

The sources of the South Branch, which is sometimes considered a tributary of the North, are just as interesting as those of its partner and considerably more varied. The primary source is Bow Lake from which the Bow River pours so gaily down the pass through Banff to Calgary and beyond. Its confluence in southern Alberta with the Oldman, whose waters come from a number of mountain sources, is taken as the beginning of the South Saskatchewan proper. This was the great river of the buffalo plains in the early days, but because (unlike the North Branch) none of it passes through forest country after leaving the Rockies, it was never of great interest to the fur-traders. The South Branch was not prolific in amphibious animals. It flows easterly past Medicine Hat, then northeast across the provincial boundary where it gathers in the Red Deer, then up through the prairie past Saskatoon and Batoche to The Forks. The total length of the South Branch from Bow Lake to The Forks is 860 miles, and the total drop is about 4,700 feet. Bow Lake is one of the highest in the Rockies, and is still frozen in early June.

Between them the two branches of this river, together with their final run as a united stream, have a length just under 2,000 miles. Between them they embrace most of the farm land of Alberta and Saskatchewan.

Most easterners, I have discovered, have no idea how historic the Saskatchewan River is, much less that it was discovered only eight years after LaSalle explored the Mississippi to the Gulf. The "Kisiskatchewan", as the Indians called it, was first visited by the Hudson's Bay Company servant, Henry Kelsey, as early as 1690 and in the following year he penetrated some distance up the river from its mouth in Lake Winnipeg. Kelsey was therefore the first European to enter the Canadian prairie. He came in by way of the Nelson River from York Factory, and from that time on the Bay men believed that the river was essentially their territory. In 1741, one of the La Vérendrye parties explored the South Branch, and in 1774 Matthew Cocking and Samuel Hearne, the latter the greatest of the Bay Company's explorers, established a post on Cumberland Lake just west of The Pas. But many years previous to this, Canadians from Montreal were competing with the Bay on the Saskatchewan, and the feat of exploring and developing its trade was largely a Canadian one, some of the men being French, some of them English. It was here that the great rivalry between the Nor'westers and the Baymen began.

> The Canadians are chosen Men inured to hardship & fatigue, under which your Present Servants would sink. A Man in the Canadian service who cannot carry two packs of eighty lbs each, one and one half leagues loses his Trip that is his Wages.

So wrote an officer of the Hudson's Bay Company from York Factory in a report to his superiors in England after seeing the feats on a Saskatchewan portage of a brigade of Canadians who had crossed the country from Montreal. The occasion of his report was probably a complaint from London that the number of pelts coming in from York Factory had been decreasing. The Baymen had little portage experience comparable to what the Canadians had, and at first did not use the tumpline, a leather band passed around the carrier's forehead in such a way that he controlled the weight by the muscles of the back and neck, and thus left his arms free and his body in balance as he walked.

Nor were the regular Nor'westers the only enemies of the Bay on the Saskatchewan in these early days. There was a French Canadian the Baymen called 'Franceways", and they regarded him as a "pedlar", or poacher, because he worked on his own. The presence of this solitary trader in that empty region at so early a date has caused some fascinated conjecture. "Franceways" is of course an English version of "François", and Harold Innis deduced (a typical example of Innis's thoroughness as a scholar) that he was François Sassevillet, a canoeman mentioned in a licence granted to one Maurice Blondeau for Grand Portage in 1772.

"He is an ignorant old Frenchman," wrote Matthew Cocking in his journal. "I do not think he keeps a proper distance from his men, they coming into his apartment and talking with him as one of themselves. But what I am most surprised at, they keep no watch in the night; even when the Natives are lying in their plantation."

This quotation does much to explain the success of the Canadians against the Bay. For the English company was always, as one might expect, class-conscious, more conservative, more averse to going native than the Canadians. The reason why Franceways kept no watch was because he had no need to. The daughter of the local chief was his woman; he had married her *au façon du nord,* and his arrangement served the same purpose as the marriages of princes and princesses in the old countries of Europe. It cemented an alliance between Franceways and the Indians, and the result was that for a time the Frenchman was able to cut off two-thirds of the Saskatchewan River trade from the Honourable Company.

In *War and Peace* Tolstoy says that in historical events it is only unconscious activity that bears fruit, and that the man who plays a vital role in an historical drama never understands the final significance of his own acts. Though this theory may not work in the case of a Jefferson or a Richelieu, it is magnificently applicable to the ironic history of Canada. It may sound strange to say that an illiterate coureur de bois like François was a maker of history, but he was. He and many of the other voyageurs knew nothing of history and cared less, but most of them were fully conscious that in their time and place they were privileged men. For they were free. They sprang from European peasants who had never been allowed to leave their villages or their lords' estates unless drafted into an army for a war they knew nothing about. But in the west of Canada they were their own masters and lived with the freedom of kings. In the Canadian service far more licence was granted to an independently minded voyageur than was ever given within the service of the Bay. That is why the Nor'westers became such great explorers.

And now, at last, I come to that extraordinary character, Peter Pond, who was born in Connecticut and entered the fur trade after four campaigns in the colonial wars.

Toward the end of his life, Peter Pond wrote a journal which has been thoroughly mined by historians. The pity is that there was not much more gold in the vein: the journal ends abruptly in mid-sentence with only a fraction recorded of an amazing life. As for its author, he died in poverty in 1807, an old man and forgotten, without anyone in his own time and place able to guess that his life's work would be remembered a century and a half later as having been vital to a nation then unborn.

It is constantly said of Peter Pond that he was an ignorant man. But was he? I know of nothing that can so close a man's mind to knowledge than the acceptance through life of the theories and methods he learned at school and university. In the case of Peter Pond the truth was the opposite. He spent his entire life in pursuit of knowledge that his meagre schooling could never have given him — knowledge through adventure, war, trade, unknown tribes and lands, and above all, the knowledge that comes from learning how to do new things. He was rough; he was probably very egotistical. But the evidence that he was guilty of two separate murders is so thin it can be discounted.

People have smiled patronizingly at the weird spelling in Pond's narrative, noting that he could seldom spell accurately four successive words. They forget that when Pond was a boy there was no English dictionary available in Connecticut where he was born; Samuel Johnson's *Dictionary of the English Language* was published in London in Pond's sixteenth year. Before spelling was standardized there could be such a variation that people almost spelled as the fancy struck them. George Villiers, Duke of Buckingham, has left behind him some dozen variants of his own signature!

When we remember this, we can learn more from the journal of Peter Pond than historical facts; we can learn how people talked in colonial New England in the middle eighteenth century. For Pond's spelling is purely phonetic. If we read him aloud, we hear in word after word the hard, broad accent of the English west country from which most of the New England colonists had come:

I was born in Milford in the countey of New Haven in Conn the 18 day of Jany 1740 and lived thare under the government and protection of my parans till the year 56. A part of the British troops which Ascaped at Bradixis Defeat on ye Bank of the Monagahaley in Rea the french fortafycation which is now Cald fort Pitmen cam to Milford. . . . Beaing then sixteen years of age I gave my Parans to understand that I had a strong desire to be a Solge. That I was detarmined to enlist under the Oficers that was Going from Milford & joine the army. But thay forbid me, and no wonder as my father had a larg and young famerly I just begun to be of sum youse to him in his afairs. Still the same Inklanation & Sperit that my Ancestors

The South Saskatchewan turns at the Batoche battlefield.

Profest run thero my Vanes. It is well known that from fifth Gineration downward we ware all Waryers Ither by Sea or Land and in Dead so strong was the Propensatey for the arme that I could not with stand its Temtations. One Eaveing in April the Drams and Instraments of Musick ware all Imployed to that Degrea that thay Charmed me. I repair to a Publick House whare Marth and Gollatrey was Highly Going on . . .

That night, Peter Pond joined what thereafter he always called "the Sarvis".

After fighting hard and well in the French and Indian Wars, seeing service under the command of General Amherst, Pond drifted into the fur trade and his first canoe was provided for him by no less a gentleman than James McGill. He went to Michilimackinac and thence to the Mississippi, where, at Portage du Chien, he saw traders "from eavery part of the Misseppey, even from Orleans". Returning to Michilimackinac in 1774, he found "a grate concors of people from all quorters". But when the American Revolution broke out, Pond had nothing to do with it. He returned to Montreal and made secure his place in the expanding Northwest trade, and it was then that his great work of exploration began.

Entering the Saskatchewan River, Pond steadily examined its possibilities and laid the groundwork of the company's food supply by discovering pemmican from the Indians and establishing a system of caching it along the banks, thus making the brigades much more independent than in the days when the men had to stop to fish or hunt. Along with Alexander Henry, Pond extended the fur trade into regions so remote from the St. Lawrence that at first the shipping of goods was a two seasons' job. He was the first white man to pass the Methy Portage into the Mackenzie basin; he was the first on the Athabaska. Now he had reached the point in the life of an active and original man when some inner force of which he may well be unconscious takes charge of him. Rough though he was, for him at this period all his past experience seems to have been an arch wherethrough gleamed "that untrav'lled world whose margins fade forever and forever as I move." He was after the Northwest Passage. In weather so cold his ink froze, he drew the first known map of the Northwest Territories. A later map he drew with the intention of presenting it to Catherine the Great of Russia when he reached her country after crossing the last of the countless horizons through which his life took him. Peter Pond's entire career, and especially the last part of it, lies solidly behind the famous voyages of Mackenzie and Fraser.

Therefore this voyageur is a perfect illustration of

The Mackenzie

INTO A FUTURE KINGDOM

In the last few years the development of the Mackenzie River country has become a matter of national and international debate, as the discovery of oil in the American and Canadian arctic seems certain to set technology loose in the far Northwest in the biggest of ways. The local Indians are probably doomed and, even when I was there, Eskimos were drinking Coca Cola in Aklavik. It was inevitable that the Mackenzie country should be settled and the question is how the settlement will come about and how the land will be treated.

But this cannot concern me here. I had the luck to live and travel on the Mackenzie when the only route of transportation above Bell Rock on the Slave was either by air or by the river itself, and I utilized both. It was an experience I have never forgotten and still cherish, for the Mackenzie I saw was still primeval—almost all of it was, and even the huge war-time invasion of American labour troops to build the useless pipeline from Norman Wells to Alaska had left so few traces behind that you would be unconscious of it had not some of the old Mackenzie hands told you their stories of it.

The day before I set out for the Mackenzie, I was on the shore of Nova Scotia facing Sambro Light and watching the Atlantic swing and ebb in crannies of those granite masses scraped bare by the glacier and polished by uncounted centuries of wind and water. In places the eastern coast of Nova Scotia looks as much a product of the glacier as the habitable parts of Greenland. Where I was lying was as far east as anyone could go on that parallel of latitude and still be in America. I lay with my back against the continent and watched a white liner that had come up over the horizon grow large and finally disappear behind the bluff of Chebucto Head on her way to dock in Halifax. I noticed that she wore the Greek flag.

Any time now, I thought, I would be leaving for the Mackenzie River and the idea of doing so still seemed strange to me. It had always seemed so far away—much, much further away than any river in Europe. Only a fortnight ago I had been in England staying with a friend on the edge of Epping Forest near London, and we had spread out maps to look at the Mackenzie country. Three of my friend's children were clustered around in some fascination, as children usually are in the presence of maps, and one of them made me promise to send her a picture of Eskimos from the Mackenzie.

"I'll have to go all the way down to here before I meet any Eskimos," I told her, and my finger came to rest at Aklavik.

The Mackenzie still seemed far away as I drove back to Halifax late that afternoon drowsy from the sun and the salt air. When I reached my mother's house, she told me I was wanted long distance by Edmonton and I made a quick calculation. It was six o'clock in Halifax; in Edmonton it was only two o'clock, so I decided to wait for half an hour to make sure my caller was back from lunch.

When the operator put me through, the call was from an official of the Northern Transportation Company which handles the movement of freight in the Mackenzie region and along the Athabaska. He told me a tow of barges would leave the vicinity of Fort Smith inside a week and would proceed down the Slave River, across Great Slave Lake, and then go down the lower Mackenzie to Tuktoyaktuk on the Beaufort Sea. There would be accommodation for me on the tugs, I was told, but I was advised to make my own arrangements with Canadian Pacific Airlines for getting out of the country at the end of the run. The barges would not wait and I was advised to depart for Edmonton immediately.

The next day I drove down Nova Scotia to Digby, where I saw Princess Margaret review a hundred fishermen on the wharf, all of them wearing yellow oilskins and sou'westers although it was a warm day of bright sun. My car was driven aboard the *Princess Helene* and I crossed the Bay of Fundy to Saint John.

The day after this I spent travelling north along the St. John River, crossed the height of land so important to the treaty-makers of 1783, reached the St. Lawrence at Rivière du Loup, and had a drink before dinner while looking across the ten-mile width of the St. Lawrence at a majestic sunset over the mountains behind Murray Bay. The next day I drove up the St. Lawrence to Montreal, finishing a journey of about eight hundred miles from Halifax.

Early the next morning I was in a plane flying across the country to Edmonton, and at that stage in my discovery of rivers, I knew so little about them that I was unaware that the plane was practically following the course of the voyageurs all the way west from Montreal.

In Edmonton I soon made the discovery everyone makes the moment he has anything to do with the Canadian north. The time-sense I had grown up with ceased to mean anything in a country which, by southern standards, is essentially timeless. I was told the tow down river had been delayed. When would it start? Well, it should start about any time now. I wanted to know precisely when in order to arrange for air transport south from

Aklavik, and at that time of the year air transport south did not seem too easy to get, since I would be coming out at the end of the season when the summer workmen would be going home. Well, I was told, it should be starting pretty soon, maybe in three days. How long would it take going down to Aklavik? It shouldn't take too long. It was hard to say, but maybe ten days.

I walked around Edmonton for more than a week, observed the North Saskatchewan in that section of its course, studied maps and figures about the Mackenzie, and called the transportation company every day. One day I went to the races and lost ten dollars, and when I came back to the hotel that afternoon the phone rang and I was told to report at Fort Smith the next day.

Edmonton is the most northerly city of any size in Canada, which means it is the most northerly of any size in North America. Yet it took the aircraft two hours and forty minutes non-stop to reach Fort Smith, then the administrative centre of the Northwest Territories, lying just over the line of demarcation between the Territories and the Province of Alberta. For a little of that journey we flew over prairie farms, but by far the most of it was over the rough mat of the northern Canadian bush, with little streams and myriads of lakes dotting the blackish-green of a forest seen from the air. It was a wonderful preparation for the Mackenzie none the less, for we were flying then over the upper basin of the entire system. So perhaps this is as good a place as any to outline what the Mackenzie system is, and to show it in relation to other great river systems of the world.

Most encyclopedias give the total area of the Mackenzie basin as 682,000 square miles, a region two and a half times the size of Texas and more than thirteen times larger than England. Later and more accurate surveys place the figure at about 700,000 square miles, which is really an immense amount of real estate. In terms of its drainage area, the Mackenzie stands about level with the Yangtse and quite a bit ahead of the St. Lawrence, Volga, and Zambesi. However, it stands well below the Rio de la Plata, the Congo, the Mississippi, the Nile, and the Lena, and far below the colossal Amazon with its basin more than two-thirds as big as the area of the entire continental United States before Alaska joined the Union.

The Mackenzie marked on the maps is the great river which issues from a north-westerly bay in Great Slave Lake and flows down to the north until it reaches the arctic sea 1,200 miles away. But this final stretch is merely the last outpouring of a system which begins more than

fifteen hundred miles farther south and from a variety of sources.

The two great tails of the Mackenzie system are the Peace and the Athabaska, and both flow out of the Canadian Rockies just east of the Great Divide. In Jasper National Park you can see the Athabaska purling, bubbling, purple-blue if the sky colour is right, throbbing down the valley from its source in the Columbia Icefield. The young Athabaska is as happy a river as I have ever seen, and even in its stripling reaches it gives you a sense of the power and mastery of the system to which it belongs. It is a strong river as it flows by Jasper determined to have its own way, and a confident river after it has descended from the mountains and begins its long north-easterly course across the Alberta plain. Most of its journey is through wilderness. Though for a time it skirts the northernmost fringe of Alberta settlement, it soon curves on into the vast forest-land of the north. It terminates in Lake Athabaska near Fort Chipewyan, which is surely one of the most historic sites in Canada west of Fort Garry. In his novel of the Mackenzie country, *Where the High Winds Blow*, David Walker has a line expressing what thousands must have felt in the presence of the Athabaska: the whole sense of the North seems to be compressed into its very name. The total length of this tail of the Mackenzie from the Icefield to the lake is seven hundred and sixty-five miles (a distance a little less than the length of the Rhine) and most of these miles are navigable.

But the Mackenzie system has another southern tail even larger, the Peace, which often is listed separately as the fifth longest river in Canada. Its birth is dramatic: it is formed by the head-on collision of the Finlay and the Parsnip in one of the wildest and most spectacular regions of the Canadian Rockies. It drives down through rapids and gorges to the plain, and then in calm and majestic solitude it winds northward through the prairie into which the homesteaders moved in the 1920s, and then into the vast northern forest which it shares with the Athabaska. Finally it gives an abrupt turn and completely takes possession of another river—indeed becomes it; this other river is the Slave.

The length of the Peace is usually given as 1,054 miles from the head of the Finlay to its confluence with the Slave. But the Slave, which coils like a smooth, cold, tranquil serpent through a forest wilderness for 310 miles until it empties in Great Slave Lake, is not really a separate river. When Samuel Hearne discovered it in 1771, naming both river and lake after the Slave Indians of the region, he had come to it from the northeast. He ended his exploration there, and he never knew that what he had called the Slave was simply the final course of a mighty river which had begun more than a thousand miles away in the Rocky Mountains. In freshet, some of the waters brought down by the Peace actually ebb southward up the Slave into Lake Athabaska.

Below Great Slave Lake begins the Mackenzie proper, or the lower Mackenzie, and it is fed steadily all the way down to the sea by a great number of tributaries.

The largest of these is the Liard which rises in Dease Lake in British Columbia near the Pacific and flows for nearly seven hundred miles through wild country until it reaches the Mackenzie at Fort Simpson. Before the entry of the Liard, the Mackenzie water is cleaner even than that of the St. Lawrence just after it leaves Lake Ontario. But the Liard has had a rough journey; it has torn its way through many a mile of sandstone and when it enters the Mackenzie its water, brown with sediment, seems to divide the mainstream into two separate sections. So great is the thrust of the Liard that all the way down to Wrigley the brown Liard water follows the left bank while the clean Mackenzie water is pressed to the right. But the streams meld finally, and thereafter the Mackenzie is stained. The Liard, like the Peace and the Athabaska, is a great stream in its own right, with many tributaries of which the wild Nahanni has tempted more than one adventurer who never returned. It also has a profound effect on the climate of the entire Mackenzie region. Down the valley of the Liard flow warm airs from the Pacific, with the result that Fort Simpson in winter has a climate little colder than that of the Laurentians north of Montreal.

But all the streams entering the Mackenzie from the east are cold, and the coldest of them is the short Great Bear River which drains Great Bear Lake, an inland sea larger than any in the hemisphere except Superior, Huron, and Michigan. Great Bear Lake seldom unfreezes before the last week in July and its river is so achingly cold it feels like melting ice. People who have come down the Great Bear River in canoes have told me that when they enter the Mackenzie, the sudden change in air temperature is equivalent to a journey five hundred miles to the south: the difference, say, between Montreal and Washington on a September day.

The true length of the Mackenzie? Of no other river in Canada does the old question make less sense. The only way to judge the Mackenzie in relation to other rivers is in terms of its drainage basin and its flow; in flow, it ranks seventh in the world, and in the western hemisphere is exceeded only by those mighty waterways, the Amazon and the Mississippi.

Our aircraft throbbed monotonously northward as I talked with the young man in the next seat. Like nearly everyone else in the plane, he was dressed in work clothes and had a dunnage bag stuffed with metal objects. At first I thought him a prospector, but he told me he was working for the government measuring rivers for velocity. A forgotten memory stirred: in Nova Scotia years before this young man was born, I had spent two weeks doing the same kind of job on a few of the little streams I used to call rivers. The routine, I gathered from the young man, has changed little with the years. You stand in the stream if it is shallow enough, or you cross it by boat or canoe held firmly in a straight line by a cable stretched across the river. You lower into the water a little propeller on the end of a long metal shaft, the current turns the propeller, and each turn registers with a click in the earphones attached to the instrument. The propeller must be lowered at a variety of depths. By counting the number of clicks against a stop-watch, and taking a series of readings at different depths all the way across the stream, you can, after averaging out all your readings, estimate the mean flow of a river. The operation must be repeated at a number of stages all the way down the stream and it is less tedious work than it sounds. Most people find it hypnotically restful to stare at moving water.

The young man was talking about the flies: "Last year I never saw anything like them. They lasted all the way through to the fall. One day they got inside my pants and I couldn't get rid of them because I was miles from camp. They bled me so bad my pants stuck to me when I took them off. This year has been a good one for flies. Where you're going, you should find them nearly all gone."

The plane seemed to be beginning a slow descent, but when I looked out I could see no sign of a post or a settlement.

"I tell you, my thighs looked like stewed strawberries. When I'd go out on the job the flies felt like grit in my eyes even when they weren't actually in them. You could hear mosquitoes on tin roofs after dark. It's the mosquitoes in this country—I mind them far worse than the blackflies, though the bulldogs hurt more. Bulldogs can bite clean through a sweater. With ordinary blackflies I've always figured the effect is psychological. If you smear 6-12 on your face they won't bite you, but they'll swarm in a haze right in front of your eyes and follow you around. It generally takes me about two days to get used to them, but there are places I've been up here in the muskeg where the mosquitoes have really scared me."

I asked him if he knew the song written by Wade Hemsworth about blackflies. It had been sung several times over the radio and it seemed to me the most authentic song I had ever heard of the Canadian north:

Oh, the blackflies
The little blackflies!
I'll die with the blackflies picking my bones
In north Ontar-eye-o-eye-o
In north Ontar-eye-o!

"I've been on the job in North Ontario and they're bad, but this country is worse. Maybe it's the permafrost that makes the muskeg so wet when it oozes through in the summer. I don't know what it is exactly, but down river where the Peel comes in, the mosquitoes are supposed to be the worst in the world."

We flew on level over the empty land, and the man leaned across me and pointed: "There's the delta of the Athabaska."

I had seen the young and happy river rise; now I was looking down at the old and experienced river going to its temporary rest in the lake. The delta of the Athabaska looks like the delta of most northern rivers, and is not an excessively large one: a maze of swamps and small channels with some principal threads of broad water which are the main courses of the stream finding their way through the obstacles the river itself has deposited. Out of the flat, brownish-black mat of the delta occasional glitters struck sharply upward as the sun was reflected from water oozing through acres of scrubby bush and marsh grass. We were too high to see the birds, but the whole region seemed mysteriously alive with the energy in it. Even with a single bucket of water, I thought, a child can make a delta. If he pours out his bucket on the sand a few yards from the water's edge, the water he pours will make its own channel just as a river does, and will form a tiny delta an inch or two wide on the verge of the sea.

A new river loomed up and it was the Slave, and after a short while I saw men on the other side staring out, crossed the plane, and had a quick glimpse of the Peace coming in from the west. The two great tails of the Mackenzie system were now united, with the so-called Slave taking Athabaska water as well as Peace water. The plane began to descend rapidly and inside a few minutes we were on the air strip at Fort Smith.

While I was finishing my lunch a man entered, asked for me, and told me he would drive me to the Company's work camp at Bell Rock. He was the manager, Joe Burkhart.

We set out in a truck for the camp along the widest dirt road I ever drove on. It went almost dead straight through virgin bush and circumvented the famous rapids of the Slave which begin at Fort Smith and last for about sixteen miles. Now this road extended all the way from Fort Fitzgerald, a total of twenty-six miles. Below Bell Rock, the main Mackenzie system is navigable all the way to the sea.

I asked Joe Burkhart why the road was so wide and was astonished by his answer.

"We have to portage tugboats and barges through here," he said, "broadside on."

The head of steel, I knew, was far south at Waterways on the Athabaska. There the freight, and even the barges and tugs in sections, were conveyed by rail, reassembled, and put into the river. They went down the Athabaska to Chipewyan in the lake, then entered the Slave, but the rapids at Smith stopped them. Hence this broad highway in a country which then had no other roads of any sort.

"You'll see a boat come over this week," Joe said. "She's in the Athabaska now."

"But they told me I'd be on the river tomorrow."

"Well, I guess it will be a little while yet."

So I waited at Bell Rock for nine days which were a strange mixture of frustration and interest. Here, at least, one could see the Canadian North in action, and the whole development depends on the diesel engine. Bell Rock camp, bulldozed out of the bush, contains quarters for the men, a large machine shop, a carpenter's establishment, a radio station, a warehouse the size of what you would expect on the dock of a modest ocean port, and the dock itself in front of which a dredger was moored lifting some of the silt brought down by the river. The Slave at this point looks small because an island faces the camp. North of the camp there was no road at all, nothing but bush for hundreds of miles. There are long, heavy slipways of baulked timber up which the barges and tugs are dragged for the winter, and down which they are pushed into the river in spring. About a hundred men work and eat in the camp all summer long, and in the fall they are flown out.

They eat like Louis XIV, but faster. Never have I seen so much food eaten so quickly by so few, and that is the prime difference between the modern Canadian frontier and the old one. Gone are the days of scouse, pork and beans, pemmican, salt codfish, and salt pork. The breakfast gong rang at 7:15 every morning, the men rushed into the mess shed and set to, and inside twelve to fifteen minutes the average man managed to work his way through tomato juice, six rashers of bacon, four or five eggs, and half a dozen flapjacks soaked with maple syrup, marmalade, or jam as the fancy took him. In the middle of the morning there was a coffee break, which meant an extra snack if you wished it. Dinner was just after twelve with hot meats, vegetables, and all the pie anyone wanted. Supper was another dinner with hot meats, vegetables, and all the pie anyone wanted—in fact, all the anything anyone wanted. At nine o'clock came coffee, tea, and cold cuts, as much as anyone could swallow.

In high summer, especially in June, the sun sets very

late in Bell Rock and it never really gets dark until summer's end. There is nothing for the men to do after 5:45 but work overtime and digest their meals. This is not the true North of the true arctic men, but the Industrial North. Why do the men overeat? I don't know. But they are amicable, they don't quarrel, and the feeling of the North, the subconscious sense that you are far away from normal living, perhaps sheer boredom, stimulates everyone to overeat, with the result that some men put on fifty extra pounds in a season. I used to take long walks along the portage to rid myself of the heavy feeling of too much food. The moment I crossed the rise of ground leading out of the camp, the moment the noise of the diesels disappeared, the immensity of the northern bush closed around me. Prairie chickens skittered about in flocks of a hundred at a time. Once I saw a black bear as heavy with food as the men in the camp, and once when I followed a jeep trail into some muskeg and bush, suddenly the whole land seemed to rise up ahead of me like a huge glossy black umbrella opening up. It was a flock of northern ravens lifting themselves from the Bell Rock dump. Those carrion ravens of the north are almost as large as capons.

A few days later Morris Zaslow came over the portage from Fort Smith in one of the Company's trucks. He was a professor of history at the University of Toronto and he had with him a three-hundred-thousand-word manuscript on the Mackenzie region. He also was going down on the tow, and for the next three weeks we were constant companions.

Naturally we met many of the men in the camp, and they came from a variety of places in Canada and other countries. There was Stoni Thorsteinsen whom everyone along the Mackenzie River knew as a good man; for years he had been a steamboat captain and now was in charge of the general river traffic of the Company. It was a very pleasant camp, comfortable, not in the least like the tough lumber camps of the east, and on the whole the men seemed content. One man told me he liked northern work because he always had something to look forward to. While he was here, he looked forward to the winter with his family in Vancouver; while he was in Vancouver, he looked forward to getting away from his family and returning to the north. Some of the men read good books. I met a radio operator reading *The Brothers Karamazov* and a chef with a copy of Spinoza, and I remember a carpenter saying to me the prophetic words: "If you ever drink Mackenzie water, you'll always want to come back."

The odd phrase moved me somewhat, for it had an origin in time which the carpenter did not know. Originally the phrase was, "If you ever drink Nile water, you'll always come back." I asked the carpenter if the words

were his own or if he had heard them somewhere, and he told me that his first year in the north he had heard them from a Sister of Charity at Fort Norman.

"If you ever drink Mackenzie water," he repeated, "you'll always want to come back."

He loved the lower river, he said, because it made him feel good, and by this he did not mean "feel good" in the sense that Hemingway used it after a drink, but that it made him feel a good man.

Waiting has always irked me, and nothing makes me feel so tired as idleness, but there was not a thing that Morris and I could do until that tow got under way. It was now well past the middle of August and I had urgent need to be back in Montreal by the end of the first week in September. I fretted. But it is useless to fret against the spirit of a timeless land. Somehow the far Northwest seems to have tamed even the meticulous time-demands of the machines it uses. Also the weather was warm and humid. Though this country can get murderously cold in January—the Slave stays frozen many days after the Liard has unlocked the middle river lower down in the north—in July and August the Fort Smith region is no cooler than Ontario. All of us were issued bed rolls, and I found mine so warm I had to sleep on top if it. Then it rained, and the next day the river silt on which the camp is built turned into a thick rich slime with a fetid odour coming from the acid in it. Wearing rubber boots, Morris and I moved outside with a sliding motion as though we were on skis, and I wondered what the river men had done in this kind of silt when they tracked. The skies were livid and somebody blamed the El Greco tints on nuclear explosions in Siberia. They were beautiful, but at times heavy and ominous, and the sense of the vastness of the North, of the viridian of endless forest dense on either side of that slow river, made me feel at times uncomfortably like a prisoner.

Then came an evening when Morris and I were walking in the clearing and he turned with a cry and pointed. The sun had just broken through clouds over the forest and was streaming horizontally in shafts like searchlights across the camp. At the very end of the portage, on the final rise of ground, we saw emerging out of the forest a white ship, broadside on. It looked huge with the sun smashing against it. I remembered the manager telling me about a ship which was coming down the Athabaska and was going to be portaged. This was it.

"Well," either Morris or I said, "I suppose that's as good an image of the modern North as either of us will ever see."

The ship's presence there was certainly evidence of what the diesel engine has done in these parts. For years this portage by the Fort Smith rapids had been one of the toughest in the whole Canadian river network. It

A "tow" of barges goes "down north" in the main channel of the Mackenzie River to the settlements on the Beaufort Sea. The author made this journey from Bell Rock to Tuktoyaktuk.

except within the camps, no roads, no telegraphs. Radio is used for all messages and they are all sent in clear, with the Bell Rock sender servicing a district several times larger than Germany. The captain, a Japanese-Canadian called Albert Irey, was trying to reach Captain Brinki Sveinson of *Radium Yellowknife* whose ship he had expected to meet here at Res Delta. On Great Slave Lake it is impossible for any tug to push the barges: the heave of the deep water would break their hawsers. On the lake the barges have to be towed in line ahead secured by a heavy steel cable to the power winch at the tug's stern, and the maximum number of barges any tug can handle is four. *Radium King* would take the four smaller barges across; *Radium Yellowknife*, a more powerful ship, would take the four larger ones.

In the wheelhouse Albert was trying to raise the captain of *Radium Yellowknife*, but all he could hear out of the ship's radio was static and gibberish.

"It might be Russia, for all I know," he said and shrugged.

"Russia?"

"We often get Russia here when we can't get our own friends around a few bends of the river. Radio is a funny thing in these parts. There's been a local black-out for several days. Brinki could be within ten miles of us and I couldn't raise him. Anyhow, let's go."

Albert yanked the signal to the engine room, and for the next half-hour he unscrambled the barges. Four were moored to the trunks of heavy trees, the other four were secured to the wire cable payed off astern, and in gathering dusk *Radium King* towed her barges out into the lake. Each barge was five hundred feet behind its leader, and the whole length of the tow was now longer than the original *Queen Elizabeth*.

I didn't like the look of the lake at all. Those steep, rapid waves of inland seas have always seemed much nastier to me than the long roll of the Atlantic. The *King* was bucking in the head-sea throwing water and the water was very cold. Above the wheelhouse the radar fan revolved, but the screen was blank except for four dots astern, which were our barges, and the line of the lake-shore we were leaving. The wind drummed hard.

"How much water does she draw?" I asked Albert.

He flashed me a quick smile caught in the light of the binnacle: "About three and a half feet."

"She'll roll," I muttered, knowing how easily I get seasick.

"By the time the night's out maybe you'll think up another word for what she does."

The helm was put over, the *King* began a long, slow turn into the cross sea, and the movement began.

"I think I'd better say good-night."

Clutching the guard rail I went down the ladder to the main deck, then I was nearly thrown down the next ladder into the cuddy where we slept. I swallowed a Gravol, felt my head spinning, and lay down on a cot with my clothes on.

I have been in a north Atlantic gale when the old *Empress of Britain*—the big one bombed to death in the Second World War—shipped it green and solid over her sixty-foot-high fo'c'sle head. Once I spent five and a half hours on a ferry between Dover and Boulogne on a day when the weather was so bad that an English paper described it in a headline which later became famous: STORM OVER CHANNEL; CONTINENT ISOLATED. On both those occasions I was deathly sick, but this night on Great Slave was worse. The *King* did not roll: balanced on the weight of her diesels, she flicked back and forth like a metronome trying to keep time to a czardas.

With eyes closed I reflected that Great Slave Lake, after all, is not a sea but a part of a river system. A little later with eyes open I remembered what had happened to the tug *Clearwater* the previous year on Lake Athabaska. Caught in a sudden storm, her captain had tried to shelter behind an island, but when he turned, the towing cable destroyed all his mechanical advantage in the water and the hammering waves capsized his ship. An air search found her the next day serving as anchor to her four barges, but all hands were lost. Then I remembered a story I had heard at Bell Rock about a war-time tow on Great Slave when the barges were carrying carbide and dynamite. The storm struck suddenly as storms do there, and as the water washed over the barges it ignited the carbide. The tugboat captain saw the flames in the night, cut his tow, and ran for it. He was three miles away when the dynamite went up, but even at that distance the shock wave was strong enough to knock him off his feet.

Then I became so dizzy I didn't care what happened and somehow I dozed off. I woke with a crash, found myself on the deck half-standing against the side of the ship, thought she was going over, and plunged for the ladder. I got on deck, seasickness forgotten, with a life-jacket in my hand, but there was no cause for alarm. The little *King* was flicking back and forth, and the water was going over her scuppers, but I realized this was no storm. It was merely a dirty cross-sea working against a ship with only three and a half feet of draught. I went up to the wheelhouse and Albert was still there.

"We're getting along all right, but the wind's freshening. Still no sign of Brinki. It looks as if he's stayed on the other side. The wind may have been heavier over there. If he was out, we should have picked him up on the radar."

When I got back to the bunkhouse I found out what had thrown me out of my bed. The rolling had smashed one leg of my cot. It was impossible to repair it in this

The Hay River hurtles over a Precambrian ledge.

not beyond doubt, I would be unable to believe the time made by those canoes. On June 29 Mackenzie left Great Slave Lake at a point very close to the place where I fished that afternoon beside the houseboat. Yet he was in the vicinity of Aklavik within two weeks and in salt water in sixteen days! The flow of the river is strong, and with favouring winds he sometimes could hoist a sail. But he and his men had to sleep at night and the channels of the river to a man who does not know them can often be confusing. The great river of the North tends to run in a long series of lake-like reaches of about three miles in length with a turn at the end. It could not have been easy always to find the quickest channel to the vital curve, for there are thousands of islands in the stream. Besides, all this journey was made in the face of grim warnings from Indians met on the course that the Eskimos at the river's end would kill them. At Great Bear Lake an Indian told Mackenzie "that it would require several winters to reach the sea, and that old age would come upon us before the period of our return."

But return he did: one hundred and two days after his departure from Chipewyan, he was back at the fort. On the afternoon when I stood beside that cold slide of water dipping off the surface of Great Slave Lake I knew that Mackenzie had accomplished this fèat, but I did not yet understand what it had involved.

For I had yet to see the rapids which Mackenzie described with precision as seething with a noise like a kettle. The Providence Rapids, the Green Island Rapids, the Clearwater Rapids do not toss and tumble; they swirl at depth and at a speed sometimes as high as twelve knots, and when you look at them the whole surface of the river seems to be quivering. The tugboats cannot control more than four barges at a time in water so swift, so they split their tows and relay them through, mooring four barges at the head of each rapid, taking four down, and then returning against the current to recover the remaining four. It took *Radium Yellowknife* barely an hour to take four barges down the Providence Rapids; with her thousand-horsepower engine making her plates shudder, it took her more than three hours to hammer her way back running light. Below the entrance of the Blackwater River is a fast stretch sixty miles long, and it took Captain Peterson in *Radium Charles* more than twelve hours to butt back against it. Below Norman Wells is the most spectacular section of the entire stream—the Ramparts, where the river pours satin-smooth and fast at a depth of two hundred feet through high limestone cliffs forming a canyon seven miles long, the sides of the cliffs virtually sheer.

The man who led this famous voyage of discovery has always seemed to me one of the most interesting and attractive personalities in Canadian history; in my opin-

ion, this man is a giant among our people. His discoveries brought him no credit from his partners in the North West Company; jealousy, which the Swedes call the royal vice, has always been the explorer's sin. But when Mackenzie's voyages were done he crossed the sea and visited London. There, with the help of a ghost writer whose formal style is marvellously unsuited to the material, he published a book with one of the longest titles in English letters: *Voyages from Montreal, on the River St. Lawrence, through the continent of North America, to the Frozen and Pacific Oceans; in the years 1789 and 1793, with a preliminary account of the rise, progress and present state of the fur trade in that country.*

In one of the most brilliant periods in English history, this book made Mackenzie a celebrity in English society. The young fur-trader, fresh from the canoes and teepees of Indians, moved with perfect ease in salons filled with men whose names shine in the history books. It was a very exciting time, for Mackenzie was in London in the period between Nelson's victories at the Nile and at Trafalgar. Yet the hitherto unknown voyageur made his place there. The leaders of the land read his book; he was given a title by the Crown; he was patronized by a royal duke; he was painted by the King's Painter-in-Ordinary.

In the context of his life on the Canadian rivers, the personality revealed by the brush of Sir Thomas Lawrence is almost startling. There is nothing rough or rugged in the face of this man who explored one of the roughest and ruggedest terrains in the world. In the countenance of Simon Fraser there is a stubborn, animal-like expression, but not in Mackenzie's. This pork and pemmican eater, this man who could drink under the table most of his fellow members of the Beaver Club in Montreal, certainly has an obstinate chin. But his face might be a poet's. His eyes, as Lawrence saw them, are quite marvellous: longing, headstrong, gentle, defiant, civilized yet making you think of an eagle. The lines put by Tennyson in the mouth of Ulysses apply well to the personality revealed by Sir Thomas Lawrence:

> *Yet all experience is an arch where through*
> *Gleams that untravelled world, whose margins fade*
> *Forever and forever as I move . . .*

With a drop in the wind the flies swarmed back, and Morris and I went back inside the houseboat. Monotonously the afternoon wore on and I wondered if we would ever get out of this place. I was becoming wearier and wearier of these endless northern delays which always seem inevitable. Once a bush plane flew overhead, but every time we scanned the horizon the lake was empty. Just after sunset, Morris rose, looked out the porthole and said: "Cheer up! The tow is arriving."

A pingo — a cone of blue ice — thrusts through the permafrost at Tuktoyaktuk, where the Mackenzie delta merges into the sea. *Below:* Inuvik ("place of the people").

of those who do go out, a few years later write the company begging to be sent north again. I have never met a true arctic hand who does not yearn to go back.

Three measures will have to be taken before this region can become habitable for a large number of people. The acids in the earth will have to be neutralized, compost will have to be worked into the soil, and the insects will have to be conquered. At various times I have referred to the insects here, but always I return to them, for they are the curse of the whole north country. Whether they are any worse than in Ungava and Rainy Lake I do not know from personal experience, but everyone I met who has travelled widely in the Canadian bush says that here they are the worst of all.

Insects are a plague even to the tugboat crews, and the chef of *Radium King* described them well:

"Insects love a bright surface, and when these tugs with their white upperworks put into the posts in June and early July, I've seen them covered with a quivering, browny-black fur of mosquitoes and blackflies. Hellish is the only word for them in swarms like that. If you breathe without your face being covered by netting, they'll choke you. I've spent hours washing them off the ship with hoses. The drowned ones have blocked my scuppers and I've had to dig them out to let the water go through."

That the insects can be conquered ultimately seems certain, but not by spraying. There are so many thousands of water surfaces in the Canadian North that you could never cover them all, nor could you keep the blackflies from breeding in running streams. The only solution seems to be biological, and several scientists have surveyed sections of this country with a view to applying methods of destroying the fertility of flies. But at the moment, with the Mackenzie region costing the country more to keep open than it can return in any form of goods and services, there is not sufficient need to inaugurate a thorough fly-killing programme.

Though I do not expect that anyone a hundred years hence will be reading these words, it amuses me to send them on through time with this prophecy. I believe there will be at least three million people living in the Mackenzie Valley. There will be hospitals, schools, and at least two universities established on sites overlooking that cold, clean river. After all, it was just under a century and a half ago that the money of a friend of Alexander Mackenzie himself was used to establish the first university on the banks of the St. Lawrence.

To bypass the rapids on the Slave River near Fort Smith, tractors haul boats of up to 300 tons across a wide bush road to Bell Rock. Great Slave Lake lies ahead.

THE
WATER ROAD

A determined man could paddle and portage from Atlantic to Pacific.
Artist Paul Kane noted this scene on the Winnipeg River in early 1846.

The river was the key to Canada. From all three bordering oceans, the river offered a water road into the furthest reaches of the land. Cartier was stopped by the rapids of the St. Lawrence, but Champlain revealed that, by adopting the birchbark canoe of the Algonkians, the European could "travel freely and quickly throughout the country, up the little streams as well as the big rivers." Where the voyageur marked the way, the settler would follow.

By open water and carrying place

Above: *They called it Mosquito Lake. The curse of the blood-sucking gnat lay on the Canadian wilds (it still does). The whites could never match the Indians' tolerance of the pest.* Below: *When Henry Youle Hind made his exploration of the West in 1858, his party was photographed on a portage along the Red.*

Above: The French River, connecting Lake Nipissing with Georgian Bay of Lake Huron, was a vital link in the fur-trade route to the beaver lands of the Northwest. The first white water in the Laduc gorge was the signal for the stocky voyageurs to start packing the 90-lb. pieces.

Below: When the timber trade boomed, the river was the road to market and even home was afloat. This raft cookhouse served gangs logging along the Ottawa River in the 1880s. The felled trees were dragged out to the frozen streams and, after breakup, were swept down to the mills.

A new era dawns. A paddle-steamer churns up the Quebec Narrows past square-riggers, a sloop, and a timber raft.

The thousand-yard gateway to a whole new world

When Jacques Cartier first saw the Rock of Quebec, in 1535, he sensed it stood at the door of a new land—and so it proved. Samuel Champlain built his Habitation here, three-quarters of a century later. Eventually, the battle for possession of a kingdom was fought on the cow pasture that we know as the Plains of Abraham—merely some fields on the slope of the mount.

The key characters in the unfolding drama of Canada went up this river road, where the salt of the Atlantic mingles with the sweet water of the inland seas. First, the priestly parties to found Ville Marie upstream, the proud Montreal of today. Then, the ships of Bourbon France, with supplies and cargoes of girls eager to be settlers' wives. Then came the British men o' war, guided by James Cook and carrying James Wolfe, those men of Canadian destiny.

Here, the lifeblood traffic flowed, in and out, first the beaver pelts, then the squared logs, then in the roundness of time the stream of golden grain from the prairies, a thousand miles distant.

The scene at left, drawn by Captain B. Beaufoy, shows a roadstead humming with traffic. The work is dedicated to Lord Seaton, the former Sir John Colborne, responsible for quelling the Quebec rebellion of 1837, later Governor-in-Chief of the Canadas.

From sail to steam: technology brings power to the river

Above: *Under sail on Lesser Slave Lake, these York boats could haul four tons. They were pulled over portages on log rollers.*

Below: *The "Countess of Dufferin" reaches St. Boniface by river in 1877. When the C.P.R. was completed, this locomotive pulled the official train carrying Sir John A. Macdonald to the Pacific. It stands on display at the C.P.R. Winnipeg station today.*

Above: *A boom of logs goes down the broad St. John River, New Brunswick, herded by a steam tug carrying its own wood fuel. As wood was rapidly consumed, at almost every concession line there was a wood-dock where farmers clearing forest from their lands stockpiled wood for passing steamers. The ruling price in mid-Victorian times was $3 per cord, and the captains had to pay out hard cash.*

Below: *The stern-wheeler played a role both romantic and useful in the Canadian West, much as it did on the Mississippi of Mark Twain. The "Inlander" is shown at full throttle in the British Columbia interior in 1911. Massive stern-wheelers, burning a cord of wood an hour, opened the 2,000-mile Yukon to commerce. Two of these "river queens" are preserved at Dawson today as relics of a bygone age.*

In the roadless hinterland, the river was the highway

This homely ferry is included in the unique record of French-Canadian country life left to us by painter Cornelius Krieghoff.

The native Indians of Canada never knew the wheel. Without the incomparable network of rivers permitting travel and transport, the development of the country would have been barely begun before the railway age. Horses could not negotiate forest, rock, or muskeg. Metalled roads were still a novelty in the middle of the 19th century. But the rivers provided a free and sparkling summer route and, when winter fell, an even easier path for the sleigh.

The Saguenay

A RIVER OF SURPRISES

On the north shore of the St. Lawrence estuary, on the upper lip of the great Saguenay fjord which cuts directly west into the high plateau of central Quebec, lies the most picturesque, historic, and still-recognizable village in all North America, Tadoussac. Nestling in a small half-moon bay, the mouth of the Saguenay being just short of a mile wide, Tadoussac is the eye and focus of an enormous scene.

At this point the St. Lawrence has long ceased to be a true river. It is almost twenty miles wide and its waters are salt enough to accommodate the white porpoise known as the beluga. The waters are so cold they can be dangerous for swimmers. They are so deep that German submarines, or at least one German submarine, hunted successfully in them during the Hitler War. Only forty miles below Tadoussac, on May 29, 1914, though nearer the other side of the St. Lawrence, the liner *Empress of Ireland* was the victim of one of the worst marine disasters in history. The Norwegian collier *Storstad,* inward bound with 10,000 tons of coal from Sydney, N.S., rammed and sank the *Empress* in one of the dense fogs which so often cover the estuary when the air is warm and the water is frigid. 1,024 people were drowned. One of my earliest memories is the horrible apparition of the telescoped bow of the *Storstad* moored in Sydney harbour near the coke ovens at Whitney Pier. We looked at her as though she was an evil spirit.

Washed by rains but bright when the sun shines and sky and water are blue, little Tadoussac has rested here for more than three centuries. On May 24, 1603, the year Queen Elizabeth died and Shakespeare wrote *Much Ado About Nothing,* Henri IV still on the throne of France, Champlain anchored in Tadoussac bay on his first voyage up the St. Lawrence. From then until the end of the sailing-ship era, ships of war and ships of commerce used to call at Tadoussac to take in fresh water or merely to wait for a fair wind to blow them upstream. There is much sand here. Even the cliffs are sandy and the scene is so maritime that Tadoussac's classically proportioned white church, its roof and cupola Sienna-red, its small square tower surrounded by a widow's walk, could easily be mistaken for a lighthouse. It seems suspended over the scene, and I wonder if there can be any place in the world where the angelus bell is more moving than here.

Since this is the twentieth century and the scenery is famous, it was inevitable that Tadoussac should also acquire its luxury hotel and luxury golf course, but in the immensity of the surrounding they are not very obtrusive. Behind and about Tadoussac is spread the mythical "Kingdom of the Saguenay", which Jacques Cartier believed, or pretended to believe, contained more gold and precious jewels than the land of the Incas, or even Cathay. As usual, the reality has turned out to be more interesting than the fable.

What is known today as the Saguenay country extends roughly from Murray Bay all the way northeast to the Moisie River which reaches salt water at Sept Iles. It includes the magnificent "North Shore" containing the Bersimis and Baie Comeau, a land of immensities. But its, heart is the Saguenay River system itself. No part of Canada embraces such a close concentration of the paradoxes out of which this country grew and with which she must live. The Saguenay has all the aspects of a hard sub-arctic land with an average of only 100 frost-free days a year; yet Tadoussac is in fact nearly two hundred miles farther south than London. Sharp contrasts appear in the landscape. Lower down, closer to the great trough of the St. Lawrence, the retreating glacier has left behind giant tors and piles of mangled rocks. But higher up, in the territory above Chicoutimi and Arvida and around the wide shores of Lac Saint-Jean, most of the farmland is rich and smiling.

Paradox is also visible in the social and economic structure of the Saguenay, for this land of Maria Chapdelaine is on the one hand so traditional of old Quebec that it is sometimes called the conscience of the province, yet at the same time it is utterly dependent on Anglophone and American industry. And the Saguenay air — in its natural state it is as clean and astringent as Labrador's, but in most of the towns anyone with sensitive nostrils may often have to sleep with closed windows to keep out the reek from the pulp mills and the aluminum smelters. Contrasts are audible in the noise of rapids and cataracts and the stillness of deep waters ponded by dams. On the tributary streams trout snick at flies cast by men in silent canoes, moose drink in streams within smelling distance of the pulp mills, and belugas swim up past the bauxite ships in Ha Ha Bay. Finally, as Walt Whitman noted almost a century ago, this is a land of echoes — of resonances which literally reduplicate themselves, merging with one another to create a sound different from the original source of the echo. Like Canada herself.

The Saguenay is not a tributary of the St. Lawrence but a system in its own right, draining some 30,000 square miles of the central Quebec plateau, its principal source Lac Saint-Jean. Nor again is the spectacular part of the Saguenay a river, but as authentic a fjord as can be found in Norway.

In one of those chances of a lifetime, a physical infirmity combined with perfect weather to present me with a single instantaneous panorama of the entire fjord from its beginning to its end. The infirmity was the distant vision of middle-age which finally forced me to abandon my beloved tennis because it turned my eyes into telescopes which blur objects at close range but enable me to see miles farther than I could when my eyes were normal. On a cloudless August afternoon, the air as translucent as the glass in Cartier's window in Fifth Avenue which gives the passer-by the illusion that he can reach in and pick up a tiara worth a million dollars, the plane was flying down the central St. Lawrence channel at 39,000 feet. Looking out a starboard window I suddenly saw it—the entire Saguenay fjord cutting straight westerly into the plateau, all of it caught in a single vision-frame from Tadoussac to some bauxite ships docked at Port Alfred or moored in Ha Ha Bay.

From this altitude and in this light the plateau looked more barren than Labrador because there are hardly any glacial ponds between the St. Lawrence and Lac Saint-Jean and the land has been more cruelly twisted by the ice sheet. If an ocean could ever acquire the colour of a spruce forest, it would look like this when a hurricane was churning it. The great master-waves of the rock structure are everywhere contorted by hummock waves. There was hardly any sign of habitation—just that wonderful fjord and the thin white line of the road that leads through Laurentide Park from Quebec City. I thought, though this may have been auto-suggestion, that I could see the shadows cast on the water by Capes Trinity and Eternity. For two incredible minutes I was looking at about seventy miles of that water lane that leads to the very gates of the Saguenay Kingdom. Then the south wall of the fjord interposed itself between the water and my line of vision and the spectacle vanished from my eyes. It will never vanish from my mind.

Of all glacial legacies, fjords are the most stimulating to the imagination because they combine in dramatic juxtaposition the contraries of great height, great depth, and the sense of mysterious intimacy created, often, by their narrowness. Literally, they are cracks in the basic rock structure of tablelands facing the sea, and often their walls are sheer cliffs which the retreating ice has gouged and polished. Relieved of the weight of the ice sheet, the land has lifted up; in some places for thousands of feet. But the cracks have remained, as deep as they ever were, and into them the sea has poured to drown what otherwise would have been deep, narrow valleys threaded by small rivers of the sort you find in the Rockies. Fjords are common in Scotland (where they are called "firths" or "lochs"), in Alaska, Greenland, Antarctica, and the South Island of New Zealand. In Norway,

British Columbia, and Patagonia, they are the chief features in the coastlines. They tend to be relatively shallow near their mouths but farther inland their depths can be enormous. A stretch of the great Sogne fjord just north of Bergen is 4,000 feet deep. The Saguenay at Tadoussac is of variable depth, not much more than fifty feet near the village, but close to six hundred toward the other side of the mouth. Near Cape Eternity the depth is around nine hundred feet—depth enough, though far short of the thousands of feet recorded by legend and hearsay.

Lost in the brine of this mighty fjord is the fresh water that has drained out of the upper Saguenay, Lac Saint-Jean and its tributaries, and the separate stream which has passed through the turbines of the Shipshaw Dam.

For years, white excursion steamers used to ply the Saguenay from Montreal to Chicoutimi and back, but lately the only passenger ship to include the Saguenay in its cruising schedule has been the Russian *Alexandr Pushkin*. Hundreds of thousands of tourists have marvelled at Trinity and Eternity, sometimes shouting in unison to set the echoes ringing. And of all the writers who attempted to describe the Saguenay in words, the most vivid and successful was Walt Whitman, who made a leisurely voyage from Niagara to Chicoutimi in the August of 1880 and recorded his impressions in his *Specimen Days in America*. As Walt's books are now in the public domain and as *Specimen Days*, if not out of print, is at least very hard to obtain, I shall now pillage it. I wouldn't dare challenge the performance Walt puts on:

"Up these black waters over a hundred miles long—always strong, deep, hundreds of feet, sometimes thousands—[evidently Walt believed the legends about the depth; he even seems to have mistaken the tide for the flow of a true river] at times a little like some parts of the Hudson, but much more pronounced and defiant. The hills rise higher—keep their ranks more unbroken. The river is straighter and of more resolute flow, and its hue, though dark as ink, exquisitely polished and sheeny under the August sun. Different, indeed, this Saguenay from all other rivers—different effects—a bolder, more vehement play of lights and shades. Of a rare charm of singleness and simplicity (like the organ-chant from the old Spanish convent in *Favorita*—one strain only, simple and monotonous and unornamented—but indescribably penetrating and grand and masterful). Great place for echoes; while our steamer was tied at the wharf at Tadousac waiting, the escape-pipe letting off steam, I was sure I heard a band from the hotel up in the rocks—could even make out some of the tunes. Only when our pipe stopped, I knew what caused it. Then at Cape Eternity and Trinity rock, the pilot with his whistle producing similar marvellous results, echoes indescribably weird, as we lay off in the still bay under their shadows."

Whitman deals with the famous capes in a separate passage: "But the great, haughty, silent capes themselves: I doubt if any crack points, or hills, or historic places of note, or anything of the kind elsewhere in the world out-vies these objects—(I write while I am before them face to face.) They are very simple, they do not startle—at least they did not me—but they linger in one's memory forever. They are placed very near to each other side by side, each a mountain rising flush out of the Saguenay."

The actual distance between the capes is about two miles, the same distance as the length of the Bay of Eternity into which discharges la Rivière Eternité. But let Walt continue: "A good thrower could throw a stone on each in passing—at least it seems so. They are as distant in form as a perfect physical man or a perfect physical woman. Cape Eternity is bare, rising, as just said, sheer out of the water, rugged and grim (yet with an indescribable beauty) nearly two thousand feet high. Trinity rock even a little higher, also rising flush, top-rounded like a great head with a close-set verdure of hair. I consider myself well repaid for coming my thousand miles to get the sight and memory of the unrivalled duo. They have stirred me more profoundly than anything of the kind I have yet seen. If Europe or Asia had them, we should certainly hear of them in all sorts of back-sent poems, rhapsodies etc a dozen times a year through our papers and magazines."

Whitman continued to Chicoutimi and Ha Ha Bay: "Life and travel and memory have offered and will preserve to me no deeper-cut incidents, panorama or sights to cheer the soul, than those at Chicoutimi and Ha Ha Bay and my days and nights on this savage river—the rounded mountains, some bare and gray, some dull red, some draped close all over with matted green verdure or vines—the ample, calm, eternal rocks everywhere—the long streaks of motley foam a milk-curd on the glistening breast of the stream—the little two-masted schooner, with patch'd sails set wing-a-wing, nearing us, coming saucily over the water with a couple of swarthy, black-haired men aboard—the strong shades falling on the light and yellow outlines of the hills all through the forenoon as we steam within gunshot of them—while ever the pure and delicate sky over all. And the splendid sunsets and the sights of evening—the same old stars (relatively a little different, I see, so far north) Arcturus and Lyra, and the Eagle and great Jupiter like a silver globe, and the constellation of the Scorpion. Then the northern lights every night."

Whitman next considers the people he met in the Saguenay country, and he does so with the warmth that never failed him when his sympathies were aroused. How he managed to think that the typical people of the Saguenay resemble Anglo-Saxon Americans beats me—though certainly the young girls of Roberval, in my own eyes, are just about the loveliest and most gracious I have ever seen in Canada or anywhere else. Anyway, back to Walt once more:

"Grim and rocky and black-water'd as the demesne hereabout is, you must not think genial humanity, and comfort, and good-living, are not to be met. Before I began this memorandum I made a first-class breakfast of sea trout, finishing off with wild raspberries. I find smiles and courtesy everywhere—physiognomies in general curiously like those of the United States—(I was astonished to find the same resemblance all through the province of Quebec). In general the inhabitants of this rugged country (Charlevoix, Chicoutimi and Tadousac counties and Lake St. John region) a simple, hardy population, lumbering, trapping, furs, boating, fishing, berry-picking and a little farming." To this I should add, as anyone would know who read *Maria Chapdelaine,* that around Lac Saint-Jean there is much more farming now than there was in 1880.

He continues: "I was watching a group of young boatmen eating their early dinner—nothing but an immense loaf of bread, had apparently been the size of a bushel measure, from which they cut great chunks with a jackknife. Must be a tremendous winter country, this, when the solid frost and ice fully set in."

It was toward the end of the winter of 1878, two years before Whitman's visit to the Saguenay, that a near-fatal accident occurred which resulted, finally, in the famous statue of the Virgin which stands on a ledge of Cape Trinity. The statue was carved in wood by Louis Jobin in 1881 and it took a work crew four weeks to build a kind of skidway to hoist the statue to its final perch on the promontory. As the statue measured thirty feet in height, they had to hoist it in sections and reassemble it on the ledge. Behind the creation of this statue, now known as Notre Dame du Saguenay, is a story perfect of the time when les *Québécois* believed in God rather than in the State, and expressed themselves in the limitlessness of poetic symbolism instead of the banal literality of TV.

In those days on the Saguenay, the only agents of trade were pedlars, and one of these was Charles Napoleon Robitaille. In the late winter of 1878, seeking to visit the settlers across the Saguenay from Chicoutimi, Robitaille drove his horse and sleigh across the ice. As happened to many Canadians in that era, the ice suddenly gave way, the sleigh began to sink in the deep water, and the horse reared frantically. Robitaille prayed to the Virgin Mary to save him. While still praying he suddenly discovered that he, the horse, and the sleigh were safe on the far side and he had no idea how he had reached it. But

The town of Tadoussac (Algonkian for "breasts"), oldest settlement in Canada (c. 1600), guards the entry to the Saguenay River. This photograph, a print from a coated glass negative, was made about the time of Confederation by William Notman.

2359 TADOUSAC, FROM SAGUENAY

he was soaking wet, the air was cold, and the water froze in his clothing. He was remote, and by the time he reached a house and a doctor could be found for him, pneumonia threatened and the doctor pronounced his case hopeless. Once again he had recourse to the Virgin, asking Her to grant him enough life to bring up his children. And just as sudden as his escape from the river, the fever left him and he was whole. He believed it a miracle.

It was then that Charles Napoleon Robitaille resolved that a statue to the Virgin should exist on the most famous point of the entire Saguenay fjord, on Cape Trinity itself, and he commissioned Louis Jobin to sculpt it, the lower St. Lawrence being a great breeder of sculptors in wood. Robitaille was a poor man, and neighbours helped him raise the necessary $7,000—a large sum in those days—and finally in 1881, just a year after Walt Whitman's visit, Dominique Racine, Bishop of Chicoutimi, publicly blessed the statue on Cape Trinity, and for years afterwards the people of the region prayed to it.

Long after I had first heard this famous story, while looking out over Ha Ha Bay in the sunset and well to windward of the scents of sulphur and the smelter, remembering the deeply gentle expressions in the faces of the Saguenay people (did Ringuet have them in mind when he wrote that the *Québécois* women "smile with their eyes, not with their lips"?) I recalled one of the loveliest folk songs I ever came upon. I had found it thirty years earlier in Jakob Wassermann's great novel *Christian Wahnschaffe*, in the English translation called *The World's Illusion*. At that time the novelist's son, Charles Wassermann, now a distinguished foreign correspondent for the C.B.C., happened to be my pupil in my days as a teacher at Lower Canada College. When I asked Charles about the origin of the song, he told me his father had heard it sung by a flower girl in Antwerp and that it was evidently an ancient folk song of the old Christian Europe. I thought how natural it would have seemed to the people of the Saguenay, at least in the early days. It might well have been sung by the young Maria Chapdelaine when she was working in the kitchen:

> *Où sont nos amoureuses?*
> *Elles sont au tombeau.*
> *Dans un séjour plus beau*
> *Elles sont heureuses.*
> *Elles sont près des anges*
> *Au fond du ciel bleu,*
> *Où elles chantent les louanges*
> *De la Mère de Dieu.*

The terrain of the upper Saguenay, a drainage basin of some 30,000 square miles, is a smaller and more temperate version of the Labrador Plateau. There is a similar pattern of glacial debris and lakes whose shapes remind you of microbe colonies or the ink blots of a Rorschach test, but there are fewer lakes and with the exception of Lac Saint-Jean, they are smaller than Labrador's. No single river has the power and volume of the Hamilton.

Central to the entire system is Lac Saint-Jean, of wonderful beauty and exceptional regularity of contour, four hundred miles in area and thirty miles across at the widest point. Legend has it that this bowl-shaped lake was created by the fall of a giant meteor, but there is nothing in this story except imagination. Lac Saint-Jean and its surrounding farmlands are relics of the Champlain Sea, which once flooded the whole area. When the waters drained out of the land, they left behind a deep sediment fertilized by the octillions-plus of organisms that had lived and died in it, so making it possible for indefatigable land-breakers like Samuel Chapdelaine to create farms here.

Lac Saint-Jean collects the main tributary waters of the Saguenay system, some forty brooks and rivers which come coiling out of the wilderness on all sides. It releases its overflow in the cataract at Alma known as La Grande Décharge, whence the waters flow with violence down the channel of the Saguenay proper to tidewater at Shipshaw. The most important tributary is almost a third longer than the English Thames. This is the Péribonka, which flows for 300 miles out of the northern wilderness until it comes home in the lake. Not far from the Péribonka, but flowing in a meandering channel out of the northwest, is the 200-mile-long Mistassini. From the south, Lac Saint-Jean receives the Metabetchouan and the beautiful Ouiatchouan. The Shipshaw is on its own. When its waters have passed through the turbines of the great dam opposite Arvida, they enter the topmost reach of tidewater in the fjord. Nor again is the Chicoutimi River, properly speaking, a member of the Saguenay system because it plunges directly into the fjord just above Ha Ha Bay.

Though the Saguenay is a modest river system, containing only a fraction of the amount of water ponded in the Smallwood Reservoir of Labrador, in the eyes of aspiring hydro-electric engineers early in the twentieth century it promised more than the Crown jewels multiplied by several millions. It also had the advantage of being easily reached both by water and by rail, to say nothing of a large resident labour force when the population had become too large to be supported by the farms. As the engineers saw this country, the upper Saguenay formed "a giant stairway which began at upstream reservoirs 1,400 feet above sea level", with a final plunging drop of 320 feet in the main Saguenay channel between Lac Saint-Jean and tidewater at Shipshaw. All that was necessary to turn the dream into reality was to interest men with many millions of dollars.

American tycoons of the highest magnitude, including J. B. Duke and Arthur Vining Davis, were persuaded to visit the Saguenay. Though Duke had made his vast fortune out of tobacco, he had the nose for the future and his nose told him that the coming industry was aluminum. There is a photograph of Duke and a few other millionaires seated uncomfortably on plank cross-benches bolted to the floor of a flat car somewhere near Chicoutimi. All of them are wearing the drab, stiff city suits, the starched high collars, and the over-sized stiff fedoras that made all North American businessmen of the first two and a half decades of the twentieth century, great or small, look like morticians in a middle-western small town. But their expressions are not those of morticians. They are the cautious, hungry, triumphant expressions that sometimes creep into the countenances of those very rare, special men who understand precisely the difference between $200,000,000 and $200,100,000. They were in the process of knowing a good thing when they saw it. Mr. Duke and Mr. Davis were interested in the Saguenay. Shortly after they left it, the financial spillways were opened, and with the blessings of the Quebec government, the "development" of the Saguenay began.

There can be few places on our planet where the masters of technological nitty-gritty (which I define as the ability to marry the maximum technological know-how to the maximum financial profit) have so thoroughly put flowing waters to work for them. The principal tributary, the Péribonka, is "developed" at three different sites before it finally reaches Lac Saint-Jean, the three powerhouses producing a combined total of 1,165,000 kilowatts. At Alma, where the lake passes through La Grande Décharge into the main Saguenay stream, the Isle Maligne dam is worth 402,000 kw. A short distance farther down, the Saguenay itself is dammed at Chute-à-Caron for 240,000 more kilowatts, and finally there is the famous dam on the separate Shipshaw River—a beautiful thing, actually, and in a majestic setting—which generates 896,000 kw for the city of Arvida and the awe-inspiring smelter on the opposite side of the river. If I counted correctly, this smelter mounts, in a compact space, approximately as many smokestacks as Admiral Jellicoe commanded at Jutland when he deployed his Grand Fleet of twenty-four battleships across Scheer's line of advance, the British battle line extending from one horizon to the next and the ships making so much smoke they soon were unable to see anything to shoot at.

The manufacture of aluminum requires a prodigious amount of electricity and this is what the Saguenay provides. Above Shipshaw the energy of the flow of every cubic foot of water is harnessed *five separate times*. Though the power produced by the whole system is little more than half the power produced at Churchill Falls in full

operation, there can be no doubt that we have here a technological package which can have few rivals anywhere. It does no apparent harm to the water and not much to the landscape. What it does to the air is of course another matter and Arvida is the place to savour it.

The manufacturing city of Arvida is a city which was itself manufactured. Founded in 1926, it takes its name from the first two initials in the three names of the famous general manager of the Aluminum Company of America (in bureaucratic newspeak, "ALCOA"), ARthur VIning DAvis. It was built to plan by ALCOA's Canadian subsidiary, the Aluminum Company of Canada (in newspeak, "ALCAN").

Arvida's location is superb, some six miles above Chicoutimi on the escarpment opposite Shipshaw Dam. It is beautifully landscaped with barbered lawns and crescent streets, and many of its houses and buildings are designed in the antique style of pre-industrial Quebec. The Manoir du Saguenay, known as the Saguenay Inn before the days of biculturalism and bilingualism, was originally intended as a guest-house for visiting magnates. Now it is a luxury hotel with the most attractive exterior design and interior furnishings I have seen in any hotel in Canada. A charming little city, Arvida. But from every point of the compass from which the wind can blow, it cannot fail to blow into Arvida the perfumes of the industries which now are the backbone of the Saguenay's economy. Besides the smelter, the largest of its kind in the universe, which exudes a strange, sickly-sweet smell one engineer told me he finds quite pleasant, the whole region is seeded with pulp and paper mills which reek of heated rotten eggs.

This is the price that had to be paid for employment and prosperity, and in land-poor Quebec, unemployment has been a major problem for more than a century. Indeed, unemployment was the cause of the original Saguenay development.

As early as the third decade of the nineteenth century, Charlevoix County contained more people than its beautiful but barren land could feed; not until the 1950s did *les Québécois* dream of limiting the provincial birth-rate. So a society was formed in Charlevoix County called "Les Vingt-et-Un", its purpose being to explore and colonize the Saguenay. In 1838, some fourteen men, many of them bearing the name Tremblay, one of them the French-speaking descendant of a Highlander called Murdoch, arrived in Ha Ha Bay near the site of the present Chicoutimi and the colonization began.

Before this date the only white men to visit the Saguenay had been missionaries, trappers, and William Price, who founded the vast lumber industry of the whole Saguenay region. The French-speaking new-comers of Les Vingt-et-Un were woodsmen and land-breakers. They and the many who followed them cleared all the arable land northwest of the modern Arvida and about the shores of Lac Saint-Jean. They built their houses in the fine tradition of habitant Quebec, they built their barns and their churches, and their achievement was a noble one. The tradition of land-breaking lasted here into the early years of the twentieth century and has been celebrated by Louis Hémon in his *Marie Chapdelaine*, which he finished only thirteen years before the founding of Arvida.

Now, as they say in the Saguenay country, "The Twenty-One" have become "The Three Hundred Thousand" and that is a number far too large to live off the limited arable land. Only industry could support such a population, and the two industries here are based on wood products and aluminum, the bauxite brought into the country in those large, long ships with SAGUENAY written on their sides, brought in from the Caribbean and lately even from Africa. But long before chemists learned how to turn soft woods into newsprint, the forests of the Saguenay had been supplying timber to the world, and the story of how it began is impressive.

In Chicoutimi there is a statue of William Price, who sometimes has been called "The Father of the Saguenay". The first William Price (the name has been repeated down several generations of this distinguished Quebec family) was born in Hertfordshire and was one of the several Englishmen sent out to Canada to purchase masts for the Royal Navy during the years when Napoleon's Berlin Decrees were cutting England off from her usual source of timber in Scandinavia. Price was barely 21 when he arrived in the New World and he went first to the Ottawa.

This was a man of rare courage and physical endurance; during the War of 1812, there being no other means to get there, he walked all the way from central Canada to Halifax. In 1830 he came to Chicoutimi, and from then until his death in 1867 in Quebec City at the age of 78, his entire life was bound up with the Saguenay country. When he first came here, not even the fourteen outrunners of Les Vingt-et-Un had arrived. There were no supplies save what a man could obtain for himself or by bartering with the Indians and there were occasions when he nearly starved. All these years he had to fight the Hudson's Bay Company, which naturally wished the land to remain a wilderness for the sake of the fur trade. Before he died, William Price had established lumber industries in thirty different places and he held his operations together by travelling in winter with dog teams.

Price had fourteen children, so what he founded was more than a great timber industry; it was virtually a dynasty. Though the sons knew hundreds, perhaps thousands, of people in the Saguenay country and could converse with them in *joual*, they were princely, and princes visited them. When still Prince of Wales, Edward VII appeared in the Saguenay country in the mid-1860s and there is a delightful drawing of the period which shows the portly young prince seated astride the shoulders of a Price who is carrying him across a shallow stream, Price smoking a pipe and the prince airily brandishing a cheroot. Years later, Edward's brother the Duke of Connaught also came to the Saguenay, where he was introduced to the old man who earlier had served the young Edward as a guide. The guide's first name was Napoléon (quite possibly his surname was Tremblay) and when he was introduced to Connaught he gave him a smile, clapped him on the back, and said, "J'ai bien connu ton frère!"

For the lumber trade, as for the pulp and paper and aluminum industries which followed it, the prime geographical asset was the deep Saguenay fjord which permitted the largest of ships to penetrate all the way inland to Ha Ha Bay and Chicoutimi. By now these industries have changed the essential character of the entire land and people. Out of them have grown a cluster of some dozen cities and towns, nearly all of them company towns, of which the largest is Chicoutimi with a population of 50,000 if you add to the old town the newer Chicoutimi-Nord. The comfortable, sure old world of Samuel Chapdelaine has been turned inside out.

By one of the ironies common enough in history, the scene of the first important novel of Quebec was set on the northern shore of Lac Saint-Jean and described the very last moments in a way of life which Hémon believed would endure for centuries, but then was on the verge of being all but obliterated. Hémon, a native of Brest who had spent some years in England as a journalist and sportswriter, came to Canada in 1911 for the sake of his health. He spent his second Canadian winter at Péribonka, Saint-Gédéon, and Roberval and worked on the farm of Samuel Bédard, one of the last of the Saguenay land-breakers. He completed *Marie Chapdelaine* in 1913 and in the summer of that year he was killed in a railway accident at Chapleau, Ontario. Before his death he had sent the manuscript to the editor of *Le Temps* in Paris, who published it as a serial in the winter of 1914, the last installment appearing only six months before the outbreak of the war which started the break-up of Christian Renaissance Society and opened the gates to what we live with now. Maria's famous paean which ends with the words, "Au pays de Québec rien ne doit mourir et rien ne doit changer" has therefore a double poignancy, for the 1914 war was merely the first of the many hammer blows which were to fall upon the Quebec *habitant*.

The townsmen of the modern industrial Saguenay

country are far more prosperous than their forebears. They have television, and supermarkets, but not many of them have the old contentment or even the old hope of heaven with the belief that Jesus and His Mother love them and will take care of them. It would be hard to find any young man of the modern Saguenay land who would spend more money than he possessed in order to have a statue made to the Virgin he believed had saved his life. It is said that the majority of the young people of the region are now separatists and this may well be true. Politics is the unfailing surrogate for a lost other-worldly religion, and nationalist politics the inevitable riposte to a materialist culture which has overthrown the one in which a people's forebears have lived. The most revolutionary book, and one of the angriest, among the many books which appeared in Quebec in the 1960s, came out of the Lac Saint-Jean region. It was *Les Insolences du Frère Untel*, written by a young man in religious orders whose actual name was Desbiens. Desbiens is also the name of a small town on the south shore of Lac Saint-Jean.

We were sitting in the library of La Société Historique de Saguenay and Monseigneur Victor Tremblay, the director of the society, was explaining something which had always puzzled me. It was the origin of the peculiar place name "Ha Ha", which sometimes is written "Ha! Ha!" In 1947 Monseigneur Tremblay had published a learned monograph on the word and he was kind enough to give me a rescript of it. Like most Canadians, I had assumed that "Ha Ha" was of Indian origin and had something to do with laughter. "Minnehaha", I was told in school, meant "laughing waters". On the Saguenay the magnificent indentation of the fjord just below Chicoutimi called Ha Ha Bay, a majestic bight of deep water framed by high cliffs cutting at a sharp angle to Bagotville and Port Alfred as you sail up the fjord, is more than one of the regions's grandest sights: it is a natural harbour almost comparable to Halifax. Tradition has it that it was called "Ha Ha Bay" by the first voyageurs who naturally turned into it on their way upstream and then laughed at themselves when they found it was a *cul de sac*. Only a desk-bound researcher could come up with an explanation like that. A stream of oaths would have been a far more human response than "a merry laugh".

"The word," said Monseigneur "has nothing whatever to do with laughter. It means 'surprise' — but also the kind of surprise which presents some sort of obstacle."

"Désagréable?" I asked him.

"Désagréable, mais aussi il peut être agréable."

In the purest sense of the word, it was a "Ha Ha" for me when this learned scholar went on to inform us that the word was not Indian, never had been Indian, but was pure Old French. He had traced it through many centuries all the way back to Joan of Arc. In 1429, when in Poitiers, she had written thus in Old French to the English invaders: "Se ne voulez croire les nouvelles de par Dieu et la Pucelle [i.e., Jeanne d'Arc herself] en quelque lieu que trouverons, nous ferons dedans at y ferons un si grant hahaz, que encore a-il mil ans que en France ne fut si grant."*

What a sentence that is! Apart from revealing Joan as the fierce, implacable warrior and patriot she certainly was, so utterly different from the pathetic and simpering Victorian schoolgirl offered by Bernard Shaw, this sentence offers us the spelling of "grand" as "grant". What else can this suggest but the origin of the name of the Scottish Clan Grant? It perfectly clinches the meaning of the word "Ha Ha" and is one more illustration of the truth that the earlier French Canadians did indeed retain the language of their distant ancestors. In my copy of Larousse, the word "Ha Ha" does not even occur.

Of Ha Ha Bay (which he thinks should be written in French as La Baie des Hahas) Monseigneur Tremblay writes that for those who mounted the Saguenay "it was a surprise that defeated them, a perfect and magnificent 'haha' of a character that could escape nobody." Likewise for travellers descending from the higher country above, "whether by the route leading from Lake Kenogami and de Laterrière, or the crossing from Chicoutimi, paths frequented in the days of the missionaries and fur traders just as by men of today, the bay offers a sudden and large opening. This is an 'haha' in the very first sense of the word."

I have noticed flying from a few flagstaffs in the Saguenay country a beautiful flag I have never seen anywhere else. It has been adopted as the flag of the Saguenay country and Monseigneur himself was its designer. It is based on a cross formed by strong red lines, just as in the Cross of St. George. But these red lines contain within themselves another cross of silver-grey. He explained that the red is symbolic of the electricity the region generates, the silver-grey of aluminum. as in the Cross of St. George, there are also four separate oblongs, two above and two below the cross-bar. The two oblongs above are green, the two below are golden; the upper ones symbolize the forests of the Saguenay, the lower — the golden ones — the ripe harvests of autumn which supported the people before the industry came.

When we rose to leave, Monseigneur, knowing that we were going to Lac Saint-Jean early next morning,

---

* *"If you refuse to believe the tidings that come from God and the Maid, in any region that we find, we will make in it, and at it, such a big HaHa that never in France these thousand years has there been one so big."*

space exceeded the violence of the Niagara Whirlpool. Not even after escaping from the canyon did the Hamilton find peace. It is a very young river because the glacier receded from Labrador less than seven thousand years ago. Almost immediately after leaving the canyon it forms still another rapid. Though it is steadied by a long reach called Lake Winokapau, with depths in places up to four hundred feet, this tranquillity is abruptly broken by the Mouni Rapids and after another calm stretch by the Horseshoe Rapids. For a distance of about eighteen miles it is steadied again by Gull Lake, only to go thundering down over the Muskrat Falls. Thereafter it widens into the final flow to the estuary at Goose Bay. The Hamilton was a very tough river for craft of any kind and in the spring run-off it carried a formidable amount of debris down to the sea.

Well into the twentieth century the Grand Falls were little more than an adventurer's goal, and an expedition to them was as dangerous as an attempt to conquer Mount Everest. An American called Leonidas Hubbard lost his life on a disastrous trip in 1903. As late as 1937 a forestry engineer named Paul Provencher saw the Falls and described them brilliantly, but on his return, one of his Indian guides deserted him; he and his partner were lost in the lake-maze for quite a while and seriously feared they might starve to death. The two Bowdoin students who had seen the Falls in 1891 wrote down their names and the date, placed the slip of paper in a large glass fruit container, wire-sealed it, and left it prominently visible on a rock slab near the tree line on the eastern brink of the Falls, with the invitation to later travellers to leave their names in it also. When the jar was presented to Premier Joey Smallwood in 1960, it contained only eighty-four names.

The first good photograph of the Falls (a few years later it appeared on a Newfoundland stamp) was taken in 1925 when two Yale undergraduates, James E. Hellier and Varick Frissell, together with two local Indian guides, paddled and portaged up the Hamilton from Goose Bay. Their aim was to see the Falls and then to explore a river which enters the Hamilton just below the canyon. So little was known about it that it was called, and still is, the Unknown River.

Like their few predecessors, these two young Americans had a rough trip. They lost one of their canoes with all its gear in the Mouni Rapids, and as they went farther inland such maps as they had were of small use to them. It took them sixteen days to cover the 190-mile distance from Muskrat Falls to the well-named Disaster Rapids just below the discharge of the Unknown into the Hamilton. They suffered such miseries from blackflies that Hellier could wince at them forty-five years later.

After travelling a short distance up the Unknown they came upon a strong cataract formed in the shape of a Y which they called the Yale Falls after Yale University, and here their exploration ended. They smelled smoke and saw at night the glare of a large forest fire started by one of those violent thunderstorms which strike central Labrador during its short summer. They had heard stories of Indians burned to death by lightning fires, so they got out in a hurry and returned to Goose Bay. Had they travelled seventeen miles farther up the Unknown they would have discovered another twin fall almost the duplicate of the one they named after their university.

The Unknown, like the Hamilton, issues from a lake, but the Hamilton is fed by a network of lakes so labyrinthine it was impossible to chart them accurately until aerial photography became an exact science.

I never saw the Grand Falls of Labrador. I was a year too late. When I reached the region for the first time in August 1972, I had read much about the new Churchill Falls development, but I entered the country with no clear idea of just what kind of a development it was.

To some extent my confusion was caused by the decision of Premier Joey Smallwood's Newfoundland government to rename the Hamilton after Sir Winston Churchill. Like many other people, I had believed that what now is called the Churchill Falls was the old Grand Falls of Labrador. It's not. And to avoid still further confusion with the famous and much larger river of the Northwest, which has been known as the Churchill for more than two centuries, I will continue to call the principal river of Labrador the Hamilton.

It still has a tremendous waterfall, but you can't see it. From a height of more than a thousand feet, the water descends silently through a granite cliff at a point fifteen miles distant from the original Falls (which now are reduced to a harmless trickle), and when it reaches the bottom this enclosed water has acquired a pressure of 450 pounds per square inch. After passing through eleven enormous turbines the waters enter an underground surge chamber the size and shape (almost) of a great cathedral. Here they heave with a dark and thunderous hissing before discharging through a pair of tall races carved out of the granite for a distance of more than a mile. They enter the lower river almost silently, their presence betrayed only by a few hovering gulls.

This hidden cataract, funnelled down through eleven penstocks carved out of the cliff, is Churchill Falls. Nature created the water and the terrain, the Labrador Plateau served as a gigantic dam, but the Churchill Falls themselves were built by engineers. On June 16, 1972, they were formally declared open by the Prime Minister of Canada; the Premier of Newfoundland, and the Prime

Minister of Quebec. From now on, the central plateau of Labrador will become increasingly known, for ever since 1969 the new community of Churchill Falls has had an airport large enough to handle the largest jets in service.

Although most of Labrador until very recently was a region less explored than Tibet, paradoxically it was visited by early navigators before any other part of continental Canada. It is almost certain that Vikings landed in Labrador about the same time William the Conqueror landed in Kent. The Portuguese navigator Corte Real skirted the eastern coast of Labrador in 1500, thirty-four years before Jacques Cartier saw it and called it 'The Land of Cain'. When I was a schoolboy in Nova Scotia I was told that the name "Labrador" indicated that the early explorers believed its interior was filled with gold mines. Evidently my grade-school teacher had a textbook which confused the place with the sales-talk fabricated by Cartier about the mythical Kingdom of the Saguenay. Anyway, the name 'Labrador' is derived from a Portuguese word for "laborer".

Geographically, Labrador is "the Northeast Peninsula of the North American Continent", a fact which has been a kind of doom, for though all the peninsula save the northern tip of Ungava lies south of the Northwest Territories, the climate of nearly half of it is truly arctic. A combination of two natural forces of huge import to our planet is responsible for this. The Labrador Current pours out of the Arctic Ocean down the northeastern shoreline carrying on its surface a perpetual fleet of icebergs, a few of them five miles long and two thousand feet high. The effect of this gelid sea water is further increased by the airs that come down from the Baffin and Greenland icecaps. The climate, no less than the terrain, explains why most of Labrador is still empty of human habitation.

Though the new town of Churchill Falls has every modern convenience, and lies on the same parallel of latitude which crosses the rich dairy farms of Denmark, its growing season is so short that it would be useless to attempt a crop even if there were enough topsoil to plant it in. Most life grows slowly in Labrador. In the rivers discharging into Ungava Bay an arctic char takes ten years to reach maturity. The valley of the Hamilton River has plenty of ground cover, but the birches are spindly, the grass is coarse and sparse, and much of the surface is covered by caribou moss. The blackflies could not be more pestiferous than they are in Siberia and the Northwest Territories, but they certainly meet the competition. This is glacial country—cruelly or beautifully, depending upon your mood, it is glacial country still. If regular night frosts be accepted as the determinant of winter, even central Labrador has a winter not much shorter than ten months and flash snow-storms have occasionally fallen in August.

Here the glacial legacy has been somewhat different from what you find in the Northwest Territories. There are no inland seas like Great Bear and Great Slave, no vast river system like the Mackenzie, no true mountain ranges like the Mackenzie and the Franklin. Instead there is a tumbled plateau drained by about sixteen medium-sized rivers, of which the Hamilton is the most important. The plateau is broken up by hundreds of thousands of glacial ponds. They vary in size from Lake Michikamau, which was about sixty miles long before it was threaded into the Smallwood Reservoir, and myriads of twisted sliver-lakes, shallow ponds, and string bogs which make any large-scale map of Labrador resemble the seething patterns of microbe colonies that leap to your eye when you squint at a culture through a microscope.

Here is another phenomenon that makes you wonder whether the eighteenth-century Rationalists, with their conviction that the mind of God operates exactly like a super-colossal human mind, may just possibly have nudged an intimation of a truth that will always elude us. No matter what the area of thought, the human mind cannot help thinking in patterns which bear at least a family resemblance to one another. In this sense, what could be more human than the emergence through the glacial agent of hundreds of thousands of small lakes, ponds, and string bogs in the shapes of streptococci, spirochetes, staphylococci, and Koch bacilli, those even more interesting products of the Divine Intelligence?

But to return to the suburban safety of verified science. The Labrador Plateau has been so architected by the glacier that it drains in three directions—east, west, and north—with altitudes rising in places to more than 2,000 feet above sea level. As the ice cap melted off Labrador only a few hours ago in geologic time, the plateau may rise even higher unless the ice should soon return. It well may. The balance of precipitation in Central Labrador—an average of 154 inches of snow per year against only 16 inches of rain—indicates how narrow is the margin of safety even now.

Cold, barren, and useless to man—ever since Jacques Cartier this was the universal verdict on Labrador. But it did not discourage the politicians; they have disputed its possession for more than three hundred years and are still at it.

For two centuries Labrador was a bone between those two old imperialist dogs, France and Great Britain. The British got it along with all of Canada in 1763. Thereafter it was disputed between Newfoundland and Quebec for nearly a century and a quarter until a decision of the British Privy Council settled the argument by the traditional appeal to a convenient watershed. Newfoundland, then a Crown colony, was awarded the 112,000 square miles of the peninsula which drains into the Atlantic, nearly all the waters carried to the sea by the Hamilton River. Quebec got the rest, which amounted to three-quarters of the whole, though up to his death in 1959, Premier Maurice Duplessis insisted that the decision was invalid and printed maps of Quebec which included the 112,000 square miles owned by Newfoundland, while Premier Joey Smallwood laughed at him.

At the time of the Privy Council decision, Labrador's total population was slightly less than four thousand souls; leaving out a handful of Indians, they all lived in tiny fishing settlements and Grenfell missions along the coast. As many of these were Eskimos, they had no representation in the Newfoundland legislature, which regarded its share of Labrador as a protectorate.

The world's opinion of Labrador as a useless territory changed abruptly in the early 1950s with the decision to build the Quebec North Shore and Labrador Railway from Sept Iles to Schefferville and the iron mines of the Labrador Trough. Sept Iles became a thriving city, a year-round port to which ore-carrying ships came and went while long trains with cars filled with the dark, mustard-coloured ore rumbled through the wilderness to the docks. Soon Sept Iles was the richest town per capita in all Canada, to be surpassed in the late 1960s by Labrador City in the Newfoundland section. At the moment the new town of Churchill Falls may well be the third richest per capita.

Then came the James Bay Development, announced in a polito-financial atmosphere of such exceptional murkiness that the public was unable to know much more about it beyond the astronomical costs that were projected. Between six and nine *billion* dollars, we were being told even a year after the first announcement of the arrangement between the Quebec government and Wall Street financiers. It is intended to be the greatest hydro-electric project ever and the chief recipients of the power, one presumes, will be some of the American eastern states. On paper, at least, the terrain offers some promise for a hydro-electric site. La Grande Rivière has a drop of about three hundred feet over a distance of twelve miles, which is a ratio of distance to drop approximately equal to Niagara. But here the comparisons end.

The Grand River flows through spruce forests and a terrain serrated with muskeg and permafrost, and from the beginning many scientists argued that if the permafrost is flooded it will probably turn into a muddy porridge. The project calls for a reservoir of some 3,400 square miles and the Grand River lacks the water to flood so large an area. The projectors therefore decided to do something on a scale nobody had ever dared attempt before: to divert the waters of large rivers, some of them hundreds of miles distant, the chief of which would be the Kaniapiscau. This river in its natural state flows *north*, and is the main feeder stream of the Koksoak which discharges into Ungava Bay. Until it actually happens, nobody can possibly know what the result of such a diversion could mean to the entire northern Labrador environmental balance. What it would mean to the Ungava Eskimos, however, is all too clear.

Since the mind of man runneth not to the contrary, whales have swum thirty-five miles up the Koksoak to Fort Chimo and the local Eskimos have depended upon them for food as the Haida Indians depended upon the Pacific salmon. If the Kaniapiscau is diverted, the Koksoak will not have enough water to float a whale. The Eskimos' traditional way of life will end and they with it. As one of their spokesmen told a smiling law court in Montreal, "We can't eat the white man's food. It makes our stomachs sick."

There were also many Indians and Innuits in the Grand River valley and figures given of their numbers varied between 2,000 and 12,000. If the planners had spared them even a moment's thought before making their decisions, they gave no sign of it. Suddenly the native peoples found the bulldozers and earth-moving machines among them, destroying their trap-lines and changing the whole region. They protested that the only way of life they knew would be ruined. So once again the whole question of who owns Labrador came into the courts, with the poor and primitive Indians confronting the lawyers and advocates of the government.

The basic morality of our post-Christian era is Jeremy Bentham's Utilitarianism, often typified by the well-known (if misquoted) phrase, "the greatest good is the happiness of the greatest number." As an ethic, this is of course preposterous. If, for example, it contributed to the happiness of a Roman mob of 80,000 people to watch lions and wild dogs kill and eat a hundred slaves and Christians in the Colosseum, this could be regarded as perfect morality. But let's not be too neat. Common sense would certainly declare that if a small and hopelessly backward people denied its land to a more advanced people who needed it for the service of many millions, in such a case the claims of the vast majority would be valid within the context of evolution.

But from this argument it does not follow that Indians or any other human beings should be totally disregarded, while it *does* follow that any government or power group is under the obligation to make damned well sure in advance that what they propose to do is going to be many times worth the human price the unfortunates must pay.

And this is something the power men seldom consider. In Canadian history the classic case was that of the *métis* in the prairies toward the end of the nineteenth century, which culminated in the hanging of Louis Riel. It was a very ugly story because of the politics involved, and it is still debated bitterly. Yet here, when it was an issue between a transcontinental railway and putting the buffalo plains to the plough, the semi-nomad *métis* were doomed by history. For all that, however, the Canadian government of the time behaved to them with a singularly callous indifference, and Canadian national unity has suffered ever since.

That is what usually happens in such cases. My own Highland-Scotch ancestors were even more callously dispossessed a century and a half ago and I could not help watching the James Bay proceedings with a distaste I lacked the language to express. The Highlanders were evicted from their glens for the usual reason: as their own chiefs and the economists of the day pointed out, their presence in the territory where their ancestors had lived for centuries served no economic purpose. The ruling economic idea was to burn out the crofts, evict the occupants, leave them to starve, emigrate, or serve as cannon fodder in the armies, and turn the glens into sheep runs. The victims never had a chance against the power men. Those who resisted were hanged or transported to Australia. The majority sailed to Canada in starvation ships, which turned out to be a fine thing for their descendants but was a cruel betrayal of the original sufferers.

For years the stirrings of racial memories prevented me from visiting the Highlands, but when finally I did so they were just as I had been told they were. Were it not for the tourists and the shooting boxes of rich Englishmen, Lowlanders, and Americans, the glens would be almost as empty as modern Labrador. No matter how the baloney is sliced, it can't be sliced into a pattern to prove that the evictions did Scotland any real good. It did not take long before the golden economic future based on sheep rather than men faded into the mists of Glencoe and Loch Duich. With this knowledge in the memories of several million living Canadian citizens, it is all the more disgusting to be exposed to the old argument that in the long run eviction is going to be the best thing for the Indians and the Eskimos. Their situation is very different from the one which faced my ancestors, to whom the challenge was at least clear. It was this: when you reach Canada, Root, hog, or die! They were lucky enough to find a land still virgin enough to root in. Rich soils awaited them in Ontario, the Townships, Prince Edward Island, Pictou and Antigonish counties in Nova Scotia. Once the Selkirk settlers had survived the horrors of the early years, they were able to inherit some of the richest wheatland on earth.

But what awaits the Indians and Eskimos? A highly organized, over-urbanized technical culture which can offer them nothing better than welfare, with its usual concomitants of boredom, Coca Cola, canned foods, and potato chips; to the younger ones, going down the road to the slums and tenements of Montreal and Toronto. I wish the bureaucratic planners would remember, or even know, what happened when Fawcett recruited a group of Brazilian Indians to help him explore the Amazon. After travelling for miles into the jungle, the Indians beached their canoes, sat down beside them, and refused to move. "We have travelled very fast, very far," they said. "We have left our souls behind us. Now we must wait until our souls catch up."

When the lawyers of the Labrador primitives argued that more than half of Quebec's share of Labrador rightfully belonged to them in law, the judge seemed to accept this claim. But I cannot believe the law will save them. What is our law, after all, but a complex refinement of what the Romans called *mores maiorum*, "the customs of our ancestors"? Among white North Americans is any custom more ingrained than the one which assumes that if ever a native's habitat stands in the path of the white invader's idea of progress, it must be held expendable even if the progress may be Gadarene? Which is another way of saying that unless the James Bay Development turns out to be a tremendous success, and does no serious damage to the environment, it will be worse than the crime it will have committed; it will be a blunder

This long digression cannot help suggesting that the Churchill Falls Development is another ecological outrage, but it is not that. Instead, it is a shining example of what technology can do if the men who apply it have great ability and a genuine reverence for the environment. In the long record of misplaced dams, unnecessary dams, reckless engineering, and destructive dams, Churchill Falls turned out to be an inspired marriage between technology and art. Nobody was dispossessed here. Though the caribou herd had to shift its migration in some places, it did not suffer. The only thing destroyed was the pure spectacle of the original Falls. But after these were tied off, the lower Hamilton gained immensely. The river's flow was controlled and actually increased. At the same time the power produced by the new, artificial Churchill Falls is sufficient to send some seven million horsepower of non-polluting hydro-electric energy to the power-hungry, polluted cities of the south.

'The clouds are reflected, pure white in a perfect mirror, but they do not shine up to me from the mirror's surface. They are buried in it. They shine up *through* it, up

"A marriage of technology and art"

The central plateau of Labrador — a great granite saucer dotted with lakes and drained by many rivers — sprang to life in 1953 when Brinco began harnessing the wild waters of the Hamilton.

Below:

As the "leaks" over the plateau rim were sealed, the tremendous Smallwood reservoir began to fill. All you see in this photograph is now under deep water.

For aeons, the Hamilton River crashed to waste unseen over the Grand Falls of wilderness Labrador. Men seeking vital energy for industrial nations, but also concerned for the environment, tunnelled it to eleven turbines that flash power to the teeming southlands.

Caught in a fantasy of ruined temples, the magic of concrete creates conduits for Herculean power.

Deep in the rock, a powerhouse takes form.

Brobdingnagian shapes in a cavern of granite.

Intake control structure measures water flow from reservoirs created by eighty-eight dykes.

Politically, the moving spirit was Premier Joey Smallwood of Newfoundland, who was assisted by the decision of Prime Minister Jean Lesage of Quebec to make available to Churchill Falls the power-line network of Hydro-Quebec, which even before Churchill Falls was completed was the largest single power network in the world. In this way the new power generated at the Falls could be disseminated over the entire network, some 750 miles south to Montreal and even beyond.

The main technical problem was a fascinating one. It had nothing to do with building a dam; the plateau-saucer itself created an immense head of water. It was the blocking of the gaps in the rim of the saucer through which the waters leaked. These had to be closed by dykes to the number of 88. Some idea of their massiveness can be given by these figures: altogether, the dykes have a length of more than forty miles and required 26,000,000 cubic yards of fill to form the embankments. At their highest the dykes rise some 117 feet from the bottom of the excavation and the longest of them is 3.8 miles.

The next technical problem was to knit together some of the lakes of the plateau in such a way that they unite to form a single, interconnected reservoir, also to divert a number of smaller rivers into the central catchment basin. This main reservoir now bears the name of Smallwood, and it includes a number of lakes which were marked as separate on older maps of Labrador. Sail Lake and Orma Lake used to leak over the edge of the saucer on their own; now they are held back by dykes so that they ebb back into Lake Michikamau, which in turn is united to Lobstick Lake. Near the southeastern end of Lobstick, at the point where it once was thought the Hamilton River began, the engineers built the main control structure in the entire system. It is here that the upper waters from the reservoir are released under control into the old channel of the river.

But in order to stop the biggest leak of all, the one formed by the rapids and the old Grand Falls, it was necessary to divert the flow of the upper Hamilton to an ultimate destination some fifteen miles distant from the old Grand Falls. This was done by dykes at the lower end of Jacopie Lake and no excavations were necessary to guide the water to the spot the engineers had chosen for it. In the present system Jacopie Lake is now called the West Forebay. Through a control structure at Whitefish Falls it enters the East Forebay and there is guided toward a point at the very edge of the plateau's cliff where it is poured into the mountain down eleven penstocks carved out of the cliff until it reaches the turbines with a pressure of 450 feet per square inch.

The old course of the Hamilton through its rapids and over the Grand Falls is now almost dry, though in case of an excess of water in the reservoir, a spillway at Jacopie Lake permits a little water to pursue the ancient channel down to the Falls.

So now, at the climax of its course, the most savage waterfall in North America has been transformed, fifteen miles distant from its old location, into a smooth, silent, and invisible downpouring for a distance of 1,100 feet to the great turbines at the cliff's bottom, thence into a surge chamber with a depth of sixty to eighty feet, thence into the huge mile-long tail races, and so into the old lower river which pours as it always did down to Goose Bay, Hamilton Inlet, and the sea.

There was one final knitting job—if that word is applicable to water—and it was made by means of the Gabro Control structure at the northern end of the Ossokmanuan Reservoir. This had been completed much earlier, in 1960, and was based on the Twin Falls of the Unknown River which joins the Hamilton just below the end of Bowdoin Canyon. These were the falls the two Yale undergraduates, Hellier and Frissell, failed to reach because the forest fire drove them off the plateau. The Ossokmanuan Reservoir was built originally to furnish 120,000 horsepower to the new mining towns of Wabush and Labrador City.

On July 1, 1971, when Premier Joseph Smallwood officially closed the Lobstick Control gates, the reservoir which bore his name was complete. Dotted with islands which give sanctuary to hundreds of thousands of wild geese and ducks, prowled about by wolves, caribou, and foxes, abundant in fish, alone in an utter wilderness with a total area of 2,200 square miles and a capacity of 1,000 billion cubic feet of water, the Smallwood Reservoir was the third-largest man-made body of water in the entire world. When it reaches full operation in 1975, the Churchill Falls plant could utilize 98 per cent of all the water in the reservoir. In late winter when the ice is thickest, the mean sometimes falls as low as 5,000 cubic feet per second. In the June flood—which is early spring in a region where temperatures of 50 degrees below zero have been recorded in May—the flow can rise to 300,000 cubic feet per second, and it is then that excess water will be diverted in some volume into the old channel to find its way over the old Grand Falls. The average mean flow is 49,000 cubic feet per second, and with all the penstocks flooded the outflow through the turbines and the great tail races into the lower river will sometimes be greater than the mean flow of the Fraser.

The underground installations have been blasted and carved out of the granite in the shape of cathedral naves. They can be reached by a fast elevator in what seems like

In the heart of the Labrador rock, a powerhouse takes shape.

a minute, or by a curving tunnel road more than a mile long. During the blasting period the inside of the cliff was thunderous with awesome reverberations. Here laboured a small army of workmen, engineers, drillers, truck drivers, and technicians of all kinds, with 75 per cent of the priority in jobs being given to Newfoundlanders and 25 per cent to Québécois. The powerhouse is immense: 972 feet long, 81 feet wide, and 154 feet high. When I was there they were still busy installing turbines in the Machine Hall, these being lowered into place by a huge gantry that could be moved on rails high above. The turbines drive the generators from which power is transmitted to the underground transformer gallery at 15,000 volts. The transformers increase it to 230,000 volts for transmission to a surface switchyard through six 900-foot-long cable shafts. From the switchyard power will be transmitted at 735,000 volts.

Here, in what only yesterday was the inaccessible wilderness of Central Labrador, within an astonishingly small area, was assembled the cumulus of a long and marvellous history in electrical engineering. Around 600 B.C. Thales of Miletus had discovered that when a piece of amber (*electron*) is rubbed, it acquires a new property, the ability to attract small particles, of different substances. In the seventeenth century, Boyle and Von Guericke had brought out a machine by which electricity could be produced by friction. In the early eighteenth century Stephen Gray had learned that electricity can be led from one place to another by certain substances. In 1745 the first condenser appeared in the Leyden jar, and a few years later Franklin used it to prove that electricity is what causes thunderstorms. Then came the work of Galvani and Volta on the dynamic electric current, and the road was open for the great men who followed them: Davy, Ohm, Faraday, Helmholtz, Maxwell, Hertz, Bell, Edison, and Marconi . . . and so many others. But what a task it was to assemble the children, the grandchildren, and the great-grandchildren of their inventions in Central Labrador!

The Churchill Falls plant contains twenty-nine transformers, and they vary in weight between 160 and 224 tons. They were shipped by water to Sept Iles, where a special dockside crane weighing 250 tons had to be installed to lift them off the ships to the railway cars. These also had to be built specially to carry them up the line to Esker, where the road trip through the bush to Churchill Falls awaited them. To carry the transformers over the road an entirely new kind of vehicle was invented—a giant the company called a transporter. Part of it built in France, part in the United States, each transporter was 196 feet long. At a maximum speed of three miles an hour it sauntered over that bush road, each of its twenty-two tires being seven feet, three inches tall and weighing 1,768 pounds. More than three times longer than the biggest of all the dinosaurs, the transporters moved by night as well as by day, and at night their eight huge headlights illuminated every bump on the road before them.

In order to deliver the power from Churchill Falls to Hydro-Quebec at a point near Seahorse on the Newfoundland-Quebec border, a right-of-way for the power towers and the power lines had to be cleared out of the bush of the rolling plateau. It is 126 miles long and 710 feet wide, and there are three to four towers for every mile, each varying in height from 125 to 165 feet and weighing up to 37,000 pounds. When the lines cross the river at Churchill Falls they make a leap of 6,000 feet, and here they are supported on each bank by anchor towers each weighing 170 tons.

Besides the railway, the special road, and the ships coming to Sept Iles, thousands of air flights carried in men and material from all over the continent and even from Europe, the traffic in one period equalling that of the Berlin Airlift. While the project went on, the main construction camp on the site contained fifty-five bunkhouses with twenty men in each; also one hundred and two family trailers and ten trailer units, the total number of workers being 2,300.

Also while the work was going on some of the ablest men in twentieth-century Canada died. Donald Gordon, the president and chief executive officer of Brinco, died in his sleep on May 3, 1969. An enormous man physically, he was probably the greatest organizer in Canadian industrial history, and under his direction the Canadian National Railways became the most efficient system of ground transport in the world. But the most terrible loss occurred at 6:31 p.m. on November 11, 1969, when the company's new twin-jet D-H125, coming into the Wabush airport in poor visibility after dark, crashed into the side of an open mine pit. All eight men aboard were killed instantly.

Aboard that plane, in addition to the two crew members, were Donald McParland, who had succeeded Donald Gordon as president of the company, only 40 years old; Eric Lambert, vice-president, finance, only 46; John Lethbridge, McParland's executive assistant, only 35; Fred Ressigieu, 56, general manager of Acres Canadian Bechtel; Herbert Jackson, 42, assistant general manager of A.C.B.; Arthur Cantle, 42, assistant manager of construction. McParland was succeeded four months later by William D. Mulholland who made an understatement when he reported to the shareholders: "This was surely one of the grimmest hours we shall ever experience." It was even worse; it was a moment of terrible grief, for McParland and the others had truly been loved by their colleagues. It may well be that McParland was one of the most serious human losses Canada has suffered in several decades, for not only was he a magnificent engineer, he was a lover of the land itself. As much as any single individual in an enterprise which involved several thousand individuals, Donald McParland was the originator (what the Germans would call the *Urquell*) of the project's grand design. He laid out its basic rationale in a Ph.D. thesis presented when he was still a student in the University of Toronto.

In spite of this tragedy the work went on, and at its formal opening in June 1972 the plant was ahead of schedule. By then the old construction camp had been replaced by a modern town. It is built around the Donald Gordon Centre, which contains a school, a bank, a post office, a twenty-one-room hotel, a restaurant, a gymnasium, a bowling alley, a hockey and curling rink, a swimming pool, even a theatre with fine appointments and 224 seats. And of course Churchill Falls has its hospital and inter-denominational church. And in the school the classes are conducted in French and English. The town's permanent population is expected to rest at a thousand souls.

For these who are unable, or understandably unwilling, to accept the human meaning of technology, this perfect marriage of art and technology contains within itself a message more frightening than any political revolution that has ever occurred. How can a man in the full vigour of youth and middle age survive as a man unless he has work which has value and in which he believes? The great power plant at Churchill Falls in its genesis and creation called forth a multitude of human resources; it gave pride to everyone who was a part of it. But it was also such a *perfected* creation that when it was finished it could be operated successfully *by only two men!* Allow two spares in case one of them, or both of them, might have a seizure. Allow a small maintenance staff for minor repairs. Yet the fact rests that once a great human achievement like the Sixth symphony or *War and Peace* is done well, it is *perfected*—which means, literally, that it is finished, and the man or men who perfected it become like Alexander sighing for new worlds to conquer.

I don't know what I ever did, or was or am, that my wife and I should have merited the kind of hospitality we received in Churchill Falls. At first I didn't think we'd get there at all. I was told by the Air Canada office in Cape Breton that their planes would land nobody in Churchill Falls unless his presence had been cleared by the company. I wondered if this was because they feared some madman would explode a bomb in the installations. Eventually we got tickets from Eastern Provincial Air Line on our return to Montreal and all went perfectly thereafter.

I have told you about the flight with Gerry LaFontaine and Ray Rouleau down the lower Hamilton to Goose Bay and back over the plateau. That night in the guest-house Gerry arranged a dinner for us that would have seemed absolutely futuristic in the Labrador of even ten years earlier. These were family men who loved it here and so, I gathered, did their wives. They came from all over Canada and the conversation ranged from Beethoven to international politics. Occasionally at my instigation the talk entered into precise discussions of science and technology of the kind I love when I shamelessly pick the brains of scientific colleagues in the McGill Faculty Club. If ever we were guests at a more civilized dinner, with good conversation, delicious food and wine served in a beautiful room, neither of us could remember when it happened. This was nothing like the mythical Englishman dining in the jungle in a dinner jacket. It was an effortless translation of urban amenities into a region where wolves still howl on winter nights. And of course, it would have been unthinkable without that same technology which so repeatedly scares the pants off me when it gets busy in other directions.

The next morning was radiantly clear and we looked up into the blue to watch another helicopter float down to us out of the sky. This time it was David Wilson, senior pilot at Churchill Falls, slim and blond, intensely alert with the relaxation of a trained athlete. Only a few months previous, he and his co-pilot, John MacDonald, had taken delivery of a new helicopter (perhaps this very one) at Fort Worth and flown it directly to Churchill Falls. They left Fort Worth on May 8 in a temperature of 85 degrees and after twenty-one hours of flying they landed at Churchill Falls to find the lakes still frozen, snow on the ground, and the temperature at 35 degrees.

David flew us into the wild country to the west and to the Smallwood Reservoir, and it was enormous beyond description. Once he lifted us up to 8,000 feet, for me an eerie sensation, for I seemed suspended in a transparent bubble, looking down between my spread knees through the plexiglass to the earth and water. Not even at this altitude could we see to the rim of the reservoir. The Lobstick Control gates looked minuscule and the gulls that circled its outlet were as small as snowflakes. Descending close to the water we saw a flotilla of ducks swimming along the shoreline of a small island, their ducklings beside them. Out here in the reservoir their nests were permanently safe from the foxes. Small islands were everywhere with the risen waters high on the boles of the trees. David pointed to a faintly quivering current in the reservoir and said it was the course of the river, here the Ashuanipi. The radiance was all about us and finally, after how many hours I forget, the helicopter dropped very low in its return to the east and the town of Churchill Falls appeared on the left. I glanced at David and saw his lips smile and then the moment came.

He was taking us very low down the course of the old Hamilton where it used to enter its rapids. Now this channel where the water had roared for centuries contained a few trickles no larger than you would find in a Nova Scotia brook at the end of a dry summer. David pointed out the round holes where the rocks had been swirled until they looked like cannon balls. The sight was strangely moving. The granite that had borne the terrible punishment of the river was now smooth, brown, and mostly dry. It had the exhausted, disappointed, shocked expression of a man who had lived a giant's life, had been the wonder and awe of all who had seen him, and now was old, abandoned, an empty shell and alone.

Then we hovered.

At last I was looking down at the Grand Falls of Labrador and was closer to them than any man could possibly have been until a year ago. A thin stream of water came down over the brink, whitened in its slide to the precipice, and fell flaccidly into the little pool below. David wheeled the machine at a right angle to enter the Bowdoin Canyon and I marvelled at his skill. Those huge rotors seemed almost to be scraping the sides of the gorge, but with him at the controls there was no danger.

My wife saw it but I missed it: the face of an Indian carved into the stone on one wall of the canyon, carved by wind, rain, snow, ice, and the mists that had washed it all those thousands of years when the Grand Falls were alive. She said he looked fierce. She said he looked cold and murderous in his wrath. The white man had taken away from him the thunder-voice of his Great Manitou.

Cost of progress. Grand Falls in its glory; now, it thunders silently to serve man.

FORCE

The pounding waters
gnaw at the land
as man seeks to
claim their power

"Continual dropping wears away a stone"—
LUCRETIUS (95-55 B.C.)

The Roman poet was thinking no doubt of the gentler streams of Tuscany, but his oft-quoted words apply most dramatically to those rivers of Canada where fast water cuts through rock, gouging and eroding, as it hurtles to the sea. Day by day, century by century, the land is being carved to new shapes by the rude force of water.

At Punchbowl Falls, Alberta (at left) "continual dropping" has worn a natural cup within the rock — a tourist attraction in the 4,200-sq.-mile Jasper National Park.
A muddy torrent rages through the canyon of the Fraser River (at right) as spring run-off sluices down the Rocky Mountain Trench. Between Prince George and Lytton, the river falls 1,300 feet, nearly eight times the height of Niagara. The yellow silt swept from the banks — it is soft rock ground to flour — stains the water of Georgia Strait for miles beyond the delta. The modern traveller staring down at the savage Fraser, its ceaseless roar numbing the ears, can only marvel at the courage and skill of the American-born fur trader whose name it bears. In 1808, Fraser and his party went down the river by canoe in 56 days, then turned and came back, against that current, in 34.

Aladdin's lamp is lit by abundant hydro power

Our industrial growth has been paced by the production of electricity from falling water. Power generated at remote installations flows to factory and bungalow at the flick of a switch. With this technological magic, the obstacles of

topography and climate have been largely overcome and a high standard of living made possible in a land largely hostile to humans. The dam at Whitehorse Rapids on the Yukon (below) lights the regional capital and powers vital metal mines.

The romance of the waterfall

There has always been something
to stir awe in the contemplation of
the foaming cataract. Generations
of honeymooners at the brink
of Niagara's giant horseshoe
stand silent, eager victims of the
enduring myth. Those who see
Victoria Falls on the Rhodesian
Zambesi are as mesmerized today as

was Dr. Livingstone when he first
saw the plunge in 1855.

Canada is liberally endowed with
waterfalls: from the famous—like
the 274-ft. Montmorency, close to
Quebec City—to the lesser-known,
like Newfoundland's Grand Falls
(below) on the Exploits River.

In two leaps, the Hay River goes over
Alexandra Falls on its 500-mile
journey from northeastern British
Columbia to Great Slave Lake.
By northern terms, this cataract is
easy to find. The Mackenzie Highway
follows the river along its Albertan
course and into the Northwest
Territories. The river was named
by pioneer travellers surprised
at the growth of edible grasses along
the sub-Arctic valley.

Where the Hay adds its water to the
huge volume of Great Slave—it's
the continent's fifth largest lake—
stands the hub town of Hay River.
Yellowknife is directly opposite,
seventy miles across the lake.

Cutting through the soft under-
lying sandstone formations of
south-central Alberta, the Red Deer
River has helped to create one of
Canada's most fascinating areas—the
so-called Badlands. The erosion
of water and wind has carved a
moonscape of grotesque bare slopes,
isolated towers of harder stone
(called "hoodoos"), wrinkled
gulches where only snakes and
bobcats can find a living.

Several other rivers falling from
the eastern slopes of the Rockies
have contributed to this phenomenon:
the Oldman, Milk, Frenchman, and
South Saskatchewan among them. Here
in Triassic times (sixty million
years ago) still roamed the greatest
reptiles the globe has ever known,
and dinosaur fossils uncovered in the
Badlands since the 1880s are star
exhibits in many of the world's best-
known museums. Even eggshells
have been recovered.

South of Stettler, the canyon of
the Red Deer is a mile wide and 400
feet deep. And still digging.

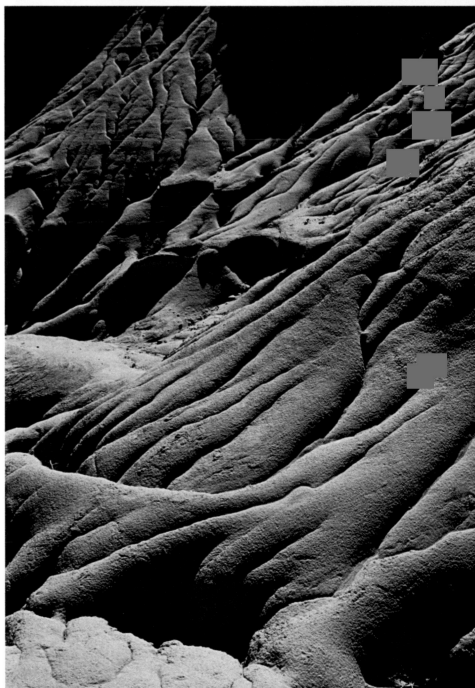

A menacing
river of ice
awaits its
next summons

There is no force on earth to match the glacier. Slow, implacable, irresistible, the rivers of ice have several times — at least four, but who knows exactly how many? — marched down from their haunts on Ellesmere Island and Greenland to grind mountain and prairie. Canada is the product of the merciless ice. The site of Toronto was once covered by an ice sheet 5,000 feet thick, and the snout of that particular glacier — the Wisconsin — furrowed its way as far south as the junction of the Missouri and the Mississippi rivers, at St. Louis.

The wild waters of B.C.

THROUGH THE PROMISED LAND

British Columbia is still the promised land, probably the only one that's left except New Zealand. I pray for her.

No matter how you try to slice the history of the first decade of the post-Christian era, it's been the age of the con man. Governments, advertisers, developers, educators, bottlers of drinks soft, medium, and hard—yea, even national banks managed by the sons of stern Presbyterian thriftarians—they promise everything under heaven to everyone on earth, from the child gawking at the tube to the pensioner propelling his arthritic limbs to the corner tobacconist who sells the Loto tickets, his last chance of dignity in the Welfare State. So the conviction has hardened that whatever anyone is promised, no matter by whom, should be taken, and that whatever any man has promised to himself should be surrendered on demand. Why not? For the world and all it doth inherit is now presumed to have been created for two purposes only—to be developed and to be consumed.

Only yesterday the promised land was California. In an America which still was promises, no question but that she was the biggest promise of them all. I shall never forget when first I saw that state.

It was in the June of 1939, Europe resigned to her torture by Hitler and Stalin but still hoping against knowledge that she might be reprieved; Canada in a daze of unreality after that royal tour which surely was one of the most remarkable investments a *Britannia moritura* ever made; the United States stirring at last out of a decade of soup kitchens and New Deals now that her masters knew that war was at hand to restore the Old Deals and what Henry Luce would soon be calling The American Way of Life. California, we were coming! For days we had been driving to you in our $450 Pontiac coupé, bought for that express purpose in the last years when it was reasonably safe to purchase a used automobile from an urban dealer. We had crossed those sections of the American dust bowl (its total area larger than all England) which lay in central Kansas, western Oklahoma, and the Texas panhandle; we had crossed the partial desert of New Mexico and the high desert of Arizona, and finally, in the canyon leading from Kingman to Boulder City, its walls the texture of slag, the thermometer dangling inside the car registered 130 degrees.

After a few hours of sleep in the humid air created by Lake Meade, the temperature down to 102 degrees but the atmosphere like steamed absorbent cotton, we set out in the dark on our final leg to the coast. At two o'clock in the morning we filled our tank at an all-night gas station in Las Vegas, where the youthful attendant wished us luck. In those days Las Vegas was a sprawling desert village whose sole distinction, according to an encyclopedia of the period, was "its fine, modern high school". In eager excitement we drove out of the splash of its lights into the Mojave and soon were alone under stars so bright that a quarter of them might have been stars of Bethlehem. In that grassless, treeless waste, just before dawn, the temperature plunged to 38 degrees and we closed the windows and turned on the heater. Dawn broke. We saw the skirts of Route 66 littered with the black fragments of the thousands of blown-out tires from the cars which had tried to cross the Mojave by day. Several squashed rattlesnakes on the pavement and hundreds of squashed jack rabbits which were the snakes' principal food. The sun rose and the mountains rimming the desert sang like bugles as its rays explored their crannies. We turned off the heater and opened the windows, and the temperature soared to 90 degrees. Then— bang!—we were through the pass and the San Bernardino Valley spread out before our eyes.

Millions of oranges glowed at us from the deep green leaves of thousands of acres of groves. The grass between the orange trees was lush and deep enough to hide the countless runnels fed by Colorado River water piped down to them from Boulder. Our dust-desiccated nostrils expanded in this new and delicious air. The little towns were smokeless, there were waves of fragrance from flowers, and the nearer we came to the coast the more wonderful California seemed to be. The people's faces shone with sunshine and health; every ranch along the highway had its little stall presided over by a teenaged boy or girl and above the stalls was written, ALL THE ORANGE JUICE YOU CAN DRINK FOR TEN CENTS! We stopped at one of them and each of us drank a half-pint, and it was real orange juice, pressed out of the sun-ripened fruit before our eyes, the vitamins alive and dancing in it. Finally, just about our normal breakfast hour, we wound our way out of the last canyon and saw the Pacific for the first time in our lives. It was Virgin Mary blue under a soft haze and its waves broke so slow and sleepy they seemed to be caressing the sands.

Yes, in 1939 America's supreme promise to herself and the world seemed fulfilled in southern California. The total population of that huge state extending from Mexico to Oregon, from the sea to the deserts, was barely seven million souls. Not even Hollywood seemed to matter much in California outside of its own precincts; the dreams it manufactured had far more effect in Chicago, Brooklyn, London, and Toronto than they had here. All the southern Californians I met that summer were simple, happy, generous people thankful merely to be alive, tending their gardens and loving the air they breathed and the warm sea in which they swam. For years, half of the American Olympic medal winners, to say nothing of the tennis champions, were bred in California. I played in the Laguna Beach tournament that August (no big deal, I assure you) and was beaten in the finals by an eighteen-year-old milkman who was six feet five and charming. At that time the singles champion of the world (who had also started as a milkman) was another Californian called Don Budge. He had beaten Baron von Cramm in the greatest of all Wimbledon finals. Six years later, after Germany had surrendered, knowing that his old rival's life was in danger, Budge flew in to save him.

If anyone had told me in the summer of 1939 that in the summer of 1969 the playgrounds of Los Angeles County would be closed on sixty-seven different days because the air was too poisonous to be breathed by children, I would have pronounced him mad. But I should have known better, for even then the future in store for southern California was visible enough. I saw it with my own eyes.

The famous highway which grew out of the old Spanish Camino del Rey leads through Long Beach, and on our way up the coast to San Francisco we passed through it. This finest of all California's beaches had been totally ruined. A forest of oil derricks sprouted out of it, spread inland and far out into the sea itself. The air reeked. Our ears were thudded with the *chunk-uhh, chunk-uhh, chunk-uhh* of oil pumps which sounded like a herd of a thousand belching hippopotamuses as they sucked up the fossil fuels which were the last earthly remains of the octillions of octillions of once-living organisms which had perished because the Great Experimenter had tried them in the balance and found them wanting, the names of their most spectacular performers being Brontosaurus, Diplodocus, Brachiosaurus, and Tyrannosaurus Rex. How ghastly appropriate it seemed to me, twenty-four years later in Naples Bay, to read the name U.S.S. *Long Beach* on the stern of the first surface warship to be armed with long-range nuclear rockets and to hear the voice of a blond Yale man, bound for Istanbul to take up his first diplomatic assignment, remark with that curious mixture of pride and guilt so characteristic of his breed and era, "Oh yes, she's got those little things. As a matter of fact, the range of her little things is 400 miles." In that year, apparently, U.S.S. *Long Beach* was not only master of the Mediterranean but of all the lands surrounding it.

And finally there is Burbank, same name as Luther Burbank who was responsible for so many of the marvellous fruits, berries, vegetables, plants, and flowers which made the very name of California beloved by the millions of northerners who depended upon its fruits for health in the long winters. Burbank today is a by-word for pollution. Yes, I should have guessed what was coming. For Archibald MacLeish, in the same poem in which he declared that "America is promises," had also written,

> *Believe*
> *America is promises to*
> *Take!*

So naturally, in an age in which men were persuaded that they themselves had ousted the Creator from the universe and taken his place, they also took the promises—just about all of them.

Beauty lies not only in the eye of the beholder but also in his mood, and it may be that I overrated the golden beauty of California because I had come to it over that long road through the dust bowl, the deserts, and the slag-textured mountains. The truth is that on the rare occasions when the sun failed to shine on the south California coast, the mesquite-clad hills looked grey-brown and pretty bleak.

British Columbia can never look like that. It is almost as lovely when the sun fails to shine, as along the coast is so often the case, as when it does.

I am a northern man; I suppose the genes of all my ancestors have been at least as northern as northern Spain ever since the great emigration from Africa before the Ice Age. And British Columbia is a northern country. What therefore delights this northern man beyond measure in British Columbia is its wild profusion, the swift contrasts between its lavishness and fearsome challenges. The magnitude of British Columbia, its multifariousness—blend of the Aegean and the Norway fjords, of the Alps and the soft airs of Devon and Cornwall, of arctic glaciers and the sage and cactus of Mexico. And those mountain lakes—Columbia, Windermere, the twin Arrows, Kootenay, Okanagan, and Kamloops!

The rivers here must vary more than any river networks on earth. There are thousands of sudden torrents white against the grey of limestone, against the black of lava rock and the heavy green of mountain forest. The wild Skeena, the savage, twisting Fraser, the blue-green Thompson, the surging flow of the Kootenay, the calm, opulent power of the Columbia master-stream as it prepares to leave Canada for the United States. The mountains of this province have never been adequately described and never will be. Orderly though they may appear to the geologist, to the layman they are a bewildering jumble of heights and trenches—sawtooth mountains, dogtooth mountains, castellate mountains, dipping-layered mountains, synclinal mountains, anticlinal mountains, matterhorn mountains—and some so impossible to define that the scientists have simply called them "complex mountains"; dalles and holes, sudden fruitful plains fenced in by rock walls eight thousand feet high, hahas of every imaginable kind, blinding white in winter, ice-capped, cloud-capped towers on the roof of the world—this is getting too extravagant but the plain truth is that British Columbia has just about everything and this worries me most of all. In a world catastrophically over-populated, desperate for more energy to waste, more water to pollute, more fresh air to turn into smoke, more happiness to con into unhappiness, more beauty to mock its spiritual poverty with, British Columbia is now a prime target, and her citizens, like all the rest of us, are children of the twentieth century.

Fraser in winter. Canada's lotusland is no stranger to snow.

The Fraser

ere occurred the climax of two centuries of canoe exploration in North America. No easterner, least of all one from the Maritime provinces, is ever likely to feel at home beside the Fraser River. It is alien to everything he knows, and so is its land. Great men have passed through its story, but they did not grow out of the country on which, for brief moments, they partially imposed their wills. Wild and amazing experiences have been recorded in some of the little towns along the Black Canyon and up tributaries like the Thompson, the Lillooet, and the Quesnel, but some of these towns are ghosts today and the descendants of the men who once thronged and brawled in them live elsewhere. It took the people of Switzerland many centuries to establish a real human relationship with the Alps. It will take Canadians of the scientific age at least half as long to do the same with the Rocky Mountains.

This is the most exciting country in Canada, and I don't see how anyone could visit any part of it without longing to return. Its beauty makes you catch your breath. But it was a westerner, Bruce Hutchison, who remarked that the beauty of the most spectacular parts of the Fraser River is that of a nightmare. This is the savagest of all the major rivers of America. It is probably the savagest in the world.

The Fraser is a mountain system, and though the area of its drainage basin is little more than 90,000 miles, here the figures are deceptively low because northern mountains catch huge quantities of snow, especially if they are close to an ocean like the Pacific. The Fraser's total length is 850 miles, its course the shape of the letter S drawn by a man in *delirium tremens*. It rises at 52° 45′ north latitude in two small branches fed by Mount Robson's glacier just west of the Divide, and the moment these feeder streams unite, they find a course in which to run. There in the absolute wilderness of the northern Rockies the drama of the Fraser begins.

Though the ultimate destination lies hundreds of miles to the southwest, the Fraser begins its career by charging northwest in a wide, wavering curve along the Rocky Mountain Trench. After about two hundred miles the rushing waters encounter the northern spur of the Cariboo Mountains, they sweep in a fierce arc around them, then they plunge directly south. Twisting furiously, with only a few brief interludes of relative calm, the Fraser roars for four hundred miles down to the little town of Hope, which began its existence as a Hudson's Bay Company post and was well named, as so many of these posts were, when one considers what awaited a traveller going north before the roads were built. At Hope the Fraser at last breaks out of its mountain trap.

To the geographer what happens here is one of the most exciting natural spectacles in Canada. Within a distance of a mile the entire character of the river changes and this tyrannosaurus of a stream turns sweet and gentle. In a broad valley shining in the sun, with a width the same as the St. John's below Fredericton, the Fraser winds calmly through the loveliest farming valley in the land. The air is balmy, the cattle as sleek as in a Cambridgeshire meadow, the snow peaks Olympian in the safe distance. During these last eighty miles the river traverses most of human British Columbia, for it is in this beautiful corner, and in the twin cities at the estuary, that the bulk of British Columbians live. At the end of its course the Fraser is old King Lear with the rage gone. But before the ocean swallows it, receiving its water through a surprisingly small delta, the river makes one final assertion of its true character. For miles it stains the clean brine of Georgia Strait with the dirty yellow silt it has torn out of the mountains all the way from the top of the Cariboo to the canyon's end at Hope.

"If a river could flow on the moon," I thought as I flew over the Black Canyon, "it would probably look like this."

The idea is not so far-fetched as it looks, because from twenty thousand feet a lot of the land around the central Fraser seems just as chaotic and devoid of purpose as the moon's surface. Those lofty, snow-clad peaks which inspire you when you stare at them from the ground are harsh, barren ridges of rock where nothing lives. The valleys where the elk browse and the little streams cascade are cruel scars. From the air the Rocky Mountains are seldom beautiful.

Yet the air is the best place to study the Fraser if you wish to understand the logic of its course. On the ground, travelling that fantastic highway which has grown out of the old Cariboo Road, the river seems to be coming at you from all directions and the road beside it twists like a spiral stair so that on a dull day, without the sun to tell you your course, you often don't know whether you are travelling north or south. But from the air the twists in the river are seen to be perfectly logical.

The necessity of every river is to get down to sea level by the shortest route possible, and this may vary from a gentle winding in a set direction to a tortured course through every point of the compass until the goal has been reached. The Fraser's terrain is the toughest of any major river in America, possibly of any in the world, and so is its problem.

From the air you see how it solves it. As all of its course save the final eighty miles lies in a mountain labyrinth where the peaks and ranges literally jostle one another, the Fraser must outflank ridge after ridge, and in some places bore its way through sheer walls of rock. From the air you see it like a very yellow, very thin snake that looks as if it had died after having had a convulsion in a rock trap. From the air there is no life in the Fraser, and it does not look like a river at all.

On the ground it explodes with life, and there is a marvellous variety in the spectacle through which it flows. Here the colours are so bold and strong—sage green, orange of sandstone, viridian of hemlock and fir, blue of translucent skies, Wimbledon green on the rare benches where the cattle graze—that a visitor from the east feels he has been translated into a larger, brighter, more exciting existence. The wild flowers are lovely along the Fraser, the wind sounds as though the mountains were breathing, the dawns and sunsets are such that you can only stare at them in silent wonder. Then you look down the steep trench—in many places you look down thousands of feet—and you see the intruder. That furious, frothing water scandalously yellow against the green—where did it come from and how did it get here?

This savage thing! On all the major rivers you expect the occasional turbulence, and you assume that all mountain streams are cataracts. Rivers like the St. Lawrence quickly calm down after their rapids, and mountain streams like the Kicking Horse are shallow and short. But the Fraser is neither short nor shallow. It is all of thirty miles longer than the Rhine, and it flows with cataract force for more than six hundred miles with only a few interludes of relative quiet. In a sense the Fraser does not flow at all: it seethes along with whirlpools so fierce that a log going down it may circle the same spot for days as though caught in a liquid merry-go-round. It roars like an ocean in storm, but ocean storms blow themselves out while the Fraser's roar is forever.

This is the most remorseless force of nature in Canada, and its effect on the person who travels beside it is curious. As you drive north in your car you twist for hour after hour around one hairpin bend after another. Some of these curves around abutments of the cliff can turn the knees of a height-shy traveller to water and I, personally, am glad I was able to travel from Lytton to Lillooet before the road was improved to the width of a super-highway. Past Yale, past Spuzzum and Boston Bar, up through Lytton to Lillooet that curving highway took us, sometimes through little tunnels in the cliff itself, once or twice around a narrow bend with an unguarded edge and a drop of thousands of feet straight down—the road is almost as exciting as the river itself, and you remember that in some of these towns, now quiet and half alive, thousands of desperate men once lived as dangerously as soldiers in war when they panned this river for gold. A little beyond Lytton the road leaves the river, and if you wish to follow the water you must abandon your car and take to the Pacific Great Eastern Railway. Miles higher up to the north, the road and river rejoin at Macalister.

All this time and all these miles the Fraser has been working on you. Sometimes you are so close to the water that its yellow malevolence boils into your subconscious, but most of the time you are so high that it looks as static as it does from the air. Almost never does it seem to belong where it is. Yet it is there, and after you have spent several days beside it, the Fraser intrudes into yourself also, and you are apt to see it in your sleep.

The Fraser River, which seems absolutely hostile to man and all his works, has been as important to British Columbia as the St. Lawrence has been to Quebec. This is another of the amazing facts about it. In his book on the river, Bruce Hutchison argues that the Fraser has practically created the province. So, in a sense, it has, and in a manner awe-inspiring to people from quieter regions.

Fraser salmon, which supported an Indian culture long before the white man came, today gives British Columbia a richer fishing industry than that of the three Maritime provinces combined. The life-cycle of the sockeye salmon is one of those natural dramas so suggestive that the very symbolism of it cuts too close to the human knuckle for mental comfort. The story of the salmon's fight up the river to spawn and die has been told so often and well that I will not repeat it here. Everyone— at least everyone in British Columbia—knows about the fish ladders at Hell's Gate, about the river visibly bulging with life when the big runs come in, about the tributaries turning blood-red as the fish expire while giving life to a new generation, about the bears that wade into the shallows to eat them, about the males fighting with each other for the privilege of dying beside the females of their choice, about the stench which pollutes the wilderness when the bodies decompose. In the upper reaches the salmon are often too far gone in the death process to be eaten by humans, and the great catches are made in the sea when the fish are bright and strong swimming in toward the estuary, or in the lowermost reaches near Mission before the final death-rush begins.

Fraser gold, discovered in 1856 or 1857 (the exact date is uncertain), caused an epic of suffering worse even than the record of the Klondike. Terrible though the Chilkoot was, it was not so cruel as the Fraser rapids down which those heroic fools tried to flounder on rafts. The amount of gold taken out of the sand-bars and lodes at Yale, Boston Bar, Barkerville, and up the Thompson and Lillooet was trivial compared to the hardship and heroism that paid for it, nor were the individual fortunes more permanent than gold-rush fortunes anywhere else.

But the Fraser gold has two by-products of infinite importance to British Columbia. The river in the end carried thousands of disappointed miners down to the estuary where they were deposited like so much sediment with neither the will nor the means to return. Many stayed permanently, and added themselves to the nucleus of humanity which built Vancouver into our third city within three generations. The second by-product was the Cariboo Road.

In 1861 Governor James Douglas, one of the most dynamic men in Canadian history, realized that unless help on a huge scale were provided for the obsessed lunatics digging and panning up the Fraser Canyon, thousands of them would die of famine and cold. He therefore ordered his Royal Engineers to build a route into the interior, and the result was the most spectacularly dangerous highway in America. When the engineers finished their work, the Cariboo Road was a ledge in the cliff sides three hundred and eighty-five miles long and eighteen feet wide. In places the drop from the unguarded lip was thousands of feet, and many a horse and mule, and quite a few men also, hurtled off and down to the end of their troubles. One imaginative teamster even introduced camels to the Cariboo, thinking they would be more sure-footed than horses and mules, but their smell so frightened the other pack animals that the camels were taken off the road.

So far as the original stampeders were concerned, this famous road probably did more harm than good: it provided an excuse for thousands more to join the hordes of gold-fevered men already working there. But when the stampede petered out and the hurdy-gurdy girls and the chisellers went south, when the roaring shack towns turned into bleaching ghost towns, the road was there and remained. It led saner men into the interior who built logging camps and established the great ranches which make British Columbia's Dry Belt a rival in stock raising to the American Southwest.

Fraser silt, deposited over millenniums in the delta and in the valley behind New Westminster, enabled the growing population of the Canadian west coast first to feed itself and later to develop an agricultural exporting industry. Acre for acre, the arable land of the lower Fraser Valley is among the richest in Canada. In recent years, with a folly not incomparable but everywhere present, this priceless heritage has been massively built over by housing developments and the Vancouver International Airport. During the same period the lovely shoreline of English Bay was covered by high-rises, spectacular when lighted after dark but in daytime the usual collection of egg crates standing on their ends.

The economic development forced on the province by the Fraser led inevitably to the construction of railways, and here again the river turned out to be the key to a tremendous engineering problem. The two transcontinental lines, after threading the Rockies from the Kicking Horse and the Yellowhead, use the canyon for their final runs into Vancouver. And the Pacific Great Eastern, the most exciting railway this side of Switzerland, swaying at dizzy heights along the cliffs, goes north to Prince George and finally links the Pacific Coast to the Peace River country.

The world knows little of the Fraser's history—nor does eastern Canada, for that matter—and I would guess there are two reasons for this ignorance. In the first place, nobody can imagine what the river is like unless he has seen it with his own eyes, for there is nothing else resembling it on this continent, and I doubt if there is anything else resembling it in the world. In the second place, modern people everywhere have been conditioned to think of post-voyageur explorations and settlements in the far west in the patterns established in the United States. From Francis Parkman's *The Oregon Trail* to the latest covered-wagon television show, the American story has been told and retold countless times. The story of British Columbia's exploration and settlement has hardly been heard at all.

It was quite different owing to the tradition of Canadian exploration and the nature of the British Columbian terrain. Though the passes through the American Rockies are sometimes difficult, horses and mules could usually negotiate them. But there is nothing in the American west like the nightmare of the Fraser Canyon. Before the building of the Cariboo Road, the pioneers of British Columbia still had to depend on the canoe or on boats, and use them on a river which no human being in his senses would try to navigate unless he had to. Later, when they built roads, they had to blast them out of sheer cliffs.

Incredibly, steamboats were used for a time in the canyon itself, and this fact alone points up the harshness of the Canadian experience in the early days of the coastal province. If anyone stands on the road above Hell's Gate—better still, if he descends to the edge of the river itself at that point—he finds it impossible to believe that anyone would even try to drive a steamboat up-river against that ferocious torrent. But as the alternative was back-breaking labour, men not only tried, they actually succeeded in using steamboats for a while. They dragged them up by means of winches on the ships with hundreds of men heaving on cables as they toiled along the ledges above the water. Many of the men on the ropes were Chinese, and perhaps some of them had worked on the Yangtse or the Yellow River in their native land. The ships' engines roared, sometimes the boilers exploded from excess of pressure, but they were hauled up the canyon against that cataract.

The pioneers of British Columbia, and later the technicians and engineers, circumvented the river's obstacles even though they could not tame the river itself. The challenges they met were never adequately described by them, nor do I think that anyone now can tell their story as it truly was. But to some extent we can guess at it by acquainting ourselves with the river itself, and by looking at some of its vital facts.

The mountains through which the Fraser finds or carves a path are far from the world's highest, but they cover a huge area and are extremely varied. For miles above Lytton the river passes through the so-called Dry Belt of British Columbia where the traveller is astonished to encounter the sagebrush, tumbleweed, and county-sized ranches associated with the American Southwest, and is warned against rattlesnakes on rocky trails. Little rain falls here, and if all the Fraser's course lay through country like this, its volume of flow would be moderate. But all of its course does not lie through country like this.

Many of the ranges sloping in chaos in the general direction of the Fraser are exposed to moist Pacific winds, and in winter they collect billions of tons of snow. By mid-June most of this snow has turned into water and the water runs. The Fraser, draining an area of 91,600 square miles, has to carry all this run-off to the sea. A geographer once told me that the mere statement of these facts tells you all you need to know about the nature of the river. It does, I suppose, to a man with a geographer's imagination. But I myself had to see it to believe it.

"When you reach Lytton," a British Columbian told me in Montreal, "be sure to stand on that little bridge where the Thompson enters. It's a wonderful sight. Thompson water is blue-green and Fraser water is yellow gumbo. You can see them both together—two separate streams in the same course."

I thought I understood what he meant, for the year previous I had been on the Mackenzie and seen the phenomenon of the Liard's brown water flowing along the left bank while the clean Mackenzie water keeps to the right. The two streams are distinguishable side by side for nearly two hundred miles below Fort Simpson. It takes the Mackenzie, one of the most powerful streams in the land, all this distance to absorb its chief tributary.

When I stood on the Lytton bridge the sight was indeed wonderful, but it bore no resemblance to anything I had expected. The Thompson is the Fraser's chief tributary, a major stream in its own right, a mountain stream also, and it does not so much enter the Fraser as smash its way into it like a liquid battering ram. From the bridge I saw its water plunging into the Fraser just as the man said, blue-green into the Fraser's yellow froth. Then it completely disappeared. The Fraser swallowed the Thompson in less than a hundred yards!

As soon as you pass beyond Lytton on the way upriver, you see evidence of the Fraser's power in what it has done to the land. Above Lillooet it has carved out a minor Grand Canyon. Farther up in the plateaux of the ranching country it is almost subterranean: you travel for miles across the ranges and think no water is anywhere and then suddenly you come to the trench and stare far, far down and there is that infernal yellow line frothing along.

But it is at Hell's Gate, its passage made still more narrow by rock-falls from railway blasting, that the prolonged violence of the river reaches its climax, and the best way I can think of describing its ferocity here is by making some comparisons with the St. Lawrence.

The mean flow of the St. Lawrence is 543,000 cubic feet per second, the Fraser's 92,600. But the width of the St. Lawrence in the Seaway section where the Victoria Bridge crosses to Montreal, *before* it has received the Richelieu, the St. Maurice, or any substantial weight of the Ottawa, is more than a mile and a half. The width of the Fraser at Hell's Gate, *after* it has received the Nechako, the Blackwater, the Chilcotin, the Quesnel, the Lillooet, the Thompson, and nearly all its less famous tributaries, is hardly more than fifty yards! This means that a good fly fisherman can cast a line across a river carrying one-fifth the flow of the St. Lawrence!

But there are days on the Fraser which are not average, days which come after steady sunshine and a succession of warm nights have melted the mountain snows in a rush. Then the Fraser becomes incredible.

During the flood of 1948 a flow of 543,000 cubic feet per second was recorded on the Fraser; in the worse flood of 1894, the flow was estimated at 600,000 cubic feet per second. In other words, there was at least one recorded occasion when 57,000 more cubic feet of water per second went through the gap at Hell's Gate than passes on an average day between Quebec and Lévis!

What this meant to the gentle valley below Hope amounted on both occasions to a national catastrophe. Thousands of acres were awash, barns and houses were carried away, cattle were drowned, and the bodies of cows were seen floating in the yellow smear spread for miles into the Strait of Georgia. But in the Black Canyon little was changed because its walls are so sheer and its trough so deep it could hold all the rivers of North America without overflowing. In the twisted gorge the Fraser boiled and roared at prodigious depths and at velocities exceeding thirty knots. It churned millions of tons of sand in its whirlpools, its backwashes tossed giant logs like splinters end over end, it killed thousands of salmon by exhausting the life out of them or by hurling them clear of the water against rocks which broke their spines. It wore several more inches off the little islands which

survive in the channel shaped like the pre-Dreadnaught battleships of the German Kaiser's High Seas Fleet.

I was not on the Fraser when these violent events occurred, but if I had flown over the canyon at those times, I would have seen nothing out of the ordinary at ten thousand feet.

This river was navigated—at least most of it was—by human beings in canoes of the North West Company, and of all the facts connected with the Fraser, this single one is the most impressive to anyone who knows the region. It was later navigated—if you can apply such a technical word to an insanely ignorant venture—by a few stampeders who built themselves rafts intending to float down the current, found themselves trapped in the canyon, and clung to the rafts because this was all they could do. But no stampeder truly navigated the Fraser any more than the logs do. Nor, for that matter, did the Frenchman who swam the river in 1958 swim it in the sense that experts swim the English Channel or Lake Ontario. Equipped with a frogman's outfit, he also was carried down like a log.

But voyageurs legitimately navigated nearly all of it. First, Alexander Mackenzie entered its upper waters in 1793 when he cut through the mountains by way of the Peace on the journey which led him to Dean Channel and the coast. When he launched his canoe on the western side of the Divide he was not sure whether the river would lead him, but he soon discovered that this was the worst river in his experience. His canoe was wrecked in the upper canyon by Fort George and he and his men were nearly drowned. They patched their canoe and continued, but at the point now called Alexandria, Mackenzie decided he had had enough. Besides being a magnificent river man, he had a poet's intuition: he abandoned the river in the nick of time and went overland to the Bella Coola. A few more miles and he would have passed the point of no return.

Boiling deep in its canyon, the Fraser is Canada's most exciting river, and perhaps the most savage on the globe. In John de Visser's photograph, we see the Trans-Canada Highway (in the track of the fabled Cariboo Road) hugging the side of the bluff while the railroad skirts the other bank. This river does not run, it races headlong to the Pacific. It was the gold of its bars and benches that quickened British Columbia to life and when the treasure was spent, settlers stayed on in the interior to farm the fertile upper river meadows.

Fifteen years later in 1808 a different type of Scot, the stolid, factual Simon Fraser, following in the path of the man he referred to tauntingly in his journal as "Sir A. M. K." (the explorer's jealousy again), passed the point where Mackenzie left the river, and kept on going. Like Mackenzie before him, Fraser also was ignorant of the river's nature and even of what river it was. He believed it was the Columbia, and he had entered it with the specific mission of exploring it to the mouth in order to establish British rights to the entire Columbia region. When he entered the Black Canyon and the waters whirled him, he knew he must go through or perish. The result was the climax of the long story of the fur-trading voyages which began when Etienne Brûlé went up the Ottawa to the Chaudière Falls. Fraser's was the most terrible and wonderful inland voyage in the history of North America.

Tiny in their birch-bark canoes, the voyageurs stared up thousands of feet at the walls of that canyon. The river roared so loud they could not hear each other speak, it twisted so fast they could not prepare themselves for what lay around the next bend. When they watched the walls of the canyon flashing past, they must have realized that no canoe, for that matter no ship hitherto built, had ever travelled for such a length of time at such a speed and survived. They were spun like tops in the whirlpools, and when backwashes swept them ashore, they portaged over cliffs thousands of feet high, for they could not survive if they stayed still—their food was running out—and they did not believe it possible to return. Finally they reached Hell's Gate, which inspired the most celebrated passage in Fraser's journal:

"I have been for a long period in the Rocky Mountains, but have never seen anything like this country. It is so wild I cannot find words to describe it at times. We had to pass where no human being should venture; yet in those places there is a regular pathway impressed, or rather indented on the very rocks by frequent travelling."

This so-called pathway had been made by Indians who had been in the region so long that the village now called Lytton claims to be the oldest permanently settled place in North America. Fraser and his men, their canoes abandoned on the shore, crawled sideways with their packs along the cliff, hanging on to twisted vines "formed like a ladder or the shrouds of a ship". Somehow they got through, and lower down they bought Indian dugouts and so reached the ocean.

It was typical of Simon Fraser that when he reached the delta he was as disappointed as Mackenzie had been when he came to the larger delta on the Beaufort Sea. Whatever else this awful river might be, Fraser knew it was not the Columbia. Not being able to foresee the future, he assumed that his mission was a failure and turned back.

The return journey was in some ways worse than the passage going down, though at least its dangers could no longer surprise them. The Indians turned hostile and bombarded them with rocks which they dropped from the cliffs above. Their supplies were nearly gone, their clothing in rags, their shoes holed and torn, their bodies exhausted, and their minds dazed with hardship and danger. Simon Fraser was not an especially attractive character, but his dogged courage was rock-like, and his powers of leadership must surely have been as great as Mackenzie's. At the moment of their bottom despair, this normally undramatic man made his Scottish and *Canadien* voyageurs join hands and take this oath:

"I solemnly swear before Almighty God that I shall sooner perish than forsake any of our crew during the present voyage."

They got through. On the northern end of Hell's Gate they found their abandoned canoes intact, and those amazing men dragged and paddled them north the way they had come. They reached Fort George in thirty-four days. This last statement should be repeated: Simon Fraser and his party, fighting their way back against that river, reached Fort George in thirty-four days!

While this voyage was taking place, the North West Company's geographer, David Thompson, was on the river which Fraser had at first believed he was on himself, and three years later Thompson explored the Columbia to its mouth.

Out of Fraser's voyage grew the story of British Columbia, which unfolded so rapidly in the next one hundred and fifty years that British Columbians themselves seem unable to realize how astonishing their advance has been. It took generations for eastern cities like Quebec and Halifax to grow, but Vancouver and the little towns of the lower Fraser Valley leaped up in a moment of time. As late as the First World War, the sole university in the province was little more than an extension department of McGill; today it is larger than McGill and one of the best institutions in the country. Vancouver is now Canada's third city; a century hence it will probably be her first, as the Pacific replaces the Atlantic in human importance.

But progress, not even with the instruments of a growing science behind it, can never change the character of British Columbia's chief river unless they dam it. Should that happen—and it well may if only because of American demands for Canadian water—the world's richest salmon fishery will disappear. At the time I write this, the men who wish to dam the Fraser have been rejected and the river is still itself. So long as it is allowed to remain so, and so long as mountain snows melt, the Fraser will roar and foam and will still be the narrowest and most savage of all the major rivers of this continent.

The Thompson

The road that leads up the Thompson River from its confluence with the Fraser at Lytton is an overture to one of the most complex river systems in the western hemisphere, a system shared by Canada and the United States, the Columbia being the master stream. Anyone who tries to follow the tributaries of the Columbia, to say nothing of the Columbia itself, will soon understand why David Thompson, greatest of all North American geographers, took four years to unravel the system and more than two to discover which stream was the actual master. Before his explorations began in this region, all that was known of the Columbia was that a great river discharged into the Pacific below Puget Sound.

Ironically, Thompson probably never saw the river which now bears his name, though it is not impossible that he crossed one of its headwaters where it was a mountain brook. The river was discovered in 1808 by Simon Fraser just before he and his party reached Hell's Gate, and Fraser named it the Thompson because he believed the geographer of his company had already explored its upper reaches. Fraser's dislike of Sir Alexander Mackenzie was the temperamental dislike of a rugged, plodding man for a dashingly brilliant man, but among those who knew him, David Thompson had not an enemy in the world.

The Thompson is a two-forked river and its North Branch comes out of glaciers in the Columbia Mountains not far west of the Yellowhead Pass. The South Branch has its source in Shuswap Lake. The branches unite at the head of Kamloops Lake, flow through it, and issue in a common channel for their final run down to the Fraser. The length of the Thompson's North Branch is 210 miles, the length of the South Branch 206 miles, the length of their united course 100 miles.

Such is the complexity of the British Columbia river systems, so narrow the margin dividing one from the other, that though the Thompson does indeed belong to the Fraser, the source of its South Branch lies so close to the Columbia that it would be easily possible for engineers to divert the upper Columbia into it, thereby turning the greatest of British Columbian rivers into a tributary of the second greatest.

We may be certain that this will never happen. Apart from what such an interference with nature might do to the ecological balance, it would result in such a commercial disaster for the states of Washington and Oregon that any attempt to divert the Columbia into the all-Canadian Fraser would be a public request for a visit from the United States Marines.

The only defence the weak have against the strong is the law and it is fortunate for Canada that her American neighbours are great respecters of legal principles.

Should we meddle with the Columbia, our neighbours would have the law on their side. In my student days I had to study a difficult but amusing speech of the Athenian lawyer Demosthenes on just such a subject. An Athenian olive farmer, living on the upper slope of one of the mountains that ring Athens, once upon a time diverted a watercourse in such a way that it washed out the house of his neighbour who lived a few hundred yards lower down. The court established the principle that a river shared by neighbours is a common property between them in respect to what each may expect in benefit from the river. True, this principle was ignored by the United States when Mexico complained that American damming of the Colorado River deprived Mexico of its rights on the lower course, but they had no chance. Nearly all of the Colorado is in the United States. Most of the Columbia is also in the United States. And in the United States' courts—our neighbours are human, after all—some rights are held to be more divine than others.

Canada also has her rights on the Columbia and its tributaries. If she is to defend them, she must be as realistic as a strong-minded woman who is intelligent enough to understand when it is necessary to be virtuous.

The Thompson River leads you also into the heart of southern British Columbia, a region as varied as it is stupendous, so wonderful, so beautiful, that no writer could possibly do it justice. He can only share his experience with his readers as best he can.

On all the occasions when I travelled up the Fraser Canyon the season was spring and the Fraser, boiling with power as it carried off the melted mountain snows, could be seen swallowing the Thompson in a single shark-like gulp. When finally we went there in mid-September after an exceptionally dry summer, the Fraser was in such low water it almost seemed tame. The shores of a river like this are almost as informative as a ship's Plimsoll line, and after studying the water marks I estimated that the Fraser was anywhere from fifteen to eighteen feet lower than during a normal June. At any rate, it gave the Thompson a chance for once. While a setting sun cast a corona of violet light over the western mountains, we watched the Thompson come flooding in under that old-fashioned iron bridge at Lytton. The Thompson was in equally low water but it seemed to have much more force, relative to the Fraser, than it has in the spring, and because it is a splendid river I felt happy for it. It flowed with a silky power into the master, a swirl on its surface, not so green as it is in the spring but gleaming nevertheless, brownish-yellow I thought, yet full of light, absorbing and reflecting the sky so that the whole effect of it was like shot silk. The Thompson's flow within the Fraser was perfectly distinct for more than a quarter of a mile. It was very moving and very beautiful.

The sunset faded and we saw fog coming up the valley and mounting to the heights as swiftly as ever I saw fog pour into Halifax harbour from the Atlantic. We could feel it in our throats and the air struck cold, so we went to a restaurant and ordered steaks to fortify us after a very long day. When the plates arrived they were completely hidden by enormous servings of meat. Eating in Greece had accustomed me to the bone structure of domestic goats but from the size of these it was clear that the animals from which they had come had been one of their wild ancestors—in other words, wild mountain goats. The meat was tough, gamy, and excellent and we could feel the nourishment in it getting to work in us.

Four men in the red shirts of hunters were at the next table and I asked the nearest of them if the hunting season had begun. With his mouth full of meat which he himself had shot, he jerked his fork in an easterly direction and said, "Yeah, but not yet on this side of the river."

It had been a weird day. We had left Montreal on a DC-8 at 10:30, Eastern Standard Time. Cloudy weather over the Shield, clearing over Superior, and after Thunder Bay glorious as we flew over the line of the voyageurs: Rainy River distinct in every bend, the turbulent, dangerous, but indispensable Winnipeg River incredibly small when seen from 36,000 feet, a twisting thread through the bush. The delta of the Red River was so blurred that I thought its appearance was caused by the jet stream until I realized that the noon daylight was so crystalline that I was looking down at the part of the delta which is actually submerged in Lake Winnipeg, that I was watching the Red in the process of making *more* delta. Cloud cover over the Rockies; a quick glimpse of the Columbia going north, a flash of Kootenay Lake; soon afterwards another glimpse of the Columbia going south; Salmon Arm; then clouds over everything, ourselves in them, finally feeling the plane descending, the lights coming on up front telling us to fasten seat belts and extinguish cigarettes; then out into brilliant sunshine and a cloudless sky, and close to starboard the Fraser coming into its delta looking calm, liberated, and mighty. At the airport we rented a car and by 3:00 o'clock Pacific Coast time we were on our way to the familiar but ever-strange highway leading up the canyon past Hope. I remembered seeing a cable car crossing the river at Hell's Gate; it wasn't there the last time I had passed. A sense of incredulity came over me as I realized that barely twelve hours after breakfasting on an egg and bacon in Montreal, we were eating wild goat at the confluence of the Thompson and Fraser, 182 miles from Vancouver.

Within a mile of the Fraser Canyon, the Thompson takes you into a country as different from what you have left as Nevada is different from the rich mountain forests of northern California. The hills here are bare of almost everything except sagebrush and most of them are as tawny as lions. Yet once upon a time all this land must have been fertile, for it contains rich grass-growing minerals. We had been up here a few years before, guests of Mr. Walter Koerner at a ranch near Ashcroft, and had seen for the first time a kind of farming I have never seen anywhere else save in south-central British Columbia.

There are magnificent natural terraces along the banks of the lower Thompson and most of them have been planted for winter and summer fodder. This is great cattle country and real cowboys ride its ranges. In a land which otherwise would be desert, water has been piped down from lakes as high as two thousand feet in the mountains to feed a network of pipes laid out along the terraces below. From some of them protrude the nozzles of sprayers, just like those you see on city lawns except for this: with that tremendous head of water, the pressure is so great that water jets are hurled as far as a hundred yards and this is a wonderful sight when the sun shines through them. When that happens, the air over the terraces of the Thompson is filled with rainbows.

"Oh yes," said the tall rancher, "there are rattlesnakes here. Plenty of them right over there in the alfalfa. But they're like any other wild animal. They get out of your way when they hear you coming."

At Ashcroft the Thompson bends toward the southwest and its valley becomes wide and spacious. It cuts a deep trench along the side of the lion-coloured foothills which mount slowly up to the high range to the west. Not far from Ashcroft you come upon a tragic reminder of the 1914-18 War commemorated by a roadside plaque set up by the British Columbia Department of Recreation and Conservation. The land roundabout is almost pure desert and the inscription on the plaque is as poignant as any war memorial in a French village with its terrible, incredibly long, list of the names of the needlessly dead:

THE GHOST OF WALHACHIN
Here bloomed a Garden of Eden. The sagebrush desert changed to orchards through the imagination and industry of English settlers during 1907-1914. Then the men left to fight—and die—for king and country. A storm ripped out the irrigation flume. Now only ghosts of flume, trees, and homes remain to mock this once thriving settlement.

When it leaves the western end of Kamloops Lake, the Thompson is deep, strong, and about 150 feet wide. I even took its temperature and found it an invigorating 60 degrees on this fine mid-September day. The lake bends off southeasterly toward a narrows—haze shot through with sun—and the city of Kamloops is at the far end. It was founded in 1812 as a fur-trading post and its name is a corruption of the Indian word *cumcloups,* which means "meeting of the waters". Kamloops citizens breathe air well tinctured with the profitable perfume that accompanies the manufacture of paper, with wonderful country all about them and a tremendous prospect where the two arms of the Thompson do not so much enter the lake as melt into it, again a silky tranquillity reflecting the high clouds of noon and catching in its mirror the outline of a mountain.

The Thompson is an overture to more than a most complex system of rivers; at Kamloops it brings you to the gates of not just one country but of many, and the magnitude, the beauty, the wildness here awes the soul; awes it almost as much as your fear of what modern man may do to it.

If you follow the course of the North Thompson, you can travel for 210 miles northwest through mountain country which man has scarcely even scratched, all the way to its source just west of Mount Robson and the Great Divide. If you follow the South Branch, the road will take you past its source in Shuswap Lake, on through Craigellachie where Lord Strathcona drove in the last spike of the C.P.R., on again through Revelstoke—range after range—to the Great Divide at Golden, whence you descend into Banff National Park. Then it is that you can see what a role the Thompson has played in the settlement of British Columbia and the west coast, for the lines of Canada's principal railway systems follow both its branches and continue along its united course into the Fraser Valley.

The other routes leading out of Kamloops take you out of the Fraser system and into the Columbia's.

The Thompson swings into a tight curve as it nears junction with the Fraser, at Lytton, B.C.

The Columbia System

When I was a schoolboy who had never heard of the Columbia River, least of all known that in the early nineteenth century most Americans called it the Oregon, a series of lines in William Cullen Bryant's *Thanatopsis* made such an impression on me that nearly fifty years later (I still can't believe I've been around that long) I was able to remember them verbatim:

> Take the wings
> Of morning, pierce the Barcan wilderness
> Or lose thyself in the continuous woods
> Where rolls the Oregon, and hears no sound
> Save its own dashings—yet the dead are there;
> And millions in those solitudes, since first
> The flight of years began, have laid them down
> In their last sleep.

It was the phrase "where rolls the Oregon" that sank those lines into my memory. Though Bryant seems never to have been west of the Alleghenies, he must have read some description of the river after the Lewis and Clark expedition and the verb he chose was perfect: "rolls" is the *mot juste* for the largest river of the Pacific slope after the Yukon, 1,214 miles of magnificent river, 459 of them in Canada. As for the dead the poet thinks of—more hundreds of thousands of Indians than historic man can guess at and some he knew: Kootenay Appee, loyal friend of David Thompson; the two Piegans whom Thompson says "were murdered by Captain Lewis"; those uncounted, unknown ones who fed on game and the fish of the best salmon river after the Fraser and died of accident or old age; the later ones who perished from the white man's smallpox; the last ones who died of broken lives after the white man took their country and drained their pride of its last drop of meaning.

From its source in Columbia Lake the river flows about 180 miles north in wild mountain country before rounding the uppermost spur of the Selkirk Range to begin its long journey southwest to the sea and its destiny. This is the Columbia's Canadian Big Bend—it has another in the States. From its source at 50° north latitude to its most southerly dip at 45° 31' near Portland and up northwest to its estuary, the total drop of the river is 2,650 feet, of which almost half are in Canada. This figure explains why the Columbia had the power behind it to carve its way through the mighty Cascade Mountains of Washington and Oregon and reach the sea. A lonely river much of it still is, in spite of some industrial developments in Canada and the celebrated dams and cities it has brought into existence along its lower reaches in the United States. A vast river lower down and not so long ago as solitary as it still is in its course from Columbia Lake and around the Canadian Big Bend.

The Columbia is a river of magnitude not only because of itself but because of its tributaries. Literally, they come into it from all points in the compass (one of them a giant in its own right and as long as the Athabaska), all of them splendid. The lovely little Okanagan, leaving its lake to flow over its falls, travels forty-three miles in Canada and seventy more in the United States before joining the Columbia about forty miles west of the Grand Coulee Dam. The Snake (called after an Indian tribe, not the reptile) is nearly a thousand miles long. Rising in Yellowstone Park in western Wyoming, the Snake follows a bending course much of the way through Idaho, then turns northwest to pour into the Columbia near the little town of Burbank, which is connected only by name with the industrial suburb of Los Angeles. The Pend Oreille, also called after an Indian tribe (in the States, generally called the Clark Fork) rises in Montana to run northwest; after staying American for 650 miles, it nips into Canada near Trail and, a dozen miles later, still in Canada but just barely, it finally unites with the master stream.

But it is in the orderly chaos of the British Columbian mountain ranges that this river system finds its subtlest expressions; no wonder it took David Thompson so long to unravel it.

In Canada the principal tributary is the Kootenay and there can be few streams on our planet which follow so wildly eccentric a course. This may be why all the estimates of its length I have researched differ one from the other. Including its passage, or sojourn, in Kootenay Lake, I would guess that its total length is about 426 miles, though for a reason I shall give later, it might be prudent to allow some forty miles more. Of its total flow, about 126 miles are in Idaho.

Most bewildering are the directions it has taken. Only a few miles to the east of the Columbia, where the master stream runs north, the young Kootenay flows in directly the opposite direction from the young Columbia—south—and at Canal Flats it misses a collision with the Columbia by little more than a mile. As the placename indicates, Canal Flats is a freak stretch of level ground running at right angles to the general line of the mountain ranges and once there was a canal cut through it. This canal was a ditch 6,700 feet long and 45 feet wide, equipped with a single lock, and it was completed in 1889 by William Adolf Baillie-Grohman, a man half-Scotch and half-Austrian. The digging work was done by Cantonese who could speak no English. When the canal was completed, it enabled small steamboats to sail from Idaho up the Kootenay into Canada, then cross over into the Columbia. The canal was abandoned in 1914.

In prehistoric time there was a union of the Kootenay and the Columbia in this region far more interesting than

Baillie-Grohman's canal. This is proved by the existence of Pacific salmon in Kootenay Lake. As it would have been impossible for the salmon to jump the succession of cataracts and waterfalls between the Columbia and the West Kootenay River and so enter Kootenay Lake, it is clear that at some time the Kootenay flooded westward over the Flats into Columbia Lake, with the result that salmon which had swum all the way up from the Pacific to spawn, crossed over into the Kootenay without knowing that they and their descendants would be trapped there for centuries, if not forever.

If the Kootenay could fool a Pacific salmon, it should be no surprise that it also fooled for such a long time the greatest geographical explorer in North American history. For several years David Thompson called the Kootenay "McGillivray's River" and used it constantly in his exploratory travels. For a time he even believed it was the river we now call the Columbia, the master stream he knew entered the Pacific below Puget Sound.

The Kootenay flows gaily out of Canada into Idaho, where it turns west, then changes its direction and turns north to come home to Canada and flow into Kootenay Lake. It does not stop even here. In a series of five separate cascades it comes surging out of the lake's western arm (here it is called the West Kootenay) and finally bursts with power into the Columbia at Brilliant, just around the mountain spur from Castlegar. I love this river. It's one of the gayest I ever saw for a stream of its size, and it may not be entirely sentimental to find it symbolic of the many Canadians who emigrated south across the border, did well there, and finally decided to come home again.

The Columbia's drainage basin is immense, and thanks to the Snake, the Pend Oreille, the Spokane, and *their* tributaries, all but 38,000 square miles of the basin's 259,000 square miles are in the United States, where in its final run the river forms the boundary between the states of Oregon and Washington.

Up to the end of his life, the knowledge that this was the case enraged David Thompson. Though the mouth of the Columbia was discovered in 1792 by Captain Robert Gray of Boston, who named the river after his ship; though in the same year it was mapped a hundred miles inland by the British naval lieutenant William Broughton, and in 1805 was reached overland by Lewis and Clark, the river's true explorer and essential discoverer was unquestionably David Thompson.

This humane and marvellous man, who also turned out to be a splendid writer of prose, was left a partial orphan in England at the age of two. His mother's poverty caused him to be apprenticed as a clerk to the Hudson's Bay Company and at the age of fourteen he landed at Churchill Factory. Almost a lifetime later, remembering his childhood emotions in his *Travels in Western North America, 1784-1812*, Thompson wrote that "When the ship sailed and from the top of the rocks I lost sight of her, the distance [from home and his mother] became immeasurable and I bid a long and sad farewell to my country, an exile forever."

Exile though he was, he was to explore and map nearly a third of the northern half of a continent. Thompson's expeditions took him hundreds of thousands of miles in canoes, on horseback, and on foot. Often he nearly died of exposure, of hostile attacks from Indians (with whom he usually got on very well), and of plain starvation. He married an Indian woman whom he dearly loved and she and "my little ones" accompanied him on many of his mountain journeys. He discovered the true source of the Mississippi and the true source of the St. Lawrence system in the little River St. Louis. In a desperate journey across the Northwest Territories in 1796, he mapped the route through Reindeer and Wollaston lakes to Lake Athabaska.

But Thompson's greatest and most difficult feat was his unravelling and mapping of the entire Columbia River System. In those years he was the official geographer of the North West Company and it was hoped that his explorations and mappings would secure for British North America the Columbia Basin, or at least such parts of it as now are contained in the State of Washington.

In one of the most concentrated single efforts of exploration in the history of the continent, working continuously from 1807 to 1811, suffering almost constant hardship, Thompson completed his task so thoroughly that almost every detail of it has stood up since. But the political gains which should have resulted were casually thrown away in London when Daniel Webster out-negotiated Lord Ashburton and between them they fixed the western international boundary with the Webster-Ashburton Treaty of 1842. Thompson was then seventy-two years old and to him this was an Esau deal which seemed to nullify much of his life's work. Years earlier he had predicted that the southern portions of the Columbia Basin were sure to become "a rich habitat for civilized man". In his *Travels* he wrote bitterly that "These fine countries, by the capitulation of that blockhead called Lord Ashburton, now belong to the United States."

Had Thompson lived on into the mid-twentieth century his bitterness would have been beyond his powers of expression. Apart from the splendid and beautiful country in Washington and Oregon, the southern Columbia River generates today more than one-third of all the potential hydro-electric power in the whole United States. There are several power developments there of which the greatest and most famous is the Grand Coulee Dam. Ninety miles west of Spokane, the Grand Coulee was completed in 1941 and enough concrete went into it to build a two-lane highway all the way from Seattle to New York City. The dam stands near the head of Grand Coulee itself, a steep-walled chasm through which the Columbia used to flow. Behind it is a 151-mile-long reservoir called the Franklin D. Roosevelt Lake, and some 3,000 people were ousted from their homes to make space for it. Though the Grand Coulee produces less than half the power that will come out of Churchill Falls in full operation, there are other dams there as well, of which the largest is the Bonneville. There are also grave problems which the international character of the Columbia System is bound to generate in the near future, and if Canada's performance in defending her rights is no better than it has been in the past, British Columbia's own share in the system could easily be sacrificed.

But I don't wish to talk here about the politics. I want to return to the river itself.

The Columbia, like the Fraser, is largely the product of the western mountain systems. Without understanding the main character of these ranges, one becomes lost and bewildered by the apparently contradictory directions taken by the tributaries of the Columbia and the master stream itself.

In the southeastern regions of British Columbia, the mountain system extends northwest for some 430 miles from the international boundary to the upper Fraser Valley. On the east, it is separated from the Canadian Rockies by the Rocky Mountain Trench. On the west, it slopes more or less gently toward the interior plateau.

Southern British Columbia is the toughest habitable terrain in all North America, as anyone knows who has read the story of the Canadian Pacific Railway. The mountain system which determines the character of the Columbia River and of all its Canadian tributaries is broad in the south where it is composed of three parallel ranges—from east to west, the Purcell, the Selkirk, and the Monashee. Each one of these is separated from its neighbours by deep trenches with the ranges standing like vast irregular walls on either side of them. There are a few—very few—transverse valleys which alone have made it possible for roads and railways to pass through them east to west and west to east.

The Purcell Range in the east is separated from the Selkirk by the Purcell Trench, which is what the geologists call "a huge fault valley" holding—God bless it!—the most beautiful inland lake on the continent, Kootenay. The Selkirk extends north and the top of it is rounded by the Canadian Big Bend of the Columbia. This range in

The Columbia begins its 1,200-mile run to the Pacific high in southern B.C. — and was once Canadian the whole way.

turn is separated from the Monashees by the Selkirk Trench, which contains part of the Columbia River and the two Arrow Lakes through which the river flows. The Monashees reach to the North Thompson River, and westerly they merge with the Fraser Plateau. Just north of the Monashees are the Cariboo Mountains, which are responsible for the upper loop of the Fraser, just as the Selkirk is responsible for the northern Big Bend of the Columbia.

These are very great mountains. When covered by snow and ice in winter—they all contain their glaciers—they are a spectacle when seen from the air that nobody could possibly describe. The Selkirk and Purcell ranges often reach to more than 10,000 feet, a low height in comparison to the Andes and Himalayas, but here they seem gigantic because frequently they rise 8,000 feet above the valley floors where the rivers run. Between them they breed the upper Columbia River System. Even the Okanagan Range, most easterly of the three ranges of the British Columbian Cascades, the general elevation of peaks being 8,500 feet, gives some tribute to the Columbia River.

What a marvellous river system this is! Is there another on our planet which contains such a galaxy of mountain lakes: in Idaho, Lake Pend Oreille; in British Columbia, the Okanagan, the twin Arrows, the Kootenay, and Columbia Lake itself? To describe them in words would make me as stupid as the pornographer who reduces what should be a transcendental experience of the senses to the dull bureaucracy of a factual report on mechanical movements and concrete measurements. Two millennia ago Catullus showed how this should be done. After a stretch of military service in Anatolia, he returned to his country home at Sirmio, a promontory on Lago di Garda which slips north into the brow of the Italian Alps. There he wrote an ode which recurs to me whenever I remember Kootenay Lake:

Paene insularum, Sirmio, insularumque
Ocelle, quascunque in liquentibus stagnis
Marique vasto fert uterque Neptunus . . .

To translate a poem of Catullus is as impossible as to translate the King James Bible into modern English, but I suppose I can give the gist of it: "Bright eyelet of all the islands and almost-islands Neptune bears in still lake waters and the vast sea—how willingly, how joyously I come to you again, hardly believing even myself that I have left the plains of Bithynia and see you in safety. Oh, what more delicious than for stress to melt away as the mind slips off its burden and tired with foreign jobs we come home to our own hearth and rest our heads on the pillow of our dreams? . . . Hail, you lovely Sirmio, and be glad for your heir. Be glad, you waters of the Lydian lake.

Laugh—laugh out loud with all the splashing laughter that's in your house!"

The Arrow Lakes—in places the mountains rise out of them like sheer walls—do not take their name from their shapes, as I had once assumed, but because numerous Indian arrowheads were found imbedded in fissures along their cliffs. Apparently the Indians had used these fissures as targets in a practice range and what a sight that must have been—braves with feathers sticking out of their hair firing fusillades of arrows against the cliffside from canoes on that miraculous, sky-reflecting lake with the ranges soaring above it.

The Okanagan

The Okanagan Valley is about sixty-nine miles long running almost directly north to south with wild forested mountains above it where cougars still hunt—I met a woman who had shot a giant cougar the winter before when she saw him trying to kill her dog. She had the pelt and the photograph to prove it and she was very angry at the growing takeover of the whole district by foreigners coming in with money. Said it was pretty nearly impossible for a native boy or girl to get a job in the hotels farther down. Said also that in those same hotels the guests were served tinned peaches imported from the south right in the middle of the Okanagan fruit season. Said it was a damned shame, the sell-out, and she didn't care who heard her say it. And certainly in that autumn of 1972 the only fresh fruit we ate came from roadside stalls where the local farmers had their stands. Certainly also every waitress we talked to in the local hotels had come up for the summer jobs from California and Oregon, the hotels, naturally, belonging to chains.

It is still a wonderful valley for fruit and vegetables, the climate permitting peaches and apricots in addition to the apples. And that long slip of a lake, in places 800 feet deep—naturally some local people insist that it's so deep its bottom has never been found—has some fine towns along its shores in Vernon, Kelowna, Summerland, and Penticton, the latter of which was home of the famous Penticton Vees, the last minor-league Canadian hockey club ever to beat the Russians decisively. These are gracious little cities and towns and it's no wonder that megalopolitans are looking them over thoughtfully these days.

Just below Penticton, the little Okanagan River goes over its falls—more of a rapid than a heavy waterfall and controlled by a small dam—and it moves south so merry, blue, and bubbling it could be the kid brother of the stripling Athabaska. Okanagan Falls is a lovely place, but after wandering around it, all alone, a sudden instinct warned me to be careful where I planted my feet. I saw nothing dangerous, but the instinct was there just the same. And sure enough. A few hours later we were on top of Anarchist Mountain where a keen wind was whistling and we stared for a long time at a panoramic view of the valley, the lake, and the line of the old Dewdney Trail used by the fur-traders and gold-hunters coming east from the coast. A little farther on a work gang was repairing the road and we had to wait for half an hour before we were allowed through. I got into conversation with a cheerful youth with ruddy cheeks and a big grin and asked him if there were rattlesnakes in these ranges. He perked up at the question.

"You want any rattlers? The place for you to go is OK Falls. OK Falls is the best place for rattlers in the whole province. The Wild Life gives you ten bucks apiece if you catch them alive."

"You do that yourself?"

"I wanted to go to Vancouver a couple of weekends ago and I needed some dough so I caught and sold four of them. You know—the old forked stick, grab them behind the ears and dump them into the sack. I got a couple in sacks at home right now."

Anyone from eastern Canada, with the built-in assumption that in North America the frontier has always moved from east to west, discovers that in many parts of British Columbia the opposite has happened. In southern British Columbia the frontier has generally moved west from the coast into the mountains. First the gold-hunters, then the forest industries, then the mines, then the smelters. At Trail, where the Columbia sweeps so splendidly out of the mountains and about the city, there stands, reeking and sweating, the Cominco smelter, which is the largest producer of lead and zinc in the world. Towns like Rossland, Kinnaird, and Castlegar—the Columbia really surging as it sweeps past the latter—are still frontier industrial towns. But still farther east, anyone who knew western Texas or Arizona thirty or more years ago rubs his eyes. Cranbrook could be Amarillo.

Except that all about these towns of British Columbia are the majestic mountains, and the moment you leave them you are in a wilderness of continuous woods. Low-lying haze of wood smoke in some of the valleys in the evening. The sudden pungency of sulphur fumes. These in the immense silence as night falls in the mountains.

The Kootenay

Though the Kootenay is certainly a part of the Columbia System, the nature of its course and its great air of independence seem to belie this fact. As I come from Nova Scotia where the estuaries are large and the rivers themselves are very small, I have always preferred to explore a river from its mouth to its source. And this is what I did with the Kootenay, first finding it as it enters the Columbia, then dodging my way eastward across the ranges to find it elsewhere.

In its final rush toward its union with the Columbia, the West Kootenay has been dammed in five different locations in a stretch of only twenty-five miles. The total production of hydro-electric power has been calculated at 302,345 kilowatts at maximum capacity, with 280,000 as the average. Though the hydro experts prefer to call these dams "head plants" or "run-of-the-river" plants, my own noun is "step-dam", which Mr. V. Raudsepp, Deputy Minister of Water Resources in B.C., was kind enough to agree was at least descriptive. For that is what they really are—a series of five huge steps which enable the Kootenay to descend to the Columbia without behaving like a drunk falling head over heels downstairs.

The western arm of Kootenay Lake is a long, narrow sleeve of deep, blue-green water enfolded by glorious mountains, and out of it pours the West Kootenay River. The highest dam, the Corra Linn with its thirteen gates, was built to control the lake level during the so-called "storage draught season" from September to March. On the way down it is backed up by the Nelson Dam, then by the two Bonningtons—wonderful spectacles, those huge washes of white, roaring water against the dark green of the mountain forest and the paler green of the river. Last step of all is at Brilliant above the confluence. And just as anyone at Niagara Falls must wish to have been born early enough to have seen Niagara in its primeval state of power, so anyone at the confluence of the Kootenay and Columbia must wish the same. Even now, the Columbia looks as if something pretty big has happened to it here. The weight of all that water coming down from Kootenay Lake makes the master stream really heave.

Kootenay Lake is the largest of all the lakes in the system within Canada, with an area of 168 square miles and depths in places of 500 feet. Along its western shore, another of British Columbia's scenic highways takes you all the way south from Kootenay Bay to Creston, near which the Kootenay River, running north out of Idaho, enters its lake. Here the river is about 130 yards wide, smooth but with a firm flow, and its valley is great farm-land almost prairie-flat between the Selkirks and the Purcells. I found myself remembering the fortnight I had spent in Sparta in my student days, taking many long walks and boning up on Plato until the fleas in my 75-cents-a-day hotel room finally drove me into a sixty-mile hike through Langhada Gorge in the Taygetus mountains and down to the sea at Kalamata. The Spartan plain is very like this land near Creston. "Hollow Lacedaemon" it was called by the people we described a few years ago as the "ancient" Greeks, our time-sense being somewhat more parochial then than it is now. In September this section of the Kootenay Valley was golden with wheat, splashed here and there with the heavy green of alfalfa, and you looked up from the river bank to the mountains.

Next you must cross the Purcell Range if you wish to discover the Kootenay flowing south again. Here the Kootenay Pass reaches to more than 5,800 feet with the mountains towering thousands of feet above it. As an aircraft flies—no crow could make it this high—the distance to old Fort Steele is little more than fifty miles. It is much farther by road, twisting and turning, climbing and descending, until you feel yourself a part of that gigantic scenery. You find a delightful haha when you descend to still another river valley where flows the Moyie, a happy little stream which rises in Moyie Lake and is one of the Kootenay's major (and one of the Columbia's minor) tributaries. With the perversity of all streams hereabouts, the Moyie flows south into Idaho before it joins the Kootenay, which at the confluence is busily flowing north into Canada.

The eastern Kootenay Valley is one of the great scenes in all Canada. Here, with the river pouring strongly south, the valley itself is so straight for many miles that it might have been laid out by a modern technocrat, wonderful, the Purcell Range high in the west, the Rockies stern and grey in the east, and straight northward you go to the Kootenay's source. Comes the moment just beyond Canal Flats where you lose the Kootenay and it's the source of the Columbia you cross as it leaves that jewel of a lake on its way north. A little farther north at Radium Hot Springs you turn abruptly eastward through the Sinclair Pass which leads you into Kootenay National Park, the mountains here pressing so close that the road is like a dry fjord between perpendicular rock walls. You emerge from the pass to confront a vast panorama—a broad, wild valley and there, far below, is the Kootenay River flickering along in the lee of mountains ten thousand feet high. These, of course, belong to the Canadian Rockies.

You descend and are beside the river again. Some fifteen miles farther north, at Kootenay Crossing, the stream marked on the maps as the Kootenay River can be seen coming out of a labyrinth of wilderness mountains, here no more than a brook. But a much stronger stream, marked on the map as the Vermillion River, so named because of the colour of some of the earth found along its banks, comes bubbling down from Vermillion Pass just west of the Great Divide. But of course the Vermillion is nothing else than the true headwaters of the Kootenay itself and, unless I'm mistaken, its source is a glacial-green marsh of spring water just west of the Divide.

This is not the most northerly source of any stream in the Columbia System; still farther north are the Blaeberry River coming out of a glacier in Yoho, the Sullivan coming out of the Columbia Icefield, the Canoe River flowing directly south to join the master stream at Boat Encampment at the very apex of the Big Bend. But when you turn east from the source of the Vermillion, the road begins to descend and after a very few miles there appears a new strong river flowing down past Mount Eisenhower to Banff. This is of course the Bow, which after Calgary is called the South Saskatchewan, river of the voyageurs. It flows across the prairies to join the North Saskatchewan east of Prince Albert, through the Grand Rapids into Lake Winnipeg, out of Lake Winnipeg into the Nelson and at York Factory out of the Nelson into Hudson Bay.

At Windermere, B.C., the Columbia is close to its headwaters in the Kootenay district.

And on to the eternal sea

I am writing now in mid-July, one year and a month since I began this book, six weeks after I completed it. Over most of North America east of the Rockies, and above all in eastern Canada, the post-winter months of 1973 have been the wettest in living memory.

Everywhere these past three months the rivers have been overflowing. The Mississippi broke its banks and levees in early spring, soon to be followed by the St. John, which rose prodigiously to turn the lower district of Fredericton into a lake. It flooded the ground floor of the Lord Beaverbrook Hotel, it invaded the museum, it flooded the main business streets. The Mactaquac Dam, built solely for power, had no effect on the flood. In May in the Eastern Townships it rained on twenty-six days; in June it rained almost as much; in the first fortnight of July it rained even more. The Magog and Massawippi rivers, draining two of the finest lakes in Quebec, were almost level with their ample banks, but they managed to carry the water off even though on one day Lake Memphremagog rose a foot and a half. The dam was opened at the Magog textile plant to save the town and the factory from a flood, and the fine, steady channel of the Magog River carried the great swell of water down to the cataract in Sherbrooke and into the St. Francis, which in turn carried it to the St. Lawrence and on to the sea whence most of the rains had come.

Thousands of rills and trickles descended the hills and some of them merged behind our cottage to mush their way down beside it to the little dirt road in front. There they created a miniature pattern of the Great Lakes, five deep puddles. Unless I did something about them, the stray cars splashing through that succession of muddy pools would have ruined my flowers and eventually eroded much of the road, so I had to make a river of my own. After an hour's work with shovel and hoe I had a splendid stream a hundred and thirty feet long, six inches wide, and eight inches deep on the average, broadening out here and there into lake-like reaches where it slowed down and deposited silt, narrowing finally as it streamed fast through the channel I had cut into the surface of the road. Finally it plunged into a deep gully filled with ferns and trees. Next I cut a canal six inches long to link the lowest of my five lakes to the river, then four more short canals to join them all up and I felt god-like, for I had created in an hour's time a genuine river system of my own which behaved exactly as the greatest of them do. Some of that water would find its way to the lake, then down the river to the St. Francis, the St. Lawrence, and the sea, and the chances were one in ninety trillion that one of the snowflakes that will land on my overcoat next January will have had its origin behind my cottage.

Immediately the dividends followed, as they always do when you co-operate with nature and do not try to force her. The birds came to wash in the river—wild canaries, Baltimore orioles, chickadees, wrens, brown thrushes, and a variety of finches; the robins found so many worms in its saturated banks that one of them grew so fat he could hardly lift himself off the ground, on which he walked with the lop-sided wobble of an elderly Bavarian brewmaster. Waking at first light in the mornings, I heard the musical tinkle of my river, but the moment the light grew, its sound was drowned out by such a philharmonic of bird songs as I had never heard before.

The maples, oaks, butternuts, hornbeams, birches, shrubs, ferns, weeds, and wild flowers proliferated like the flora of a tropical rain forest—I measured one sucker from the stump of a small red oak and found it had grown eight feet in a single month. The farmers were having an awful time and would not be comforted if anyone had told them that such a season was in the nature of things because we are still in the Pleistocene. Vegetables were going to be scarce the coming fall, in the coming winter the price of meat would rise higher still because so much of the corn had been drowned or washed out. Next year the farmers would have to pay more for their seeds, but they would still have their lands, for the overloaded rivers had saved them from turning into a Jurassic swamp.

Nature is truly harmonious, so it was appropriate that in such a season the spillways of the Watergate should also have opened and let out in a flood prime samples of the silt, debris, and fecal matter of two poisoned decades.

The writers of Scripture knew what they were doing when they turned into symbols such natural occurrences as Noah's flood and the obliteration of Sodom and Gomorrah, thereby linking them in the human mind to the great chain of being. Had I been cooped up in the city during these weeks I would have been outraged by the Watergate affair but I would have missed the whole point of it by localizing it. In the country in a season like this it seemed abundantly clear that the whole thing was inevitable, and the Watergate *dramatis personae* were obviously simple-minded, in their own context even innocent. All they had done was to behave precisely as they had been taught to behave in the post-war society in which they grew up. This was a culture essentially mindless because it had cut its moorings with the tradition of many centuries, with the result that the delicate distinctions between what used to be called right and wrong had become (to use the favourite word of the witnesses) "inoperative". As I listened to the birds singing in the dawn much more convincingly than all those witnesses sang in front of the television cameras, it became overwhelmingly clear that there is no real disorder in nature.

In a culture which invented the myth of the Common Man and pretended that this non-existent being is more important than the very real exceptional man, pretended also that the mass is more important than the individual, the image more real than reality, that God either does not exist or does not care what engineers and developers do to His universe, what else could have been expected than that sooner or later a man like Richard Nixon should have become president of a nation which still calls itself the world's greatest (as it well may be in fact) and that Nixon should have selected as his servants such men as Ehrlichman, whose name in German means "honest man", and Kleindienst, whose name in German means "small service"? The consequences of the Watergate flood are bound to last longer than those of the flood from the skies, because there were no proper channels ready to catch and control such an overflow of our post-war moral chaos. The only available drainage was found in those two supreme expressions of the Age of the Common Man: television and committees of investigation.

When I wrote a year ago that it was essential to my sanity to try to think like a river, to immerse myself in the ways, mysteries, and inexorable logic of moving water, I did not fully understand just how essential this was going to be. The succeeding fall, winter, and spring taught me, and with a vengeance.

During the long succession of months when I researched, wrote, and rewrote this book, I lived in a city which, after a long and honourable resistance, had finally joined the Gadarene rush to self-destruction which can have only one consequence—the collective, frenzied, violent insanity so obvious in the concrete jungles of Manhattan, Detroit, Chicago, and all the other concrete jungles where anthropoids are isolated from growing things and forced to live like convicts in concrete cells. It so happened that my own apartment, and above all the university where I taught, were in the very core-area of the maximum devastation.

This is not the place to describe in detail what was done to central Montreal that year, but it is a literal fact that there were more and much bigger holes in my district than in any comparable area of London during the 1940 blitz. Skyhooks were swinging everywhere, demolition engines battered, trees were butchered, dug up, and shredded, the priceless topsoil of gardens, a few of them a century old, was scooped up, dumped into trucks, and carted off to be used as fill in some other site. Clouds of mortar dust filled eyes and nostrils, the roaring of diesels and the racketing snarls of pneumatic drills tautened the nerves and produced muscular spasms, the tootings of blasting horns were followed by the dull thuddings of exploding dynamite. Worst of all was the knowledge that when these developments were completed there would be nothing beautiful in any of them, nothing conducive to a good life or even to sanity.

When I remembered the stillness of the great reservoir of lakes in Labrador, the austere majesty of HaHa Bay, the white water lacing the blue of the West Kootenay after it leaves its lake, the cosmic silence of the Mackenzie, the sweetness of alder fragrance beside the streams of Nova Scotia, it was easier—it really was—to admit the hideous knowledge that when these slab-buildings, egg-crate buildings, wall-buildings, works of architecture inspired by Hitler's bunker and maximum-security jails, stand finally complete in their holes, it will be next to impossible to see even a glint of the St. Lawrence from any point in Montreal lower than the cross on Mount Royal, and from there impossible to discern any trees lower than the ones immediately below the cross.

As with the Watergate, all this was probably inevitable. Those banal high-rises, filled with identical cubby-holes and *ersatz* carpeting, lined with identical windows, and illuminated by identical tubes of Neon—do they not express meticulously the utter banality and barrenness of the contemporary bureaucratic mind? To say, as many do, that rampant greed is responsible for them ignores the real point. The merchant princes who built Florence and Venice were among the most rapacious of men, and Bess of Hardwick counted her pence as closely as a Mafia numbers game racketeer counts the dimes and quarters he collects in Harlem. What surged to a climax in Montreal in that year must continue until the time comes—and the Watergate may be a herald that this time will come soon—when men will agree to do on a huge scale what the authorities of Kansas City did in the spring of 1973. They will blow up the worst of these new buildings.

The mayor called in experts of the United States Army's Engineering Corps to get rid of a recent housing development, fourteen storeys high, which had cost millions to build. As anyone might have foreseen, hoods and juvenile delinquents, themselves maddened by having to live in such a place, had been terrorizing the other inmates, robbing apartments right and left, raping girls in the corridors, beating up the elderly and infirm as a release for their frustrated natural impulses. It therefore seems clear to me that certain new buildings in Montreal, Toronto, and even Vancouver are sooner or later going to be demolished. It is equally clear that when this has been done the cities will recover, and the rivers and lakes will again become integrate with them. Twenty-five years ago nearly every city in Germany, and some cities in Northern Italy, were piles of stinking rubble. Since then nearly all of them have been restored.

Five days after I finished writing this book, my wife and I boarded an Alitalia plane in the late evening of a late spring day and left Montreal. We were both exhausted, and on the advice of a physician who had grown up in Czechoslovakia we were going to Italy for what the Europeans call "the cure"—specifically the thermal mud baths of Abano, just outside Padua.

Night over the Atlantic, dawn over the coast of Northern Ireland, sunrise over the tawny smog blowing across Lancashire, a slim thread of silver that was the upper Thames. Cloud over the Channel, a quick flash of the Seine west of Paris, cloud over Dauphiné and the Alps, deluging rain when we landed in Milan. Fog and rain over Lombardy while a slow train carried us eastward through Brescia, Verona, and Vicenza to Padua. In Padua the rain lifted and did not return during the following twelve days we spent in Italy.

That wonderful ancient city by the Brenta River was called Patavium when Livy was born in it fifty-nine years before Christ, and a millennium and a half later it served as the birthplace of Mantegna. Home of Petrarch and Giotto's greatest frescoes, of Donatello's equestrian statue before the six-domed cathedral which holds the bones of the city's patron San Antonio, city where Galileo taught his mathematics and Shakespeare's Portia learned her law—Padua has seen and survived most of the best and the worst that humanity can do. The Lombards destroyed it in the seventh century; the people rebuilt it and gradually civilized the Lombards. Allied bombers destroyed a good deal of it in the Second World War, but when you stroll along its colonnades today you would never suspect that this had happened.

Lombardy and the land of the Verona quadrilateral are drained by rivers famous in history military and civil. Some of these cities and all of these rivers were there when Hannibal came; they were unchanged after Hannibal was driven out. They knew the many armies of the many Roman civil wars; they knew the invading barbarian hordes, the invading Christians from Spain and Austria. They saw them in and they saw them out. They saw Napoleon in on two separate occasions and they saw him out, saw the Nazis in and out, saw finally the allied armies in and out.

All traces of the countless battles along the lines of the Po, the Ticino, the Brenta, and the Adige have entirely disappeared. The land is verdant with vines and waving wheat, the barns are white with roofs of Sienna red, the poplars always seem to have grown as a frame for something man has built, and mellow bells ring from the *campanili* as they have done for a thousand years.

INDEX

Page numbers in italic indicate photograph references.

Abitibi River, 22
Agassiz, Lake, 22, 170, 171-3, 177, 179, 182
Ainslie, Lake, 116
Aklavik, 189, 194, 198, 200, 202, 203
Alaska, 22, 188, 194, 214
Alaska Highway, 194
Albany River, Ont., *16-17*, 22, 140-4
Alexandra Falls, *243*
Algonquin Indians, 83, 84, *205*
Aluminum, 213, 219, 220, 221
Aluminum Company of America, 219
Aluminum Company of Canada (ALCAN), 219
Amazon River, 22, 53, 189, 190, 227
Anarchist Mountain, 263
Annapolis River, 95, 112
Annapolis Royal, N.S., 100
Annapolis Valley, 112, *114*
Anticosti, 68, 97
Appalachians, *14*, 24, 25, 53, 67
Arctic, Canadian, 10, 21, 188, 203
Arctic Ocean, 23, 202, 225
Arrow Lakes, 246, 262
Arvida, 213, 218, 219, 220
Ashcroft, B.C., 256
Ashuanipi River, 231, 235
Assiniboine River, 27, 32, *121*, 169, 173, *174*, 177
Athabaska, Lake, 21, 32, 189, 190, 196, 199, 259
Athabaska River, 23, *28*, 181, 185, 186, 189, 190, 192, 199, 258, 262; delta, 191, 194
Atikonak, Lake, 231
Atikonak River, 231
Atlantic Ocean, 23, 60, 171, 196, *209*, 226, 231, 254
Attawapiskat River, *16-17*, 22, 141
Aurora borealis, 202, 215
Avon River, N.S., 113
Avon River, Ont., *143*

Baddeck Lakes, 113
Baddeck River, 112, 113, 115, 116, 126
Badlands, *243*
Baie Comeau, P.Q., 213
Baie St. Paul, P.Q., *42*
Baie Ste. Catherine, P.Q., *39*
Banff National Park, *23*, 257
Batoche, Sask., *184-5*, 186, 187
Beaufort Sea, 12, 21, 188, *193*, 254
Beauharnois Canal, 54
Beechwood Dam, 94, 97
Belcher Islands, 21
Bell Rock, 188, 191, 192, *193*, 194, 195, 196, 199, *204*
Bella Coola River, 35, 252
Belle Isle, Strait of, 68
Beluga, *38-9*, 213
Belwood Dam, 147
Bering Sea, 22
Bering Strait, 21
Bic, P.Q., *38*
Black Canyon, 8, 248, 251, 254
Blackwater River, N.W.T., 200
Boiestown, 104
Boston, 24, 136, 139, 140
Bout de l'Ile, 82
Bow Lake, 182

Bow Pass, 181
Bow River, *87, 122, 162-3*, 182, 264
Bowdoin Canyon, 223, 224, 231, 233, 236
Bras d'Or Lakes, 112, 113, 116
Brazeau River, 181
British Columbia, *18-19*, 22, 34, *75, 92*, 133, *159, 211*, 214, *243*, 245, 246, 247, 248-54, *252-3*, 254, 255, 256, 257, 258, 260, *260-1*, 263; Dry Belt, 250, 251
British North America, 30
Buffalo, 126, 132, 136, 137
Burbank, Wash., 258
Bytown, 79, 82, 83

Cabot Strait, 54
Cabot Trail, 116
Calgary, *122*
California, 245, 246
Camsell Bend, 202
Canadian National Railways, 234
Canadian Pacific Railway, 12, *75*, *121*, 173, 177, *210*, 257, 260
Canagigue River, 146
Canal Flats, B.C., 258, 259, 264
Canot du maître, 32, 33
Canot du nord, 32, 194
Canol Project, 194
Canso, Strait of, 105
Cap de la Madeleine, P.Q., *47*
Cap Santé, P.Q., *47*
Cape Breton Island, 25, 111, 112, 113, 115
Cariboo Mountains, 248, 262
Cariboo Road, 248, 250, *252-3*
Cariboo Hills, 203
Cascade Mountains, 258
Cayuga Indians, 132, 133, 134, 144, 147, 148
Cedar Lake, Man., 182
Chambly, P.Q., 56
Champlain, Lake, 56, 57
Champlain Sea, 57, 60, 218, 222
Chatham, N.B., 103, 104, 108
Chaudière Falls, 26, 27, 78, 254
Cheticamp River, 115
Chicoutimi, P.Q., *40*, 213, 214, 215, 219, 220, 221
Chicoutimi River, 218
Chippawa Creek, 132
Churchill Factory, 259
Churchill Falls, 219, 224, 225, 230, 231, 233, 235; development, 224, 227, 231, 234, 235, 260
Churchill Falls, Lab., 225, 226, 235, 236
Churchill River, Man., 10, 21, 22, 32, 224
Chute-à-Caron Dam, 219
Clearwater Rapids, 200
Clearwater River, 32, 181
Colorado River, 245, 255
Columbia Icefield, 23, 57, 181, 189, 264
Columbia Lake, 246, 258, 259, 262
Columbia Mountains, 255
Columbia River, 22, 32, *159, 160*, 173, 231, 246, 254, 255, 259-60, *260-1, 264*; dams, 258; valley, 34
Columbia River System, 258-64
Conestoga River, 146
Congo River, 22
Coppermine River, 199
Cornerbrook, Nfld., 111

Cornwall, Ont., 60
Cornwall Power Dam, 54
Cornwallis River, 113
Cornwallis Valley, N.S., 113
Corra Linn Dam, 263
Coulonge River, 78
Coureur de bois, 26
Craigellachie, 257
Credit River, Ont., *151, 157*
Crowfoot Glacier, *23*
Cumberland Lake, 32, 182

Dams, 8, *16-17*, 227, 233
Danube River, 12, 36
Dean Channel, 35
Dease Lake, 190
Dewdney Trail, 263
Diamond, Cape, P.Q., *44*
Disaster Rapids, 224
Dnieper River, 21, 36
Dogger Bank, 8
Domagaya Lake, 231
Don River, U.S.S.R., 21

East Forebay, Lab., 233
Eastern Townships, 57, 111, 227, 265
Edinburgh, 21
Edmonton, *123*, 188, 189, 203
Edmundston, N.B., 94, 96
Elora, Ont., 146
English Bay, 250
Erie, Lake, 53, 57, 131, 132, 133, 144, 146, *149*
Erie Canal, 136, 137
Esker, 231, 234
Eskimos, 188, 199, 200, 203, 226, 227
Eternity, Bay of, 215
Eternity, Cape, 214, 215
Euphrates River, 9
Evolution, process of, 7, 11
Exploits River, Nfld., 111, *242*
Expo 67, 7, *48*, 68

Fargo, N.Dak., 170, 172
Farming, 103, *209*; Alta., *87*, 182; B.C., 248, *252-3*, 256, 263; Man., 170, 177; N.B., *88-9*; N.S., *114*; Ont., 78, 227; P.Q., 56, *86, 87*; on Saguenay River, 213, 215, 218, 220, 221, 222; Sask., 173, 182, 187
Father Point, 68
Fergus, Ont., 146, 147, 151
Finger Lakes, N.Y., 147
Finlay River, 189
Fisheries, coastal, 24
Fishing industries, *91, 92*, 108. *See also* Salmon fishing *and* Trout fishing
Fjords, 214; of Norway, 21, 213, 246; on Saguenay River, 213-14, 220, 221
Fort Albany, 140
Fort Chimo, 223, 226
Fort Chipewyan, 32, 34, 189, 191, 199, 200
Fort Chippawa, 137
Fort Douglas, *174*
Fort Erie, 137
Fort Fitzgerald, 199
Fort Garry, 171, 172, *174-5*, 177, 178
Fort George, B.C., 252, 254
Fort George, Ont., 132, 136, 137, 138

Fort Good Hope, N.W.T., 202
Fort Henry, Ont., *52*, 83, 132, 137
Fort McPherson, 202, 203
Fort Nelson, 140
Fort Niagara, N.Y., 132, 136, 137
Fort Norman, N.W.T., 194, 202
Fort Providence, 202
Fort Qu'Appelle, *74-5*
Fort Resolution, 195
Fort Rouge, 173
Fort Simpson, 190, 202, 251
Fort Smith, 188, 189, 191, 192, 198, *204*; portage, 192
Fort Vermilion, 32
Fort William, 30, 31, 32
Franklin Mountains, 202, 225
Fraser Canyon, 250, 255, 256
Fraser River, 8, 11, *15, 18-19*, 21, 22, 32, 36, *75*, 142, 173, 185, 233, *239*, 246, *247*, 248-54, *252-3*, 255, 256, *257, 260*, 262; gold, 249-50, *252-3*; length, 248; salmon, 249, 251, 254
Fraser Valley, 34, 250, 254, 257, 260
Fredericton, 24, 93, 94, 95, 96, 97, 100, 101, 104, *117*, 248, 265
French River, 30, 32, 77, 144, *145, 207*
Frog Portage, Sask., 32
Fundy, Bay of, *90*, 97, 100, *109*, 112, 113
Fur trade, 24, 25, 26, 30, 32, 33, 34, 53, 82, 100, 173, 176, 177, 182, 183, 185, 194, *207*, 220, 221, 254, 256, 263

Gagetown, N.B., 101
Galt, Ont., *145*, 146, 151
Ganges River, 9
Garonne River, 8
Gaspé Peninsula, *55*, 56, 97, 105
Gatineau River, *13*, 77, 78, 79
Georgia Strait, *239*, 248, 251
Georgian Bay, 144, *207*.
Glaciers, 7, 9, 21, 22, 57, 103, 110, 111, 113, 126, 140, 170, 181, 188, 213, 214, 218, 222, 224, 225, 231, 244, 246, 248, 262, 264
Goat Island, 130, 132
Goose Bay, Lab., 223, 224, 230, 233
Grand Bay, 94, 96, 97
Grand Coulee Dam, 231, 258, 260
Grand Falls, Lab., 223, 224, *229*, 231, 233, *236*
Grand Falls, N.B., 9, 94, 96, 97
Grand Falls, Nfld., 111, *242*
Grand Island, 132
Grand Lake, 97
Grand Portage, 26, 30, 31, 32, 183
Grand Rapids, 180; dam, 181
Grand River, Ont., 57, 144-7, *145*, 150, 151
Grand River, P.Q. *See* La Grande Rivière
Great Bear Lake, 10, 190, 194, 200, 203, 225
Great Bear River, 190
Great Divide, 23
Great Lakes, *16-17*, 22, 30, 53, 54, 56, 57, 60, 77, *90*, 97, 130, 136, 171
Great Slave Lake, 21, 188, 189, 190, 194, 195, 196, 199, 200, *204*, 225, 243
Green Island Rapids, 200

Greenland, ice cap, 21, 225, *244*; fjords, 214
Grondines, P.Q., *91*
Guelph, Ont., 151
Gulf of Mexico, 26, 53, 140

Ha Ha Bay, 213, 214, 215, 218, 219, 220, 221, 266
Habitat, *119*
Haida Indians, 226
Halifax, 21, 25, 110, 111, 137, 138, 221, 254
Hamilton Inlet, 233
Hamilton River, 8, 11, 218, 223-36, *228-9*; blackflies, 223, 224, 225; Horseshoe Rapids, 224; Mouni Rapids, 224; Muskrat Falls, 224
Hartland, N.B., 94
Hay River, N.W.T., *243*
Hayes River, 22
Hell's Gate, 249, 250, 251, 254, 255
Highlanders, Scottish, 27, 30, 33, 34, 61, 115, 176, 186, 227
Homesteaders, 186-7, 189
Hope, B.C., 248, 251, 256
Hudson Bay, *16-17*, 21, 22, 23, *121*, 140, 171, *174-5*, 182, 203, 264
Hudson River, 57, 67, 97, 100, 136, 214
Hudson's Bay Company, 24, 26, 27, 30, 32, 34, 36, *122-3*, 140, 176, 182, 183, 187, 194, 195, 202, 220, 223, 248, 259
Humber River, Nfld., 111
Humber River, Ont., *70*, *143*, 152
Huron, Lake, 26, 32, 53, 190, *207*
Huron Indians, 27, 144, 148
Hurricane Hazel, 152
Hwang-Ho River, 8, 9
Hydro-electricity, *16-17*, 49, 67, 94, 101, 203, 231, 232, *240-1*; Columbia River, 259-60; Hamilton River, 224, 226, 227, 233, 234, 235; Kootenay River, *263*; Robert Moses Station, 130; Niagara Falls, 126, 130, 132; Niagara River, 130, 137; Saguenay River, 218, 219, 221
Hydro-Quebec, 231, 233, 234, 235

Ice Age(s), 9, 21, 56, 57, 110, 131, 171, 246
Ile aux Coudres, *42*
Ile Jésus, 82
Ile aux Lièvres, *38-9*, *40*
Ile d'Orléans, 54, 66, 82, *87*
Ile Verte, *38-9*
Innuits, 227. *See also* Eskimos
Inuvik, N.W.T., *201*, 203
Iroquois Indians, 83, 144, 147-8
Irvine River, 146
Isle Maligne Dam, 219
Ivy Lea Bridge, *50-1*

Jacopie Lake (now West Forebay), 231, 233
James Bay Development, 226-7
Jasper National Park, 189, *238*

Kamloops, B.C., *18-19*, 256-7
Kamloops Lake, 246, 256
Kanata, 37
Kaniapiscau River, 226
Keewatin District, 57
Kennebecasis River, 94, 97
Kicking Horse River, 249, 250
Kincaid, Ont., *86*
Kingston, Ont., *50-1*, 52, 83, *120*, 139
Kitchener, Ont., 146, 151
Koksoak River, 226

Kootenay Lake, 246, 258, 259, 260, 262, 263
Kootenay Pass, 264
Kootenay River, 246, 258, 259, 263-4. *See also* West Kootenay River
Kootenay Valley, 264

Labrador, 57, *86*, 97, 103, 111, 213, 214, 218, 223, 224, 225, 227, *228-9*, 230, *232*, 233, 234
Labrador City, 226, 233
Labrador Plateau, 224, 225, 231
Lachine, P.Q., 30, 31, *48*
Lachine Rapids, 66, 72, 82, 139
La Grande Décharge, 218, 219
La Grande Rivière, 226
Lahave River, 112
Lake of the Woods, *16-17*, 32, 171, 186
LaLoche, Portage, 32. *See also* Methy Portage
LaMontagne Portage, 78
LaTraite, Portage, 181
Laurentian mountains, 25, *38-9*, 53, 190
Laurentian Shield, 22, 26, 30, 56, 60, 171, 222
La Vérendrye National Park, 78
Lawrence, Sir Thomas, 200
Lévis, P.Q., *44*
Lewis and Clark expedition, 258, 259
Lewiston, N.Y., 132, 137
Liard River, 190, 192, 251
Lièvre River, 77, 78
Lillooet, B.C., 249, 251
Lillooet River, 248, 249, 251
Lobstick Lake, 231, 233
Loire River, 9
Long Reach, N.B., 96, 97
Long Sault rapids, 31, *49*, 139; Spillway dam, 54
Lotbinière, P.Q., *46*
Louisbourg, 25, 100, 105
Louisiana Territory, 26, 67, 112, 141
Loyalists. *See* United Empire Loyalists
Lumber industry, *41*, 79, 82, 83, *85*, *86*, *88-9*, 96, 97, 100, 108, *120*, *207*, *211*, 215, 219, 220, 250
Luther Swamp, Ont., 146
Lytton, B.C., *15*, *239*, 249, 251, 254, 255, *257*

Macalister, B.C., 249
Macdonald, Sir John A., 36, *52*, 65, *210*
McGill University, 34, 61, 254
Mackenzie, Alexander, 24, 25, 26, 31, 32, 34, 35, 182, 186, 194, 199, 200, 202, 204, 252, 254, 255
Mackenzie Mountains, 202, 225
Mackenzie River, 10, 21, 22, 23, *28*, 32, 142, *166-7*, 172, 173, 180, 185, 188-204, *193*, 225, 251; blackflies and mosquitoes, 190-1, 198, 204; delta, 21, 112, 198, *201*, 203, 266.
Mackenzie Valley, 21, 203, 204
Mactaquac Dam, 9, 94, 95, 265
Madawaska County, *41*, 96
Magog River, 265
Malicete Indians, 96
Manitoba, 24, 57, *121*, 170, 171, 173
Margaree River, 116
Maritime provinces, 22, 25, 100, 249
Marne River, 8
Marquette, Jacques, 26

Mattawa River, 77, 78
Maugerville, N.B., 9, 95, 97
Memphremagog, Lake, 265
Metabetchouan River, 218
Methy Portage, 10, 32, 181, 185
Métis, 186, 227. *See also* Riel, Louis *and* Riel Rebellion
Michigan, 57
Michigan, Lake, 53, 190
Michikamau, Lake, 225, 231, 233
Middle River, N.S., 112, 116
Mills Lake, 202
Minas Basin, 113
Minnesota, 32, 169, 170, 171
Miramichi Bay, 104
Miramichi River, 22, *88-9*, 97, 102-8, *106-7*, 159
Missinaibi River, 22
Mission, B.C., 249
Mississippi River, 9, 12, 21, 22, 26, 32, 53, 54, 56, 126, 140, 144, 169, 171, 182, 185, 189, 190, *211*, 244, 259, 265; delta, 66, 112
Mississippi Valley, 30
Missouri River, 21, 22, 25, 34, 113, 171, 172, 180, *244*
Mistassini River, 218, 222
Mitchin River, 231
Mohawk Indians, 132, 133, 134, 144, 147, 148, 150, 151
Moisie River, 108, 213
Monashee Mountains, 260, 262
Montmorency, P.Q., 94
Montmorency River, 56, 242
Montreal, 22, 25, 30, 31, 34, *42*, *48*, *49*, 53, 54, 56, 57, 61, 68, 78, 83, *119*, *120*, 139, 186, 187, 190, *209*, 214, 251, 266; Island, 66, 82
Morrisburg, Ont., *49*
Mount Royal, 66, 67
Moyie Lake, 264
Moyie River, 264
Murray Bay, P.Q., *38*, *41*, 54, 213
Musquodoboit River, 113, *165*

Nahanni River, 190
Napoleonic Wars, 25, 176
Nashwaak River, 95, 96, 97
National Capital Planning Commission, 79
Nelson Dam, 263
Nelson River, 10, 21, 22, 23, 171, 177, 181, 182, 264
Neutral Indians, 144, 148
New Brunswick, *41*, 57, 93, 94, 95, 96, 97, *98-9*, 100, 102, 103, 104, 105, 108, 111, 112, 113, *117*, 141, *154-5*, *159*; University of, 104, 113, 265
New England, 57, 93, 95, 97, 112, 136, 138, 183
New France, 26, 27, *118*
New Westminster, B.C., 250
New York City, 24, 130, 136, 231
New York State, *49*, 140
Newcastle-on-Miramichi, 102, 103, 104
Newfoundland, *14*, 92, 97, 111, *160*, 222, 224, 225, 226, 231, 234
Niagara Falls, *76*, 115, 127, *128-9*, 130, 131, *134-5*, *149*, 214, 222, 223, 226, *239*, 242, 263; *Maid of the Mist*, 127; Whirlpool, 127, 132, 137, 139, 224
Niagara Falls, Ont., 130
Niagara-on-the-Lake, Ont., 130, 132, 133, 137
Niagara Peninsula, 125
Niagara River, 8, 9, 53, 60, 125-40, 141

Nile River, 9, 21, 22, 23, 112, 116, 200
Nipissing, Lake, 77, 144, *207*
Nith River, 146
Noire River, *40*
Norman Wells, N.W.T., 188, 194, 198, 200, 202, 203
North Sea, 8
North West Company, 27, 30, 31, 32, 34, 53, 139, 177, 182, 183, 199, 200, 252, 254, 259
North West Mounted Police, *123*
Northwest Passage, 26, 35, *37*, 66, 185, 199
Northwest Territories, 22, *166-7*, 185, 189, 194, 203, 225, *243*, 259
Notre Dame, Monts, P.Q., *38-9*
Notre Dame du Portage, P.Q., *41*
Nova Scotia, 57, 100, 105, 108, 111, 112, 113, *114*, 115, 116, 133, 141, 142, 144, *165*, 188, 227, 266

Ohio Territory, 24, 30, 67
Okanagan Falls, B.C., 262
Okanagan Lake, 246, 262
Okanagan Range, 262
Okanagan River, 258, 262-3
Okanagan Valley, 262
O'Law, Lake, 116
Oldman River, 182, *243*
Oneida Indians, 132, 133, 134, 144, 147, 148
Onondaga Indians, 132, 133, 134, 144, 147, 148
Ontario, Lake, 22, *52*, 53, 54, 57, 60, 77, 83, *120*, 131, 132, *149*, *151*
Ontario Hydro Electric Commission, 84
Oregon Trail, 25
Orma Lake, 233
Oromocto Island, 97
Oromocto River, 100
Ossokmanuan Lake, 231
Ossokmanuan Reservoir, 233
Ottawa, 78, 79, 83, 84, *120*
Ottawa River, 26, 30, 31, 56, 60, 73, 77-84, *80-1*, *120*, 140, 144, *207*, 251, 254; length, 78
Ottawa Valley, 57, 82, 84, 131
Ouiatchouan River, 218, 222

Pacific Great Eastern Railway, 249, 250
Pacific Ocean, 22, 23, 34, 35, *124*, 199, *210*, 226, 245, 248, 251, *252-3*, 254, 259, *260-1*
Paddlewheeler, *29*, *168*
Papineauville, P.Q., 84
Paris, Ont., 146, 147
Parliament, Houses of, 83, *120*
Parliament Hill, 79
Parsnip River, 189
Peace River, 21, 32, 189, 190, 191, 199, 250, 252; dam, 8; delta, 195
Peel River, 191, 203
Peggy's Cove, N.S., 113
Pend Oreille, Lake, Idaho, 262
Pend Oreille River, 258, 259
"Peneplain", 9
Penticton, B.C., 262
Péribonka, P.Q., 220, 222
Péribonka River, 218, 219
Permafrost, 141, 191, *201*, 202, 203, 226
Petawawa River, 10
Petitcodiac River, *88-9*, 103
Petroleum, 24
Pigeon River, 30
Pingo, *201*
Pitchblende, 194
Plains of Abraham, *68*, *209*

Pointe aux Trembles, P.Q., 54
Pontiac's Rebellion, 133, 150
Port Alfred, P.Q., 214
Port Credit, Ont., *151*
Port Maitland, Ont., 146
Port au Persil, P.Q., *41*
Port Royal, N.S., 112
Portages, 22, 27, 31, 134, 182, *206*, *210*, 223
Precambrian Shield, *16-17*, 24, *197. See also* Laurentian Shield
Prescott, Ont., *49*
Preston, Ont., 146
Prince Albert, Sask., 180, 181, 182, 264
Prince Edward Island, 111, 133, 227
Prince George, B.C., *239*, 250
Providence Rapids, 200
Pulp and paper industry, 46, *80-1*, 82, *88-9*, 94, 111, 213, 219, 220
Purcell Range, 260, 263, 264

Quebec, 67, 213, 215, 220, 225, 226, 227, 231
Quebec Act, 67, 150
Quebec City, 25, *29*, *41*, 44-5, *46*, 53, 54, 65-6, 82, 83, 84, *87*, *118-19*, *120*, *208-9*, 214, 220, *242*, 251, 254
Quebec North Shore and Labrador Railway, 226, 231
Québécois, 64
Queenston, Ont., 132, 137
Queenston Heights, Battle of, 126, 136
Quesnel, B.C., 8
Quesnel River, 248, 251

Rainy Lake, 31, 32, 171, 204
Rainy River, 10, 30, 256
Red Deer River, *243*
Red River, 9, 21, 22, 32, 93, *121*, 169-79, *174-5*, *178-9*, 181, *206*, 256; carts, 36, *123*, 187; delta, 179
Red River Valley, 170, 173, 178
Res Delta, 195, 199
Restigouche River, *88-9*, 97, 108
Reversing Falls, *88-9*, 93, 97
Rhine River, 12, 22, 53, 60, *92*, 96, 189, 231, 249
Richardson Mountains, 203
Richelieu River, 56, *86*, 139, 251
Rideau Canal, 83
Rideau Falls, 79
Rideau River, 77, 78, *120*, *156-7*
Riel Rebellion, *74-5*, 177. See also *Métis*
River of Disappointment, 199
Rivière des Mille Iles, 82
Rivière des Prairies, 82
Rivière du Loup, *40*, *41*, 54, 188
Roberval, P.Q., 215, 220, 222
Robson, Mount, B.C., 248, 257
Rockfort, *174*
Rocky Mountain Trench, *239*, 248, 260
Rocky Mountains, 22, 36, *87*, 125, 180, 189, 190, 199, 214, *243*, 248, 250, 254, 260, 264
Roosevelt, Franklin D., 95

Roosevelt, Franklin D., Lake, 260
Rothesay, N.B., 94
Royal North-west Mounted Police, 186

Sackville River, 110
Saguenay River, *38-9*, *40*, 56, 213-22, *216-17*, 225, fjord, 220, 221
Sail Lake, 233
St. Ann's Bay, 113
St. Ann's Point, 100
St. Boniface, Man., *121*, 177, 178, 210
St. Catharines, Ont., *149*
St. Clair, Lake, 53, 130, 142
St. Clair River, 53, 60
St. Fabien, P.Q., *39*
St. Francis, Lake, 54
St. Francis River, 56
Saint John, N.B., *88-9*, *90*, 95, 97, *98-9*, 100
St. John River, 9, 22, 54, *88-9*, 93-101, *98-9*, *101*, 103, 104, *117*, *154-5*, 188, *211*, 248, 265; dam, 8; length, 93
St. John Valley, 93, 100, 104
St. John's, Nfld., 140
St. Lawrence, Gulf of, 37, *38-9*, 57, *59*, 68, 105, 112, 116
St. Lawrence, Lake, *49*
St. Lawrence International Seaway, 48, *53*, *62-3*, 65, 67, 68, 125, 136, 147, 251; length, 53
St. Lawrence River, 9, 10, 12, 21, 22, 24, 25, 26, 35, 37, *41*, *42-3*, *44-5*, *46-7*, *50-1*, *52*, 53-68, *55*, *59*, *63*, 77, 79, 83, 84, *86*, *87*, *91*, 97, *119*, *120*, 130, 132, 136, 138, 139, 140, 146, *161*, 171, 185, 189, 190, 203, 204, *205*, 213, 214, 249, 251, 259, 265, 266
St. Lawrence Valley, 24, 57
St. Louis, Lake, 54, *73*
St. Louis River, 53, 54, 259
St. Margaret's Bay, 113
St. Mary River, 53
St. Mary's River, 116
St. Maurice River, 25, 56, 84, 251
St. Peter, Lake, 54
St. Siméon, P.Q., *39-40*
Ste. Anne de Bellevue, 30, 32, 78, 79, 82
Ste. Anne de la Pérade, P.Q., *91*
Salmon fishing: B.C., 249, 251, 254, 258, 259; N.B., 94, 95, 97, 101, 104, 105, 108; Nfld., 111; N.S., 110, 116
Saskatchewan, Mount, 181
Saskatchewan, University of, 187
Saskatchewan River, 21, 22, 23, 32, *164*, 170, 172, 173, 180-7; The Forks, 182; North, 23, *29*, *123*, 181, 182, 264; South, 27, 181, 182, *184-5*, *243*, 264
Saskatoon, 186
Schefferville, P.Q., 231
Seahorse, Lab., 234
Seine River, 8, 12, *92*, 267
Selkirk, Man., 178
Selkirk Range, 260, 262, 263
Selkirk Settlement, 24, 173, 179, 186, 227

Seneca Indians, 132, 133, 134, 144, 147, 148
Separatism, 61, 64, 221
Sept Iles, P.Q., *49*, 213, 226, 231, 234
Seven Years War, 112
Severn River, *16-17*, 22, 141, 142
Sherbrooke, N.S., 116
Shipbuilding industry, *86*, 105, 108
Shipshaw River, 219; Dam, 214, 218, 219
Shuswap Lake, 257
Siberia, 21, 24, 192, 225
Silver, 194
Skeena River, 246
Slave Indians, 190
Slave River, 21, 170, 188, 189-90, 191, 192, 195, 199, *204*
Smallwood Reservoir, 218, 225, 228, 233, 235
Snake River, 258, 259
Sorel, P.Q., 56
Soulanges Canal, 54
Speed River, 146, 151
Spokane River, 259
Stern-wheeler, *211*
Stewiacke River, 95, 113
Superior, Lake, 26, 53, 54, 141, 171, 190
Sydney, N.S., 213

Tadoussac, P.Q., 213, 214, 215, *216-17*
Temiskaming, Lake, 78
Thames River, England, 8, 12, 21, 66, 67, *92*, 96, 116, 142-3, 170, 198, 218, 267
Thames River, Ont., 142, *143*
Thirteen Colonies, 24, 27, 66
Thompson, David, 12, *18-19*, 25, 26, 34, 35, 53, 54, 186, 254, 255, 258, 259
Thompson River, *18-19*, 246, 248, 249, 251, 255-7, *257*; North Branch, *18-19*, 255, 257; South Branch, *18-19*, 255, 257, 262
Thousand Islands, 21, *50-1*, 54, 72
Thunder Bay, Ont., *48*
Tigris River, 9
Tobique River, 94, 97
Toronto, *16-17*, 53, *70*, 83, *120*, 130, *151*, *152*, *244*, 266
Tracking, *28*, 31, 32
Trail, B.C., 258, 263
Traverse Lake, 169, 171
Trent Canal, *91*
Trent River, *143*
Trinity, Cape, 214, 215, 218; Virgin statue (Notre Dame du Saguenay), 215, 218, 221
Trois Pistoles, P.Q., *41*
Trois Rivières, P.Q., 25, 26, *46*, 54, 56, 96, *118*
Trout fishing, Nova Scotia, 113, 115
Tuktoyaktuk, N.W.T., 188, *193*, *201*, 202
Tuscarora Indians, 147, 148
Twin Falls, Lab., 233
Two Mountains, Lake of, 78, 79

Uisge Ban Falls, 115, 126
Ungava, 225
Ungava Bay, 225, 226
United Empire Loyalists, 67, 82, 93, 95, 100, 103, 105, 113, 137, 138
Unknown River, 224, 233
Uranium, 194

Val Jalbert, P.Q., 222
Vancouver, *90*, *124*, 250, 254, 256, 266
Verchères, P.Q., 54
Vermillion River, 264
Vermont, 139
Victoria Falls, 223, *242*
Volga River, 21, 189
Voyageurs, 12, 22, 25, 26, 27, 30, 31, 32, 33, 34, 36, 78, 79, 82, 84, 145, 181, 183, 185, 186, 188, 199, 200, *205*, *207*, 221, 250, 252, 254, 256, *264*; canoes of, 26, 31, 35, *205*; *mangeurs de lard*, 33

Wabush, Lab., 233, 234
War of 1812, *120*, 133, 134, 136, 142, 220
Washington Conference of 1871, 65
Waterloo, Ont., 146, 151
Waterways, Alta., 191, 194
Webster-Ashburton Treaty, 53, 259. *See also* Ashburton, Lord *and* Webster, Daniel
Welland Canal, 136
West Forebay, 233. *See also* Jacopie Lake
West Kootenay River, 263, 266
Westmount, P.Q., 64
Whale Island, 199
Whitefish Falls, 233
Whitehorse Rapids, *240-1*
Windermere, B.C., *264*
Windermere, Lake, 246
Windsor, N.S., 113
Winisk River, *16-17*, 141
Winnipeg, Lake, 22, 23, 32, 169, 170, 171, 172, 177, 181, 182, 256, 264
Winnipeg, *16-17*, 21, *121*, 169, 170, 171, *174-5*, 178, *210*; Floodway Channel, 173
Winnipeg River, 31, 32, *205*, 256
Winnipegosis, Lake, 171
Winokapau River, 224
Wisconsin Glacier, 111, 131, 244
Woodstock, N.B., 93, 95, 96
Wrigley, N.W.T., 190
Wrigley Harbour, 198, 199, 202

Yale Falls, Lab., 224
Yamaska Rivers, 56
Yangtse River, 9, 21, 189, 250
Yarmouth County, N.S., 112
Yellowhead Pass, 255
Yellowknife, N.W.T., 194, 198, *243*
York (Toronto), 133, 136
York Factory, Man., 10, 22, 176, 182, 264
York Fort, *174*
Yukon River, *20*, 21, 22, *91*, *158-9*, *168*, *211*, *240-1*, 258

EDITORIAL SERVICES   *Lonsdale Requirement Ltd.*
ART DIRECTION   *Frank Newfeld*
PICTURE CAPTIONS   *Leslie F. Hannon*
PICTURE RESEARCH   *Bill Brooks*
PRINTING & BINDING   *Mondadori Editore, Verona*

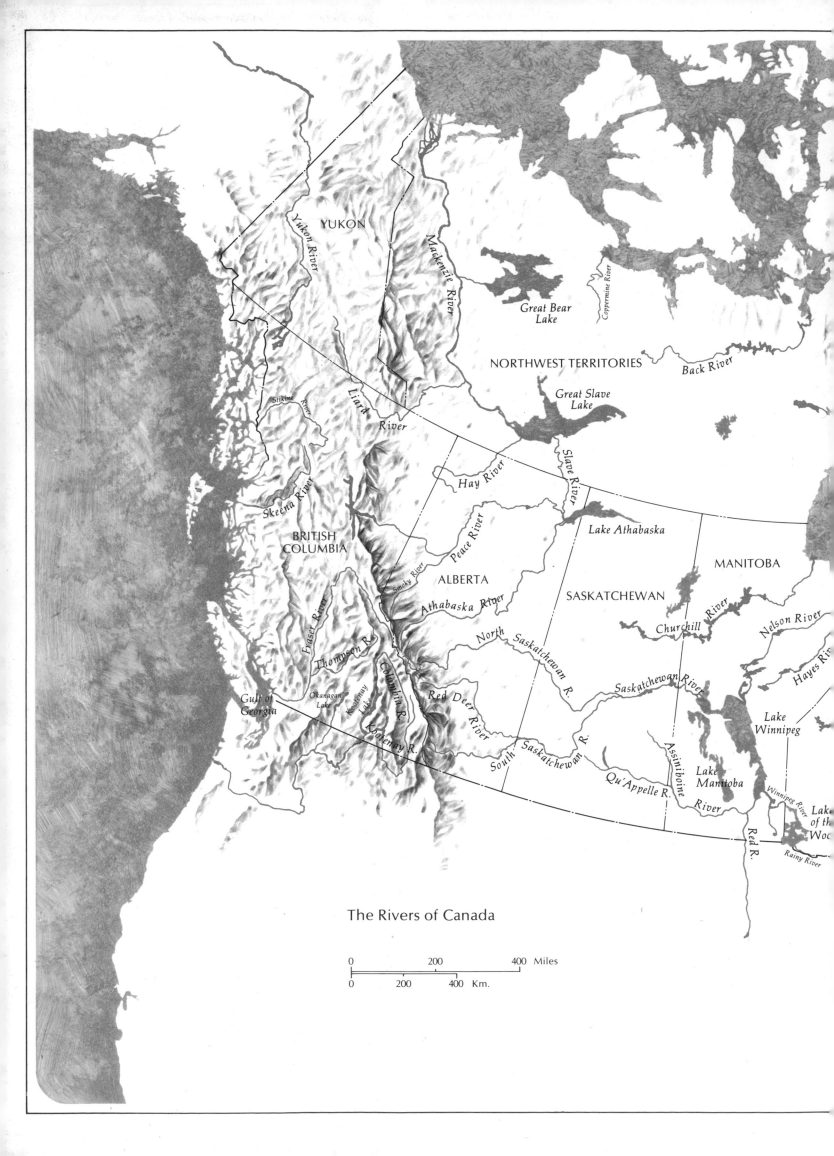

The Rivers of Canada